DEATH AND RENEWAL

SOCIOLOGICAL STUDIES IN ROMAN HISTORY
VOLUME 2

DEATH
AND
RENEWAL

SOCIOLOGICAL STUDIES IN ROMAN HISTORY
VOLUME 2

KEITH HOPKINS
Professor of Sociology, Brunel University

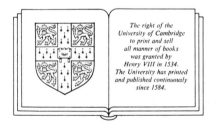

The right of the
University of Cambridge
to print and sell
all manner of books
was granted by
Henry VIII in 1534.
The University has printed
and published continuously
since 1584.

CAMBRIDGE UNIVERSITY PRESS

Cambridge

London   New York   New Rochelle
Melbourne   Sydney

Published by the Press Syndicate of the University of Cambridge
The Pitt Building, Trumpington Street, Cambridge CB2 1RP
32 East 57th Street, New York, NY 10022, USA
10 Stamford Road, Oakleigh, Melbourne 3166, Australia

First published 1983
First paperback edition 1985

Printed in Great Britain by the University Press, Cambridge

Library of Congress catalogue card number: 82–17887

British Library Cataloguing in Publication Data
Hopkins, Keith
Death and renewal   (Sociological studies in
Roman history; v. 2)
1. Social structure—Rome
2. Rome—Social conditions
I. Title II. Series
305'.0937   HN10.R7

ISBN 0 521 24991 0 hard covers
ISBN 0 521 27117 7 paperback

UP

CONTENTS

TABLES

FIGURES

PREFACE

Argument and methods

This book is about death and social renewal. It is about the social institutions which regulated the transfer of power and property in the Roman political elite. Every death created a vacancy, a gap in the social order, a place to be filled. One of the book's central problems is the degree to which the Roman senatorial aristocracy reproduced itself biologically and socially between the third century BC and the third century AD. One of our main findings is that the senatorial aristocracy achieved a surprisingly low rate of social reproduction; surprising, that is, relative to Roman ideals of hereditary succession and modern scholarly views; and low, relative to aristocracies in other societies.

The late Republic

Explanation is elusive. But several factors seem important. In the Republic (before 31 BC), a highly competitive political culture stressed not merely high birth, but also success in military leadership, wealth, ostentatious consumption, rhetorical skills and victory in successive popular elections. Capacity to succeed in most of these did not necessarily follow biological lines, or not in each generation. The inheritance of property, split equally between all surviving sons and daughters, diffused wealth away from agnates to relatives by marriage, and away from narrow lines of political succession. High death-rates left some aristocrats with no direct descendant, while others had more surviving heirs than they could afford. The fall in the birth-rate among aristocrats, which occurred probably from the last century BC onwards, increased the proportion without a single surviving son. Biological descent, the inheritance of wealth, and political succession all overlapped. But they did not coincide exactly. Their asymmetry in successive generations created a social dynamic, even within a stable political structure.

These factors in combination (and several others discussed in

Chapter 2) increased the permeability of the political elite to outsiders. Three qualifications should be made immediately. First, the senatorial aristocracy of the late Republic always had a small inner core of elite families who held strong expectations of hereditary succession to political power. Secondly, in spite of bitter civil wars between rival aristocrats and their armies, the political supremacy of senators relative to other social strata persisted. Thirdly, senators' economic supremacy was never undermined. This economic supremacy remained firmly anchored in the ownership of large tracts of Italian land and huge numbers of slaves, supplemented by investments in money-lending, urban property and shipping and by the privileged exploitation of conquered provinces.

Continuous changes in senate membership did not diminish the political supremacy of the senatorial order. Why then did shifts in senate membership matter? First, the steady turnover in member families in each generation mitigated the narrowness implied by a small senate with only 300 (from 81 BC, 600) life members. At any one time, the senate incorporated a powerful oligarchy. But in the long run, it also represented a broad stratum of Roman and Italian large landowners. This loose representativeness, for all its short-comings, was preserved in family histories and in public memories, and fostered young men's ambitions. The repeated openness of the senate to outsiders probably helped frustrate effective political opposition from potential interest groups, such as new citizen landowners, knights and tax-farmers.

Secondly, because senators and higher officers of state were elected in part for their military and political abilities, the turnover in senate members enabled the Roman state to recruit leaders who could meet the exacting requirements of acquiring, controlling and governing a large and expanding empire. A small, hereditary oligarchy in the long run would not have provided an adequate flow of talents. An open oligarchy with circulating membership recruited and rewarded those who succeeded within traditional and constitutional forms.

Thirdly, the circulation of talents into and within the Roman elite was itself the result of conflicting pressures. From one direction came aristocratic elitism and hereditary ideals; from another, a competitive political culture, which stressed both abilities and achievements; and finally, popular elections, which reflected the political rights and powers of a broad band of citizens. The democratic elements in Roman politics during the late Republic have been consistently undervalued. This balance of pressures allowed the Roman ruling classes to preserve traditional constitutional forms long after massive changes had taken place in Rome's wealth and power. The huge Roman empire of the late Republic was still being governed by the institutions of a city-state.

The Principate

In 31 BC, after years of civil strife, peace was re-established under a monarchy. In Chapter 3, we analyse the very low succession rates prevalent among the senatorial aristocracy under emperors' rule during the next three centuries. Among second-rank (*suffect*) consuls, for example, less than one in five is known to have had a consular or senatorial son. Admittedly, this conclusion is based on several samples drawn from different periods, and from incomplete data. Even so, we think that the figure is roughly right. It indicates how high the turnover between generations in the senatorial aristocracy had become. The senate under the emperors was even more open to outsiders than it had been during the Republic.

Once again explanation is difficult. Some of the factors at work during the last century of the Republic (high mortality, split inheritance, restricted fertility) persisted, and perhaps even increased in importance. But differences in succession rates between periods and between different strata inside the senate reveal the limitations of an explanation along these lines. For example, succession rates among top-rank (*ordinary*) consuls were always higher than among second-rank (*suffect*) consuls, even though they fluctuated considerably. A fall in fertility does not explain these fluctuations, nor the differences between strata inside the senate. In any case, changes in aristocratic birth-rates and changes in their death-rates (for example, through imperial persecutions) were themselves responses to social and political pressures. These pressures must also be analysed and explained.

In pursuit of this explanation, two broad changes deserve particular attention: rule by emperors and the increased integration of the whole empire into a single political system. I shall deal with each in turn. First, the establishment of monarchy fundamentally altered the ground rules of political competition within the elite at Rome. Popular elections, for example, were soon abolished. Opportunities for generals to win military glory were severely restricted, especially when the boundaries of empire were more or less fixed (by the middle of the first century AD). Opportunities for self-enrichment in the provinces or at Rome by corrupt administration were curtailed, although never eliminated. The style and location of political competition changed. Internal senatorial elections, patronage by emperors and palace intrigue all became important ingredients in political success.

The eagerness of senatorial contestants persisted. Senate membership alone raised the status of a whole family for generations. The consulship and the prestigious offices which it could bring in its train still represented the pinnacle of aristocratic achievement. But the costs were high (an impressive house at Rome, a huge retinue of slaves, the presentation of elaborate games, suburban villas). The financial rewards were uncertain. The rise in status often drained a family's resources. Politically successful fathers may have been unable to launch their son or sons into politics. Success did not secure succession.

The power of emperors overshadowed both senators individually and the senate considered as a legislative body. Emperors' entourages of influential administrators and advisers included some senators, but they also included knights, ex-slaves, wives and favourites. The palace administrators at Rome and the equestrian administrators in the provinces constituted complementary nodes of power which eventually rivalled the senate. Their growing importance reflected an increase in the complexity of imperial administration and an increase in direct monarchical intervention in areas which had traditionally been senatorial preserves. In the crisis of the third century AD, knights with military experience replaced senators as governors of important provinces. The development was symptomatic. The power wielded by parallel groups undermined the political supremacy of the senatorial aristocracy.

Secondly, the gradual integration of the whole empire into a single political system progressively removed the distinction between conquerors and conquered. In AD 212, Roman citizenship was given to practically all the free inhabitants of the empire. But long before that, members of provincial elites were allowed to compete for places in the Roman senate. It was in the emperors' interest to widen support for Roman government in the provinces and to strengthen the capacity of respected subjects to control the arbitrary exercise of power by governors of provinces. Whatever the conscious motives, the result was a significant increase in the number of candidates from all over the empire, qualified by wealth and culture, who could compete for the fixed number of places in the Roman senate.

This provincialisation of the Roman senate is well known, but its implications still need to be worked out on two distinct levels: on the level of actors' perceptions and on the level of the political system.

Preface

First let us consider actors' perceptions. Senators' sons did not go into politics, partly, we think, because a political career was very expensive relative to probable rewards, and partly because senatorial privileges could be inherited in the male line over three generations, without any descendant needing to enter the senate. Hereditary senatorial privileges thus came to be divorced from active membership of the senate.

Secondly, let us consider the political system. As in the Republic, high turnover between generations in senatorial families increased the flow of talent into the senate and so into important administrative positions. The low level of hereditary membership in the senate and the competition among the large number of qualified Italian and provincial land-owners for entry to the senate weakened the senatorial aristocracy as a privileged stratum. The emperors depended for the strength of their autocracy upon the permeability of the senate and on the rivalries inside it, as well as on rival power bases, such as the army and equestrian and ex-slave palace administrators. The failure of senators to turn themselves into a closed hereditary order, in order to defend and increase their collective privileges, was an important characteristic of the Roman political system.

Methods

These two central chapters are similar in substance and method. Both work towards an analysis of the ruling elite and of Roman political culture from a body of hard evidence (mostly lists of consuls). In both, we use standard techniques of statistical and demographic analysis in order to estimate the extent and significance of the evidence which has not survived. This tactic is possible, because in demographic history the number of probabilities is strictly finite. We can set what is observed against what can be expected. With due precautions, we can supplement what is known from surviving sources with what was probable. At this stage, theory collides with convention. Modern historians of the Roman world conventionally authenticate each event in Roman history, and often their interpretations, with references to a surviving text or artefact. Writing a history of the ancient world is thus often presented as though it were chiefly a matter of mastering the sources and modern commentaries on them, and of ironing out ambiguities and differences in their accounts. One general implication is that if there is no evidence, there can be no authentication, and therefore no history. At first sight, this may seem a reasonable deduction. But a false corollary is often, perhaps unconsciously made: what is known is equated with what happened; what is not known did not occur. As one school text-book disarmingly put it: 'In the second century [AD], nothing much happened.'

We are not suggesting that history should normally cover what is not known, let alone what did not happen and what might have been. Occasionally each is tempting. In limited areas, but not just in demographic history, if probabilities are finite or if the size of the universe is known or can be estimated (as is the case with consuls or the senate), it is worthwhile systematically analysing what our sources did not report and what the Romans did not do. And in general, the absence of evidence on particular points of Roman 'failure' to do certain things which we find in other pre-industrial states (such as harnessing horses effectively, or making private loans to the state) can be the start of profitable investigations. The search for what is missing stimulates us to consider what we or the Romans took for granted, or wanted to keep hidden, or had not thought of doing. To turn a well-known phrase, the Roman emperor was not only what the Roman emperor did, but also what he did not do and what he did but he was not reported to have done.

Rituals and emotions

The rest of the book, Chapters 1 and 4, are both very different from the central chapters in substance, method and style. They are both heavily dependent on direct citation of classical sources, and present in effect a collage of quotation and interpretation, in the hope of arousing the reader's empathetic imagination. Another objective is to place Roman feelings and perceptions in a social and political context. Chapter 1 deals with the wilful slaughter of men and animals as popular entertainment, mainly in the city of Rome. Chapter 4 deals with grief, with Roman rituals of burial and mourning and with the transmission of property by legacies at death.

The concern with politics is still there. Gladiatorial combats, for example, can be envisaged as political theatre, as bloody and dramatic enactments of emperors' power in front of, and occasionally in conflict with, a huge audience of temporary courtiers. And legacy-hunting in the Roman elite can be understood as an adaptation to the high cost of political life, to the restriction on ways of self-enrichment in the political elite, and to the asymmetry between biological and social reproduction, which we discuss in Chapters 2 and 3. Roman legacy-hunters exploited some of the difficulties which this asymmetry caused for the transfer of wealth between generations.

Preface

The main underlying problem in these two chapters is to understand, and to develop ways of expressing, Roman experience. This involves wondering 'What was it like to be Roman?', and 'In what ways were their experiences and reactions different from our own?' In tackling these questions, we are exploring the limits of the value of empathy as a tactic of historical analysis.

I chose death as a central topic, not only because it was a breaking-point in the transmission of power and property, but also because it aroused strong feelings, ranging from grief to relief, from triumphant excitement at bloody slaughter to greed and jealousy over dividing a dead relative's possessions:

> I was chatting to my mother...about the property left to me by my father...in his will, when she oppressed by the consciousness of what she had purloined – furnishing, stores and a lot more besides – set upon me with her sister's husband Serenus...and not only abused me, but also ripped my clothes, all because they want to rob me of what is mine. (Extract from a formal complaint to a local magistrate in AD 194 from Hermopolis in Roman Egypt; P.Ryl. 116.)

The quotation is immediately attractive. What makes it so alluring? In part, I think, it is because we can imagine ourselves to be there, at least as sympathetic or shocked observers. The plaintiff's psychological insight that his mother's guilt about her theft had provoked her aggression (that is how I interpret it) seems strikingly modern. By modern, I mean that we can readily recognise similar emotions in ourselves or in others. But that very recognition underscores a problem of method. How can we understand Roman experiences, especially when those experiences are mediated to us in sophisticated literary works? Ideally, we need a key for translating Roman literary expressions back into the original experiences. But that is impossible. We have to rely instead on the cumulative impression of selected texts, interlaced with interpretative commentary. The limitations and dangers of this method are considerable. Interpretations are subjective, translations into English unavoidably reflect English, not Roman culture, excerpts are necessarily cited out of context, the criteria for the selection of each quotation cannot be made explicit, and finally, the total impact is probably as much or more the product of each reader's perceptions as it is of the author's intentions. But then history is often more art than science.

Preface

Structure and action

This summary of arguments and methods raises more questions than it answers. Reviewers and students in a hurry (for whom this preface is particularly written) are encouraged to discover that some of these questions are answered in the book. The mixture of experimental and conventional techniques may seem inconsistent. But methods depend on problems. The main problem in the two central chapters is to discover and analyse persistent elements in the selection and renewal of the Roman political elite. For this, we draw considerably on aggregate, statistical data, which are at some remove from actors' predominantly short-term and egocentric perceptions. In the two outlying chapters, by contrast, an important problem is to understand how some Romans perceived and coped with death. For this empathetic reconstruction, we put more stress on actors' perceptions and what is directly reported in surviving ancient sources.

The division between the two methods should not be exaggerated; they overlap and are intertwined. Each reflects a different axis of analysis, a different starting point. In one, we regard Roman behaviour as determined, or at least as moulded by a political system; but we also take account of individual perceptions, ambitions and achievements. In the other, we see individuals as controlling, or at least as being responsible for their own actions; but we also take account of the conventions and institutions within which they worked. The two methods reflect the old and still unresolved problem of structure and action.

ACKNOWLEDGEMENTS

I should like to thank Brunel University and the Social Science Research Council for funds which enabled me to employ research assistants. Graham Burton worked with me for two years before going on to better things at Oxford and Manchester. I am very grateful to him, not only for all his hard work and scholarship, but for his patience and for his tactful correction of many errors in fact and logic, not only in the two central chapters on which we worked together. Melinda Letts helped me considerably with Chapter 1 as well as with Chapter 4.

My thanks to the Classics Faculty of Cambridge University, who invited me to give the J. H. Gray lectures in 1977; these lectures formed the foundation of Chapters 2 and 3. Professor P. A. Brunt invited me to give a paper on the same topic to his seminar at Oxford,

Preface

and read each chapter with his usual and exceptional critical acumen. It is reassuring that he has now come to similar conclusions by a different route (*Journal of Roman Studies* 72 (1982) 1ff). Mary Beard, John North and Simon Price each helpfully improved different chapters. Finally, I should like to say how much I have benefited from the friendly and helpful academic atmosphere created among ancient historians by Fergus Millar at University College, and the Institute of Classical Studies, London.

This book is dedicated to Sir Moses Finley, who first excited my interest in ancient history, as he has excited the interest of so many others. I am grateful to him for many discussions and insights, and particularly for his unerring selection, from a morass of arguments, of the problems which matter most. It is that capacity, and much else, which makes him a great teacher and historian.

London   K.H.
January 1983

LIST OF ABBREVIATIONS USED

AE	*Année Epigraphique.*
ANRW	*Aufstieg und Niedergang der römischen Welt*, ed. H. Temporini *et al.*, Berlin 1972– .
CIL	*Corpus Inscriptionum Latinarum*, ed. T. Mommsen *et al.*, Berlin, 1863– .
CJ	*Codex Justinianus*, ed. P. Krüger, Berlin, 1877.
CPL	*Corpus Papyrorum Latinorum*, ed. R. Cavenaille, Wiesbaden, 1972.
C.Th.	*Codex Theodosianus*, ed. T. Mommsen, Berlin, 1905.
D.	*The Digest of Justinian*, ed. T. Mommsen, Berlin, 1870.
DS	*Dictionnaire des antiquités grecques et romaines*, ed. C. Daremberg and E. Saglio, Paris, 1877–1919.
e_0	Average expectation of life at birth (in years).
ESAR	T. Frank *et al.*, *An Economic Survey of Ancient Rome*, Baltimore, Md., 1933–40.
FIRA	*Fontes Iuris Romani Anteiustiniani*, ed. S. Riccobono *et al.*, Florence,[2] 1940–3.
ICUR	*Inscriptiones Christianae Urbis Romae*, ed. J. B. de Rossi, Rome, 1922–75.
IG	*Inscriptiones Graecae*, Berlin, 1873– .
ILS	*Inscriptiones Latinae Selectae*, ed. H. Dessau, Berlin, 1892–1916.
Kaibel	*Epigrammata Graeca ex lapidibus conlecta*, ed. G. Kaibel, Berlin, 1878.
OGIS	*Orientis Graeci Inscriptiones Selectae*, ed. W. Dittenberger, Leipzig, 1903–5.
ORF	*Oratorum Romanorum Fragmenta*, ed. H. Malcovati, Turin,[3] 1967.
PG	*Patrologia Graeca*, ed. J.-P. Migne, Paris, 1857–66.
PIR	*Prosopographia Imperii Romani*, ed. E. Klebs, H. Dessau, E. Groag, A. Stein, Berlin, 1897–8; 2nd edition, Berlin, 1933– .
PL	*Patrologia Latina*, ed. J.-P. Migne, Paris, 1844–64.
P.Oxy.	*The Oxyrhynchus Papyri*, ed. B. P. Grenfell *et al.*, London, 1898– .
RE	*Real-Encyclopädie der klassischen Altertumswissenschaft*, ed. A. F. von Pauly *et al.*, Stuttgart, 1894– .
SEG	*Supplementum Epigraphicum Graecum*, Leiden, 1923– .
SHA	Scriptores Historiae Augustae.

To find standard editions of classical authors, see *The Oxford Classical Dictionary*, ed. N. G. L. Hammond, Oxford,[2] 1970, or W. Buchwald *et al.*, *Tusculum Lexikon griechischer und lateinischer Autoren*, Munich, 1963. For translations and texts, see the Loeb Classical Library; many useful translations are also in The Penguin Classics. Selected sources are translated with commentary in N. Lewis and M. Reinhold, *Roman Civilization*, Harper Torchbooks, New York, 1966, two volumes.

Abbreviations

MEASURES AND COINS

The following rough equivalences are used:

1 *modius* = 8·62–8·67 litres = 6·5 kg wheat.

4 HS (*sesterces*) = 1 *denarius* (*dn*) = 1 *drachma* (*dr*).

The notional normal price of wheat was 3 HS per *modius*, so that an average urban family of four persons could live at the level of minimum subsistence, consuming roughly 1,000 kg wheat equivalent per year, at a cost of about 450–500 HS. This calculation is very rough, but it helps give some meaning to ancient prices from about 100 BC–AD 200. The cost of living in the city of Rome was appreciably higher.

To
Sir Moses Finley

Teacher and Friend

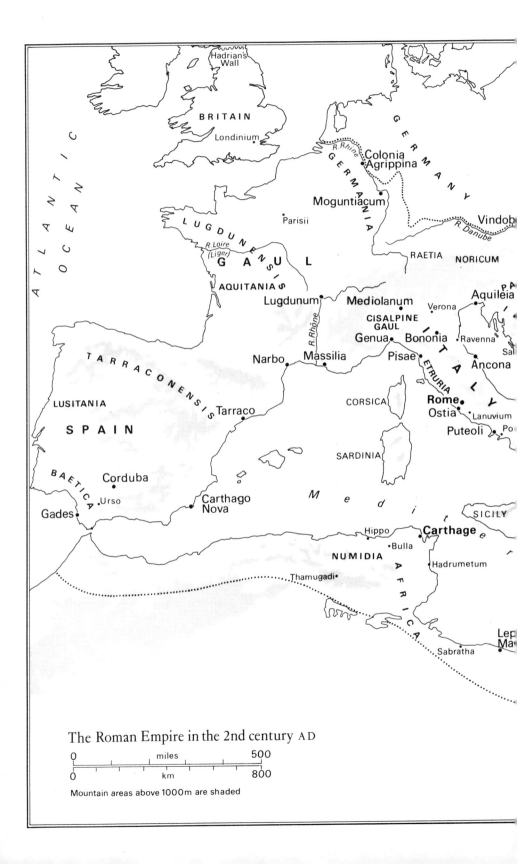

The Roman Empire in the 2nd century AD

```
0          miles        500
0           km          800
```

Mountain areas above 1000m are shaded

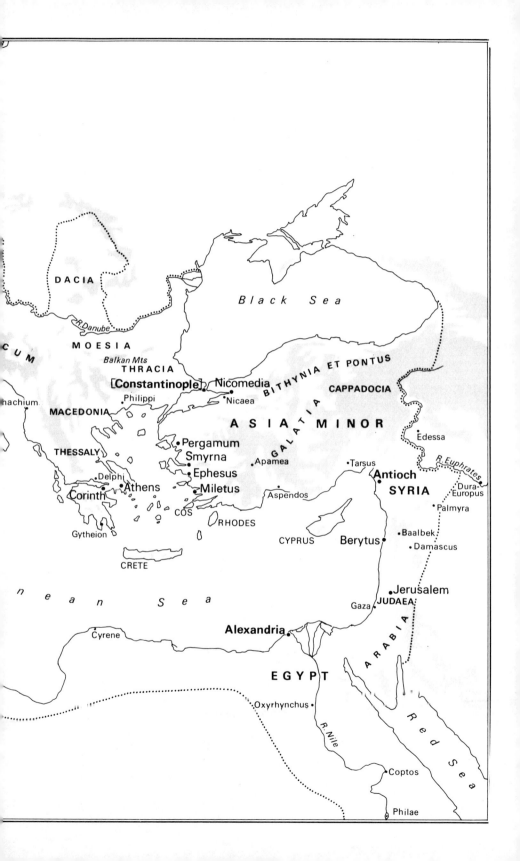

1

MURDEROUS GAMES

I INTRODUCTION

Rome was a warrior state.[1] During two centuries of imperial expansion following the second war against Carthage, that is in the last two centuries BC, Rome conquered the whole of the Mediterranean basin, and incorporated the conquered territory and its inhabitants, perhaps one fifth or one sixth of the world's then population, within the Roman state. These victories were bought at a price, paid by hundreds of thousands of men killed in war, and by captive slaves, and by soldiers who owed their victory to training and discipline. Decimation illustrates the point well. If an army unit was judged disobedient or cowardly in battle, one soldier in ten was selected by lot and cudgelled to death by his former comrades (Polybius 6.38). Decimation was not merely a terrifying myth, told to enforce compliance among fresh recruits. Decimation actually occurred, and often enough not to be particularly remarked on (e.g. Dio 41.35 and 48.42). Roman soldiers killed each other for their common good.[2] Small wonder then that they executed military

---

1 For Rome as a warrior state, see *Conquerors and Slaves* 25ff and W. V. Harris, *War and Imperialism in Republican Rome 327–70 B.C.* (Oxford, 1979) 9ff. On the close involvement of emperors, senators and knights in feats of prowess, as well as in chariot-racing, animal-killing and gladiatorial fighting, see particularly L. Friedländer, *Sittengeschichte Roms* (Leipzig,[10] 1922) vol. 2, 1–162. This chapter owes a great deal to that unsurpassed work of scholarship and insight. The article in DS *sv Gladiatores* is very useful, while M. Grant, *Gladiators* (London, 1967) offers a serviceable but unannotated review. G. Ville's monograph, *La gladiature en Occident* (Rome, 1981) reached me when this book was already in press. I have been much influenced by C. Geertz' brilliant essay 'Deep play: notes on the Balinese cockfight', in his *Interpretations of Culture* (London, 1975) 412ff. Indeed, in some respects this chapter is written in direct imitation of that essay.

2 'When every tenth man from a defeated army is beaten with clubs, the lot falls also on the brave. Making an example on a grand scale inevitably involves some injustice. The common good is bought with individual suffering' (Tacitus, *Annals* 14.44). As always, it is difficult to deduce frequency of practice from frequency of mention in our surviving sources. Tacitus (*Annals* 3.21) recorded an instance of decimation in about AD 20, and commented that it was rare in that period. Yet the existence of the word, *decumo* – choose one in ten – first

deserters without mercy; or that prisoners of war were sometimes forced to fight in gladiatorial contests, or were thrown to wild beasts for popular entertainment. Public executions of prisoners helped inculcate valour and fear in the men, women and children left at home. Children learnt the lesson about what happened to soldiers who were defeated. These were the rituals which helped maintain an atmosphere of violence, even in peace. Bloodshed and slaughter joined military glory and conquest as central elements in Roman culture. They persisted as central elements, even when the Roman peace (*pax Romana*) was established under the emperors in the first two centuries AD. It was a period when the mass of Roman citizens living in the capital were divorced from the direct experience of war. Real-life battles occurred much less frequently. And those which did occur, were fought on distant frontiers.

Then, in memory of their warrior traditions, the Romans set up artificial battlefields in their cities and towns. They re-created battlefield conditions for public amusement. The custom spread from Italy to the provinces. Nowadays, we admire the Colosseum in Rome and other great Roman amphitheatres, such as those at Verona, Arles, Nîmes and El Djem (Tunisia), as architectural monuments, while choosing to forget, I suspect, that this was where Romans regularly organised fights to the death between hundreds of gladiators, the mass execution of unarmed criminals and the indiscriminate slaughter of domestic and wild animals. The enormous size of the amphitheatres indicates how popular these exhibitions were. The Colosseum which seated about 50,000 people is still one of the most impressive buildings in Rome. It is also a magnificent feat of engineering and design. In ancient times, amphitheatres must have towered over cities, much as cathedrals towered over mediaeval towns. Public killings were a Roman rite, legitimated by the myth that gladiatorial shows 'inspired a glory in wounds and a contempt of death, since the love of praise and desire for victory could be seen, even in the bodies of slaves and criminals' (Pliny, *Panegyric* 33).

The lure of public spectacles was hard to resist, but not everyone approved. 'There are special vices peculiar to this city which children seem to absorb, almost in the mother's womb: a partiality for the theatre and a passion for horse-racing and gladiatorial shows'

attested in this period suggests that the practice had been common, while other evidence, albeit not good evidence, suggests that the practice continued (SHA, *Macrinus* 12). For a brief but guarded account, see G. R. Watson, *The Roman Soldier* (London, 1969) 117ff and *RE sv decimatio*.

Introduction

(Tacitus *Dialogue on Oratory* 29). Seneca tells us of a visit he once paid to the arena in Rome. He arrived in the middle of the day, during the entertainment staged in the interval between the wild-beast show in the morning and the gladiatorial show of the afternoon. He expected to find some light relief 'from the sight of human blood'. Instead, he found himself watching the mass execution of criminals. With a mixture of moral outrage and excitement, he described to a friend how degrading he had found the whole experience:

All the previous fighting had been merciful by comparison. Now finesse is set aside, and we have pure unadultered murder. The combatants have no protective covering; their entire bodies are exposed to the blows. No blow falls in vain. This is what lots of people prefer to the regular contests, and even to those which are put on by popular request. And it is obvious why. There is no helmet, no shield to repel the blade. Why have armour? Why bother with skill? All that just delays death.

In the morning, men are thrown to lions and bears. At mid-day they are thrown to the spectators themselves. No sooner has a man killed, than they shout for him to kill another, or to be killed. The final victor is kept for some other slaughter. In the end, every fighter dies...And all this goes on while the arena is half-empty.

You may object that the victims committed robbery or were murderers. So what? Even if they deserved to suffer, what's your compulsion to watch their sufferings?

'Kill him', they shout, 'Beat him, burn him.' Why is he too timid to fight? Why is he so frightened to kill? Why so reluctant to die? They have to whip him to make him accept his wounds. (Seneca, *Letters* 7.2ff)

Seneca wrote that he went away from the experience feeling 'more callous and less human'. He also acknowledged the danger of being sucked in by the crowd's enthusiasm. Over three hundred years later, St Augustine recorded in his *Confessions* how a Christian friend who swore that he would have nothing to do with such things was forced along to the amphitheatre by his companions, opened his eyes when he heard the crowd shout, and became an eager devotee of gladiatorial shows (*Confessions* 6.8).

II GLADIATORIAL SHOWS: ORIGINS AND DEVELOPMENTS

Gladiatorial fights originated apparently as an element in funeral games. 'Once upon a time', wrote the Christian critic Tertullian at the end of the second century, 'men believed that the souls of the dead were propitiated by human blood, and so at funerals they sacrificed prisoners of war or slaves of poor quality bought for the purpose' (*On the Public Shows* 12). It was also thought that gladiators

3

were originally imported from Etruria or from Campania. Stories about origins are notoriously unreliable. Yet repeated evidence confirms the close association of gladiatorial contests with funerals. The first recorded gladiatorial show in the city of Rome is attributed to the ex-consul D. Iunius Brutus Pera and his brother in 264 BC; it was held in the ox-market (*forum boarium*) in honour of their dead father. Only three pairs of gladiators took part. Over the next two centuries, the scale and frequency of gladiatorial shows steadily increased.³ In 65 BC, Julius Caesar gave elaborate funeral games for his long-dead father, involving 320 pairs of gladiators, and condemned criminals equipped with silver weapons who were forced to fight with wild beasts (Pliny, *Natural History* 33.53; Plutarch, *Caesar* 5). At his next games in 46 BC, in honour of his dead daughter and of his recent triumphs in Gaul and Egypt, Caesar presented not only the customary fights between individual gladiators, but also fights between detachments of infantry and between squadrons of cavalry, some mounted on horses and others on elephants; the contestants were gladiators, prisoners of war and criminals condemned to death (Dio 43.23).

Up to this time, gladiatorial shows had always been put on by individual aristocrats at their own initiative and expense, in honour of dead relatives. The religious component in gladiatorial ceremonies continued to be important. For example, attendants in the arena were sometimes dressed as gods; slaves who tested whether executed criminals or dead gladiators were really dead or just pretending, by applying a red-hot cauterising iron were dressed as the god Mercury, while those who dragged the dead bodies away were dressed as the god of the underworld, Pluto, or as Charon (Tertullian, *In Defence*

³ On the gladiatorial contest of 264 BC, see Livy, *Summary of Book* 16, Valerius Maximus 2.4.7; Servius (on Virgil, *Aeneid* 3.67) commented that gladiatorial fighting developed out of human sacrifice, and through forced contests held between prisoners of war at funerals. On Etruscan origins, see Nicolaus of Damascus cited by Athenaeus, *Banquets of the Philosophers* 4.153 and an Etruscan funeral urn of the third century BC depicting gladiators (reproduced in DS *sv Gladiator* 1564). The later testimony is spasmodic, presumably noting only special gladiatorial shows given by great nobles at funeral games. For example, in 216 BC the three sons of M. Aemilius Lepidus, twice consul, gave funeral games in his honour, which lasted for three days and included fights between 44 gladiators (Livy 23.30, cf. 28.21). In 200 BC and 183 BC, two funeral games included fights between 50 and 120 gladiators (Livy 31.50 and 39.46). Under 174 BC, Livy recorded: 'Several gladiatorial shows were given that year. Some were small. But one was notable above all the rest, namely that given by Titus Flamininus to mark the death of his father [an ex-consul]. There was a public distribution of meat, a feast and theatrical performances. The whole ceremony lasted four days. The climax of the show, which was large for the period, was fighting between 74 gladiators spread over three days' (41.28).

of Christianity 15). During the persecutions of Christians, from the second century AD, the victims were sometimes led in a procession around the arena dressed up as priests and priestesses of pagan cults, before being stripped naked and thrown to wild beasts.[4] The welter of blood in gladiatorial and wild-beast shows, the squeals of the victims and of slaughtered animals are completely alien to us and almost unimaginable. For some Romans, there must have been associations with battlefields, and more immediately for everyone, associations with religious sacrifice – except that after gladiatorial shows the victims were not eaten. In gladiatorial contests and in wild beast shows, the Romans came very close, even at the height of their civilisation, to performing human sacrifice. Purportedly it was done in commemoration of their dead.[5]

In the city of Rome, in the late Republic and early Principate, the religious and commemorative elements of gladiatorial shows were increasingly fused with, even eclipsed by the political and the spectacular. Gladiatorial shows at Rome were public performances, held mostly, before the amphitheatre was built, in the ritual and social centre of the city, in the Forum.[6] Public participation, attracted by the splendour of the show and by the distributions of meat (*visceratio* – Livy 41.28), magnified the respect paid to the dead and the honour of the whole family. Aristocratic funerals were political acts. And funeral games had political overtones, particularly during the Republic, because of their popularity with citizen electors. Indeed, the growth in the splendour of gladiatorial shows was largely fuelled by political competition between ambitious aristocrats. It

---

[4] For Christians this added insult to injury; presumably that was its purpose. See *The Martyrdom of Perpetua and Felicitas* 18 in H. Musurillo, ed., *Acts of The Christian Martyrs* (Oxford, 1972) 106ff. Perpetua managed to persuade the officer in charge that they should be allowed to parade in their normal clothes. I imagine that most martyrs were not granted this privilege, and that pagan victims were also forced to parade in a religious procession before being killed.

[5] On the large-scale ritual slaughter of prisoners of war and slaves by Aztecs, and their later consumption, see the stimulating essay by M. Harris, *Cannibals and Kings* (London, 1978) 110ff; he also discusses the social functions of torture among some North American Indians, both as public entertainment and as instruction on the benefits of fighting bravely in order to avoid capture.

[6] According to Vitruvius (*On Architecture* 5.1), it was ancient tradition for gladiatorial shows to be held in the Forum, that is in the political and cultural centre of the city. Under the Forum, modern archaeologists have discovered extensive and well-planned corridors, built towards the end of the last century BC, and the remains of mechanical hoists situated in these corridors G. Carettoni has plausibly connected these corridors and hoists with the presentation of elaborately staged gladiatorial shows; the combatants were winched up from below suddenly to appear in the centre of the arena. See his 'Le gallerie ipogee del Foro romano', *Bulletino della commissione archelogica di Roma* 76 (1956–8) 23ff.

spilled over from their traditional competition in the provision of regular games, which included theatrical shows and chariot-races. Scipio Africanus and Julius Caesar, for example, gave splendid funeral games in honour of the dead, which also celebrated their own victories, enhanced their family's prestige, advanced their political careers and reputations, and presumably both pleased and excited their supporters.

In 42 BC for the first time, gladiatorial fights were substituted for chariot-races in official games (Dio 47.40). In the city of Rome, thereafter, regular gladiatorial shows, like theatrical shows and chariot-races, were given by officers of state as part of their political careers, as an official obligation and as a tax on status.[7] Extra gladiatorial shows and wild-beast hunts were given by the emperors themselves. The first emperor, Augustus, as part of his general policy of limiting aristocrats' opportunities to court favour with the Roman populace, severely restricted the number and size of the regular gladiatorial shows (Dio 54.2). So after 22 BC, in his reign, there were perhaps only two regular gladiatorial shows per year. In the fourth century AD, we know from an official calendar that there were ten per year.[8] But for the very long period in between, we know little about fluctuations in the frequency of regular gladiatorial shows. And perhaps exact frequency does not matter much; Christmas comes

[7] In 22 BC Augustus allocated the provision of up to two gladiatorial shows per year to the praetors (Dio 54.2); the emperor Claudius transferred this obligation to the quaestors, the youngest members of the senate; soon afterwards, it was returned to the praetors and then back to the quaestors; it stayed with them from the end of the first century AD onwards (Tacitus, *Annals* 11.22 and 13.5; Suetonius, *Domitian* 4). The reasons for these transfers are obscure. In the fourth century AD, some shows were paid for, perhaps only in part, by the treasury, while others were wholly paid for by the quaestors who had been specially chosen by the emperor (*candidati Caesaris*); see SHA, *Severus Alexander* 43 confirmed by the Calendar of Furius Filocalus, ed. A. Degrassi, *Inscriptiones Italiae* 13.2 (Rome, 1963) p. 261.

[8] We should be wary of taking for granted that this regulation was systematically enforced until the date when our scanty sources next tell us something about gladiatorial shows at Rome. And yet this is very often how ancient historians work, perforce. The next emperor also fixed the size of gladiatorial shows (Suetonius, *Tiberius* 34). The number of regular gladiatorial shows during the first two centuries AD is unknown; see best Friedländer's cautious comments: 'The number of days given over to Games in the course of the year cannot be ascertained for any period, because the regular games were shifted from time to time, and the extraordinary games cannot be systematically counted' (vol. 2, 11). Finally, in spite of the clear distinction between circus games (*ludi circenses*), theatrical shows (*ludi scaenici*) and gladiatorial shows (*munera*), gladiatorial contests were occasionally slotted into games normally devoted to chariot-racing (e.g. Dio 59.14).

Origins and developments

only once a year; frequency and significance are not Siamese twins. Gladiatorial shows were always something special, and happened regularly only a few times each year. The actual events were magnified beforehand by expectations and afterwards by memory. Street advertisements, painted on plastered walls, stimulated excitement and anticipation.[9] In surviving literature, art and artefacts (frescoes, mosaics, sculptures, graffiti, bronze figurines, glazed vases, terracotta lamps and engraved glasses), there are frequent references to and depictions of gladiatorial fights and of wild-beast shows. In Latin proverbs and sayings, and even in our own language, gladiatorial contests have left their mark: thumbs down – *verso pollice*.[10] In conversation, in daily life, chariot-races and gladiatorial fights were all the rage; the historian Tacitus commented, presumably with some rhetorical exaggeration: 'How often will you find anyone who talks of anything else at home? And when you enter the lecture-halls, what else do you hear the young men talking about' (*Dialogue on Oratory* 29) A baby's nursing bottle, made of clay, and found at Pompeii was stamped with the figure of a gladiator. It presumably symbolised that the baby should imbibe a gladiator's strength and courage.[11] Gladiatorial shows suffused Roman life.

Cost and splendour

We know very little about the normal cost of regular gladiatorial shows presented under the emperors. Augustus tried to take all the games produced in the city of Rome out of the sphere of political competition by granting sponsors a subvention from state funds, by forbidding any one official from spending more on them than his colleagues, and by limiting the size of regular shows to only sixty pairs of gladiators (Dio 54.2). Fragmentary testimony suggests that these

[9] Several such advertisements survive from Pompeii; an example in red letters runs: '20 pairs of gladiators belonging to D. Lucretius Sater Valens, lifelong priest of Nero Caesar, son of Augustus, and 10 pairs of gladiators belonging to D. Lucretius Valens his son will fight at Pompeii on April (8 9 10 11 and 12). There will be a wild-beast show as allowed by law and awnings (over the seats)' (*CIL* 4.3884, cf. 7995). For commentary on this and similar texts see P. S. Tumolesi, *Gladiatorum Paria* (Rome, 1980) 24ff and more generally A. Mau, *Pompeii, Its Life and Art* (New York, 1899) 215ff.
[10] On gladiatorial elements in several Latin sayings, see A. Otto, *Die Sprichwörter und sprichwörtlichen Redensarten der Römer* (Leipzig, 1890) 396. On artefacts, see conveniently *Enciclopedia dell'Arte antica sv gladiatore*; for graffiti, see still R. Garrucci, *Graffiti di Pompeii* (Paris,² 1856).
[11] Mau 1899: 366.

7

regulations were evaded.[12] The pressure for evasion was simply that aristocrats were still competing with each other, for prestige and for political success. The splendour of their public exhibitions could make or break their social and political reputations. As the aristocratic Symmachus wrote to a friend: 'I must now outdo the reputation earned by my own shows; the recent munificence of our house in my consulship and the quaestorian games of my son allow us to present nothing mediocre' (*Letters* 4.60). In frequent letters, he enlisted the co-operation of powerful friends in the provinces and some help from the emperor's aides, so that he finally managed to procure antelopes and gazelles (*Letters* 6.144), leopards and lions (4.12 and 2.76), bears from Dalmatia (9.142), some emaciated bear-cubs (2.76) and even crocodiles, which only just survived to the beginning of the games, because for fifty days they had refused to eat (6.43). Moreover, twenty-nine Saxon prisoners of war strangled each other in their cells, 'their necks broken without a noose', on the night before their final scheduled appearance (*Letters* 2.46).[13]

The total cost of procuring all these men and animals must have

[12] Caligula, for example, in order to increase revenues, encouraged extra numbers of gladiators to be sold and extra bouts to be given at the Circensian games (Dio 59.14). Costs: in the mid-second century BC, Polybius (31.28) claimed that a grand gladiatorial show, fit for a leading aristocrat's funeral, cost 720,000 HS, a seemingly huge sum for the period. An untrustworthy source reported that the future emperor Hadrian, when praetor, spent 2,000,000 HS on his games (SHA, *Hadrian* 3), while Martial in an epigram (10.41) sneered that a praetor might just get away with spending 100,000 HS on his main games. This is all fragile testimony, but better evidence comes from the provinces. A senatorial decree of *c*. AD 177 indicated that a show of 120 gladiators would cost nearly 700,000 HS for the gladiators alone, without taking account of gifts to the crowd or of wild-beast shows or processions. This estimate is based on new maximum legal prices, but presumably actual prices had previously been higher (see below, note 20). Symmachus in the fourth century AD is said to have spent 2,000 Roman pounds of gold (655 kg) on his son's praetorian games (Olympiodorus frag. 44) – a sum equivalent to 9,000,000 HS, enough to feed *c*. 20,000 families for one year at minimum subsistence. This figure is often cited, but should it be believed? However that may be, it seems probable that Roman senators by the middle of the first century AD spent very substantial sums on the presentation of official gladiatorial shows and games, perhaps twice as quaestors, aediles or praetors in the early part of their senatorial careers.

[13] Symmachus was consul in AD 391. Is it reasonable to cite his comments and experience as illustration of aristocratic attitudes during the previous four centuries? I think so, because of significant persistencies in the political structure, and because parallels can be found in earlier literature (cf. Apuleius, *The Golden Ass* 4.13 and 10.18). The dangers of such a tactic are obvious. But then a historical method, which uses excerpts from fragmentary surviving texts not merely as illustration, but more often as alleged authentication of arguments, is fraught with dangers. Besides, logically, there is little difference between citing a later text as evidence of an earlier practice, and citing an earlier text as evidence that the practice persisted until later!

been enormous. A few years before, in AD 384, the emperor Theodosius had, like the first emperor Augustus, tried to control senatorial expenditure on games. Symmachus thanked him fulsomely: 'When disgraceful ostentation had brought ruin to senatorial office because of reckless expenditure, you restored ancient sanity to our habits and costs, so that giving a modest show does not now bring stigma to colleagues who cannot afford more, nor does thoughtless extravagance bankrupt those who out of shame try to do more than they can afford' (*Letters* 10.8). But emperors' repeated attempts to control the cost of games given by senators failed because games brought popularity (Symmachus, *Letters* 10.9 and *C. Th.* 15.9). Games were part of the political order. That was why emperors' orders were evaded. Aristocrats knew that, when they presented gladiatorial contests and wild-beast shows, their political standing was at stake. Each presentation was, in Goffman's strikingly apposite phrase, 'a status bloodbath'.[14]

The most spectacular gladiatorial shows were given by the emperors themselves in the city of Rome. For example, at the dedication of the Colosseum in AD 80, the emperor Titus gave games which lasted 100 days and included the slaughter of 5,000 or 9,000 animals in a single day (some killed by women), plus individual and mass gladiatorial fights and pitched battles, including a naval battle on an artifically flooded site. One day's fighting alone involved 3,000 men. Spectator interest was heightened by the emperor, who threw small wooden balls (*missilia*) into the crowd, each marked with a sign indicating that it could be exchanged for food or clothes, or for silver or for slaves (Dio 66.25). Trajan, to celebrate his conquest of Dacia (roughly modern Romania), gave games in AD 108–9 lasting 123 days, in which 'some eleven thousand animals wild and tame were killed and ten thousand gladiators fought' (Dio 68.15).[15]

By their very nature, these were exceptional shows, enormously costly to prepare and to present. And self-liquidating. At least, all

[14] E. Goffman, *Encounters* (Indianapolis, 1961) 78. On Symmachus, see J. A. MacGeachy, *Quintus Aurelius Symmachus and the Senatorial Aristocracy of the West* (Chicago, 1942) 87ff.

[15] Roman emperors and aristocrats were, so it seems, much concerned with giving precise figures recording their achievements. For example, the formal lists of imperial acts surviving from Ostia state for AD 109: 'November 1 emperor Trajan finished his gladiatorial show which had lasted 117 days with 4,441½ pairs of gladiators. November 11 emperor Trajan inaugurated a naval battle lasting 6 days involving 127½ pairs of gladiators' (*Fasti Ostienses* in A. Degrassi, ed., *Inscriptiones Italiae* (Rome, 1947) vol. 13.1, p. 201). Similarly, Augustus in his formal life-record stated that he had given 26 wild-beast shows in Rome during his reign, in which 3,500 animals had been killed (*My Achievements* 22).

9

wild-beast shows were, even if gladiatorial contests left some survivors. To produce another show one had to start all over again, practically from scratch. The whole empire was scoured for fierce and exotic animals, for gladiators and for condemned criminals who could fight. Hence the rule: 'A provincial governor should not release criminals condemned to the beasts in order to curry favour with the populace. If the condemned have such strength and skill that they are worth exhibiting to the people in Rome, the governor should consult the emperor' (D. 48.19.31pr – Modestinus). The demand for prisoners for simple execution or to train as gladiators, to fight with wild beasts or to take part in mass battles was enormous. For example, in AD 52, the emperor Claudius presided in full military regalia over a battle on a lake (Fucino – just over 100 km from Rome) between two naval squadrons, manned for the occasion by 19,000 forced combatants. The palace guard, stationed behind stout barricades, which also prevented the combatants from escaping, bombarded the ships with missiles from catapults. After a faltering start (the men refused to fight), the battle 'although between criminals was fought with the spirit of free men; after much bloodshed, those who remained were spared extermination' (Tacitus *Annals* 12.65, cf. Dio 60.33).

The quality of Roman justice was occasionally tempered by the need to satisfy the demand for the condemned. Christians, burnt to death as scapegoats after the great fire at Rome in AD 64, were not alone in being sacrificed for public entertainment.[16] Slaves and bystanders, even the audience itself, ran the risk of becoming victims of emperors' truculent whims. The emperor Claudius, for example, dissatisfied with how the stage machinery had worked, ordered the stage mechanics responsible to fight in the arena. A spectator, who made a witty remark at the expense of Domitian during a gladiatorial show, was, at the emperor's command, dragged from his seat and thrown to the dogs, with a mocking placard round his neck (Suetonius, *Claudius* 34, *Domitian* 10, cf. *Caligula* 35). One day, when there was a shortage of condemned criminals, Caligula commanded that a section of the crowd should be seized and thrown to the wild beasts instead (Dio 59.10). Isolated incidents, but enough, I imagine,

---

[16] Nero gave his Gardens for the spectacle: 'A vast number of them were convicted, not so much of incendiarism as of hatred of the human race. And as they died, they were made laughing-stocks: some were dressed up in animal skins and given to the dogs to be torn apart; others were tied to crosses, and when daylight faded, were set alight to illuminate the night' (Tacitus, *Annals* 15.44). Tacitus went on to say that Nero's obvious enjoyment of cruelty eventually made people pity the Christians, in spite of their guilt. For other Christian martyrdoms as public entertainment, see Musurillo 1972 and Eusebius, *History of the Church* 5.1.

to intensify the excitement of those who attended (cf. Dio 72.20). Imperial legitimacy was reinforced occasionally by terror.

As for animals, their sheer variety symbolised the extent of Roman power, and left vivid traces in Roman literature and art (for example, in the beautiful mosaics at Piazza Armerina in Sicily). Already in 169 BC, 63 African animals (probably lions or leopards), 40 bears and several elephants were hunted down in a single show (Livy 44.18). New species were gradually introduced to Roman spectators – tigers, crocodiles, giraffes, lynxes, rhinoceros, ostriches, hippopotami – and killed for their pleasure (Pliny, *Natural History* 8.65ff). Not for Romans the tame viewing of caged animals in a zoo. Instead, slaughter and murder were acted out in front of their eyes and ears. Wild beasts were set to tear criminals to pieces as a public lesson in pain and death, or to kill each other, stimulated if necessary by firebrands. Finally, skilled hunters pursued and killed any animals which survived. Sometimes, as a variation, elaborate sets and quasi-theatrical performances were prepared, in which as a climax a criminal was devoured limb by limb (e.g. Strabo 6.2.6; Martial, *On the Public Shows* 7). Such spectacular punishments, common enough in other pre-industrial states, helped reconstitute sovereign power; the deviant criminal was punished; law and order were re-established.[17]

The labour and organisation employed to capture animals on the scale required and to deliver them alive to the city of Rome must have been enormous and effective. Even if these animals were more plentiful then than now, single shows with 100, 400 and 600 lions plus other animals in the last century BC seem amazing (Pliny, *Natural History* 8.53, cf. Dio 39.38). By contrast, after Roman times, no hippopotamus was seen in Europe until one was brought by steamship to London in 1850; it took a detachment of Egyptian soldiers to capture it, and a five-month journey to bring it from the White Nile as far as Cairo.[18] And yet the emperor Commodus, a dead shot with spear and bow, himself killed five hippos, two elephants, a rhinoceros

---

[17] On wild-beast shows, see best Friedländer 1922: vol. 2, 77ff. Strabo, during the reign of Augustus, had himself seen in the Forum at Rome the execution of a Sicilian robber who was dropped from an elaborate scaffold into wild-beast cages below (6.2.6); cf. the elaborate sets prepared for the magic ass, when he was to have intercourse in the arena with a female criminal, who was then to be devoured by a wild animal, as described in Apuleius' novel, *The Golden Ass* 10.29ff; see similarly, Tertullian, *In Defence of Christianity* 15. On animals in Roman art, see B. Pace, *I mosaici di Piazza Armerina* (Rome, 1955) and J. M. C. Toynbee, *Animals in Roman Life and Art* (London, 1973). On public punishments, see the brilliantly suggestive work of M. Foucault, *Discipline and Punish* (London, 1979).   [18] Friedländer 1922: vol. 2, 80.

Murderous games

and a giraffe in one show which lasted two days (Dio 72.10), while
on another occasion he killed 100 animals, lions or bears, in a
morning with exactly one hundred spears, from safe walk-ways,
specially constructed across the arena; 'a better demonstration',
wrote a contemporary historian, 'of accuracy than of courage'
(Herodian 1.15). The slaughter of exotic and fierce animals in the
emperor's presence, or exceptionally by the emperor himself or by
his palace guard (Suetonius, *Claudius* 21), was a spectacular
dramatisation of the emperor's formidable power: immediate, bloody
and symbolic.

Obligatory shows

Outside Rome, in Italy and in the provinces, gladiatorial shows were
given by individuals, sometimes in the traditional manner to
commemorate a death or to preserve a dead man's memory. This is
stated on inscriptions (e.g. *CIL* 11.6366), and also implied by
elaborate tombs which depict fiercesome gladiatorial shows –
presumably those which had been held to celebrate the death of the
dignitary buried inside.[19] In one Italian town, Pollentia, a crowd
prevented the burial of a high-ranking soldier (*primipilaris*) until his
heirs were forced to agree to provide a gladiatorial show out of his
estate; the emperor Tiberius reacted fiercely to the news by sending
soldiers to capture the town and enslave 'the greater part of its people
and town-council' (Suetonius, *Tiberius* 37). This story is interesting,
because it illustrates again the arbitrariness of imperial power and
the strength of popular demand for gladiatorial shows, grafted onto
the old tradition of funeral games. Several later inscriptions mention
gladiatorial shows celebrated 'by popular request'; others note that
gracious permission (*indulgentia*) had been received from the emperor
(e.g. *CIL* 10.1211, 4760 and 6012). Over time, the occasions thought
suitable for gladiatorial shows broadened: for example, a local
dignitary's birthday (*CIL* 9.1156) or the opening of a public library,
celebrated by a fight between twelve pairs of gladiators (*CIL* 3.607).

[19] The tomb of A. Umbricius Scaurus found at Pompeii, dating from about AD 50,
has fine reliefs. The two main panels show eight pairs of gladiators and two armed
men fighting wild animals; minor panels above show two athletic-looking naked
men also in some way engaged in fighting animals. The outcome of two
gladiatorial contests is depicted by blood pouring from the wounds of the
vanquished. For commentary and good reproductions, see F. Mazois, *Les ruines
de Pompeii* (Paris, 1824) vol. 1, 47ff and Plate 32, and Mau 1899: 410–12. For
the text of the inscription on this tomb, see *CIL* 10.1024 plus *CIL* 4.1182: the
local town-council voted 2,000 HS towards the cost of the funeral of this man,
who had been joint mayor (*duovir*), and an equestrian statue in the town-square.

It seems unlikely that all gladiatorial shows required or received imperial permission, especially those which were on a very small scale in country towns (for example, a show with four pairs of gladiators – *CIL* 9.4208), or those which were put on by itinerant entrepreneurs for a paying audience.[20]

But most gladiatorial shows in small towns were not given voluntarily. As in the city of Rome, they were produced by leading citizens as a tax on status, at once an obligation and an opportunity for self-enhancement. For example, in the Foundation Charter of the Roman colony at Urso in Spain, dating from 44 BC, the four chief annually elected magistrates were required to give fourteen days of gladiatorial shows or dramatic spectacles in honour of Jupiter, Juno and Minerva, largely at their own expense, but with some subvention from municipal funds (paras. 70–1 = *FIRA* vol. 1, 182–3). Similar arrangements were probably made in other Roman colonies; and the custom spread to other towns in both eastern and western provinces. The larger the town, the larger the gladiatorial show, the greater the burden on the donor. The very largest shows were closely associated with emperor worship, so that the donor's glory overtly subserved the religious and political order.[21]

---

[20] The mere existence of a special term *munera assiforana* (penny shows) for these travelling gladiatorial shows for a paying audience is evidence enough for their existence and frequency. A decree of the senate of *c.* AD 177 indicates that the state treasury got revenues of about 20–30 million HS per year, perhaps from the sale of condemned criminals to exhibitors of gladiatorial shows and from tax on other sales of gladiators; see J. H. Oliver and R. E. A. Palmer, 'Minutes of an Act of the Roman Senate', *Hesperia* 24 (1955) 330 and 332, lines 8 and 29 = *FIRA* vol. 1, 295 and 297. The scale of the treasury revenues suggests a huge overall expenditure on all gladiatorial shows, even though individual shows cost less than 30,000 HS for a travelling show and up to or even over 200,000 HS for other shows (*ibidem*).

[21] In an excellent if encyclopaedic study of the surviving evidence from the eastern provinces, L. Robert, *Les gladiateurs dans l'Orient grec* (Paris, 1940) 270 concluded that most gladiatorial shows there were connected with emperor-worship. They also bolstered the donor's status or were intended to; see the two attempts by local notables to give grand shows worthy of their wealth and status, replete with wild beasts and the best gladiators available, recounted by Apuleius in *The Golden Ass* 4.13 and 10.18; cf. the long search for gladiators recorded in an inscription of *c.* AD 100, ed. G. E. Bean, *Journeys in northern Lycia 1965–67* (Vienna, 1971) 18ff. Hundreds of honorary inscriptions once erected prominently on or near public buildings or on tombs, proclaimed the donor's generosity. For example: 'To L. Fadius, joint mayor, most generous citizen, to celebrate the honour given him by the council, in the year of his election, he exhibited 30 pairs of gladiators and a hunt of African beasts, and a few months later in his town of office as joint mayor, with a contribution of 13,000 HS from the town, he exhibited a complete hunt and 21 pairs of gladiators, and then after his year of office he gave theatrical shows with his own money. The priests of the imperial cult gave this site in accord with a decree of the council' (*CIL* 9.2350 – Allifae in central Italy).

13

Murderous games

An extract from a senatorial debate in about AD 177 reveals how hard hit some provincial aristocrats had been by the obligation to give magnificent gladiatorial shows while they were serving as chief priests of the imperial cult; the senatorial decree aimed at lightening the burden by fixing the prices at which condemned criminals were to be sold to gladiatorial trainers, and the prices at which gladiatorial trainers could then sell on their gladiators to those who produced the shows. The senate's decree also abolished the tax collected on such sales, in spite of the treasury's objections that it made 20–30 million HS per year from this source. It declared:

> Why should the treasury of Marcus Aurelius and Lucius Commodus be supported by a connection with the arena? All the money of these emperors is clean, not stained with the splashing of human blood, not soiled with the filth of sordid profit, and it is as innocently produced as it is collected. (*FIRA* vol. 1,295)[22]

Impeccable sentiments, but gladiatorial shows continued, and continued to be closely associated with emperor worship.

III GLADIATORIAL SHOWS AS POLITICAL THEATRE

Gladiatorial shows provided an arena for popular participation in the city of Rome. This was explicitly recognised by Cicero, when he declared that 'the judgement and wishes of the Roman people about public affairs can be most clearly expressed in three places: public assemblies, elections and at plays or gladiatorial shows' (*contione, comitiis, ludorum gladiatorumque consessu* – Cicero, *In Defence of Sestius* 106). He went on to describe how at a packed gladiatorial show in 57 BC, one political figure was cheered, while another, the praetor Appius Claudius, was hissed (*ibidem* 124–7, cf. *Letters to Friends* 8.2). In private, Cicero professed to despise the rabble which attended these public meetings, but he was pleased enough to receive their cheers himself (*Letters to Atticus* 1.16.11 and 2.19.3). He challenged one opponent: 'Give yourself to the people. Entrust yourself to the Games. Are you afraid of being hissed?...Are you terrified of not being applauded?' (*Speech against Piso* 3). The crowd had the important option of giving or of withholding applause, of hissing or of being silent.

[22] Adapted from the translation of the whole text with valuable commentary by Oliver and Palmer 1955: 340. These minutes were published on a bronze plaque in Italica, Spain, but refer in detail to Gaul and Italy. Fragments of another copy, on marble, have been found in Sardis, Asia Minor. Such finds suggest wide interest in cutting the costs of giving gladiatorial shows.

Political theatre

Under the emperors, as citizens' rights to engage in politics diminished, gladiatorial shows, games and theatre together provided repeated opportunities for the dramatic confrontation of rulers and ruled. Rome was unique among large historical empires in allowing these regular meetings between emperors and the massed populace of the capital, collected together in a single crowd, not just strung along the public streets. To be sure, emperors could mostly stage-manage their own appearance and their reception; they gave extravagant shows, threw gifts to the crowd, occasionally had their own claques, and were attended by armed guards. Mostly they received standing ovations and ritual acclamations.[23]

Things did not always go their way. Sometimes the theatre-crowd objected vociferously, for example, against the high price of wheat (Tacitus, *Annals* 6.13), or demanded the execution of an unpopular official (Plutarch, *Galba* 17); on one occasion, it demanded that the emperor Tiberius return a statue which he had taken from some public baths to decorate his palace; in response to public pressure, he gave it back (Pliny, *Natural History* 34.62). The theatres provided the best opportunities for nuances and caricature, all the more so when a bold actor or comedian suited his lines and the crowd its reaction to contemporary events. For example, an actor in the reign of Nero recited the pedestrian line 'Good-bye father, good-bye mother' with accompanying gestures of drinking and swimming, clear references to the public knowledge (or suspicion) that Nero had poisoned his father and attempted to drown his mother; the actor

---

[23] '...the whole theatre will rise to show you its respect' (Pliny, *Panegyric* 54, cf. Propertius 3.18.18). The history of acclamations is fragmentary, so that it is difficult to be sure about normal practice from the incidents reported. In the reign of Tiberius, a theatre crowd chanted: 'Rejoice O Rome; you are safe because the emperor is safe' (Phaedrus 5.7.27). Nero brought a very large claque of soldiers to the theatre for his own performances, which induced the crowd in general and prominent aristocrats in particular to join with apparent alacrity in shouts of 'Glory to Caesar...No One Surpasses You' (Dio 61.20, cf. Tacitus, *Annals* 16.4). Dio recounted how he himself and other senators under Commodus at a gladiatorial show were ordered to shout repeatedly: 'You are Lord, the Foremost and the Most Blessed of Men' (Dio 72.20). Similar slogans were shouted by senators as part of their political activities; for example, when Commodus was dead, the senators shouted in a long chant: '...Enemy of the Gods, Enemy of the Senate, Enemy of the Gods. To the Morgue with the Gladiator. He killed the Senate. Drag him away with the Hook...Save us, O Jupiter Best and Greatest, Save Pertinax for Us...' (SHA, *Commodus* 18, seemingly confirmed by Dio 74.2; see similarly in Trajan's reign, Pliny, *Panegyric* 75.2). The whole subject of ritual acclamation as part of Roman politics deserves thorough study; see already J. Colin, *Les villes libres de l'orient gréco-romain et l'envoi au supplice par acclamations populaires* (Brussels, 1965) 109ff and M. P. Charlesworth, 'Pietas and Victoria – The Emperor and the Citizen', *Journal of Roman Studies* 33 (1943) 4ff.

Murderous games

was only sent into exile, either, Suetonius thought, because Nero
was impervious to insult or because he did not want to sharpen malice
by showing resentment (*Nero* 39).

These are isolated and selected incidents. At first sight, they may
seem trivial, and not the proper stuff of serious political history. Two
points should be made. First, these incidents were reported by
serious-minded ancient historians, often as weapons of attack against
emperors they disliked (e.g. Dio 72.18). Indeed, history was one
arena created by upper-class Romans for the judgement of dead
emperors. There they could avenge humiliations by vilifying an
emperor's reputation. Secondly, the Games at Rome provided a stage
for the emperor to display his majesty – luxurious ostentation in
procession, accessibility to humble petitioners, generosity to the
crowd, human involvement in the contests, graciousness or arrogance
towards aristocrats, clemency or cruelty to the vanquished. When the
emperor entered the amphitheatre, or decided the fate of a fallen
gladiator by the movement of his thumb, at that moment he had
50,000 courtiers. He knew that he was Caesar Imperator, the
Foremost of Men. Reciprocally, the crowd, protected by its mass,
could outvote the emperor. The amphitheatre was their
parliament.[24]

Even in the Circus, where the huge audience of 200,000 was strung
out long the track, there could be powerful demonstrations. Dio,
senator and historian, was present at one in AD 195 when the crowd
first shouted the appropriate ritual hurrah 'Immortal Rome', but
then shouted 'How long are we to be at war?' Dio was amazed that
tens of thousands of people shouted in unison together 'like a
well-trained choir' (75.4). Similarly, the Circus crowd appealed to
Caligula once to cut taxes. He refused. 'And when they shouted
louder and louder', he sent soldiers into the crowd to arrest anyone
seen shouting, with orders to execute him immediately (Josephus,
Jewish Antiquities 19.24–7). Understandably, the crowd became
silent, but sullen. This popular reaction, according to Josephus,
strengthened the conspirators' resolve to kill the emperor. Dio also
reported on the hostility towards Caligula at theatrical and
gladiatorial shows, and on the tension between an 'angry ruler and
antagonistic people' (59.13).

Similar hostility developed between emperor and spectators in

[24] For a more detailed and very interesting analysis along these and other lines,
see P. Veyne, *Le pain et le cirque* (Paris, 1976) 675–730; cf. A. Cameron, *Circus
Factions* (Oxford, 1976) 157ff to which I owe a great deal and the conclusions
of T. Bollinger, *Theatralis Licentia* (Winterthur, 1969) 72–3.

other reigns. Dio recounted how with his own eyes he saw the emperor Commodus cut off the head of an ostrich as a sacrifice in the arena, then walk towards the congregated senators whom he hated, with the sacrificial knife in one hand and the severed head of the bird in the other hand, clearly indicating, so Dio thought, that it was the senators' necks which he wanted. Years later, Dio recorded how he had kept himself from laughing (out of anxiety I imagine) by chewing desperately on a laurel leaf which he plucked from the garland on his head (72.21). The amphitheatre held terror occasionally for prominent spectators as well as for chosen victims.

Gladiatorial shows were political theatre. The dramatic performance took place not only in the arena, but also between different sections of the audience. Their interaction was part of Roman politics, and should be included in any thorough account of the Roman constitution. They are usually omitted, simply because in our own society, mass spectator sports count as leisure. The politics of metropolitan control included 'bread and circuses' (Juvenal, *Satires* 10.81). 'The Roman people', wrote Fronto, 'is held together by two things: wheat doles and public shows. Control is secured as much by amusements as by serious things' (2.216 – Loeb edition).

Consider how the audience in the amphitheatre sat: the emperor in his gilded box, surrounded by his family; senators and knights had special seats, and came properly dressed in purple-bordered togas.[25]

[25] The segregation of seating at public shows by social rank at Rome is a symptom of the increasing and overt stratification of Roman society. The senate sat separately for the first time at the Roman games in 194 BC (Livy 34.44 and 54); Livy commented on the mixed reaction to the innovation: some thought it a 'long-overdue tribute to a most honourable rank; others thought that what had been added to the majesty of the senate, had been subtracted from the dignity of the people'. The innovation was seen by some as a threat to social harmony, liberty and equality. 'What has suddenly happened to make senators unwilling to mix with the plebs, to watch a show, or to make a rich man despise a poor man as his neighbour in the audience?' In 67 BC, knights were by law given special seats in the theatre. But this segregation of seats by social rank was not universally applied. Laws were renewed. For example, Augustus instigated a decree of the senate, reserving special seats for senators at all spectacles (Suetonius, *Augustus* 44), and we know from several sources that knights still had fourteen rows of seats reserved for them in the theatre and special seats in the Circus (Dio 55.22 and a senatorial decree of AD 19 edited by M. Malavolta, *Sesta Miscellanea* (1978) 347ff). And yet Claudius is reported to have assigned special seats for senators in the Circus (Dio 60.7), whereas previously they had been allowed to sit anywhere (Suetonius, *Claudius* 21), while Nero did the same for knights (Tacitus, *Annals* 15.32). It seems reasonable to conclude that seating was generally but not uniformally by rank; over the long time-period with which we are concerned, habits changed. It is therefore dangerous to assume that a law was obeyed, or that a custom persisted from the time when it is first mentioned in a surviving source until the next time that it is mentioned. But then what else can one do?

Soldiers were separated from civilians. Even ordinary citizens had to wear the heavy white woollen toga, the formal dress of a citizen, and sandals if they wanted to sit in the bottom two tiers of seats; married men sat separately from bachelors, boys sat in a separate block with their tutors in the next block. Women, and the very poorest men dressed in the drab grey cloth associated with mourning (*pullati*), could sit or stand only in the top tier (Suetonius, *Augustus* 44). Priests, such as the Arval Brethren and the Companions of Augustus (*sodales Augusti*) and the Vestal Virgins (honorary men), had reserved seats at the front.[26] The formal dress and the segregation of ranks underlined the formal, ritual elements in the occasion, just as the steeply banked seats reflected the steep stratification of society. It mattered where you sat and where you were seen to be sitting.

The emperor was the centre of everyone's attention, usually welcomed, cheered with ritual chants of praise. In return, the crowd was showered with gifts and often provided with food and drink (Statius, *Silvae* 1.6). Ideally, gladiatorial shows put the whole metropolitan population in a good humour (Fronto 2.216). When a gladiator fell, the crowd would shout for mercy or dispatch (either *missos* or *iugula*). The emperor might be swayed by their shouts or gestures, but he alone, the final arbiter, decided when the fighting was to stop and who was to live or die.[27] This dramatic enactment of imperial power, repeated several times a day on several occasions a year, before a mass audience of citizens, conquerors of the world, helped legitimate the emperor's position. And yet, the crowd's potential for legitimation and support contained an inherent risk of subversion and resistance. To be sure, the crowd could be placated, bought off with tokens, commanded or bullied into silence. But it could also resist, or slip out of control. Yet the dangers of political confrontation were lessened by the crowd's lack of coherence, by its own volatility, and by the absence of an ideology which could bind

[26] Inscriptions found at the Colosseum indicate clearly that certain seats were allocated for knights, boys, teachers, state guests, and that space was allocated, curiously, by the foot (*CIL* 6.32098). The Acts of the Arval Brethren for the year AD 80, the year of the Colosseum's opening, show that they were allocated seats in each tier; those in the upper tiers were presumably for dependants (*Acta Fratrum Arvalium* ed. W. Henzen (Berlin, 1874) cvii. On the ambiguous sexual status of Vestal Virgins, see the excellent article by M. Beard, 'The sexual status of Vestal Virgins', *Journal of Roman Studies* 70 (1980) 12ff. On their seats, see Suetonius, *Augustus* 44. On seats for the poor, see Calpurnius Siculus, *Poems* 7.26–7.
[27] In one long fight between two equally matched gladiators, Priscus and Verus, 'the crowd shouted loud and often for both to be released. But Caesar obeyed his own law: "Fight on until the finger is raised"' (Martial, *On the Public Shows* 29).

it together in a sustained programme of action. If the crowd became too vociferous, emperors could just stay away or leave the city; for example, Nero, immediately after he had killed his mother in AD 59, delayed returning to Rome, reportedly because he was anxious about popular reaction (Tacitus, *Annals* 14.13); Tiberius, who had little interest in public shows, withdrew for several years to the island of Capri, and by his absence disfranchised the crowd (Suetonius, *Tiberius* 47; Tacitus, *Annals* 4.67).

Even so, given the decline under the emperors of all the other Republican traditions of popular participation in politics, it is surprising that the tradition of the emperor's attendance at the Games persisted. If he was in Rome, he was expected to go to the Games regularly, and to watch attentively. By and large, emperors did. For example, when Augustus could not attend, even for a few hours, he customarily sent his apologies for his absence, and appointed a substitute to preside; the fact was, as he himself admitted, he enjoyed watching (Suetonius, *Augustus* 45). Augustus set the style of overt respect by emperors to the only surviving assembly of citizens. Tiberius attended public shows assiduously in the early years of his reign, in spite of not being interested in them, 'both in order to honour those who put them on and to keep the populace in order, by seeming to share their fesitivities with them' (Dio 57.11, cf. Suetonius, *Tiberius* 47). By no means all emperors followed their example, as we have seen; Caligula in a rage wished out loud that the Roman people had but a single neck (Dio 59.13) and rushed out of one show in a tantrum, tripping over his toga, 'fuming and shouting that the people who were the masters of the world gave more honour to a gladiator' than to their emperor (Suetonius, *Caligula* 35). But Claudius called the people 'My masters' and joked with them, sometimes explaining his decision to them on placards.[28] He gave frequent gladiatorial shows, during which 'he acted as one of the people and was quite relaxed; he even counted out loud in time with

---

[28] This is what happened in the famous case of Androclus and the lion, reported by Apion who saw it with his own eyes; the story is relayed to us by Aulus Gellius (*Attic Nights* 5.14). Androclus was an escaped slave of the provincial governor of Africa. He was recaptured and sentenced by his master to death by wild beasts in the Circus at Rome. The lion, a magnificent specimen, instead of attacking Androclus, gently licked his feet and hands; in fact, the two greeted each other like long-lost friends. Caligula, who was presiding, summoned Androclus to explain this extraordinary behaviour. Androclus said that when he escaped, he had taken shelter in the lion's cave, and had removed a splinter from its foot. The lion had appeared not fierce, but grateful, so that he had stayed in its cave for three years. But when he left, he was soon recaptured. The emperor had this story written out on placards and carried round the Circus (cf. Dio 69.16).

the crowd, and on the fingers of his outstretched left hand, marked off the number of gold coins paid to the victors' (Suetonius, *Claudius* 21). By his enthusiastic involvement, he outperformed expectations and so earned censure from some aristocrats and historians who thought that emperors should be more discreet and discriminating in their pleasures.

IV GLADIATORS AS HEROES

Enthusiastic interest in the Games and in gladiatorial shows occasionally spilled over into a desire to perform on the stage or in the arena. Two emperors were not content to be spectators-in-chief; they wanted to be prize performers as well. Nero's histrionic ambitions and success as musician, singer, actor and dancer were notorious; he also prided himself on his abilities as a charioteer, and after a private exhibition in front of 'his slaves and the dregs of the plebs' he gave a public performance in the Circus Maximus (Suetonius, *Nero* 21–2 and 54). Commodus also fancied himself as a charioteer, but as such performed only in private. He practised as a gladiator at home, killing or maiming several opponents; in the amphitheatre itself, he took part as a gladiator in preliminary bouts with blunted weapons and won all his fights; he charged the treasury a million HS for each appearance. Eventually, he was assassinated, when he was planning to be inaugurated as consul (for AD 193) dressed up as a gladiator (Herodian 1.14–17; Dio 72.19–22). Such behaviour was even then regarded as a reflection of 'madness and paranoia' (Herodian 1.14).

Commodus' gladiatorial exploits were an idiosyncratic fall-out from a cultural obsession with fighting, bloodshed, ostentation and competition. After all, Commodus was not alone. At least seven other emperors (Caligula, Titus, Hadrian, Lucius Verus, Didius Julianus, Caracalla, Geta) practised as gladiators or fought in gladiatorial contests. And so did senators and knights, occasionally but repeatedly. Attempts were made to prohibit senators and knights from appearing in the arena by law, but the laws were evaded. Our sources are uniform in their moral condemnation, and try to explain away their behaviour by calling them desperadoes, forced into the arena by degenerate emperors, or by the dissipation of their patrimony (Suetonius, *Nero* 12; Seneca, *Letters* 99.13).[29] In such a steeply strati-

[29] On emperors' involvement in gladiatorial shows, see Friedländer 1922: vol. 2, 61 and Suetonius, *Caligula* 32 and 54; Dio 59.5 and 66.15; SHA, *Hadrian* 14; *Marcus Aurelius* 8; *Didius Julianus* 9; Dio 76.7. On the involvement of senators and knights, see Dio 48.43; 51.22; 56.25; 57.14; 59.10; 61.17; 67.14; Seneca,

fied society, it seemed outrageous for men of high status to throw away privilege, to declass themselves, even if 'in this way they achieved death instead of dishonour' (Dio 56.25).

It is difficult to know why senators and knights performed as gladiators. I suspect what attracted them was the opportunity to display their military prowess, their courage and their skill, plus the desire for victory, and the shouts of the crowd. At the risk of death, it was their last chance to play soldiers in front of a large audience. In spite of the opprobrium and perhaps because of the risk, a minority tried. The emperor Septimius Severus openly rebuked the senate for its hypocrisy in criticising Commodus so severely for his activities as a gladiator: 'And do none of you fight as gladiators? Why then have some of you bought his shields and those golden helmets of his?' (Dio 75.8). Gladiatorial fighting was more popular among the Roman upper classes than modern scholars readily admit.

Gladiators were glamour figures, culture heroes. The probable life-span of each gladiator was short. Each successive victory brought further risk of defeat and death. But for the moment I am concerned more with image than with reality. Modern pop-stars and athletes (tennis-players, gymnasts and footballers) have only a short exposure to full-glare publicity. Most then fade rapidly from being household names into obscurity, fossilised in the memory of each generation of adolescent enthusiasts. The transience of the fame of each does not diminish their collective importance. So too with Roman gladiators. Their portraits were often painted; and occasionally even walls in public porticoes were covered with 'life-like portraits of all the gladiators' in a particular show (Pliny, *Natural History* 35.52). Names of individual gladiators survive in dozens, scratched or painted on the plastered walls of Pompeii. The ephemera of AD 79 have been preserved by volcanic ash. For example:

> Celadus the Thracian, thrice victor and thrice crowned, the young girls' heart-throb
>
> Crescens the Netter of young girls by night. (*CIL* 4.4342 and 4353)[30]

Letters 87.9, cf. his *Investigations into Nature* 7.31 about rich men who choose which kind of gladiator to become and 'hired for death, choose an obscene type of armament in which they work off their sickness'. See also Suetonius, *Augustus* 43, *Tiberius* 35; Tacitus, *Annals* 15.32 and 2.62; SHA, *Marcus Aurelius* 12. I apologise for the list of references; they illustrate the frequency of mention. One can only guess if performances by senators and knights in the arena went even more often unrecorded.

[30] The words Thracian and Netter (*retiarius*) refer to different types of gladiator. The name Celadus is probably a stage-name, meaning crowd's roar; so Robert 1940: 302. For gladiatorial inscriptions, see *CIL* 4 passim or *ILS* 5083ff and A. Mau, 'Iscrizioni gladiatorie di Pompei, *Römische Mitteilungen* 5 (1890) 25ff.

The victorious gladiator, or at least his image, was sexually attractive. The word *gladius* – sword – was vulgarly used to mean penis. Even the defeated and dead gladiator had something sexually portentous about him. It was customary for a new bride to have her hair parted with a spear, at best one which had been dipped 'in the body of a defeated and killed gladiator' (Festus L55 *sv caelibari hasta*). A stone relief from southern Italy (Beneventum) shows a heavily armed gladiator fighting a huge penis; besides him are written the words of the crowd: 'Free him. Kill him' (*missos iugula; CIL* 9.1671). I am not at all sure how to interpret the significance of all this; such customs and artefacts can mean so many different things to different people, and even to the same person.[31] But this evidence suggests that there was a close link, in some Roman minds, between gladiatorial fighting and sexuality.

Other evidence corroborates this association: for example, a terracotta gladiatorial helmet shaped suggestively like a penis, and a small bronze figurine, from Pompeii, of a cruel-looking gladiator, fighting off with his sword a dog-like wild-beast which grows out of his erect and elongated penis; five bells hang down from various parts of his body and a hook is attached to the gladiator's head, so that the whole ensemble could hang as a bell and perhaps as a talisman in a door-way or from a ceiling.[32] Once again, interpretation is speculative. It seems as though gladiatorial bravery for some Roman men represented an attractive yet dangerous, almost threatening, macho masculinity.

Gladiators' strength and bravery, their risk of death, attracted some Roman women. Yet to pursue and love slave gladiators was socially dangerous, even disastrous. Even if they were free men by

---

[31] Festus himself suggested various interpretations of the custom of parting the bride's hair with a spear dipped in the blood of a dead gladiator: '...just as the spear had been conjoined with the body of the gladiator, so should she be with her husband; or...; or because it was a sign that she might give birth to brave men; or because by the rights of marriage a wife is subject to the commands of her husband' (55L); cf. J. G. Frazer, Commentary on Ovid's *Fasti* (London, 1929) vol. 2, 441 and Plutarch, *Roman Questions* 87 (= *Moral Essays* 285c). I have no idea how many Romans believed in or thought of these interpretations of custom.

[32] For the terracotta of a gladiator's helmet, see conveniently *Enciclopedia dell'arte antica sv Gladiatore* p. 940. For the bronze figurine, see M. Grant, *Erotic Art in Pompeii* (London, 1975) 143 for a good picture, especially of the gladiator's face, but see also Colonel Fanin, *The Royal Museum at Naples, Erotic Paintings, Bronzes and Statutes* (London, privately printed, 1871) plate 22. Woe betide anyone who wishes to see the pictures or objects nowadays. They lie protected by the Museum's creaking administration, dingily dust-covered in a dark room. Very dirty pictures.

birth or socially distinguished by origin, as gladiators they were déclassé, outcasts. Indeed, because they were in such close contact with death, they were polluted and sometimes therefore, like suicides, excluded from normal burial (see *CIL* 11.6528). They were, according to Tertullian, both loved and despised; 'men give them their souls, women their bodies too...they are both glorified and degraded...' (*On the Public Shows* 22).

In spite of these social dangers, or perhaps because of them, even aristocratic women fell for gladiators. In a vicious satire, Juvenal ridiculed a senator's wife, Eppia, who had eloped to Egypt with her favourite swordsman:

What was the youthful charm that so fired Eppia? What hooked her? What did she see in him to make her put up with being called 'The Gladiator's Moll'? Her poppet, her Sergius, was no chicken, with a dud arm that prompted hope of early retirement. Besides, his face looked a proper mess, helmet-scarred, a great wart on his nose, an unpleasant discharge always trickling from one eye. But he was a Gladiator. That word makes the whole breed seem handsome, and made her prefer him to her children and country, her sister, her husband. Steel is what they fall in love with. (*Satires* 6.102ff)

Satire certainly, and exaggerated, but pointless unless it was also based to some extent in reality. Modern excavators working in the armoury of the gladiatorial barracks in Pompeii, found eighteen skeletons in two rooms, presumably of people caught there in the ash storm; they included one woman who was wearing rich gold jewellery, and a necklace set with emeralds.[33] Women's identification with gladiators sometimes went further. Women, even women of high status, fought in the arena as gladiators (Tacitus, *Annals* 15.32).[34] In the British Museum, there is a small stone relief, depicting two armed female gladiators, one with breast bare, suitably called Achillia and Amazon; both had been honourably discharged from the ring (*Greek Inscriptions in the British Museum* 911 – from Halicarnassus).

For all their idealised glamour, most gladiators were slaves or condemned criminals (*ad ludum damnati*). The same excavations in the

---

[33] A. Mau 1899: 157–8.
[34] Cf. Dio 61.17; 75.16. In some instances, women gladiators were classed as oddities with dwarfs (Dio 67.8 and Statius, *Silvae* 1.6.51ff); and in one reported instance, a man directed in his will that the most beautiful female slaves he owned and the boy slaves whom he had once loved should all fight in the arena. But the populace would not allow it This story has an implausible ring to it (Nicolaus of Damascus in Athenaeus, *Banquets of the Philosophers* 154A). Yet the other cases seem well authenticated. What made wives of knights or senators fight as gladiators?

gladiators' barracks at Pompeii revealed iron stocks, presumably for the confinement and punishment of gladiators (Mau 1899: 157). Even free men who volunteered to be gladiators (*auctorati*) bound themselves by a fiercesome oath 'to endure branding, chains, flogging or death by the sword' (Petronius, *Satyricon* 117; Seneca, *Letters* 37).[35] For the fixed duration of their service, free gladiators became like slaves, although they could always in principle buy themselves out. But when released, they were prohibited, like convicted criminals or tricksters, from holding public office, even as small-town councillors (see the so-called Julian Law on Towns of 44 BC = *FIRA* vol. 1, 149). At Rome, criminal gladiators were sometimes freed by the emperor at the crowd's insistence (Fronto vol. 1,118), and in any case they could be freed after five years of fighting – if they survived that long (*Comparison of the Laws of Moses and the Romans* 11.7.4 = *FIRA* vol. 2, 572). With slaves, there were legal problems. In strict law, even emperors could not just free another man's slave in response to the crowd's roar. Tiberius, for example, would not free a slave pantomime dancer under popular pressure until the owner had agreed to sell him the slave (Dio 57.11). Hadrian replied to the crowd's clamouring for the manumission of a slave charioteer by sending a placard round the Circus with the message: 'It is not right for you to ask me to free a slave belonging to someone else, nor for the master to be compelled' (Dio 69.16). Incidentally, such evidence implies widespread literacy. Finally, Marcus Aurelius ruled that manumission of slaves provoked by 'the shouts of the people', even if the owner consented, was invalid (D. 40.9.17 – Paul). Under less scrupulous emperors and away from Rome, such rulings were often, one suspects, ignored. And many

---

[35] The existence of the word, *auctorati*, for freeborn gladiators suggests that they were commonplace. This is corroborated by the presence of free names (e.g. Q. Petillius) in surviving advertisements or programmes of gladiatorial contests (e.g. *CIL* 4.2508). In one list, 9 out of 28 gladiators are apparently free men (*CIL* 9.465–6). We have no idea that this proportion was typical. The motives for free men to become gladiators probably ranged from poverty to prodigality (Tatian, *Against the Greeks* 23 = *PG* 6.857). Manilius, writing in the early first century AD, ascribed volunteering to pleasure in bloodshed and slaughter, and wrote of those 'who now sell themselves for the risk of death and for murder in the arena, and make enemies out of each other in times of peace' (4.220–6; cf. Dio 74.2). Masters could, until the early second century AD, send slaves to be gladiators without redress. The future emperor Vitellius, for example, tired of a boy lover, sold him to a gladiatorial school, then changed his mind, rescued him, and when he was emperor made him a knight (Suetonius, *Vitellius* 12). We hear of this story only because of its dramatic resolution. Hadrian apparently restricted a slave owner's right to sell a slave to a gladiatorial school (SHA, *Hadrian* 18). But who was there to enforce such laws systematically?

ex-slaves, once freed, continued to do what they did best; they fought on. 'Just think', wrote Petronius, 'we are going to have a magnificent gladiatorial show lasting three days during the holidays; no cheap touring show, but lots of ex-slaves' (*Satyricon* 45). Graffiti at Pompeii confirm this and point up the predictable ending:

Severus ex-slave 13 victories   Killed
Albanus once slave of Scaurus, freed, 19 victories   Won   (*CIL* 4.8056)

or more sadly, age and experience bowed out to youthful vigour:

Spiculus of Nero's school, first fight   Won
Aptonetus ex-slave 16 victories   Killed   (*CIL* 4.1474)

All gladiators, whatever their formal status, received cash for winning, crowns for bravery, and if they were fortunate the wooden cudgel (*rudis*) as a symbol they they need never fight in the arena again (Martial, *On the Public Shows* 29). The crowns were important. A painting from the amphitheatre at Pompeii, now lost, shows preparations for a gladiatorial combat; the gladiators are arming themselves, while in the background two winged figures of Victory hold out garlands for the prospective victor.[36] And in graffiti at Pompeii, crude but touching line-drawings trace the outcome of gladiatorial fights; the contestants are identified by name, by the number of their fights or victories (it is now impossible to tell which) and sometimes by the number of crowns which they have won; for example:

Hilarus of Nero's School   14 fights 12 crowns   Won
Creunus   7 fights 5 crowns   Discharged   (*CIL* 4.10237)

Similarly, street advertisements for forthcoming shows put out by the producers and programmes (*libelli*), which spectators bought, listed combatants by gladiatorial type (*Thracian, Myrmillo, Hoplomachus* – all heavy-armed; *Essedarius* – chariot-fighter; *Retiarius* – light-armed Netter), and by previous record. In several graffiti, the outcome of the bouts was also noted. For example:

THRACIAN *vs* MYRMILLO

Won	Pugnax of Nero's school	3 fights
Killed	Murranus of Nero's school	3 fights

HOPLOMACHUS *vs* THRACIAN

Won	Cycnus of the Julian school	8 fights
Discharged	Atticus of the Julian school	14 fights...

[36] Mau 1899: 208.

25

CHARIOT-FIGHTERS

Discharged	P. Ostorius	51 fights
Won	Scylax of the Julian school	26 fights
		(*CIL* 4.2508)

Without the results this reads, I suggest, like a guide to form. Spectators needed to know the combatants' capacity to survive and their experience, as a guide to betting (Ovid, *The Art of Love* 1.168). The emotional glue of Roman gladiatorial shows, what drew the crowd, was not merely the spectacle and the slaughter, but also gambling.

On the day before the contest, the gladiators were given a grand last banquet; curious bystanders were allowed in to watch them eat (Plutarch, *Moral Essays* 1099B). When the time came, the gladiators entered the arena in a showy parade. A sarcophagus from Pompeii depicts the procession: gladiators carrying their helmets, a small forge, a placard-bearer, trumpeters. A mosaic discovered at Nenning (Germany) shows a gladiatorial combat accompanied by a portable water-organ. To recapture the experience, we have to blend sight, sound and smell. Yet we should be careful not to exaggerate the grandeur. Petronius satirically described a small-town contest of cheap, broken-down gladiators. Only one had any spunk, and he held back under instructions. The upshot was that all of them were publicly flogged with the crowd shouting encouragement (*Satyricon* 45). The cultural divide between us and the Romans is difficult to cross. A magistrate at Minturnae in Italy was honoured with a statue; the inscription at its base recorded his achievements and the fine gladiatorial show which he had given: 'Over 4 days he showed 11 pairs, from these 11 of the best gladiators of Campania were killed, and 10 bears killed cruelly' (*crudeliter – CIL* 10.6012).

Behind the brave façade and the hope of glory at the best shows, there still lurked the fear of death. 'Those about to die salute you, Emperor' (Suetonius, *Claudius* 21). Only one account survives of what it was like, from the gladiator's point of view. It is from a rhetorical exercise; the raconteur, typically enough, is a rich young man who had been captured by pirates and then sold on as a slave to a gladiatorial trainer:

And so the day arrived. Already the populace had gathered for the spectacle of our punishment, and the bodies of those about to die had their own death-parade across the arena. The presenter of the show who hoped to gain favour with our blood, took his seat...Although no one knew my birth, my fortune, my family, one fact made people pity me; I seemed unfairly matched. I was destined to be a certain victim in the sand...All around

I could hear the instruments of death: a sword being sharpened, iron-plates being heated in a fire [to stop fighters retreating and to prove that they were not faking death], birch-rods and whips were prepared. One would have imagined that these were the pirates. The trumpets sounded their foreboding notes; stretchers for the dead were brought on, a funeral parade before death. Everywhere I could see wounds, groans, blood, danger...' (Quintilian?, *Rhetorical Exercises* 9.6)

He went on to describe his thoughts, his memories in the moments when he faced death, before he was dramatically and conveniently rescued by a friend. That was fiction. In real life, as gravestones tell us, the outcome was different:

To the Revered Spirits of the Dead. Glauco born at Mutina fought seven times, died in the eighth. He lived 23 years 5 days. Aurelia set this up to her well-deserving husband, together with those who loved him. My advice to you is to find your own star. Don't trust Nemesis; that is how I was deceived. Hail and Farewell. (*CIL* 5.3466)[37]

V   CONCLUSIONS

Why did Romans popularise fights to the death between armed gladiators? Why did they encourage the public slaughter of unarmed criminals? What was it, asked Tertullian, which transformed men who were timid and peaceable enough in private and made them shout gleefully for the merciless destruction of their fellow men (*On the Public Shows* 21)? Part of the answer may lie in the social psychology of the crowd, which helps relieve the individual of responsibility, and in the psychological mechanisms by which some spectators identify more readily with the victory of the aggressor than with the sufferings of the vanquished. Slavery and the steep stratification of society must have helped. Slaves were at the mercy of their owners. Those who were destroyed for public edification and entertainment were considered worthless (cf. Tacitus, *Annals* 1.76), as non-persons; or like the Christian martyrs, they were considered social outcasts and were tortured as if 'we no longer existed' (Eusebius, *History of the Chuch* 8.10).[38] The brutalisation of the audience fed on the dehumanisation of the victims.

---

[37] Another tombstone, set up by wife and child to a dead gladiator, maintained pride in his accomplishments: 'He won and killed his opponent, but died – a valiant hero' (Robert 1940: n° 191, cf. 55: 'no opponent killed me, but by myself I died, and my gracious wife placed me here').

[38] Cited also by Musurillo 1972: 322. On the persecution of Christians, see particularly Eusebius, *History of the Church* 5.1 on the martyrs of Lyons, executed in AD 177 (Musurillo 1972: 62ff); for commentary, see W. H. C. Frend, *Martyrdom and Persecution in the Early Church* (Oxford, 1965) 1–30.

Rome was a cruel society. Brutality was built into its culture, in private life as well as in public shows. The tone was set by military discipline and by slavery, to say nothing of wide-ranging paternal powers (on fathers' traditional 'power of life and death', see below, p. 243). Perhaps because of this paternal independence and slave-owner's rights over their slaves, the state did not establish an early monopoly of legitimate violence, and only in the second century AD did it acquire a legal monopoly of capital punishment (Gaius 1.53). So, for example, rich Romans could give and regularly gave private gladiatorial shows of two or three pairs at dinner-parties: 'when they have finished dining and are filled with drink, they call in the gladiators; as soon as one has his throat cut, the diners applaud with delight' (Nicolaus of Damascus in Athenaeus, *Banquets of the Philosophers* 4.153, cf. Strabo 5.4.13). At their master's whim, as we have seen, slaves could be sold to gladiatorial schools or sentenced without trial and thrown to wild beasts. Owners could, if they wanted, on their own initiative, crucify their slaves publicly. Seneca recorded from his own observations the various ways in which crucifixions were carried out, in order to increase pain (*Letter of Condolence to Marcia* 20).

But there were limits, even though the limits were not where we would set them. For example, the story is told that a Roman knight, Vedius Pollio, had a fish-pond stocked with huge lampreys which he fattened on the flesh of slaves who offended him in any way. Once when Augustus was dining with him, a young slave dropped a precious crystal bowl. His master ordered him to be seized and thrown alive to the lampreys. The boy slipped from his captors' grasp and threw himself at the emperor's feet 'to ask only that he be allowed to die some other way, not as human bait'. Augustus was so shocked at Vedius' cruelty that he pardoned the boy, and ordered that all Vedius' crystal bowls be smashed there and then, and that the fish-pond be filled in (Seneca, *On Anger* 3.40). The truth or falsity of the story does not matter much. There are numerous other examples of cruelty, most of them reported casually, without critical comment.[39] What matters here is that these stories circulated. They

[39] See for example, Suetonius' chilling account of Claudius' love of cruelty (*Claudius* 34), and Augustus, after defeating Sextus Pompey in the civil wars, sent back 30,000 runaway slaves to their masters for punishment; those for whom no masters could be found were publicly impaled (Augustus, *My Achievements* 25; Dio 49.12). But again, there were limits; in a famous incident in AD 61, a master was killed in his house by one of his own slaves; by Roman law, all the slaves in the household were to be tortured and executed. There were 400 of them. The populace objected. There was an earnest debate in the senate. Tradition

were instruments of social control. Feeble enough in all conscience, but they helped set the boundaries to the open cruelty which could be socially condoned in the private domain. It is worth stressing that we are dealing here, not with individual sadistic psychopathology, but with a deep cultural difference. Roman commitment to cruelty fuelled popular interest in gladiatorial shows. The cultural divide makes the modern historian's normal tactic of empathetic imagination particularly difficult.

The popularity of gladiatorial shows was a by-product of war, discipline and death. Rome was a militaristic society. For centuries, it had been devoted to war and to the mass participation of citizens in battle. They won their huge empire by discipline and control. Public executions were a gruesome reminder to non-combatants, fellow-citizens or subjects, that vengeance would be exacted if they betrayed their country, rebelled or were convicted of serious crimes. For example, in 70 BC, after the slave rebellion by Spartacus, himself an escaped gladiator, had finally been crushed, 6,000 slaves captured alive were crucified all the way along the road from Capua to Rome, a distance of about 200 km (Appian, *Civil Wars* 1.120).[40] The objective was deterrence (D. 48.19.28.15). Public punishment ritually re-established the moral and political order. The power of the state was dramatically reconfirmed.

When long-term peace came to the heartlands of the empire, particularly after 31 BC, these militaristic traditions were preserved at Rome in the domesticated battlefield of the amphitheatre. War had been converted into a game, a drama repeatedly replayed, of cruelty, violence, blood and death. But order still needed to be preserved, and the fear of death still had to be controlled or assuaged by ritual. In a city as large as Rome, without an adequate police force, disorder always threatened. And without effective medicine, death-rates must have been very high. No one was safe. Sickness spread occasionally like wild-fire through crowded apartment blocks. Gladiatorial shows and their accompanying executions provided opportunities for the reaffirmation of the moral order through the sacrifice of criminal victims, of slave gladiators, of Christian outcasts and wild animals. The enthusiastic participation by spectators, rich and poor, raised and then released collective tensions, in a society which traditionally idealised impassivity (*gravitas*). The gladiatorial

won over pity for innocence. But the decision could not be executed because of angry crowds, armed with stones and firebrands, until the emperor (Nero) had the route lined with soldiers (Tacitus, *Annals* 14.42–5).
[40] Cf. M. Foucault, *Discipline and Punish* (London, 1979) 48.

shows provided a psychic and a political safety valve for the population of the capital. The risk for the emperors, as we have seen, was an occasional political conflict, but the populace could usually be diverted or fobbed off. At the psychological level, the gladiatorial shows provided a stage (as television news does for modern viewers) for shared violence and tragedy. They also gave spectators the reassurance that they themselves had yet again survived disaster. Whatever happened in the arena, the spectators were always on the winning side. 'They found comfort for death', wrote Tertullian, 'in murder' (*On the Public Shows* 12).

2

POLITICAL SUCCESSION
IN THE LATE REPUBLIC (249–50 BC)

by Keith Hopkins and Graham Burton

I INTRODUCTION

When Julius Caeser was thinking of setting himself up as king of
Rome, or so rumour had it, Brutus was repeatedly reminded by
graffiti scrawled on his tribunal: 'Brutus are you asleep?' and 'You
are no true Brutus.' These slogans recalled the deeds of his distant
ancestor, who over four hundred years previously had killed the last
king of Rome.[1] In AD 22, Brutus' sister Junia, the widow of Cassius
(the other leading assassin of Caesar), finally died; the busts of twenty
leading families, to whom she was related by blood or marriage, were
paraded in her funeral procession, though out of political tact to the
emperor Tiberius Caesar the busts of both Cassius and Brutus were
omitted (Tacitus, *Annals* 3.76). The public display of noble ancestry
was 'a matter of pride among the ancients, and was considered a
mark of status and success'.[2] Noble descent enhanced a man's status
and political prospects. Cicero, for example, once taunted an
opponent, Piso:

You crept into office by mistake, on the recommendation of your smoke-
blackened family busts, with which you have nothing in common except
colour...When you were made aedile, it was a Piso who was elected by the
Roman people, not you. The praetorship too was bestowed on your
ancestors; they were famous, though dead; you were alive, but as yet no
one knew of you. (*Speech against Piso* 1–2)

1 Plutarch, *Brutus* 9; cf. R. MacMullen, *Enemies of the Roman Order* (Harvard, 1967)
   7ff for a sympathetic account of the pressures on Brutus.
2 So Servius, *Commentary on Virgil, Aeneid* 6.861 on the six hundred busts in the
   funeral cortège of Marcellus, Augustus' nephew and the reported six thousand
   busts in the funeral of Sulla; cf. Tacitus, *Annals* 4.9 on the funeral of Drusus,
   and in general see Chapter 4 below, p. 201. Scholars have argued that the word
   nobilis was used in Latin only in a strictly technical sense to mean a man, one
   of whose ancestors in the male line had been a consul, so M. Gelzer, *The Roman
   Nobility* (Oxford, 1969) 27ff (translated from the original German edition of
   1912 = *Kleine Schriften* (Wiesbaden, 1962) vol. 1, 39ff). But as Gelzer himself
   admitted, there is no ancient definition of *nobilis*, and we doubt that most
   Romans were so strict in their usage (and see note 18 below).

From evidence such as this, many modern scholars have concluded that Rome in the Republic was ruled by a stable, hereditary nobility stretching back for many generations into antiquity.

A sketch of the argument

We shall argue that this view is significantly mistaken. But first a note about terms; for better or worse, we use the words aristocracy and aristocrat throughout this chapter rather loosely to cover several upper layers of Roman society, including (*a*) the political elite, comprising high officers of state and leading senators, (*b*) lesser senators, and (*c*) a set of wealthy families with high social status, but at any one time not actively involved in elite politics. We use the English word noble with some implication of inherited status, but without suggesting hereditary right or a prediction about political success – in short, we do not use it in a technical sense (see note 2). Other terms are defined as we go along.

We shall show that there was continuous movement into and out of the Roman political elite during the last two centuries of the Republic. This conclusion is based on a study of consuls, the chief elected officers of the Roman state. One third (35 %) of all consuls elected in the period 249–50 BC had no direct consular ancestor in the previous three generations (no consular father, uncle, grandfather or great-grandfather); barely one third (32 %) of all consuls had a consular son. Political success did not guarantee political successors. We extended our investigation to cover praetors, the elected magistrates who ranked second to consuls. Praetors' chances of having politically successful sons were much lower than consuls' chances. The results of our research imply that the Roman senate was wide open to outsiders, that is to men who were not themselves the sons of senators. Conversely, many sons of senators, who survived well into adult life, did not enter the senate. Where did they go? Where did the new senators come from? How should we perceive Roman political life and Roman social stratification in the light of these findings?

In the first part of this chapter, we briefly review traditional scholarly opinion about the Roman senatorial aristocracy. Next we describe the design of our research on consuls and praetors, and its limitations. In the third section, we present our findings, partly in tables, which do not make for easy reading. Those who hate statistical analysis will be able to get a good general picture of our argument by skimming the first sentence or so of each paragraph. The next two

Introduction

sections deal with the problems of fertility and mortality: how many sons did senators have? How many of these sons died before reaching the minimum age required for election to political office?[3] We have surprisingly good indicators of the fertility of consuls and (for a limited period) of praetors, at least once the figures have been manipulated! But we repeatedly need to test the Roman evidence against comparable demographic evidence from other societies. For example, it is important that about one third of senators probably had no son surviving into adult life.

In the final section, we stress the competitive elements in Roman political life. The political elite was elected by Roman popular assemblies. To become consul, one had to win at least three, and often five elections, spread over fifteen years. Elections presuppose winners and losers. Historians have understandably concentrated on the winners. And their victories have become more predictable in retrospect. In our view, losing elections was tolerable to upper-class Romans, because it involved only political, not social demise. Senators' sons were not necessarily or predictably their fathers' political successors. But they did inherit their estates. It is conventional and convenient to describe the highest social stratum in Rome as an 'aristocracy' or 'nobility', words which unavoidably have resonances in our own language and history. It is obvious, but we need to stress how very different the Roman senatorial aristocracy was from the nobility of post-feudal Europe, where status and title were automatically passed from generation to generation. The Roman senate can best be seen, not as a separate Estate, nor even as a distinct social stratum at the top of the Roman social pyramid, but rather as the prestigious political arm of a broader class of Roman and Italian land-owners.

This is a summary of our arguments. Necessary qualifications will be discussed in the main body of the chapter. But before we begin, a brief sketch of Roman political organisation may be useful.[4] The

---

[3] By fertility, we refer to the actual numbers of live children born (as distinct from fecundity – the capacity to conceive and bear children). The minimum legal age for election to quaestor was perhaps 27 years, perhaps raised to 30 years in 81 BC; for praetors, it was established in the early second century BC at 39 years and for consuls at 42 years; see further note 24 below. The law was sometimes by-passed, and it is likely that some were above the minimum legal age.

[4] For a concise and lucid introduction, see H. F. Jolowicz and B. Nicholas, *Historical Introduction to the Study of Roman Law* (Cambridge³, 1972) 8ff. The systematic account by T. Mommsen, *Römisches Staatsrecht* (Leipzig³, 1887) remains fundamental. For modern discussions, see F. de Martino, *Storia della costituzione romana* (Naples², 1972–3) vols 1–3; less formally, J. Bleicken, *Die Verfassung der römischen Republik* (Paderborn, 1975) and C. Nicolet, *The World of the Citizen in Republican Rome* (London, 1980) 207ff.

government of Rome depended on the senate and on popular assemblies. The senate was strictly speaking an advisory body, which in effect controlled state policy (relations with other states, the size of armies, the levels of taxation and of expenditure); its decrees (*senatus consulta*) were not laws, but nevertheless had considerable force. All laws and declarations of war were voted by popular assemblies (comprising all adult male citizens), which also elected the executive officers of the state (the magistrates). The chief magistrates, the consuls and praetors, who acted as generals and judges, were members of the senate and were elected annually by a popular assembly and held office for only one year. The junior magistrates (quaestors) were also elected each year, although by a different popular assembly. In the late Republic, after 81 BC, the senate consisted of all past and present quaestors; in other words, from that time, membership of the senate depended upon popular election. Even before then, most senators and all powerful senators were magistrates or ex-magistrates, who had been successful in popular elections.

Elections were not based on the principle of individual votes. Instead voting was by sets.[5] For example, in one assembly (the *comitia centuriata*), which elected censors, consuls and praetors, the whole body of voters was divided into seven sets of property-holders, split in accordance with their traditional military role into cavalry and infantry: (i) cavalry (*equites*), (ii–vi) five classes (Latin: *classes*) of infantry, and (vii) the proletariat. The richer and much smaller sets had disproportionate voting power; the cavalry and the first class of infantry had 88 votes out of the total of 193 votes, whereas the poorest and single largest set, the proletariat, had only one vote. In elections, often bitterly contested by rival candidates, voting in the upper sets must usually have been split; but on legislative issues affecting the distribution of land or the allocation of tax burdens, the voting power of the richer sets ensured a conservative bias. Even though few issues can have stimulated massive popular participation in assemblies, the element of democracy in Roman elections and legislation was important. Only members of a powerful minority actually competed for political office, but it was the common people, men with a modicum or more of land and property who held the balance of power between these competitors.

Originally, the senate had consisted only of patricians, members

---

[5] The exact weighting of votes and the history of changes in voting practice are much disputed by modern scholars; see Nicolet 1980: 207ff and L. R. Taylor, *Roman Voting Assemblies* (Ann Arbor, 1966).

of a few clans (*gentes*), that is patrilineal kin groups, identified by a common name, such as Claudius, Fabius, Julius. In the fifth and fourth centuries BC, patrician exclusiveness had been breached by the simple tactic of a mass walk-out by the *plebs*. As a result, plebeians, that is non-patricians, secured their own magistrates, the tribunes of the people, who could intercede on behalf of a citizen against any magistrate and could bring state business to a complete halt with a veto. Plebeians also secured the right to stand as candidates for the highest office; from the middle of the fourth century BC onwards, one consul each year came from a plebeian clan. By the beginning of the third century BC, leading (and rich) plebeian families had become firmly entrenched in the political elite, so that the constitutional distinction between patricians and plebeians was no longer a major axis of political conflict. Patrician privilege was gradually eroded. In 172 BC, for the first time, both consuls came from plebeian clans. Thereafter, that happened often.

By 200 BC, Rome had spread its influence over the whole of central and southern Italy and had conquered large territories overseas. The incorporation of Italy into Roman territory and imperial expansion overseas continued. In their train they brought problems which deeply affected the political economy of Italy (see *Conquerors and Slaves*, Chapter 1). Three aspects of these broad changes particularly concern us here. First, the conquest and administration of a growing empire demanded from Roman leaders political and military capability both at home and abroad, capacities which were often not inherited. Secondly, the range of administrative tasks to be performed increased considerably. One reflection of this was the increase in the number of elected magistrates: the number of praetors elected increased from 2 per year to 4 (227 BC) to 6 (from 197 BC) to 8 per year (from 81 BC); the number of quaestors increased from 8 to 20 per year over the same period, so that the total size of the senate doubled. Outside the senate, the successful operation of the Roman state depended upon a whole complex of lawyers and financiers of public works particularly in the city of Rome, and of soldiers, their suppliers and tax-collectors in the conquered provinces. The men directly and most successfully involved in financing state contracts and the farming of taxes were rich Roman land-owners, with the status of knights. One symptom of the increased wealth and importance of these land-owners was their formal involvement as knights in jury service (after 123/2 BC).[6] Our main point here is that the

---

[6] We should stress first, that even though most rich tax-farmers were Roman knights, most knights were land-owners not heavily involved in tax-farming, and

number of positions of responsibility and profit in the upper levels of the Roman status hierarchy expanded, just as the Roman state expanded in size, complexity and wealth. Thirdly, the incorporation of all Italy into the Roman state during the last two centuries BC roughly trebled the number of citizens. The mass enfranchisement of allies after 89 BC and of northern Italians in 49 BC constituted dramatic steps in that direction; but before that and less noticeably, wealthy Latins, Etruscans and Italians from other regions had infiltrated, and had become absorbed into the Roman political elite. In these conditions of expansion and change, it is difficult to see how the Roman political elite could have been preserved as a strictly hereditary body.

The traditional view

Yet in ancient and modern times, the traditional view of Roman politics has been that the Roman senatorial aristocracy in the last two centuries of the Republic was dominated by a tight circle of hereditary *nobiles*. These *nobiles* were the descendants of consuls, the top rank of magistrates, elected annually ever since the foundation of the Republic in 509 BC. According to the historian Sallust, the *nobiles* '...passed the consulship down from hand to hand. Any new man, however distinguished he might be...was considered unworthy of this honour and was spurned as if polluted' (*War against Jugurtha* 63.6). Cicero was immensely proud that he was himself allegedly the first man for thirty years, whose family was new to the senate, and who had crashed through the defences protecting the consulship.[7]

Distinguished modern scholars, such as Gelzer, Syme, Taylor and Scullard have all stressed the power of the hereditary nobility, their privileged access to the consulship, and their exclusiveness. All make a point of the fact that it was rare for men from families which were new to the senate to achieve the consulship.[8] Between 250 and 50 BC,

secondly, we think that there was no deep social, political or economic divide between senators and knights in general. See further *Conquerors and Slaves* 43ff and the literature cited there: best E. Badian, *Publicans and Sinner* (Oxford, 1972) and C. Nicolet, *L'ordre équestre à l'époque républicaine* (Paris, 1966) vol. i.

[7] '...under my leadership, you (the people) have opened up the consulship, which the nobility held securely protected and defended by every method, and you have shown your wish that in future it should be open to talent' (Cicero, *On the Agrarian Law* 2.3). However, Cicero's memory is here, as at other times, selective. A consul of 83 BC, C. Norbanus, was certainly a new man. On Cicero's exploitation of historical examples, see T. P. Wiseman, *New Men in the Roman Senate* 139 BC–A.D. 14 (Oxford, 1971) 107ff.

[8] See particularly Gelzer 1969: especially 35 and 50–2; R. Syme, *The Roman Revolution* (Oxford, 1939) 10–12; L. R. Taylor, *Party Politics in the Age of Caesar*

Introduction

only 11 such men were elected consul.[9] According to Syme (1939:11), nobles guarded the consulship jealously: '...the conservative Roman voter could seldom be induced to elect (as consul) a man whose name had not been known for centuries.' De Sanctis made a similar point: in the hundred years before 133 BC, only ten out of over four hundred clans (*gentes*) filled 99 out of 200 consulships.[10]

There are several reasons for the traditional emphasis on the inheritance of elite status. First, the large hereditary element in the Roman senatorial aristocracy in the last two centuries of the Republic is undeniable. Nobles from great families repeatedly played a central role in Roman politics. Some noble families provided high-ranking magistrates in each generation. They expected to be elected to the highest offices, as of right. 'Distinguished origin brought even indolent men to the highest honour', commented Asconius (23c). Roman nobles had huge influence and power. They dominate our surviving sources. Nobles clothed their values and expectations in an idealisation of their own virtues; they were simply the best men (*optimates*). Other Romans accepted this evaluation or paid lip-service to it. Yet we should be wary now of deducing from the real prominence of some nobles and from their idealisation, that all surviving sons of nobles became candidates for public office, or that all noble candidates succeeded in popular elections. Neither deduction is true.

Secondly, the common practice among modern historians of analysing political power in terms of clans (*gentes*) has exaggerated continuity in Roman political life. It has obscured the rise and fall of particular families which formed the segments of clans.[11] The gaps

(Berkeley, 1949) 3: 'The families which held the Consulship formed the hereditary nobility': similarly, H. H. Scullard, *Roman Politics 220–150 B.C.* (Oxford[2], 1973) 11: 'Once the patricio-plebeian aristocracy had established its ascendancy, members of unennobled families seldom climbed to highest office.' Very strong statements of the traditional view are also made by E. Gruen, *The Last Generation of the Roman Republic* (Berkely, 1974) 162ff.

[9] This is the number given by Gelzer 1969: 51–2, but see the sensible qualifications by H. Strasburger in *RE sv Novus Homo*.

[10] G. de Sanctis, *Storia dei Romani* (Florence[2], 1969) vol. 4.1, 486–7, but see our discussion of clans and consuls below (note 11). The total number of clans (*gentes*) containing Roman citizens is unknown, but in the period 249–50 BC, nearly 400 clan names (e.g. Valerii, Aelii) and 500 clan segments (e.g. Valerii Flacci, Aelii Tuberones) are known to have produced magistrates. And the lists of magistrates are incomplete, so that it seems justified to reckon that more than 400 clans existed at any one time. For the lists, see T R S Broughton, *The Magistrates of the Roman Republic* (New York, 1951–60).

[11] Clans were social groups united by the possession of a single family name, such as Claudius, Fabius, Iulius. Clan segments comprised kin who traced descent from a specific member of the clan, and so had a social existence separate from

in our evidence have contributed to this confusion, by allowing those who stress the hereditary character of the Roman elite to assume that the sons and grandsons of consuls, about whom we know nothing, became the praetors and ordinary senators of whom no record survives. But it is equally possible that many of them stayed out of the senate, and that is what we think happened. Besides, during the last two centuries of the Republic, clans were no longer effective political units (see below, p. 54). Moreover, statistical analysis by clan reveals a considerable opening up of the consulship in the last century of the Republic (see below, Table 2.1).

Thirdly, Romans who wished to join the political elite usually claimed traditional virtues, and sometimes fictional descent. Because of this, their intrusion did not appear to break the nobles' stranglehold; rather it seemed to reinforce the nobles' superiority.[12] Similarly, the notion that a consul ennobled his descendants in the male line tempts us to treat even distant descendants of consuls as noble. There is ancient testimony which appears to make this legitimate. But it disguises the very real difference between men whose father and grandfather had both been consul, and someone like Catiline whose

---

that of the clan as a whole. Clan segments also split up. For example, the Cornelii Scipiones Asinae were distinct from the Cornelii Scipiones Nasicae by the third century BC; Iunius Brutus Bubulcus was distinct from and not closely related to Iunius Brutus Pera and Iunius Brutus Scaeva. The last names (*cognomina*) in these cases were soubriquets meaning Ass, Large Nose, Ploughman, Bag, Left-hander. For anecdotes about their origins, see Macrobius, *Saturnalia* 1.6.24ff. We do not know why clans and segments split up. R. Develin in a study which is similar in purpose to our own (*Patterns in Office-Holding 366–49 BC* (Brussels, 1979) analysed consuls 366–180 BC, unfortunately by clan only. But he rightly emphasised the greater chances which patricians had of becoming consul in this period, because of their relatively small numbers, their traditional power, and because they had a single consulship reserved for them each year (down to 173 BC). Even so, Develin noted (p. 56) that succession to the consulship from fathers to son over more than one generation was rare.

[12] Cicero, for example, rhetorically assimilated a new consul to the establishment by calling him 'the consul designate from an old and illustrious family' (*In Defence of Murena* 17), and referred to the historic 'rich and honourable plebeian families' originally put in power by the mass walk-out (*secessio*) of the plebs in the fifth century BC (*ibid.* 15). L. Licinius Murena had been charged with bribery in securing his election to the consulship of 62 BC; he was the son, grandson and great-grandson of praetors, but the first of his clan segment to be elected consul. His accuser, a defeated aristocratic candidate, took his defeat as *prima facie* evidence of Murena's electoral corruption. Cicero defended the alternative and old Roman tradition of electing able new men to high office. Some scholars have used the concept patronage to help explain 'the power of the nobility to control the expansion of their circle as they saw fit' (Gelzer 1969:52, 62ff; cf. Syme 1939: *sv* patronage). This formulation is tautological; any case fits; good generals win battles. We do not doubt that patronage occurred, but we do doubt its explanatory value. Presumably those who lost elections also had patrons.

only claim to nobility rested on his descent from consular tribunes three hundred years earlier. Cicero tells us of a similar case, Servius Sulpicius Rufus, later consul (in 51 BC):

Your nobility, although of the highest, is known chiefly to historians and to the highly educated (*litteratis*) and is obscure to the people and to the voters. Your father was a knight, and your grandfather was not renowned for any brilliant deed. So knowledge of your nobility cannot be gained from the everyday talk of men, but must be unearthed from the history of antiquity. (*In defence of Murena* 16)

In theory, Sulpicius was a noble. But, in fact, Sulpicius' family had not gained consular office for over three hundred years. Should we consider him as a noble or as a new man? This formulation of the problem is not new, as can be seen in the comments reported by Asconius about M. Aemilius Scaurus, a noble who was elected consul in 115 BC: '...neither his father, nor his grandfather nor his great-grandfather had gained honours, I think, because of shortage of money and lack of effort.' This Aemilius Scaurus had to work to achieve success, Asconius continued, 'just like a new man' (23c).

Fourth, as so often, the experience of Cicero's generation, mirrored in his brilliant and voluminous writings, has dominated our understanding of political institutions throughout the late Republic. But political competition in the last generation of the Republic was atypical; Sulla's reforms in 81 BC had doubled the size of the senate and had increased the number of men qualified to compete for the consulship by a third. The temporary outcome was an increased restriction of the consulship to insiders, a response perhaps best understood as a last-ditch defence of noble privilege. Cicero's view of politics has had another, more surprising and less excusable consequence. Cicero never tired of repeating that he was himself a new man, who had succeeded in becoming a consul. 'In the strict sense of the term', wrote Syme (1939:11), new man (*novus homo*) means 'the first member of the family to secure the consulate and subsequent ennoblement.' Hence the most common criterion of Roman nobles' exclusiveness and power has become the rarity with which men without senatorial ancestry achieved the consulship. But the use of this definition diverts attention from the large numbers of new men who were the first members of their clan or clan segment to enter the senate, but who never achieved high office,[13] And

---

[13] Wiseman 1971 gives a very useful and readable account of the Republican evidence; he concentrates on men whose families were new to the senate, but consciously avoids statistical inference or hypothesis.

Cicero's own exceptional and dramatic achievement diverts us from appreciating the considerable achievements of those senators who came from merely senatorial families, but who then secured election as praetor or consul. This slow and continuous percolation into the Roman political elite constitutes a central theme of this chapter.

The openness of the Roman senate to outsiders has been known for a long time. For example, according to Willems (1878:396), one quarter of the consuls elected between 178 and 82 BC came from clans or from clan segments which had never produced a consul before.[14] But this is an aspect of Roman politics which is seldom stressed. The lower echelons of the senate were recruited from an even wider range of families.[15] And there seems to have been a rapid turnover. The evidence is patchy, but it suggests that many families sent only one or two representatives to the senate over several generations. It is difficult to trace this marginal mobility in individual families over long periods of time, because we are often uncertain about exact lines of descent, and we do not know whether the absence of a family member from the fragmentary lists of lower magistrates is due to a gap in the sources, or to political demise. But in principle, it is easy to recognize that in some cases, early death, lack of funds, lack of political ambition, lack of ability or the loss of an election, to say nothing of a father's lack of sons, created vacancies. Complementarily, since the size of the Roman senate was roughly fixed, places given to outsiders excluded sons of senators – unless the senate as a whole was not reproducing itself. And that would not be so much an explanation, as another problem to be explained.

Implicitly, we have been arguing that there were three complementary, but competing sources of recruitment to the Roman senate:

(*a*) sons of senators;

---

[14] P. Willems, *Le sénat de la république romaine* (Louvain, 1878) vol. 1, 396. See also the confused argument of Gelzer who delineated 'the exclusiveness with which the *nobiles* kept their hold on the consulship' and claimed that 'the principle of exclusiveness operated within fairly wide limits. Every senator's son was admitted [to candidacy for the consulship?] without serious opposition' (1969: 35).

[15] The variety of senatorial recruitment is clear from the nearly 400 clans (*gentes*) and nearly 500 clan segments (see note 11) which are known to have produced magistrates, some of them admittedly pre-senatorial, in the period 249–50 BC. For surviving names of magistrates, see Broughton 1951–60. C. Nicolet, 'Les classes dirigeantes romaines sous la république: ordre sénatorial et ordre équestre', *Annales* 32 (1977) 726ff, accepts the traditional view of the exclusiveness of the high nobility, but also stresses the openness of the lower ranks of the senate, and concludes that the senatorial and equestrian orders formed a single governing class. We agree with these last two conclusions.

(*b*) descendants of men who had been senators in a previous generation;

(*c*) new men, that is men without senatorial ascendants.

With appropriate changes, the same can be said about the recruitment of consuls. Individuals from each of these sets, according to their family's status and wealth, and their own ability, achievements and good fortune, had different chances of achieving entrance to, and success within the senate. We decided to examine the surviving evidence, in spite of its obvious deficiencies, to see if we could, even roughly, estimate the relative size of each set.

Our first approach was both statistical and demographic. Statistics were necessary so that we could get an overview of what was normal, normal that is in the statistical sense. That may seem an obvious objective and unobjectionable. Yet it is rarely sought after in Roman history, partly because the primary data seem so defective, partly because of fashions in writing history. Traditionally, Roman political history concentrated on legal and constitutional issues, or was dominated by great men, such as Marius, Sulla, Pompey and Julius Caesar, who strutted across the stage of history with only a small supporting cast. Their exceptional qualities precluded any easy generalisation about what was common-place in the Roman world. In recent decades, Roman political history has been heavily influenced by prosopography, the detailed study of the individual careers, political alliances and family relations of almost every Roman whose name has survived in our sources. The historical stage is now crammed with thousands of minor characters, about most of whom we know next to nothing.[16] We have traded a shortage of humdrum details for an overdose. Nor do prosopographers typically aim at generalisation; they seem more interested in attaining a delicate mastery of intricate detail. Even so, they often illustrate their writings with examples, and in so doing sometimes fall foul of what we can call the Everest fallacy, that is a tendency to illustrate a category by an example which is exceptional. The exceptional nature of the illustration is not made clear, and the illustration veils rather than reveals the normal. For example, Mount Everest is a 'typical' mountain, Cicero is a 'typical' new man, M. Aemilius Lepidus becomes a 'typical' noble.

[16] This may seem harsh criticism, but the indexes and pages of recent scholarly histories bear it out. Proper names may be redolent with meaning for *cognoscenti*, and in skilful hands they may be a useful tool. But more often they are an obstacle to good history, closer to a cricket scoreboard or a biblical list. For a polemical elaboration of these views, see K. Hopkins, 'Rules of evidence', *Journal of Roman Studies* 68 (1978) 178ff.

It is against this background that we thought it worthwhile to resort to statistics, because summary statistics transform individual fragments of data into usable aggregates, and subordinate the exceptional to the normal. To be sure, in this process we lose the drama of great men; and it may seem ungrateful to have criticised prosopographers, when we use all their hard work in constructing our statistical tables. Finally, statistical tables do not make for thrills. They cannot be a replacement for conventional history, only a supplement. They do not by themselves offer solutions to questions about recruitment to the Roman senate. But they do help us pose some new questions.

We turned next to demography, so that we could assess the extent of some gaps in our evidence. Usually, historians concentrate almost exclusively on those sources which survive. Understandably enough. What does not survive, what we do not know, what did not happen are all compressed into a single order of non-events, and so seem to be equally immeasurable. But in demographic history, in matters of birth and survival, the number of probable (and possible) patterns is finite. This finite probability opens the way for a special type of investigation, which can be helped along with the better data available from comparable societies.

One of our objectives here was the resuscitation of missing persons. For example, within a set of stated assumptions, we can estimate how many consuls probably had brothers surviving to consular age (consuls had to be at least forty-two years old). Put another way, we can estimate the probability that consuls (or senators) had many more surviving sons than we know about. The probable extent of their existence, hitherto we think largely unsuspected, surprised us. Our admittedly speculative findings raise two cognate problems. First, what happened to the politically unsuccessful sons of senators and consuls? Secondly, from which social stratum did their replacements come?

The scale of mobility into and out of the Roman political elite suggests further questions. Nobles in other pre-industrial states have typically ensured that at least one son as of right inherits the title previously held by his father, and in many societies all sons of nobles as of right inherit some social or political privileges.[17] Such comparative evidence tempts us to wonder why the Roman aristocracy was different. In the last two centuries of the Roman

---

[17] A useful collection is A. Goodwin, ed., *The European Nobility in the 18th Century* (London², 1967); L. Stone, *The Crisis of the Aristocracy 1558–1641* (Oxford, 1965) is brilliant and suggestive for students of the Roman aristocracy.

Republic, less than half of all the consuls are known to have had one consular or even praetorian son. This failure to secure hereditary succession at the top was an important and deep-seated factor in Roman political organisation. Our statistics suggest a principle: the higher the status of the father within the senate, the greater the chances of his son(s) succeeding to the status of the father. That is only to be expected; but its inverse is suggestive: the lower the status of the father within the senate, the less the son(s) chances of succeeding to the father's status. If this corollary holds, and we think it does, then sons of those senators who never became consul or praetor had an even lower rate of succession than sons of consuls (that is, *much* less than half). The question then arises: Why did the Roman political elite and the aristocracy as a whole fail to ensure their sons' political future?

The question arises out of the statistical evidence, and we shall discuss it at length in the last section of this chapter. But it may be helpful to summarise some elements of our answer. Roman politics were highly competitive. Top jobs in the Roman political elite, such as the command of Roman armies, the governance of conquered provinces, required considerable ability, which might not be inherited. These two factors alone might have prevented fathers from pushing all their sons into politics. There were other factors which inhibited succession. Participation in politics was expensive, especially for families whose wealth made them marginal members of the senatorial aristocracy. For them, the Roman custom of splitting inheritance more or less equally between all children (sons and daughters) was especially undermining. It jeopardised the social status of each child. Moreover, a sizeable minority of senators did not have a single son surviving to reproductive age, just as many fathers died before their sons were of an age to enter politics. These demographic factors brought about the biological extinction of some families in each generation, and precipitated the social downfall of others: but they also created circumstances which helped a sole heir who inherited his parents' total estate to achieve a dramatic social rise. They provided an arbitary dynamic within the Roman political system, like atomic flux within a stable structure. A realistic portrait of the Roman elite must incorporate both the stability and the flux.

Paradoxically, the ideal of inherited status encouraged fluidity. Among the Roman nobility, the ideal existed that status could be inherited, even after a gap of generations; the very fact that the great-grandson of a noble, or even a more distant descendant, could claim noble status in order to enhance his chances of political success indicates that noble families did not have to participate in politics in each and every generation. To be sure a few of the top noble families sent a son or sons into politics in each generation. That helped preserve the ideal of inherited status. But for the other families of the elite, there was a gap between ideals and actual practice. That is what ideals are for. Some elite families stayed out of the senate and active politics, even for generations, and still found entry easier than did outsiders. The implications are interesting. We see the Roman political system as one in which some noble families sent a son into the senate in each generation, while other senatorial families provided a senator less often or only occasionally. This gap between the ideal of inherited status and practice was recognised institutionally. Sons of senators ranked as knights, until they became or if they did not become, senators. Nobles, senators and knights were three layers in a broad elite, which had no well defined external boundaries.[18]

Three main points emerge. First, the Roman senate was an aristocracy of office, elected by the Roman people, and so unlike the hereditary nobility found in post-feudal European societies. Secondly, there was a broad stratum of elite families from which the senate was recruited. The concept elite is unavoidably, but in this context suitably, vague.[19] It comprised the descendants of consuls, senators and knights,

---

[18] Each of these terms (*nobilis, senator, eques*) has a specific meaning, but we doubt that they were always used exactly. Gelzer (1969: 27ff – see note 2 above) argued that Cicero used the word *nobilis* strictly for men with consular ancestry; but he also noted some exceptions and was reduced to treating those in Livy as thoughtless lies (p. 39). The term senator was unambiguous enough, but sons of senators were knights. Yet they were classed with senators in the law of 218 BC restricting the size of ships owned by senators and their sons (Livy 21.63), and in the legislation of G. Gracchus (123/2 BC), sons of senators like their fathers were made liable for prosecution for extortion before juries manned by knights, from which they were excluded (*FIRA* vol. 1, 86 and 88 – heavily restored). Nevertheless, in general usage, the *ordo senatorius* comprised senators but not their descendants or relatives. This changed in the early Principate; see below, Chapter 3, pp. 193ff and A. Chastagnol, 'La naissance de l'*ordo senatorius*', *Mélanges de l'école française à Rome* 85 (1973) 583ff. There is a great scholarly dispute about the boundary line between knights with the required minimum fortune (property valued in the census at 400,000 HS) and knights given a horse at state expense – reflecting the knights' origins in the cavalry. The modern dispute probably reflects the vagueness of Roman usage.

[19] Roman authors used numerous words to classify status in addition to those already discussed in note 18; let us mention *boni* – good men, *honestiores* – the more honourable men, later devalued to include lower social strata, *clarissimi* – the most distinguished, gradually devalued to include all senators, *potentes* – the powerful. Usage varied, just as criteria of status cut across each other. Surviving Roman authors and modern scholars seem to have paid more attention to minute differences in the upper reaches of the elite, than to the boundary line between the elite and the prosperous and respectable strata of lesser landowners. See further below and Nicolet 1973: 738.

and some successful outsiders. The elite was itself internally stratified, and marked off from the rest of society by landed wealth, style of consumption and social esteem (of which prestigious descent was an item). But because this broad elite had no fixed external boundaries, no fixed membership, no legal status as a stratum, and no common rituals, it was permeable to outsiders. And because of the various factors which we have mentioned above (the competitiveness and expense of politics, the need for real ability in some top political jobs, and the arbitrary incidence of the birth of sons and of their deaths), there was considerable mobility, percolation we could call it, both up and down within the elite. Thirdly, method. Lists of important office-holders provide us with a partial record of senate members in the last two centuries of the Republic. They are biased towards the successful. But the universe is finite; the size of the senate is roughly known. We can therefore tentatively estimate the number of missing persons and their significance. We can complement striking illustrations taken from fragmentary data with summary statistics. Similarly with excerpts taken from ancient authors, we must avoid treating statements about ideals as a trustworthy guide to actual practice; in fact, the one may, unintentionally, disguise the other.

II THE RESEARCH DESIGN AND ITS LIMITATIONS

We wanted to see how far holders of high office in Rome were either recruited from or themselves created consular families. From the Republican period, our analysis concentrates on consuls. We have taken praetors into account as well, when that was practicable. We have a complete list of the names of the two consuls elected each year. Their names were carved on marble and prominently displayed in the centre of the city of Rome. Fortunately, the main surviving list has in many cases preserved all six parts of the traditional Roman name: first name, clan name, father's first name, grandfather's first name, segment name and soubriquet, if any (for example, L. Cornelius Cn.f. L.n. Lentulus Lupus – Lucius Cornelius Lentulus the Wolf, son of Cnaeus, grandson of Lucius). Thus we have much of the information necessary to work out if consuls had consular brothers, or were sons and grandsons of consuls, or had consular sons and grandsons; consular uncles, nephews and cousins, if they were linked through males (for example, father's brother's son), can also be traced.

Our main focus is on the 364 men elected consul between 249 and

45

50 BC.[20] Our research for most important purposes goes back three generations before and three generations after each set of consuls. We thus cover seven generations for each consul. We have not tried to do original research on genealogies. We have followed what has been set out by prosopographers in standard works.[21] There are obviously gaps in what is known. The identification of some links is only tentative, sometimes barely plausible.[22] In individual cases, we may occasionally have been wrong. In aggregate, and that is what we are concerned with here, the impact of our decisions in disputed cases or of changes suggested by very recent scholarship, is small. If anything, there has probably been a general tendency for genealogists to assign men of uncertain origins to known ascendants. Consuls are better known than non-consuls. The standard genealogies are therefore likely to have overstated hereditary connections.

Praetors. We have a full list of praetors only for the years 218–166 BC.[23] Our main source is Livy, who for the most part gave no patronyms and no names of grandfathers. The identification of relationships to people with similar names is therefore tentative. Nevertheless, the list expands our knowledge of the Roman political elite significantly. It provides the names of 174 praetors who never became consul. The period covered is just long enough for us to see how far these praetors-never-consul elected at the beginning of the

---

[20] This number excludes 48 second, third and subsequent consulships, but includes 12 supplementary (technically called *suffect*) consuls. In each sub-period (e.g. 249–220 BC), first consulships only are counted.

[21] Articles in *RE* were the basic sources, supplemented by Broughton 1951–60; F. Münzer, *Römische Adelsparteien und Adelsfamilien* (Stuttgart, 1920) and for the last period of the Republic, Syme 1939 and E. Groag, A. Stein *et al. Prosopographia Imperii Romani* (Berlin², 1933–70). We started by going back only two generations for Republican consuls, but later and for some purposes only, looked at consuls' great-grandfathers.

[22] For example, Q. Caecilius Q.f. L.n. Metellus Macedonicus, consul of 143 BC, on the basis of Pliny, *Natural History* 7.54 is taken by Münzer as the son of Q. Caecilius L.f. L.n. Metellus, consul of 206 BC, in spite of the 63 year gap. Against our better judgement, we have followed this convention.

[23] We know less than a fifth of the praetors-never-consul 165–141 BC, less than third 139–80 BC, and about two-thirds 79–50 BC; all estimates are drawn from lists in Broughton 1951–60. We counted the numbers known in these three periods as 18, 68, 117+ respectively. Second praetorships were excluded. To avoid double-counting, it seems important to separate consuls, who were nearly always ex-praetors from praetors who never became consuls. Gruen 1974: 508ff did not do so; his figures on praetors contain data on consuls and this affects his interpretation. Of 185 praetors-never-consul elected 78–49 BC, 62 are unknown. Of the rest (N = 123), 40 came from ever-consular clans or segments, 20 from known praetorian clans or segments, and 63 (just over half of those known) came from families not known to have achieved the praetorship. Given the gaps in our information, this is difficult to interpret, but to us it suggests a high degree of mobility into the praetorship.

period (218–198 BC) had praetorian or consular sons, and how far
the praetors-never-consul who were elected at the end of this period
(190–166 BC) had praetorian or consular fathers.

Consuls and praetors together provide a sound basis for the
analysis of the Roman political elite, because from 197 BC onwards
about half of all the entrants to the senate were eventually elected
praetor. This estimate rests upon several assumptions, which seem
reasonable, but are not certain. The senate before 81 BC probably had
about three hundred members. This would have required on average
just less than 12 entrants each year aged about thirty (as we calculate
later from comparable demographic data: see Table 3.11). We
assume, without being certain, that thirty was the normal age of entry
to the senate. Thirty-nine was the minimum legal age for election
to the praetorship, with forty-two years the minimum legal age for
election to the consulship; this was fixed by the *lex Villia Annalis* of
180 BC; in some respects, this law seems only to have legalised
contemporary practice, since three years was the median interval
between the two offices, among those elected consul in the twenty
years before the law's enactment. We do not know how commonly
men achieved high office at or even before the minimum legal age.
Tiberius Gracchus, for example, was quaestor when he was twenty-
four or twenty-five years old.

If we rely on the simplifying assumption that entrants to the senate
were usually thirty years old, we can calculate that by the age of
thirty-nine, on average about one sixth (17%) of the original 12
annual entrants to the senate would have died (see Table 3.12). Thus
on average until 82 BC, 10 senators became eligible for election to the
praetorship each year.[24] From among these, only 6 were elected

[24] Professor Badian has kindly persuaded us that well before the time of Sulla (who
raised the number of quaestors from 81 BC to 20 per year), the administration
of the provinces required 12 quaestors annually, although some quaestors may
have served for longer than one year. This fits with an assumption that the senate
was filled with about 12 senators each year, aged about 30. If new senators were
on average more than 30 years old, then the number of senatorial recruits would
have been larger – or the senate smaller. Formally, the censors (who held power
in theory every 5 years) selected senators from among those who had served in
the army (? or who had been available for military service) for 10 years, and
who had been elected quaestor or tribune of the people. This supports a
mimimum age of 27, and an average age of least 30 at entry to the senate. Pompey
fixed rules in Asia Minor that no one should be senator in a provincial city before
the age of 30 (Pliny, *Letters* 10.79); perhaps this reflected practice at Rome. On
Tiberius Gracchus, see A. E. Astin, 'The Lex Annalis before Sulla,' *Latomus* 17
(1958) 61ff. On intervals between praetorship and consulship, see Astin *ibid.* 16
(1957) 588ff; the average interval was 4.0 years for the periods 200–180 and
179–160 BC.

47

praetor. From 81 BC, there were 20 entrants to the senate each year; if one sixth of these also died before reaching the age of thirty-nine, then again about half (8 out of 17 survivors) could on average secure election to the praetorship. We know very little of those who failed to become praetor and who remained mere senators (called *pedarii*, because they voted with their feet and had no right to talk in senate meetings). Our calculations make it seem unlikely that all these relatively unsuccessful senators were sons of consuls or of praetors or even of senators, or that all the sons of senators, praetors and consuls whom we cannot trace, became mere senators. Other things being equal, we should expect more newcomers among mere senators than among praetors and consuls.[25]

Some limitations of the research design

Our research suffers from several limitations. They may induce cautious scepticism about some of our results. Nevertheless, we think that most of our results are valid. One limitation is that we have taken no account in our figures of relationships in the female line: no maternal grandfathers, no mother's brothers, wives, fathers-in-law or brothers-in-law, nor any similar affine descendant. The evidence on such relationships is available only in a tiny minority of cases and we saw no way of incorporating it meaningfully. This is obviously a drawback; how much does it matter?

In the prosopographical literature, relationships by marriage figure prominently. Many first marriages, divorces and remarriages appear to have been governed by political considerations.[26] Alliances between noble families were forged or cemented by marriage. For example, Pompey and Caesar strengthened their new alliance of 60 BC by breaking off the existing engagements of their daughters; instead, Pompey married Caesar's daughter, her ex-fiancé married Pompey's daughter, while Caesar married the daughter of the consul designated for the next year. Like many often-quoted examples, this is an extreme case, but it illustrates the reinforcement which the elite secured by intermarriage. And, in an elite of fixed size, fertile intermarriage limited the upward mobility of outsiders.

[25] We argue this in more detail below, pp. 66ff.
[26] 'In her dynastic policy she (Servilia) ruthlessly employed the three daughters of her second husband, whom she gave in marriage to...' (Syme 1939: 69). As often, Syme's attribution of motive and style is suspect. For words of caution against regarding all marriages as political, see D. R. Shackleton Bailey, 'The Roman nobility in the Second Civil War', *Classical Quarterly* 10 (1960) esp. 266–7; see also below, pp. 86ff.

Several nobles are known to have married off their sons or daughters to spouses of lower status.[27] Successful new men are known to have climbed socially by marrying well. For example, P. Sestius, son of a tribune, when he was perhaps not yet even a senator (the date of his marriage is uncertain), married the daughter of Scipio Asiaticus, consul of 83 BC, admittedly exiled but of very noble family. Interpretation is difficult; did Sestius rise successfully to praetor because of his marriage to a consul's daughter and the connections which it brought, or did she marry him because he had the ability to rise? We have insufficient evidence to make a choice. Both factors may have played a part. What matters here is that although 'good marriages' may have been an important channel of upward mobility for some men, they are not a sufficient explanation of their mobility. Why were these men chosen as husbands instead of others? Marriage offers no better explanation than patronage. If we assume that both successful and defeated candidates had powerful patrons and allies, then the common attribution by prosopographers of success as due to a marriage with the daughter of X or to the patronage of Y, offers less explanation than is sometimes implied. Why then did the protégé of Z fail? Statistics and prosopography should be allies and not alternatives.

We dealt with adoption by counting the adoptive father only; this was sometimes unsatisfactory, but we saw no easy way around it. For example, a consul, himself the biological son of a consul, but adopted by a praetorian father (e.g. the consul of 179 BC: L. Manlius Acidinus Fulvianus – i.e. born Fulvius) is counted in our figures as upwardly mobile! Fortunately, known cases like this are rare and do not seriously distort our findings. Overall, to judge from their names, only 15 (4%) of the consuls 249–50 BC were adopted, mostly in the second half of the period; there may have been other cases no longer easy to spot. Thus the incidence of adoption was apparently quite low. But its effects were doubly important. It enabled fathers without surviving sons to keep the family name alive (in other cases done by insisting that a son-in-law took his wife's family name). Complementarily, it provided fathers who had too many surviving sons with a way of maintaining a son's status from someone else's funds, and of widening family alliances. Of course, it did not always work out as well as intended. In one notable case, L. Aemilius Paullus, twice

---

[27] Wiseman (1971: 53ff) gives a fascinating account of marriages in the late Republic. Our knowledge is patchy, but several examples of marriage of nobles to the obscure are recorded. Cf. Münzer 1920: 328–47 and 425ff, who also dealt with adoptions (154, 235 etc).

consul (182, 168 BC) gave two of his four sons away to be adopted by leading nobles. The two remaining sons died, the adopted survived. The father died legally childless. A cautionary tale, then as now. In spite of such risks, adoption contributed significantly to the social survival of several noble families.

Another shortcoming of our research design is that we go back only three generations, or roughly a century. This means that we put men with only distant consular ancestors into the same category as new men. For example, M. Iunius Brutus (consul in 178 BC) whose nearest direct consular ancestor was apparently consul in 509 BC, is equated with M. Porcius Cato, consul in 195 BC, the first of his line ever to enter the senate.[28] Yet Roman consciousness of a family's past glory went a long way back. Even distant consular ancestry was a political advantage, though not an overwhelming one.[29] In Cicero's usage, a solitary consular ancestor three centuries back entitled a descendant to be called *nobilis*. Why did we not take this into account? First, because the further back one goes, the more likely one is to mistake connections, especially if no members of the family are attested in the intervening generations. Segmentation of clans obscured genaealogies, so that often we are not sure of the relationship between men of the same clan with different segment names (*cognomina*); they are sometimes direct linear descendants (for example, C. Servilius Vatia was apparently the grandson of M. Servilius Geminus), sometimes not.

Secondly, the discontinuites in the Roman consular elite are themselves interesting; gaps of more than a century should not be ignored. We did not want to put consuls with consular fathers into the same category as men with a putative consular ancestor more than a century before. Every research design has boundary problems. The cost of our decision was that our statistics occasionally lump together new men, who are the traditional subjects of studies of upward social mobility, with descendants of noble families, whose members had not ostensibly been successful in politics for more than a century.

There was a third reason for this decision. With the lapse of time as the gap between a consul and his descendants lengthened, so in some cases, the probability grew that there were a number of people

---

[28] For this purpose, we disregard other sub-segments of the Iunii Bruti, the Iunii Bruti Bubulci and Iunii Bruti Scaevae, who produced four consuls between 325 and 291 BC.

[29] Cicero discussed the relative claims of virtue and birth in his speeches, *In Defence of Plancius* 12 and *In Defence of Murena* 16.

The research design

who could effectively claim descent from the consul. Even our fragmentary sources, which are biased towards the successful, preserve the names of a large number of unsuccessful men with aristocratic names. L. Valerius Flaccus, for example, was the name of four consuls (261, 195, 152, 100 BC); it was also the name of the son of a centurion in the civil wars of Julius Caesar.[30] The decision of any one descendant to capitalise on his distinguished ancestry, real or fictive, must have been the result of many considerations other than the ancestry itself (such as his ability, wealth, connections and social acceptability). Noble descent was obviously important; the majority of consuls had some real or putative connection with a consular ancestor. But noble descent was neither a necessary nor a sufficient condition of a successful political career. By the same token, it seems probable that many sons of noble descent either did not enter or failed in political life. As we argue below, a significant number of men who could claim consular ascendants did not enter the senate.

So far we have left faked ancestry out of our account. There is little evidence about it in Republican Rome and even less modern discussion, as though it is somehow irreverent to suggest that Republican Roman nobles faked their ancestry. English and Chinese nobles certainly did. Why should the Romans have been less successful (in similar conditions) in claiming noteworthy ancestors?[31] We have more evidence from the Principate and Late Empire; in the first century, some nobles claimed descent from Trojan heroes or from early Roman kings; in the fourth and fifth centuries AD, Gallic nobles traced their ancestry back to Italian heroes of the late Republic or early Principate; metropolitan Roman nobles claimed Scipio, the Gracchi or the Fabii, and less modestly Agamemnon as ancestors.

---

[30] Professor T. P. Wiseman very kindly prepared for us a list of 37 Romans with high-sounding names (for example M. Claudius Marcellus, A. Popillius Laenas, P. Terentius Varro, M. Valerius Messalla) who were probably either soldiers or Italian town-councillors (NB not ex-slaves who took the names of their masters). He did not claim that his list was exhaustive; it is predominantly Republican. Cf. the comments of E. Badian (*Historia* 12 (1963) 136) against the facile identification of senators with other men bearing the same name. Lists of such men in L. R. Taylor, *The Voting Districts of the Roman Republic* (Rome, 1960) 288, cf. 184ff; R. Syme, *Historia* 13 (1964) 157 and 163ff; Taylor and Syme regard these men as Roman nobodies stealing distinguished names, a view which is complementary to, but no more plausible than our proposition that noble ancestors had some unsuccessful descendants.

[31] T P Wiseman seems readier than most to accept Roman faking; see his 'Legendary genealogies in late Republican Rome', *Greece and Rome* 21 (1974) 153ff; cf. Stone 1965: 23ff and M. Freedman, *Lineage Organization in South-eastern China* (London, 1958). On confusion about distant ancestry, see an interesting example in Aulus Gellius, *Attic Nights* 13.20.

51

After conversion to Christianity, nobles sought their origins in early Christian martyrs.[32] The pressures to enhance status, and the solutions, were probably similar in the Republic, even if the process by which these fictions became accepted remains mysterious. Cicero thought that laudatory funeral speeches, public occasions in which the nobility of a family was competitively displayed, encouraged distortions which then became part of history:

> ...much is set down in them which never occurred, false triumphs, too large a number of consulships, false parentage (*genera*) and false transitions of patricians to plebeian status, by which men of humble birth claimed that their blood blended with a noble family of the same name, although in fact quite alien. (*Brutus* 62)

Clans, clan segments and families

Finally, our concentration on consuls' and praetors' direct ancestors and descendants in the male line precludes us from considering their wider connections with clansmen, that is with fellow aristocrats bearing the same name (*nomen*). Major scholars, such as De Sanctis and Scullard, have taken for granted in their analysis of Roman political institutions that clans (*gentes*) were politically powerful units even in historical times. Their statements that ten clans held roughly half the consulships in the century before the Gracchi, must assume that the clan was an effective focus of political organisation.[33] By a clan, they mean, for example, all Aemilii, Cornelii, or Valerii. This is unrealistic.

Nevertheless, we thought that we should analyse the origins of consuls by clan. Table 2.1 sets out the results for the last two centuries of the Republic (232–33 BC). The periods are arbitrary, but not

[32] Several examples are given by L. Friedländer, *Sittengeschichte Roms* (Leipzig[10], 1922) vol. I, 120–1; see also K. F. Stroheker, *Der senatorische Adel im spätantiken Gallien* (Tübingen, 1948) 10–11. A distinction should be drawn between well-established families acquiring fictitious distant ancestors (as the Julii acquired Aeneas) and an upstart family fictitiously claiming descent from noble ancestors. Cf. Seneca: '...when they review their ancestors, wherever an illustrious name is missing, they foist in a god' (*On Benefits* 3.28).

[33] So De Sanctis 1967–69: vol. 4.1, 473 and Scullard 1973:9ff and Syme 1939:492. But *contra*, for scepticism of the unity of clans, see F. Cassola, *I gruppi politici romani nel III secolo a.c.* (Trieste, 1962) 20–2. His critique has been well received, but this has apparently not led to the rejection of the old ideas, if only because most ancient historians are oriented primarily not to hypothesis, proof and refutation, but to scholarship and insight. Of course, we know that M. Tullius Cicero was not a member of the patrician Tullii, just as we know that P. Sulpicius Quirinius, consul of 12 BC, had nothing to do with the patrician Sulpicii (Tacitus, *Annals* 3.48); how many such cases do we not know?

misleading, in the sense that altering the first period to 249–200 BC and the last period to 99–55 BC did not change the general picture. The main finding is that, in terms of clan, entry to the consulship in the last two centuries of the Republic became much more open.

Let us take a quick look at the changes set out in Table 2.1. All the indices move more or less consistently in the same direction; and so, for the sake of simplicity, we shall compare the first 50-year period (232–183 BC) with the last period (82–33 BC). This simplification is not misleading. The number of patrician clans with consuls declined from 13 to 7 (row A), while the number of plebeian clans with consuls rose from 25 to 39 (row B). The number of clans with only one consul in the 50-year period increased from 17 to 24 (row D), while the number of clans producing a consul, which had not produced a consul in the previous 50-year period, rose from 14 to 22. These are symptoms of the fragmentation of power and of discontinuity in tenure. Admittedly, the changes in raw numbers may seem small, but

Table 2.1. *During the last century of the Republic, access to the consulship opened up considerably. Analysis by clan* (gens)

	232–183* a	182–133 b	132–83 c	82–33 BC* d
A Patrician clans with consuls	13	11	10	7
B Plebeian clans with consuls	25	28	40	39
A + B All consular clans	38	39	50	46
D Clans with only one consul in this period	17	17	30	24
E Consular clans with no consul in previous 50 year period	14	14	21	22
Number of consuls†				
F Patrician consuls	47	34	22	20
G Plebeian consuls	43	53	67	65

* The figures for the fifty year periods 249–200 BC and 99–50 BC were very close to the figures here for columns *a* and *d*.

† Suffect consuls and second or third consulships excluded.

they are significant in proportional (percentage) terms. We should stress that the units of analysis, clans, are crude and that these findings are accordingly weak. But they all point in a single direction. The power of the nobility, if measured by its exclusive tenure of the consulship, declined during the last two centuries of the Republic.[34] More clans shared in the exercise of power at the top.

The most obvious argument against analysis by clan is that in the historical period most Roman clans were divided into segments, and even segments were split (see note 11). We do not understand the factors which made a Roman family decide to distinguish a segment as a separate entity from other segments or from the main clan; nor do we know what demands members of a clan or segment normally made on each other. But segmentation suggests that the whole clan was not united. Even common membership of a segment was no guarantee of political support. The conflict between Pompey and Caesar brought members of the same segment into conflict with each other; L. Iulius Caesar, for example, was on Pompey's side.[35] Besides most aristocratic members of a segment were dead, which heightened their ritual importance, but lessened their immediate political usefulness. One needed living allies as well. Even if common membership of a segment or clan legitimated some claims for political support, the claims of the clan or segment had to be balanced against other claims, for example, from relatives by marriage, from clients, or from friends (*necessarii*), against the interests of the state, and against the benefits which each might bring. In general, we imagine, the closer the family relationship, the greater the probability of co-operation. But the rivalry of brothers was legendary (Romulus and Remus), to say nothing of tension between fathers and sons (see Chapter 4, pp. 244ff).[36] And the more complex the society and its political system, the greater the need to secure support from others besides kinsmen.

In sum, the first part of our analysis is statistical, a complement

[34] For example, the five clans with the most consulships in the century before 133 BC held 61 consulships in that period; the equivalent number in the next century was 48 consulships, a decline of 21 %; it is a symptom of the dispersion of power.

[35] See notably Shackleton Bailey 1960: 254ff; cf. the expulsion of an ex-consul, P. Cornelius Lentulus Sura by the censor of 70 BC, P. Cornelius Lentulus Clodianus. L. A. Fallers, *Bantu Bureaucracy* (Chicago[2], 1965) esp. 1–20 and 225–50, gives interesting ideas on the tensions between clans and state.

[36] One could not always count on help from relatives; for the proverbial hatred between brothers (*solita fratribus odia*), see Tacitus, *Annals* 4.60, cf. 13.17. For a prosopographical treatment of political or kin relationships, see particularly Münzer 1920 and Syme 1939; since the evidence on distant kin and affines is fragmentary, it is better handled prosopographically than statistically.

to and perhaps a framework for prosopographical studies. Our research is restricted mainly to consuls, their consular ascendants and descendants in the male line over seven generations supplemented by a study of praetors. In so far as it was possible, we included in our survey brothers, agnatic uncles (father's brothers), cousins and nephews. But we took no account of agnatic collaterals at more than one remove (such as second cousins), of links through females, of connections with wider clan segments or clans, nor of distant ancestry, whether real or claimed. Let us now turn to the results.

III ANALYSIS OF FINDINGS

The best summary of our findings is set out in the Tables 2.2–2.7. They appear formidable because they contain more data than we can analyse here. Our purpose has been to provide descriptive statistics which scholars can use for their own purposes. We have tried to avoid statistical figments, such as an average of grossly disparate figures. The mass of data presented in the tables will enable the reader to qualify, as necessary, the generalisations which we make about the consuls of the last two centuries of the Roman Republic.

Interpretation of the tables is difficult, since we are often trying to say in words what is better expressed in figures. Some of the tables' limitations will be clear from the titles of columns and rows, and they should be read first. In this chapter, we concentrate on general patterns rather than on variations between small periods, and dwell on only one or two conclusions derived from each table. We indicate the figures referred to by column and row, and by heavy type in the tables. We regret that this section does not read easily, but we are convinced that statistical analysis is helpful; it affords rough orders of magnitude and reveals dimensions of social behaviour which are often ignored through lack of testimony. It also directs our attention to fresh problems, which may then be advanced by traditional historical techniques.

Consuls in the last two centuries of the Republic did not form an exclusive, hereditary clique. Only two fifths of consuls (Table 2.2, col. *h*) had a consular father. Only one third of consuls had a consular son. Two thirds of consuls had no consular son. These patterns are very roughly stable throughout the last two centuries of the Republic.

Continuity and discontinuity in consular familes. It was extremely rare for a family to produce a consul in each of six successive generations. Only 4% of consuls (Table 2.3, col. *a*) came from such

Table 2.2. *The inheritance of consular status: consular ascendants and descendants of Republic consuls (249–50 BC)*

Consuls with consular:	Consuls of:							Total
	249–220	219–195	194–170	169–140	139–110	109–80	79–50 BC	249–50 BC
	a	*b*	*c*	*d*	*e*	*f*	*g*	*h*
				(per cent)				
A Grandfather	15	35	40	38	32	43	35	34
B Father	38	38	30	42	**57**	41	36	**40**
C (research generation of consuls)	100	100	100	100	100	100	100	100
D Son	32	38	38	38	**27**	**31**	**24**	**32**
E Grandson	30	32	24	30	13	16	12*	24
F Great-grandson	13	30	18	27	10	8	12*	16
N =	53	37	50	55	60	51	58	364

* Suffect consuls in the Principate excluded.
This table shows the percentage of consuls of any one period (*a–h*) who had consular father, grandfather, etc. For example, of the consuls of 169–140 BC, 42% had a consular father, and 38% had a consular grandfather. To see how many consuls had only a consular father, or both a consular father and consular grandfather, see Table 2.4.

a family. The Metelli and the Claudii Pulchri may seem archetypal Roman aristocrats, but they were exceptional; and we should not allow the famous to obscure the normal. A quarter of the Republican consuls (27%; row A) had only one representative as consul in the six generations covered by our research. Another fifth (20%; row B) had consuls in only two adjacent generations, father and son. Thus almost one half (47%) of consular families flourished briefly and then disappeared from the centre of the political stage at least for a century, or for ever.

How many consuls had consular ascendants? Throughout the last two centuries of the Republic, just under one third (32%; Table 2.4, col. *h*, rows K and L) of consuls, that is 116 out of 364 consuls secured election without the help of immediate consular antecedents, that is, without consular father, grandfather or great-grandfather, without consular uncle or brother. Known praetorian fathers, admittedly very incomplete information, 'explain' a further 18 (5%) of these 116 consuls. The inner sanctum of the Roman elite was penetrated

Table 2.3. *Continuity and discontinuity in consular families*

Consuls came from families with consuls in how many generations* out of six:	Consuls elected in:		
	249–50 *a*	249–140 *b*	139–50 BC *c*
	(per cent)		
A one only	27	28	26
B two adjacent	20	19	22
C two not adjacent	12	12	13
D three	19	17	23
E four	13	15	11
F five	4	5	3
G six	4	6	2
N =	364	198	166

* The data cover grandfathers and fathers of consuls and their sons, grandsons and great-grandsons in the male line only.

Our research covered six generations ($uvwxyz$): the grandfather and father of each consul, his sons, grandsons and great-grandsons. The consul of any given date is in generation w, his father is in generation v, son in x. Two adjacent generations in row B are either generations vw or wx.

more than is often thought, both by men whose ascendants had achieved nothing memorable in a century, and by new men. On the other hand, it is easy to stress continuity; we can 'explain' the election of over half the consuls (53 %; col. *h*) by their consular father or grandfather.[37]

Consuls and Praetors. From the next table (Table 2.5), we draw two main conclusions. First, when sons of praetors and consuls competed for political office, sons of consuls were more likely to win, but they were often beaten by sons of praetors. Secondly, even after the number of top political posts (consuls plus praetors) was increased from six to eight per year from 197 BC, many consuls and praetors-never-consul did not have politically successful sons. These results are based on the analysis of praetors elected in the only period for which

[37] Like most explanations in history and sociology, this 'explanation' is retrospective. There may well be other, unknown factors, which help 'explain' the consulships of both father and son, such as wealth, ability or connections. In sum, it is a very limited 'explanation'. Nor can it be transformed into a statement that 53 % of sons or grandsons of consuls became consul.

Table 2.4 *How far can the election of consuls be 'explained' by consular ascendants?*

Consuls with:	249–220 *a*	219–195 *b*	194–170 *c*	169–140 *d*	139–110 *e*	109–80 *f*	79–50 BC *g*	All consuls 249–50 BC *h*
				(per cent)				
A Consular father and consular grandfather	8	22	20	24	23	25	17	**20**
B Consular father only	30	16	10	18	33	16	17	**21**
C Consular grandfather only	8	8	16	11	5	12	16	**11**
D Consular great-grandfather only	2	5	0	4	2	8	16	5
E Consular grandfather and praetorian father only	0	5	4	4	3	6	3	4
F Consular great-grand-father and praetorian father only	0	0	0	4	2	0	5	2
G SUB-TOTAL*	47	57	50	64	68	67	74	62
H Previous consular brother	8	3	8	4	2	0	0	3
J Consular uncle	0	8	4	4	8	0	3	4
K Praetorian father	0	0	10	9	5	4	5	5
L None of the above	45	32	28	20	17	29	17	**26**
TOTAL	100	100	100	101	100	100	99	100
N =	53	37	50	55	60	51	58	364

* Percentage sub-totals (row G) are recalculated from raw numbers; this accounts for discrepancies in addition.

NB. To avoid double-counting, each successive row applies only to consuls not yet counted. For example, row H shows consuls who had consular brothers but had none of the consular ancestors listed in rows A–F.

we have a complete list of praetors (218–166 BC). In other periods, our knowledge is defective and is biased towards those who later became consul. As we mentioned before, the period 218–166 BC is fortunately just long enough for us to be able to study how many of the praetors-never-consul elected in the first part of this period

Analysis of findings

Table 2.5. *Consuls and praetors: their fathers and sons*

		Consuls			Praetors-never-consul	
	249–220	219–195	194–170	169–140 BC	218–198	190–166 BC
	a	*b*	*c*	*d*	*e*	*f*
Consuls or praetors with:			(per cent)			
A Consular grandfather only	8	8	16	11	4	8
B Consular father	38	38	30	42	30	14
C Father praetor-never-consul	n/a	n/a	16	16	n/a	20
D SUB-TOTAL			62	69		42
E Consular son	32	38	38	38	22	6
F Son praetor-never-consul	27	32	n/a	n/a	24	n/a
G SUB-TOTAL	53*	62*			40*	
N =	53	37	50	55	50	50†

* 6% of fathers in col. *a*, 8% in col. *b* and 6% in col. *e* had both consular and praetorian sons.

† Based on a one in two sample (n = 50) out of 101 praetors-never-consul; full data on praetors are available only for 218–166 BC.

NB. Row A does not include consuls whose fathers were consul or praetor.

(218–198 BC; N = 50) had consular or praetorian sons, and how many praetors-never-consul elected in the last part of the period (190–166 BC; N = 101) were of praetorian or consular origin.[38]

Consular halo. More consuls (62%–69%) than praetors-never-consul (42%) had immediate consular or praetorian ancestors (Table 2.5, row D). Overall, as we should expect, sons of consuls were more successful politically than sons of praetors-never-consul (row G;

[38] We fixed the dates for each cohort of praetors to take account of the increase from four to six per year in 197 BC, and to maximise the chances of including praetors who were the sons of praetors (therefore 190–166, not 197–166 BC). We used the lists of Broughton 1951–60. Scullard 1973: 306–8 conveniently lists praetors of this period, but he omits to note some of their subsequent consulships. We analysed all the praetors-never-consul elected 218–197 BC. But we took a one in two sample (50 out of 101) of praetors-never-consul elected 190–166 BC. N denotes a universe, n denotes a sample. On the dangers and benefits of sampling, see Chapter 3, pp. 130–3.

53 %, later 62 % of consuls had consular or praetorian sons, compared with 40 % of praetors-never-consul). We could call this the consular halo effect. But the halo's power was limited; politically successful sons of consuls were almost as likely to finish up as praetors as to achieve the consulship (compare rows E and F: 38 % of consuls had consular sons, 32 % had sons who became praetor-never-consul). Praetors-never-consul had roughly the same chance of having a consular son as of having a son finish up as praetor (22 % and 24 %). Moreover, the sons of praetors-never-consul with immediate consular ancestry were no more successful politically than sons of praetors-never-consul without consular ancestry.[39] Not great findings, but they indicate that consulars and praetorians did not come from stable, segregated strata of noble and non-noble families. They were interwoven.

These succession rates were low enough to leave a considerable number of vacancies free to be filled by those who were not sons of consuls and praetors. Our argument rests upon two inter-related points: first, many sons of mere senators and of non-senators became praetors and consuls; secondly, and this is more difficult to prove, consuls and praetors had a significant number of sons, surviving to consular age, who did not become consuls or praetors, or even mere senators.[40] At this stage in the discussion, the increase in praetorships from four to six per year from 197 BC can be turned to our advantage, because it gave sons of consuls and of praetors an unprecedented chance of achieving political success. Yet the 79 consuls and praetors of 218–198 BC had only 52 sons who became praetor or consul, although there were 126 vacancies (up from 84 vacancies) over an equal period of time. In the period 190–166 BC (admittedly exceptional because of the new vacancies), two thirds of praetors-never-consul were sons of neither consuls nor praetors (Table 2.5, col. *f*); the top ranks of the Roman political elite were wide open to outsiders. By outsiders, we mean as always in this chapter, men with sufficient money, status and ability to compete in Roman politics, who were not sons of consuls or praetors, or of mere senators.

[39] We divided the praetors-never-consul of 218–198 BC into (a) those with consular father or grandfather (N = 17), and (b) those without (N = 33). Slightly fewer (6/17) of group (a) had consular or praetorian sons than in group (b) (13/33). The numbers involved are very small, and not much can be made of this.

[40] By mere senators, we mean senators who never became praetors, but who survived past praetorian age. We think that a significant number of non-senators, including some descendants of mere senators, praetors and consuls, lived on terms of rough social equality with senators. They constituted a broad stratum of respectables, with sufficient status and resources occasionally to compete in politics.

Table 2.6. *Self-replacement of consuls and praetors* 249–50 BC

	Consuls		Praetors-never-consul	Consuls			All consuls
	249–220	219–195	218–198	194–140	139–80	79–50 BC	249–50 BC
	a	*b*	*c*	*d*	*e*	*f*	*g*
			(per cent)				
A FSM*	53	**62**	**40**	(48)	(43)	(34)	(46)
B Consular sons	36	51	24	48	32	24	38
C Praetorian sons	28	35	30	(11)	(21)	(12)	(19)
D B + C = SRP*	**64**	**86**	**54**	(59)	(52)	(36)	(57)
E B/C†	1·3	1·5	0·8	4·2	1·5	2·0	2·0
N =	53	37	(n = 50)	105	111	58	364

* FSM is the Rate of Family Status Maintenance; FSM answers the question: What proportion of consuls had a consular or praetorian son? SRP is the Rate of Social Reproduction in Politics; SRP answers the question: How many sons of a given cohort of consuls reached the consulship or praetorship? For example, col. *a*, 53 % (FSM) of consuls 249–220 BC had politically successful sons; these sons totalled 64 % (SRP) of consuls 249–220 BC.
† B/C shows the ratio of consular to known praetorian sons.
  Numbers in brackets are based on defective data for praetors; only about one third of all praetors-never-consul are known for 139–80 BC, but about two thirds are known for the period 79–50 BC.

How many politically successful sons did consuls and praetors have?[41] This is the question which we answer in Table 2.6 (row D). Here we are concerned to find out the extent to which consuls and praetors-never-consul reproduced themselves politically (not biologically – we turn to that in a moment). We must distinguish this problem from our previous question: How many consuls and praetors had consular and praetorian sons? In order to underline the distinction, we have used special, and rather inelegant, terms for each: the rate of Family Status Maintenance (FSM) measures how many consuls or praetors had at least one son who became praetor or consul, in other words, how many families maintained their high political status over two generations. The rate of Social Reproduction

[41] We use the term politically successful and success in politics in this chapter as a literary variation to mean consuls and praetors-never-consul.

in Politics (SRP) measures how many consular or praetorian sons each cohort of consuls and praetors elected in successive periods had; the total number of politically successful sons is expressed as a proportion of the whole cohort to which their fathers belonged.[42] We are analysing the extent to which cohorts or sets of consuls and of praetors-never-consul reproduced themselves politically. We can then compare the two rates; for example, 62 % of the consuls elected 219–195 BC had at least one son who then became consul or praetor (FSM = 62 %); the same cohort of consuls (N = 37) had altogether 32 consular and praetorian sons, giving a rate of Social Reproduction in Politics of 86 % (N = 32/37; Table 2.6, col. *b*). Among praetors-never-consul elected 218–198 BC, the succession rates were much lower: FSM = 40 %, SRP = 54 % (Table 2.6, col. *c*).

But what rates of succession and reproduction might we expect? We shall argue later (pp. 99ff) that in Roman conditions of high mortality, in a biologically self-reproducing population, we should expect that roughly one third of the adult males surviving to forty had no son surviving to the age of forty years, one third had one such son, and one third had more than one such son. Our formulation here is consciously crude, in order to underline the rough and ready nature of this estimate, especially because we are dealing with small numbers of consuls and praetors, who were frequently engaged in war. Nonetheless, the above formula can serve as a useful guideline. It implies that if a group was self-reproducing and did not recruit outsiders, we might expect a maximum rate of Family Status Maintenance of 67 %, and a Social Reproduction rate of 100 %; in this group, two thirds of the males surviving to the age of forty years would have a brother who had reached or who would reach the age of forty.

Let us now compare our observations (Table 2.7) with these expectations. To do this well, we sub-divided consuls into two sets, (*a*) the inner core, and (*b*) other consuls. By inner core, we mean consuls with both a consular father and with a consular grandfather. The results provide striking confirmation of the unsurprising principle that a father's high status improved his son's chances of political success. The inner core of the elite (249–195 BC) had a rate of Family Status Maintenance of 83 %, other consuls 53 %, praetors-never-consul (218–198 BC) 40 % (Table 2.7, row A). Similarly with the rate of Social Reproduction in Politics: the inner core scored 125 % (more sons than fathers, but the numbers are very small), other consuls

---

[42] By cohort, we mean a set of people who experienced the same event (e.g. birth) in the same time period (e.g year).

Analysis of findings

Table 2.7. *Succession rates of inner elite, other consuls and praetors compared*

	Inner elite*	Other consuls	Praetors-never-consul	Inner elite*	Other consuls	Inner elite*	Other consuls
	249–195 BC		218–198 BC	194–140 BC		139–80 BC	
	a	*b*	*c*	*d*	*e*	*f*	*g*
	(per cent)						
A FSM†	83‡	53	40	61	43	52	40
B SRP†	125‡	65	54	83	52	63	48
C N =	12	78	50	23	82	27	84

* The inner elite here comprised consuls with consular father and consular grandfather.
† FSM is the Rate of Family Status Maintenance; FSM answers the question: What proportion of consuls had a consular son or praetorian son?
SRP is the Rate of Social Reproduction in Politics; SRP answers the question: How many sons of a given cohort of consuls reached the consulship or praetorship?
‡ Deductions from so small a number of consuls should be cautious.

65%, and praetors-never-consul 54% (Table 2.7, row B). The same principle holds in the next period, 194–140 BC, for which our data on praetors-never-consul are seriously defective. If our information on praetors were complete, the succession rate would be higher than those reported (inner core: FSM = 61%; SRP = 83%; other consuls: 43% and 52%). The incomplete figures are still suggestive.

Fertility was high in the inner core of the Roman political elite, at least until 140 BC. Their observed rates of Family Status Maintenance and of Social Reproduction in Politics in the whole period 249–140 BC, at 69% (FSM) and 97% (SRP), matched what we would expect (67% and 100%) in a biologically self-reproducing population. To be sure, the numbers are small; 35 consuls from the inner core of the elite had 34 consular and praetorian sons. The other consuls elected in 249–195 BC, a period for which we have full information on their politically successful sons, had a FSM rate of 53% (Table 2.7, col. *b*), which was also close to what we would expect in a biologically self-reproducing population (67%). The significantly lower rate of FSM, 40%, among praetors-never-consul elected in 218–198 BC, was surely because of their lower status, and not because they had lower fertility than consuls. The lower a father's status, the lower his sons's chances of political success. The implications of this principle are important.

We can now show that consuls and praetors probably had a large number of sons who did not themselves become praetor or consul. This conclusion rests principally upon the following argument. Let us assume that all consuls and praetors-never-consul had on average a similar number of sons ever-born and surviving to the age of forty. This seems a reasonable assumption, because in Roman conditions of high fertility and mortality, parents were somewhat at the mercy of chance as to how many sons were born and how many died before reaching maturity (we discuss this probability in detail in section V of this chapter).[43] In Roman conditions, it would have been very difficult for consuls to have achieved the recorded high rates of FSM, without many of them also having more than one son surviving to the age of forty. If all this is roughly right, we can measure the extent to which sons of 'other consuls' and of praetors-never-consul existed, but did not succeed in politics. We simply subtract the known SRP of other consuls and of praetors-never-consul from the SRP of inner-core consuls.[44]

The result is surprising: by this measure, 33 % of the sons of other consuls (249–195 BC), who survived to the age of forty, did not become praetor or consul; and 44 % of the sons of praetors-never-consul (218–198 BC), surviving to the age of forty, did not become praetor or consul (derived from Table 2.7, row B).[45] This conclusion rests upon the differences in the recorded succession rates of inner-core consuls, other consuls and of praetors-never-consul. Many of their surviving sons did not succeed in politics.

This is an exciting finding. The politically unsuccessful sons of consuls and praetors are not mentioned singly by name, or even as a category in surviving Roman histories. As far as we know, their existence has also been unsuspected by modern historians. Yet we think that politically unsuccessful sons of consuls and praetors existed, and in significant numbers. Indeed, their existence helps us to understand the apparent disappearance of elite families from

[43] Fertility was high, and some parents had more daughters than sons, and vice versa. It was difficult to predict or to control how many of each sex would survive. Many of these children would have been born before a man knew whether he would become consul or praetor, and besides there was considerable social overlap between consuls and praetors-never-consul.

[44] We recalculated the rate of Social Reproduction in Politics of inner-core consuls for the period 249–140 BC as 97 % (Table 2.7, col. $a+d$:$(125 \% \times 12) + (83 \% \times 23) = 97 \%$ of 35).

[45] The calculations are as follows (cf. note 44): $\frac{97-65}{97} = \frac{32}{97} = 33 \%$; $\frac{97-54}{97} = \frac{43}{97} = 44 \%$.

Roman politics, and their reappearance on the political scene after an absence which lasted sometimes for centuries.[46] Some of these disappearances may be due to the defects in the surviving evidence. But not all. The persistent differences in the rates of succession according to father's status corroborate the reasonable proposition, that the lower the status of the father within the political elite, the lower his son's chances of maintaining or improving upon his father's status.

The same evidence can be viewed in yet another perspective, and again seems to corroborate our conclusions. It was difficult for lower status senators, even for some consuls, to secure political success for more than one son. To be sure, there were exceptions, especially in what we have called the inner core of the elite. For example, Q. Caecilius Metellus Macedonicus (cos. 143 BC) had four consular sons; Appius Claudius Pulcher (cos. 212 BC) had three consular sons. But in general, other consuls and praetors-never-consul had fewer politically successful sons that we would expect demographically. In a cohort which replaced itself biologically and politically, as the inner core of the elite (249–195 BC) was apparently doing, we would expect about half those with one politically successful son surviving to over age forty years to have had more than one surviving son. That is what happened to the inner core of the elite (249–195 BC). But among other consuls (249–195 BC) and praetors-never-consul (218–198 BC), only 27 % and 30 % of those with one consular or praetorian son had more than one such son.[47] The known incidence is just over half of what

---

[46] Servius Sulpicius Rufus, M. Aemilius Scaurus and L. Sergius Catilina have already been mentioned (p. 39 above). There was a gap of a century between the consulship of M. Popillius Laenas (316 BC) and the legateship of P. Popillius (210 BC); no Popillii are known in between. The Cornelii Cethegi are known as consuls in 204, 197, 181 and 160 BC and then again in AD 24 and 170; senators of this name are known in the first part of the first century BC. Cf. such rarely recorded senatorial names as Curiatius, Furnius, Nautius, Petillius.

[47] We are assuming again that one third of aristocrats surviving to the age of 40 years had no son surviving to the age of 40, one third had one such son, and one third had two such sons. This is a rough calculation. The proportions with no son may be slightly too low, and the proportion with two sons may be slightly too large. It depends on the extent to which consuls and praetors, survivors to age 40, were demographically exceptional because of their survival, and so had more surviving heirs than Roman adult males on average. The average figures for all adult males in a self-reproducing population with high mortality are of the order: no son – 40 %; one son – 32 %; two or more sons – 28 %. See further section v of this chapter, especially note 85 and Table 2.11.

Among all consuls 249–50 BC, only 10 % are known to have had more than one consular or praetorian son, very much less than we would expect (but the evidence is defective). Put another way, in a cohort which was reproducing itself biologically and politically, we would expect two thirds of those who reached

we should expect. Some of these surviving sons may have stayed as senators-never-praetor, a probability which we tackle in a moment. But the general implications of our argument are serious. If sons and brothers of the consuls and praetors, who were unsuccessful in politics or who did not enter the senate, had as many sons as their politically successful fathers and brothers, then in the course of several generations, many descendants of consuls and praetors were outside the senate. It follows, therefore, that aristocratic descent was not a sufficient condition of political success, and should not be used as a sufficient explanation.

Some speculative conclusions

At this point our argument becomes speculative. We need to estimate the probability that sons of consuls and praetors, surviving to praetorian age, became senators-never-praetor; we shall call them: mere senators. At first sight, such a calculation seems impossible, because we know very few of these mere senators by name, let alone enough to make generalisations about their origins, or about their rates of succession.

But we do have a guiding principle: the higher a father's status, the greater his son's chances of achieving political success, and its inverse corollary, the lower a father's status, the lower his son's chances of political success. It follows from this principle that sons of mere senators, and sons of non-senators, both stood a lower chance of becoming praetor or consul than of becoming a mere senator. These guidelines, taken together with the rates of succession which we have just examined, help us considerably, even though they do not give us absolutely certain answers.

In order to illustrate probabilities, and to cut short calculations, we now present a single set of speculative figures. Purposely, our figures err on the side of high succession rates among consuls, praetors and mere senators. Even so, they still imply that over one fifth of consular and praetorian posts, and over one third of mere senatorial positions were open in each generation of the late Republic (from 249 BC) to sons of non-senators. We reckon that these are underestimates. We must also stress that these figures are in some senses

---

praetorian age eventually to have had a praetorian or consular brother. That was what happened in the inner core of the elite (249–195 BC), but among the sons of other consuls (249–195 BC) and of praetors-never-consul (218–195 BC) combined, the rate was only 44%. It was perhaps the influence of brothers, as distinct from fathers, which kept it as high as that.

66

only rash guesses; but we do not see how reasoned argument could plausibly arrive at figures which were substantially lower. Our basic evidence is the succession rates of consuls from 249 BC onwards and of praetors-never-consul from 218 BC onwards. After 140 BC, the evidence on consuls and praetors-never-consul suggests even greater openness at the top.

Let us go over our reasons for these conclusions. We start with an imaginary cohort of 120 senators, enrolled in any ten-year period in the second century BC. For convenience, we assume that they all entered the senate when they were thirty years old; before they reached the normal minimum age for the consulship, about a fifth (21 %) would have died.[48] We are therefore left with 95 senators over a ten-year period who would surivive to consular age; roughly 20 would become consuls, 40 would become praetors-never-consul, and 35 were senators-never-praetor, mere senators. What about their sons? We know that the rate of Social Reproduction in Politics (SRP) for consuls (249–195 BC) was 73 % (derived from Table 2.6, row D); for praetors-never-consul (218–198 BC) it was 54 %. That was the rate for maintaining or improving on father's status. Thus 20 consuls had 15 consular or praetorian sons, while 40 praetors-never-consul had 22 such sons (see Figure 2.1). Their sons filled 37 out of 60 vacancies for praetor and consul. Unfortunately, we do not know for certain how many sons they had who became mere senators.

We can speculate. There were 35 vacancies for mere senators in the second generation. We have to leave some vacancies free to be filled by sons of mere senators, to say nothing of sons of non-senators. Two principles may help. First, men probably had a greater chance of maintaining than of improving on their father's status. And secondly, in a hierarchical system, sons had a greater chance of going up one step than of going up two (especially if the higher steps hold roughly the same or fewer people). So we have to finish up with a result which (*a*) gives sons of mere senators a lower chance of maintaining or improving their status than sons of praetors-never-consul (< 54 %); and (*b*) which gives sons of non-senators a greater chance of becoming mere senators than of becoming praetor or consul.[49]

As an experiment, without commitment, just to see where it leads

[48] On probable rates of death of senators at ages over 30, see Table 3.12; on numbers entering the senate each year, see note 24 above.

[49] Readers may get a better idea of the constraints, if they themselves juggle around with the figures; the results should be compatible (*a*) with the principles stated, unless they can be improved, and (*b*) with known FSM and SRP of consuls and praetors-never-consul.

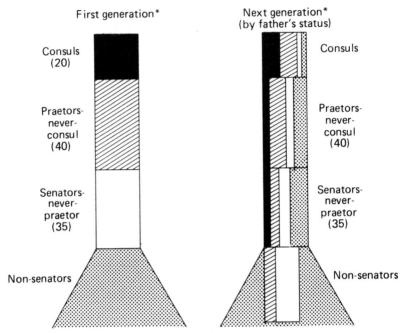

Figure 2.1. Fathers and sons: probable succession rates.
* Surviving to age forty, in a stationary self-reproducing population, at attested and extrapolated rates of succession. Numbers are for a ten-year cohort.

us, let us *guess* that consuls had a total succession rate of 100%, praetors-never-consul 75% and mere senators 50%; let us further suppose that half of these sons of mere senators finished up as consuls and praetors, the other half as mere senators. Two points must be stressed; first, we are dealing here only with survivors to consular age, and secondly these rates are experimental; they are not a description of what happened.

These experimental rates (see Figure 2.1) imply that 77% of consuls and praetors (N = 60), and 63% of mere senators (N = 35), surviving to consular age, were sons of our imaginary cohort. Complementarily, sons of non-senators and of senators who died early filled 23% of consular and praetorian posts (N = 14), and 37% of mere senatorial positions (N = 13). But these experimental figures slightly contravene our first principle, that men had a greater chance of maintaining than of improving on their father's status; they imply that sons of non-senators gained roughly equal numbers (14 and 13) of higher (consular and praetorian) and lower (mere senatorial) posts. The fault probably lies in the succession rate experimentally suggested for mere senators (50%); it should be lower. Our experiment probably overestimated the number of senators of all ranks who were sons of mere senators, and complementarily underestimated the proportion who were sons of non-senators. Finally, we probably over-estimated the succession rate for consuls; by no means all their sons became senators.

Enough of speculation. Rates of succession below par, when a hundred fathers had less than a hundred sons of the same or higher status, provided opportunities for outsiders. The surviving evidence does not allow us to know the exact proportions of mere senators and leading senators who came from non-senatorial families. For the moment, we want to stress that in each generation a significant number of senators regularly came from a wider status group of social respectables outside the senate. And various factors, such as the growth of empire, the increased cost of competing in Roman politics, the assimilation of Latins and later of Italian notables into the upper echelons of Roman society, the murder of aristocrats in civil war, to say nothing of frequent death by endemic and epidemic disease, all militated against a high rate of hereditary succession in the Roman political elite.

IV   MORTALITY AND FERTILITY

In the next three sections of this chapter, we try to explain why the Roman political elite was so open to new members. We begin by examining a matrix of demographic and social factors which obstructed both the biological reproduction of the elite and its social self-replacement. For example, we argue that high mortality was in itself a major obstacle to high rates of hereditary succession in politics. Even if the Roman elite had been biologically reproducing itself (and for a time there is evidence to suggest that it was), even so a significant minority of families would have had no surviving male heir. In addition, two social factors militated against succession to high office: the costs of competition and the practice of splitting estates by inheritance more or less equally between all children of both sexes. Finally, in this section we argue that the fertility of the Roman elite probably fell in the last century of the Republic, so that it was no longer reproducing itself biologically. High mortality and lower fertility in combination created numerous vacancies in each generation for new-comers to the Roman political elite. In section v, which is somewhat technical but important for our discussion, the parameters of these arguments are explored. We set what we know of Roman succession rates in the political elite against rates of survival in model populations. This allows us to say to what extent Roman succession rates corresponded to high or low fertility. In the penultimate section of the chapter (VI), we set the problems of the social reproduction of the political elite in the wider context of the political culture of the last centuries of the Republic.

Biological reproduction in conditions of high mortality – some problems

When death-rates are high, any elite of fixed size faces considerable difficulties in remaining both hereditary and exclusive.[50] Mortality in the Roman political elite during the last two centuries of the Republic was high. Normal mortality due to disease was aggravated by deaths in battle, and towards the end of the Republic by judicial murders (called *proscriptions*) and by civil wars. For example, over 40 senators and 1,600 knights were sentenced to death and their property confiscated by Sulla in 82 BC (Appian, *Civil Wars* 1.95); by the time he retired from power in 79 BC, it is reported that 90 senators, 15 consulars and 2,600 knights had been killed or banished (*ibid.* 1.103). Similarly, about 300 senators and 2,000 knights were sentenced to death in 43 BC (*ibid.* 4.5.). Some of those convicted escaped and subsequently recovered their property. Even so, death on this scale cut across hereditary succession.

In general, no satisfactory evidence survives which allows us accurately to estimate average expectation of life at birth in the Roman aristocracy. Our best tactic, therefore, is to begin by assuming that it probably lay within the relatively narrow range normally found in pre-industrial societies before the modern demographic revolution. This range runs from an average expectation of life at

---

[50] We have been concentrating in this chapter on three tiers of the political elite: consuls, praetors and mere senators. During the Republic, the size of each tier remained constant for longish periods, with a big break in 81 BC, when the size of the senate was doubled from about 300 to 600 senators (Appian, *Civil Wars* 1.100). The number of praetors went up from 4 to 6 per year from 197 BC and to 8 per year in 81 BC. The number of new senators per year was perhaps on average 12 per year before 81 BC and 20 per year from 81 BC. There were no mechanisms to ensure that the top two tiers were replenished exclusively from sons of mere senators. At all levels, there was considerable looseness in succession. Prosperous Italian land-owners, some of whom were engaged in financing tax-farming or state contracts, and who had the status of Roman knights (*equites*), constituted a reservoir for new senators. For many purposes of social analysis, senators and knights can be considered members of the same social class.

birth of 20 years to about 40 years (e_0 = 20–40 years). If the average expectation of life at birth is less than 20 years, then it is difficult for a human population to reproduce itself. The upper limit (e_0 = 40 years) was consistently exceeded in England and other western countries (USA, France, Holland and Scandinavia) only from about 1830 onwards.[51] Among the bulk of the population of the Roman empire, ineffective public medicine, poor hygiene and vulnerability to infection probably put average expectation of life towards the bottom end of this range. That said, comparative evidence suggests that there probably were significant regional variations and sizeable short-term fluctuations; there could even have been important long-term shifts in mortality and fertility; but about those, because our evidence is so wretchedly thin, we can only speculate.

We should also expect some differences in average expectation of life between social classes – not huge differences, because the upper classes for all their better nutrition, were still liable to infectious diseases. In the next chapter, we present some slight evidence from the early Principate on the expectation of life of senators. Very tentatively we conclude that in relatively peaceful circumstances (i.e. excluding large-scale persecutions by the emperors), senators had an average expectation of life at birth of about 30 years. This was similar to the average expectation of life at birth found in European ruling families and British ducal families in the seventeenth century.[52] In the last two centuries of the Republic, when senators and their sons were more often involved in wars, their average expectation of life was probably lower.

All we can reasonably aim for is a band of probability. To the professional ancient historian, trained to document facts from ancient sources, this whole procedure may seem fragile, inapplicable and dangerous. Historical demographers, on other hand, are accustomed

[51] E. A. Wrigley, *Population and History* (London, 1969) 171 and E. A. Wrigley and R. S. Schofield, *The Population History of England 1541–1871* (London, 1981) 230.

[52] Among European ruling families, average expectation of life at birth for males was 33 years for those born in the sixteenth century, 28 years in the seventeenth century, and 36 years in the eighteenth century (see S. Peller in D. V. Glass and D. E. C. Eversley, edd., *Population in History* (London, 1965) 98. Such evidence is worth citing in detail because it shows both the general level of mortality and variations over time. T. H. Hollingsworth in a study of British ducal families (*ibid.* 358–9) revealed an average expectation of life at birth for males born between 1480 and 1679 of 27 years; 1680–1729: 33 years; 1730–1779: 45 years. Violent deaths were numerous for cohorts born before 1680. Hollingsworth's broader study of sons of British peers showed an average expectation of life at birth for those born in the late sixteenth century of 35.9 years, and of 31.7 years in the seventeenth century (*The Demography of the British Peerage, Population Studies, Supplement* to vol. 18 (1964) 56).

Table 2.8. *Survivors to exact ages in a stationary population with different expectations of life at birth**

Male survivors to exact age (in years):		Expectation of life at birth $(e_0 = 20-35)$		
	20 *a*	25 *b*	30 *c*	35 *d*
A	0	1,000	1,000	1,000	1,000
B	1	668	710	744	775
C	10	445	524	589	646
D	20	392	472	541	603
E	40	242	318	392	464
F	60	79	132	194	263

* Derived from U.N. model life-tables in *Methods of Population Projection by Sex and Age*, U.N. Population Studies 25 (New York, 1956) 76.

to aggregating awkwardly incomplete statistical data and to extrapolating from model populations; so for them, the techniques used here and the probable margins of error are commonplace and relatively unproblematic. For us, the game seems worth the candle, because it is important to know, or to imagine roughly how long Romans lived. We do not need to know exactly, partly because the pattern of death by age was similar at any probable average expectation of life. Infant mortality, for example, was very high (at least 200 deaths in the first year of life per thousand live births); child mortality was high, and even among young adults, there were significant losses of life from natural causes. If average expectation of life at birth was twenty-five years $(e_0 = 25)$ among the aristocracy in the late Republic, then about one third (33%) of twenty year old males died before the age of forty, and about three fifths (59%) of forty year olds died before they reached sixty years. In Table 2.8, we have set out the variations in rates of survival according to different assumptions about the average expectation of life at birth. We ourselves, ignoring fluctuations, place the mass of the population of the Roman empire towards the left of this table, and put the Roman aristocracy roughly in the centre of the table. But for most historical purposes, what is important in this respect is that death-rates were high, and average expectations of life were low.

High death-rates by themselves constituted a major obstacle to high rates of political succession between one generation of the political elite and the next. The trouble was not merely that death-rates were high, but also that the incidence of death was unpredictable. In some families, all the sons ever-born died; some in infancy, others when grown up, either through sickness or in war; some families were truncated by the premature death of a father or mother, and were left with an only son, or with a daughter, or with no heir at all. In these conditions, successful family-planning was difficult; the best-laid plans were undermined by sudden death.[53] To be sure, political elites in all pre-industrial societies have faced, and have coped with similar problems. The Roman political elite confronted an additional difficulty: a high age-threshold. In order to achieve the same status as his father, the son of a praetor (in the late Republic) had to survive, as a general rule, to the age of thirty-nine years; the son of a consul had to survive at least until he was forty-two years old. A similar high age-threshold operated for consuls and their sons in the Principate. In the English peerage, by contrast, the eldest son of any age inherits his dead father's title. And if there is no son, continuity is preserved, broadly speaking, by conferring the title on the closest agnatic relative. Only if no male heir can be found among close relatives, the title lapses. The Roman political elite was fixed in size, had a high age-threshold for entry, and had to cope with high death-rates and the unpredictable incidence of death. All these factors made it impossible to achieve universal hereditary succession within the elite, and so opened up wide avenues for sons of non-senators.

Let us now consider fertility. For the moment, let us suppose that the Roman political elite reproduced itself biologically. To do that, in the prevailing conditions of high mortality, consuls and praetors should have had, on average, roughly speaking five or six children

---

[53] E. A. Wrigley in a brilliant article, 'Fertility strategy for the individual and the group' in C. Tilly, ed., *Historical Studies of Changing Fertility* (Princeton, 1978) 135ff discussed the conflicts of interest which arise between individuals and the group in conditions of high mortality, when individuals do not want more than one surviving male heir. Given the time gap between births of sons, and the fact that the greatest risk of death is in the early years of life, it might have been possible for some fathers with one or two sons who had survived the early years, to prevent the birth of subsequent children without too much risk of leaving themselves childless. That may have happened in restricted social circles, if family limitation was effective. But it could not have happened in the whole society, without a drastic fall in population. Many large families are needed to balance the many small families caused by low fecundity or by marriages broken by the early death of parents. On the incidence of death, see the excellent article by J. Fourastié, 'De la vie traditionelle', *Population* 14 (1959) 417ff; L. Stone, *The Family, Sex and Marriage in England 1500–1800* (London, 1979) 54ff.

ever-born.[54] This average high fertility would have secured the biological succession of the group as a whole, but not of every family within it. In these conditions of high mortality and if the group was reproducing itself biologically, at least one third of all families had no son surviving to age forty, one third had one surviving son, and somewhat less than one third of families had two or more sons surviving to age forty (see above, note 47, and below, note 85). The hereditary exclusiveness of the elite could then be preserved, only if all those families with two sons secured political success for both. Hence the importance of marriage as a means of transferring resources from families without sons to those with more than one. Hence also the potential importance of adoption as a mechanism for distributing surviving sons throughout the elite, so that they could inherit the property and status of families without male heirs; (but note that only 4% of consuls 249–50 BC were adopted). If fathers could not provide adequately for younger sons, or if younger sons failed to fill the places left vacant by childless senators, then these places were open to outsiders. All the more so, of course, if the fertility of the political elite as a whole fell below the level of biological replacement. And in the last century BC we think it did.

The costs of high status and partible inheritance

Two more obstacles to exclusiveness deserve attention: the costs of high status and the normal pattern of inheritance. Senators needed to be rich, because they were expected to live grandly; in order to enhance their status, they spent ostentatiously. The high costs of elections and the rewards of office in the Republic are well known. For the moment, we want to stress the risks and the losses. It seems likely that in the period of rapid imperial expansion (the last two centuries BC), many Italian landed families failed to secure an increase in income, which matched the dramatic rise in living standards of the Roman elite. By no means all senators secured appointment to a profitable position in the provinces, or kept expenditure within income. In the late Republic, the censors dis-

---

[54] Calculation of the fertility required to keep a population stationary depends upon age-specific death-rates, the proportion of ever-married, the age of marriage, the rates of remarriage, and the incidence of sterility, so that exact specification is difficult. The higher the rates of non-marriage, or of marriages interrupted by death, the greater the burden of fertility on those who did reproduce, if the population or sub-population was reproducing itself. Consuls and praetors, because they survived at least until the ages of 42 and 39 years respectively, should have had above average fertility.

74

missed a significant number of senators from the senate. Our sources give us occasional figures, which suggest rather surprisingly that senators had roughly a one in ten chance of being expelled.[55] Indeed, in one famous incident in 70 BC, 64 senators were expelled all at once from a senate which probably had about six hundred members. The grounds for expulsion were usually debt, impoverishment, immorality, whether real or alleged, and political enmity.

The impoverishment and social demise of senators continued in the Principate. Augustus raised the minimum property qualification for senators to one million HS (roughly 2,000 times the annual income of a poor peasant family). To be sure, many senators had much more than the minimum, but some could not support their status and appealed to the emperor for help. Marginality was a recurrent problem. In AD 4, Augustus gave 80 senators enough money to reach the required minimum (Dio 55.13). Tiberius assisted several senators, but not all those who asked. In one dramatic case, Hortensius brought his four children to the doorway of the senate-house and pleaded to the full meeting of the senate: 'I had these children whose number and youth you see, not of my own accord, but because the emperor advised it' (Tacitus, *Annals* 2.37). In the changed political conditions of the Principate, he argued, he could neither inherit money, nor earn it through popular favour. He pleaded for financial help. Tiberius surlily objected both to the timing of the plea (during a debate on something else), and to its implications as a precedent.

[55] The evidence on the expulsion of senators is slender, and in annalistic accounts is usually tied to the activities of censors, who were appointed ideally at five-year intervals, and whose job it was to review the membership of the senate. Between 209 and 169 BC, according to Livy, the censors were three times 'strict' or 'severe' in their review, and on three other occasions (204, 194 and 174 BC) they expelled in total 19 senators ($7 + 3 + 9$). For sources, see Broughton 1951–60: *sv* censors. This works out (19 senators expelled in 15 years) at an expulsion rate of 1.2 senators per year. But we have no idea if these figures were typical. Nicolet 1977: 731 thought that expulsions averaged 2–3 per year in the second century BC. He dismissed this as small-scale and unimportant, because the yearly average involved less than 1 % of the senate's total membership (300). There are other ways of looking at the same figures. First, senators were expelled every five years in clumps. No one knew how many would go or who. Did senators really feel that their chances of expulsion were negligible? Secondly, we can calculate the chances of a senator being expelled before death, if we assume that expulsion was random to age (it also matters whether those expelled were replaced by new senators). If on average 1.2 senators were expelled each year and if average expectation of life at birth was 25 years, and so at age thirty further expectation of life averaged 22.5 years, then the chance of expulsion before death was 9 % ($1.2 \times 22.5/300$), if their average expectation of life at age thirty, on entry to the senate, was a further 25 years ($e_0 = 28.5$ years), and the expulsion rate was 2.5 senators per year, as Nicolet suggested, then the chances of expulsion before death were ($2.5 \times 25/300$) 21 %, one in five, a significant risk.

But in response to the senators' general sympathy, he finally offered to give each son 200,000 HS.[56] We know about these cases, because emperors used state funds to help preserve some old aristocratic families. In the Republic, there was no such safety net; it seems likely that some noble families just fell.

Roman senators did not protect the integrity of their estates by primogeniture. Entail and strict settlements, by which the English aristocracy preserved their estates entire for future generations, were in Roman law illegal.[57] This is an important point, but it is hard to prove. Very few Roman wills survive; it is difficult to know how much those which survive are typical; it is usually impossible to quantify the relative value of estates or farms left by name to particular children, and it is impossible to tell whether testators have taken into account gifts already made before death (for example, the dowry given to a daughter). That said, the surviving evidence by and large suggests that children, irrespective of sex or birth order, were treated equally in inheritance.

In addition, four arguments imply a general expectation among Romans that all children should be treated equally in inheritance. First, the rules of intestacy. If a father made no will, then his estate was split equally between his children, sons and daughters, as next of kin.[58] These rules of intestacy surely reflect a social norm. But

---

[56] Cf. Tacitus, *Annals* 2.48 on the removal of impoverished prodigals with distinguished names (Marius Nepos, Appius Appianus, Cornelius Sulla) from the senate by the emperor Tiberius. Similarly, impoverished senators were expelled in AD 47 by the emperor Claudius, and reportedly most went willingly because they were poor (Dio 60.29); cf. Suetonius, *Vespasian* 17. It is noteworthy that gifts between husband and wife (*inter vivos*) were generally prohibited by law, except when a wife helped a husband to meet the minimum census qualification for a senator or knight (D. 24.1.42-second century AD).

[57] For a clear exposition of the law, see Gaius, *Institutes* 2.152ff and J. A. Crook, *Law and Life of Rome* (London, 1967) 98ff. Even trusts (*fideicommissa*) set up to circumvent the law restricting inheritances were declared invalid in the early second century AD (Gaius, *Institutes* 2.287), though they were attempted (D. 31.88.15; cf. 35.1.102). See further, M. Kaser, *Das römische Privatrecht* (Munich², 1971) vol. 1,761 and the literature cited there, and M. Amelotti, *Il testamento romano* (Florence, 1966). For comparative evidence, see J. Goody, ed., *Family and Inheritance* (Cambridge, 1966).

[58] If a widow had been married under the old form of marriage (*cum manu*), then she ranked with the children as a daughter. Under the later and eventually predominant form of marriage (*sine manu*), a widow had only a distant claim on her dead husband's estate. If he made no will, she counted after his children and after any agnatic relative as far as the sixth degree. On the other hand, she still belonged to her own family of origin, so she could inherit from her own father and brother, if they died intestate. If a mother, who was no longer in the power of her father, left no will, then her estate fell to her nearest agnate, of whom her brother was in the first rank. Only after AD 178, following the *senatus consultum*

76

making wills was common among the propertied classes at Rome. Testators, in principle and in practice, had considerable freedom of action. Did they use this freedom mainly to decide how much to leave to outsiders as against family heirs ('How much time we spend and how long we debate with ourselves about how much we shall bequeath and to whom', Seneca, *On Benefits* 4.11), or did they commonly leave substantially different amounts to each of their children? We do not know for sure. A father could, and reportedly many fathers actually did disinherit specific children (D. 5.2.1 and cf. p. 237 below). But then a child who had been disinherited without good cause could try to get his father's will invalidated. The underlying assumption in allowing such suits was that fathers should treat each child fairly.[59] That is our second point. The third point can be made briefly. There are no references in Roman literature to the younger son as someone who was normally under-privileged, or to the eldest son as someone who was especially privileged. That is presumptive evidence that children were normally treated equally. Finally, one might expect that Roman daughters were treated less favourably than sons. It probably happened. But we also know that dowries in the Roman upper classes were large, and that daughters were considered expensive.[60] In spite of political objections and legal

Orfitianum, were a mother's children given preference in succession over her agnates, again if there was no will. To be sure, husband, wife, mother, father could by will leave their property to each other and to their children. For details, see best Jolowicz–Nicholas 1972: 124ff and 249ff and Kaser 1971: 668ff and 701ff. The important point which informed the detailed rules of intestacy was that under the new form of marriage (*sine manu*), a woman, even after a long marriage and the birth of children, still for strict legal purposes remained a member of her family of origin, to whom she returned on her husband's death with her dowry. Only in the second century AD, did she acquire legal rights in her children's property, and they in hers. All these rules matter, we suppose, but what people actually did matters more. We suspect that many prosperous husbands and wives made provision in their wills for their surviving spouse, even if traditional law remained conservatively agnatic long after practice had become broad-mindedly cognatic. Proof seems impossible and so does tracing the extent and date of these changes.

[59] A father could evade a suit for disherison by giving a disinherited son one quarter of what he would have received under intestacy (D. 5.2.8.8 – Ulpian). See Kaser 1971: vol. 1, 711ff and Chapter 4, note 47.

[60] It is difficult to generalise from patchy evidence; for example, Scipio Africanus gave his daughters 1.2 million HS as dowry, which was considered a lot by the standards of the mid-second century BC (Polybius 31.27; Valerius Maximus 4.4.10); Cicero had considerable difficulty in paying his daughter's dowry (for her third marriage); it clearly was a significant sum (*Letters to Atticus* 11.1–3); the emperor Tiberius gave a dowry of one million HS to the rejected candidate for Vestal Virgin (Tacitus, *Annals* 2.86). Such examples suggest that dowries in the Roman upper classes were large; the minimum census for a senator was also one million HS. For several anecdotes, neatly put together, see J. P. V. D.

obstacles, a significant number of Roman women inherited and controlled large fortunes.

The net effect of splitting inheritances equally or nearly equally among all children was that a Roman aristocrat with more than two surviving children faced the prospect of sub-dividing the family property. He risked lowering the status of each surviving child. Aristocratic fathers who wanted to preserve both the family line and the family's status were caught in a dilemma. If they tried to secure the biological survival of their families by having lots of children, they ran the risk that more children would survive than could be provided for adequately. Or, if they restricted their fertility in order to make sure that their heirs had fortunes, then they risked the biological extinction of the family in the male line.

Fertility in the late Republic

Did Roman aristocrats conceptualise this problem clearly, or in this way? The Greek historian Polybius, who lived for a long time as a hostage in the city of Rome, wrote in a passage lamenting the decline of the Greek cities in the second century BC, that men there did not wish to marry, 'or if they married, they did not wish to rear the children born to them, or at most one or two, so as to leave them prosperous' (36.17).[61] It seems likely that Roman aristocrats had similar thoughts and put them into effect. We shall argue on general grounds that there was a significant reduction in fertility in some sections of the Roman upper classes, at least from the last century BC onwards. We cannot prove this, and the contemporary testimony which can be adduced to corroborate it is slight. Better testimony comes from later periods. Yet citing something which happened later to corroborate or to explain something which happened earlier is problematic, even if it can be justified in particular circumstances. More of that later.

For the moment, our best method of proceeding is to put our arguments in a general form first, and then to discuss the surviving testimony. Our general argument is that four inter-related changes – increased competition for status, individuation, secularisation and the higher status of women – all encouraged a reduction in fertility.

Balsdon, *Roman Women* (London, 1962) 186ff; for the law on dowries, see Crook 1967: 104–5 and in more detail, P. E. Corbett, *The Roman Law of Marriage* (Oxford, 1930); A. Watson, *The Law of Persons in the Later Roman Republic* (Oxford, 1967) 57ff.

[61] Polybius went on to note that in cases where there were only one or two children, there was the risk that one was killed by war and the other by disease (36.17).

78

Each of these processes is problematic, in the sense of being difficult to describe and to analyse. We find it difficult to be precise about their timing, their effects and their significance. But that does not mean that they should be ignored. We think that individually and in combination these changes were important in Rome in the late Republic. Let us deal with them in turn.

First, increased competition for status. The expansion of the empire in the last two centuries of the Republic raised standards of living in the Roman upper classes tremendously. The size of private fortunes, the luxury of houses and their furnishings, private expenditure on works of art, jewellery, clothes, exotic foods and on domestic slaves all increased; so did expenditure by private individuals on public works, such as roads and temples, and on festivals including gladiatorial shows.[62] According to contemporary moralisers, this new-fangled luxury was Rome's undoing (Polybius 31.25, Livy, *Preface* 12). But the increased cost of living also stimulated competition for political office, because the rewards to be won out of high office, the command of an army or of a province, increased enormously. The costs of political competition also soared; the costs included not merely direct electioneering expenses but also, in the longer term, the cost of expressing and maintaining high social status in the city of Rome by ostentatious expenditure. Living standards, competition and the cost of competition among aristocrats all increased together. This social competition must have spread beyond senatorial aristocrats to the broader stratum of social respectables, from which new senators were recurrently drawn. All must have known that one son could be launched into politics more cheaply than two.[63]

Secondly, individuation; this is an interesting concept, but difficult,

---

[62] On the increasing grandeur of gladitorial shows and wild-beast hunts, see Chapter 1 above, pp. 4ff. On Roman luxury, see Freidländer 1922: vol. 2, 266ff, and on attempts to stop increased expenditure by law in the late Republic, see I. Sauerwein, *Die Leges Sumptuariae* (Diss. Hamburg, 1970). Pliny, *Natural History* 33, esp. 133ff and 36.48ff and 101ff described increasing expenditure at Rome, from the mid-second century BC, on silver plate, statues, marble, buildings. Aulus Gellius, *Attic Nights* 2.24 traced the increases in legally permitted expenditure on banquets during public festivals (including those given by aristocrats for each other) from 40–48 HS in 161 BC, 50 HS in 101 BC, 300 HS in 81 BC and 1,000 then 2,000 HS in the reigns of Augustus and Tiberius.

[63] H. Bergues *et al.*, *La prévention des naissances dans la famille* (Paris, 1960) 384 pointed to the clear connection in France during the seventeenth and eighteenth centuries between the residence of aristocrats in Paris, their competitive expenditure there and their consequent curtailment of their fertility, on the principle: 'two more lackeys, one less child'. Or as the poet Martial put it at the end of the first century AD, when discussing a knight's fortune (legal minimum 400,000 HS): 'Divide 400, go on divide a fig; do you think that two brothers can sit on one horse?' (5.38).

as sociologists say, to operationalise; in other words, we do not know exactly what it means or what index we can safely use to show that there was more or less of it. That is a complication, but it does not rule the concept wholly out of court. After all, the same charge can be levied against the modern concepts of love, courage and anger, yet each is in widespread use. Our idea about increased individuation is that educated Romans, at some stage, increasingly pursued their individual ambitions, independently or even contrary to the interests of the collective or state.

On the political scene, one indication of increased individualism was the degree to which individuals felt entitled to divert profits of war to their personal advantage. In the early second century BC, victorious generals usually handed over booty to the state (it was a very important source of state revenues – *ESAR* vol. 1, 141). For example, when L. Aemilius Paullus conquered Macedon in 168 BC, he captured more than 6,000 talents of gold and silver and handed it over to the state (Plutarch, *Aemilius Paullus* 28); when he died, a few years later (in 160 BC), his heirs had difficulty in repaying his widow's dowry of 25 talents out of his estate (Polybius 18.35). Similarly, Publius Scipio Aemilianus, final destroyer of Carthage in 146 BC, took absolutely nothing for himself out of its immense treasures (Polybius 18.35, cf. Fronto vol. 2, pp. 44–6 on Cato = *ORF* 70). These are notable cases, and we should be careful not to romanticise early Roman virtue and incorruptibility. That said, Polybius was very impressed in the mid-second century BC by the lack of corruption shown by most Roman leaders, in spite of the temptations offered by foreign conquest (18.35).

Over the next century, there was a sea-change. Well before the end of the Republic, it became common practice for Roman provincial governors and generals to use the profits of administration and war principally to line their own pockets. Roman corruption and the rapacity of its generals in the provinces became notorious (Cicero, *On the Manilian Law* 45; *Conquerors and Slaves* 41ff). Inside Italy, Marius and Sulla, for example, used political victories, which they had achieved by armed attacks on the city of Rome itself, as opportunities to enrich themselves and those who had helped them to power. They punished their political rivals by judicial murder and confiscation and rewarded their lieutenants with cheap property and official appointments (Appian, *Civil Wars* 1.55ff). Julius Caesar used his booty-raising conquests in Spain and Gaul as a means of paying off his personal debts, for winning political support through bribes at Rome, and for reconfirming the personal loyalty of his troops to himself (Appian, *ibid.* 2.17 and 26). Personal advantage gained precedence over collective or state benefit. Catiline and his fellow conspirators in 63 BC aimed at seizing power for themselves in the chaos created by setting fire to Rome; its leaders were to be murdered. Political generals, like Marius, Cinna, Sulla, Caesar, Antony, each felt justified in pursuing his individual interest by declaring civil war. Repeated civil wars were at once a symptom of extreme political individualism, and a mechanism for disrupting old social ties between kinsmen and friends, and for destroying traditional values and obligations; the civil wars and political discord provided the excuse and the social space for individuals to pursue their own advantage. That is one aspect of what we have called increased individuation.

Individuation was reinforced by secularisation. Secularisation is a dangerous concept. It implies that later there was less religion or belief in the supernatural than before, or that people came to care less about religion and the supernatural, or that in deciding about what to do, they increasingly thought more about means and ends in this world (what Max Weber called *Zweckrationalität*) and less about the religious evaluation of their acts (*Wertrationalität*). In the modern world, secularisation is often used to imply that science and technology have displaced religion.[64]

The dominant conventional view of traditional religion in the late Republic is that it declined.[65] Three main processes are usually invoked. First, the old state religion comprised a set of formal rituals which decreasingly fulfilled the emotional needs of the People for individual contact with the divine, all the more so because state rites became increasingly and cynically subordinated to the factional politics of the elite. Secondly, the introduction of Greek and 'Oriental'

---

[64] On the inadequacies of the concept secularisation, see D. A. Martin, *The Religious and the Secular* (London, 1969) 9ff; on Max Weber's distinctions between different forms of rationality, see *The Theory of Social and Economic Organization* (Glencoe, Ill. 1947) 115ff.

[65] The traditional view is carefully set out by W. Warde Fowler, *The Religious Experience of the Roman People* (London, 1911) 223ff and by K. Latte, *Römische Religionsgeschichte* (Munich, 1960) 264ff. See also J. Bayet, *Histoire politique et psychologique de la religion romaine* (Paris, 1957) 144ff and A. J. Toynbee, *Hannibal's Legacy* (Oxford, 1965) vol. 2, 374ff. His views are representative: 'There was an ever-widening gulf between the personal religion for which the individual craved and the official religion...The Roman people was long-suffering, and the Establishment will have congratulated itself on having succeeded in conditioning the People to live on stony spiritual fare' (378) or 'The people of Italy were still craving for some religion that would give them personal support and consolation' (390). The style is perhaps somewhat old-fashioned, but the logical form is unfortunately still very common.

deities (e.g Magna Mater, Dionysus, Attis) reflected the inadequacy of traditional Roman religion. Thirdly, the introduction of Greek philosophy and of other religious experiences legitimated explicit criticisms and scepticism about the native religious tradition, at least among educated Romans.

Our main objections to these views are, first, that they seem to presuppose a particular and ethnocentric view of what constituted a satisfying religion. They seem to suggest that formal rites, punctiliously performed, are essentially unsatisfying, whereas 'Oriental' religions, by offering men and women a personal relationship with God, were a step forward along the path of social evolution and towards Christianity.[66] Secondly, the close interaction of religion and politics is not necessarily evidence of religious atrophy. Far from it. For example, the involvement of the Catholic Church and of devout Catholics in political struggle in contemporary Poland is not evidence of religious decline. In the last century BC, the scope of political struggle in Rome widened immensely, and some contestants in desperation used any weapons which came to hand, including religious rites. But using religious rites in political conflicts made sense only if some or many people thought that religious sanctions should be effective. Finally, are only the educated sceptical? Besides, those who are sceptical in their formal thought often nonetheless find comfort and satisfaction in conventional religious observance, or look up their fate in the stars (cf. *Conquerors and Slaves* 232ff). Scepticism is not conclusive evidence of disbelief.

Let us now turn from argument to evidence. The evidence used to corroborate or to illustrate the decline of traditional Roman rites is fragmentary and anecdotal. For example, Roman orators once customarily began their speeches with an invocation to the gods, but by the last century BC that practice had died out (Servius, *Commentary on Virgil's Aeneid* 11.301). Similarly, the custom of taking auspices before commencing private business seems to have died out by the last century BC (Latte 1960: 264). Cato said that he was amazed that one soothsayer (*haruspex*) could look at another without laughing (Cicero, *On Divination* 2.51). The poet Ennius wrote scathingly of 'superstitious prophets and shameless soothsayers...who do not know their own futures, but point it out for others and promise them wealth, while asking for a tip' (cited by Cicero, *ibid.* 1.132). The consul P. Claudius Pulcher in 249 BC was about to fight a sea-battle, but the omens were bad; the sacred chickens refused to

---

[66] For a trenchant and sensitive critique, see J. A. North, 'Conservatism and change in Roman religion', *Papers of the British School at Rome* 44 (1976) 1ff.

eat; so he threw them into the sea, saying 'if they won't eat, let them drink' (Valerius Maximus 1.4.3). The priesthood of Jupiter, one of the most ancient and prestigious sacred offices in Rome, was left vacant for seventy-five years in the last century BC, until filled in the reign of Augustus (Tacitus, *Annals* 3.58). Julius Caesar's fellow consul of 59 BC, M. Calpurnius Bibulus, tried to stop Caesar's legislation by 'watching the heavens' for omens; by religious tradition, this meant that no public business could be transacted. Caesar simply ignored his obstruction and the laws were passed. When Augustus came to power, he found eighty-two temples in the city of Rome in disrepair and had them restored (28 BC – *My Achievements* 20). The Epicurean poet, Lucretius (died 55 BC) attacked traditional religion as the result and the cause of ignorance and anxiety (*On the Nature of Things* 5.1194ff). The jurist Servius Sulpicius, consul in 51 BC, wrote a treatise on how to avoid ancestral rites (Aulus Gellius, *Attic Nights* 7.12). And so on.

Such evidence poses problems. First, it is slight relative to the general changes claimed. Secondly, the chronological fit is slack. Thirdly, much of the evidence can be interpreted in several ways. For example, the consul who threw the sacred chickens into the water lost the ensuing sea-battle disastrously; the moral was that arrogant impiety met with divine revenge. Moreover, the story may have been a later confection.[67] Or to take another example, the known rate of temple decay and of new dedications in different periods depends considerably on the type of surviving source. For the early period, we have the annalistic account by Livy, which was partly based on public records; for the next period (after 167 BC), very few sources survive; and then from the middle of the last century BC we have Cicero's letters and speeches, which for all their variety do not provide a list of temple-building. From this and similar evidence, we try to depict broad changes in religious attitudes in the total population of Roman Italy. The task must seem hopeless, all the more so because of the bias in several ancient authors, who themselves interpreted the changes which had taken place in Rome by the late Republic as a moral decline from an earlier, golden age of pristine piety (Sallust, *Catiline* 9ff; Livy, *Preface* 9; cf. Polybius 6.56).

In spite of all these difficulties, the total body of evidence for secularisation seems impressive. We think that there probably was a decline in traditional religion, both in observance and in belief, and a growth in scepticism in the Roman upper classes during the last

---

[67] T. P. Wiseman, *Clio's Cosmetics* (Leicester, 1979) 85 ff.

two centuries BC. We write this in full awareness that these changes cannot be proved. But they can be illustrated, and not only by the evidence just cited, but also by long term secularising trends, such as the separation of civil from priestly law (discussed in *Conquerors and Slaves* 85ff). To be sure, we do not want to exaggerate. Secularisation reinforced individuation, but the extent of the changes was limited. Secularisation was only partial. Ancient intellectual scepticism was not underwritten, as modern scepticism is, by technological revolution. Upper class Romans were still very much at the mercy of natural forces and accommodated their vulnerability by placating the divine. Some increased individuation was lodged within religious beliefs; witness, for example, the spread of beliefs about individual survival in life after death (see below, pp. 226ff). Even so, secularisation and individuation helped some upper class Romans slip out of their traditional collective obligations, such as ancestral rites. They were no longer simply links in the great chain of being, gaining identity by virtue of being the son of their father, and the progenitor of sons, all in some collective clan interest.[68]

The reason for these changes are unknown, but a variety of factors probably contributed: the impact of Greek philosophy, broader intellectual horizons, the growing complexity of Roman society and the increased variety of social roles which upper class Romans could play as the society became structurally more differentiated; and, above all perhaps, the political conflicts of the last century of the Republic.[69] These factors in combination gave leading Romans more social space and greater freedom of action; they felt freer, we imagine, of traditional beliefs, and freer of the social and political ties which those traditional beliefs legitimated. Whatever the reasons, secularisation and individuation together provided a context favourable for lower fertility, by helping to foster the belief among upper class Romans that the external world in general, and their own sexual behaviour and fertility in particular was, to some extent at least, under human as well as divine control, and could be manipulated to an individual's advantage, irrespective of the collective or public interest.

Personal relations between men and women were also affected by the growth in individualism, with implications for the average levels

[68] The fusion of identity between son and father is beautifully illustrated by E. Gellner, *Thought and Change* (London, 1964), 1–2. Over time, a son in telling a story about his youth, changed from describing his father as he, into calling him I, since by that time he too had become a bearded father, while he described himself (as we think) when he was a young son, not as I but as he.

[69] On structural differentiation in the late Republic, see *Conquerors and Slaves* 74ff.

of fertility achieved in the Roman upper classes in the last century BC. Surprisingly, some of the best evidence for this change in personal relations comes from Roman poetry. In the last century BC, for the first time, Latin poets wrote personal love poems, and whole series of poems about their love affairs. This art form was the particular invention of Catullus (*c.* 84–54 BC) from Hellenistic models. But our interest here is not in origins, nor even (regretfully) in Catullus' exquisite expression of individual feelings, especially ambivalence:

> Odi et amo. Quare id faciam, fortasse requiris;
> nescio, sed fieri sentio et excrucior. (*Poem* 85)
> I hate and love her. Perhaps you'll ask me why;
> I don't know, but I feel it happening, and it tortures me.

We are interested here more in Catullus' experiments with the Latin language to express unaccustomed feelings, and with the social implications of his message. His need to experiment with language indicated the novelty of expressing loving and passionate emotions to a woman; for example, in describing his relationship with his beloved, he often used terms derived from social relations with men, or from public life (e.g. *foedus* – pact, *officium* – duty, *benefacta* – favours, *fides* – loyalty, see *Poem* 76). Catullus' message that passionate love for a particular woman outside marriage could be quasi-legitimate, a properly improper social obligation, was itself revolutionary.[70]

There was a limitation. Romantic love, as it was expressed in love poems, remained outside marriage. The object of Catullus' love was Lesbia, a pseudonym for Clodia, a married woman, who was an aristocrat, but morally déclassée, so that she appears to have been a member of the Roman demi-monde. And in the genre of love poems as a whole, by Propertius, Ovid and Tibullus, it is revealing that the women addressed were courtesans rather than unmarried girls or respectable widows or divorcees. This convention partly reflects the custom of early marriage for Roman girls.[71] On average, they married when they were only about fifteen years old, so that they could not have been much pursued before marriage, nor even had a great say in the choice of their first husband. The love poets' convention may also reflect the convenience of expressing socially dangerous romantic emotions in a context which did not appear to

---

[70] See the interesting discussion by R. O. A. M. Lyne, *The Latin Love Poets* (Oxford, 1980) 19ff. The pressures on later poets to convert their moral message to fit in with Augustus' moral ideals is discussed by G. Williams, 'Poetry in the moral climate of Augustan Rome', *Journal of Roman Studies* 52 (1962) 28ff.

[71] See K. Hopkins, 'The age of Roman girls at marriage', *Population Studies* 18 (1965) 309ff.

threaten the basic pattern of property transfer and political alliance forged by marriage.

But ideas cross boundaries. Of course, it is difficult to know whether or where literary style and convention overlap with the real world, and to what extent the emotions expressed in poems were emotions commonly felt. Romantic poems are only romantic poems. And the image of romantic attachment was only one among several images available to Roman upper class men and women; the traditional ideals of life-long marriage to one man (*univira*), obedience and fidelity also persisted.[72] But what the love poets offered, at least to highly cultured Romans, and what they also reflected, was the availablility of an alternative image, of how a man and a woman could interact with love, commitment and passion. It was an image by which actual relationships inside traditional marriage as well as those outside marriage could be tested.

Traditionally, aristocratic marriage was more a union of two families than a union between two persons. The very young age of Roman girls at first marriage is a symptom of their subordination to the collective family interest. In ancient times, the bride was transferred with her dowry in an indissoluble marriage (*confarreatio*) into the household and power of the husband or of his father. For reasons which are obscure, this form of marriage was gradually displaced in the last two centuries BC by a new form of marriage (*sine manu*), in which the daughter remained legally in her father's power even after marriage.[73] One consequence was that an aristocratic father who wanted a political return for his payment of a large dowry could exercise influence by threatening to withdraw his daughter from the marriage, with her dowry. Under Roman law, the marriage could be dissolved by the bride's father, even against her and her husband's wishes. And in the last century BC, there were several notable cases of divorces and remarriages, executed in the political interests of parents.

---

[72] See G. Williams, 'Some aspects of Roman marriage ceremonies and ideals', *Journal of Roman Studies* 48 (1958) 23ff and in more detail, the excellent work of M. Humbert, *Le remariage à Rome* (Milan, 1972) 59ff.

[73] Corbett 1930: 90ff argued on quite slender grounds that the new form of marriage (*sine manu*) was common by 204 BC. Watson 1967: 21 argued, again on slender grounds, that the old-fashioned marriage (*cum manu*) was rare by the middle of the last century BC. And this has become the generally accepted view; we have no quarrel with it, but wish to stress that its foundations are flimsy. One noted case of marriage *cum manu* in the middle of the last century BC is mentioned in the famous obituary of Turia – see note 64 in Chapter 4. On a father's right to make a daughter or a son divorce, even against her or his will, see Watson 1967: 52–3.

Two well-known examples can serve to illustrate Roman practice. They are both drawn from Plutarch's *Lives*, so that the attribution of motives may be suspect, but the bare facts, as it were, speak for themselves. First, in 81 BC, Pompey was only 25 years old, but he had already achieved considerable success as a general. Sulla, who was then dictator, wanted to bind Pompey to himself through a marriage alliance. So Sulla persuaded Pompey to divorce his wife Antistia and to marry Sulla's step-daughter Aemilia, even though Aemilia was already married to Manius Acilius Glabrio and pregnant by him. 'The marriage was therefore dictatorially imposed and suited the interest of Sulla more than it fitted the disposition of Pompey. Aemilia was married to him when she was with child by another man, while Antistia deserved pity because she was divorced without honour' (*Life of Pompey* 9). Her sense of grievance was aggravated because her father had recently been murdered because of her connection with Sulla through her marriage to Pompey. And as a result of the divorce, Antistia's mother committed suicide. To complete the tragedy, Aemilia died in childbirth just after she had moved into her new husband's home.

Secondly, Plutarch tells the following story about Cato the Younger. One of Cato's many 'lovers and admirers' was the orator Q. Hortensius (born 114 BC). Hortensius wanted a marriage alliance with Cato. So he asked Cato to let him marry his daughter Porcia, who was then married to Bibulus and had borne him two sons. He admitted that his argument was unconventional, but on first principles, it was absurd for a woman of youth and beauty either to restrict her fertility (*argein to gonimon aposbesasan*) or to burden and impoverish her husband by having more children than was enough. If Bibulus was deeply attached to his wife, then Hortensius volunteered to return her immediately after she had borne him a child (he already had a surviving son). Then Cato, Bibulus and Hortensius would all be closely connected through their common children. Cato refused, saying that it was inappropriate to talk of marriage with a daughter who had already been given to someone else. So Hortensius then proposed that he marry Cato's own wife, Marcia; Cato had enough heirs, he argued, and Marcia was still young enough to bear children; indeed she was even said to be pregnant by Cato at the time. Cato demurred, but was reluctant to refuse. He insisted that the agreement of the wife's father, the consul L. Marcius Philippus, was also needed. The father agreed. Cato then divorced his wife, and jointly with her father gave her to Hortensius, who was 58 years old. Six years later, Hortensius died. Cato then remarried Marcia, who had become very rich, since she was Hortensius' heir (Plutarch, *Life of Cato the Younger* 25 and 52). Interestingly, in another context, Cato had vehemently and publicly protested against the use of marriages to cement political alliances (Plutarch, *Life of Caesar* 14).

In spite of these practices, and there are several more well-known examples, we think that Roman aristocratic women gradually moved from being the pawns in the power games of others, to being socially and politically powerful themselves. In the new form of marriage (*sine manu*), they were not legally in their husband's power, but remained attached to their family of origin, and in the power of their father. So at their father's death, they became legally independent (*sui iuris*), albeit subject to the authorisation of a guardian (of which more in a moment), and they could inherit substantial property and income by the rules of intestacy or by will, often sharing roughly equally, as we have seen, with sons. Daughters could also inherit by will from their mother. On a husband's death also, widows automatically reclaimed their dowry and in addition could be provided for by will, legacy or trust. For example, in the case just cited, Hortensius left his widow substantially richer (Plutarch, *Cato the Younger* 52); or to take a much earlier example, the widow of Scipio Africanus 'used to display great magnificence' in the religious processions which women attended. When she died (*c*. 162 BC), she left her considerable fortune probably by will to her grandson by adoption, Scipio Aemilianus. Out of this inheritance, he provided sizeable dowry payments (1,200,000 HS) to his adoptive aunts and made a substantial gift to his natural mother. When she died, she left her fortune to him by will, but he again gave some of it generously to his sisters (Polybius 31.26–8). Two points stand out. First, some women received substantial property through wills. And secondly, women themselves dispersed their property by will when they died.[74] In the course of a life-time, in different roles

---

[74] We do not know when women acquired the right to make, or receive under, a will, but women's capacity to receive by intestacy went back to the fifth century BC (Gaius 3.1). Even in historical times, down to the early second century AD, a woman had to go through a special ceremony (*coemptio*) in order to make a will with her guardian's authority (Gaius 1.115a, cf. Aulus Gellius, *Attic Nights* 1.12.9 on the special rights of Vestal Virgins, presumably once denied to other women). See B. Biondi, *Successione testamentaria e donazioni* (Milan,² 1955) 92ff and 119ff, and A. Watson, *The Law of Succession in the Later Roman Republic* (Oxford, 1971) 22ff and 1967: 153–4. If a woman was married *cum manu* and received something by will, then that was incorporated notionally in her dowry and returned to her on her husband's death (Cicero, *Topica* 23). The passage from Polybius cited in the text is well discussed by S. Dixon, 'The family feeling of Scipio Aemilianus' (unpublished paper); she concluded that in the second

as daughter, widow, sister, niece, surviving women could pick up sizeable shares in dead relatives' estates. It is difficult to calculate the chances of all this happening. So much would depend on particular circumstances (the age of the widow, the existence of children, wills as against intestacy, who else survived, personal preferences, social pressures). But it is worth remembering that there was roughly a one in five chance that a father had no son, only a daughter or daughters surviving him when he died (see note 85 below). There must have been many occasions when the closest surviving relative was female.

There was nothing new about the survival of female relatives. But three interlinked developments lent old demographic patterns new social significance: the increase in wealth which followed on imperial expansion, the dissolution of clan ties, and the weakening of guardians' control over female wards. Let us deal briefly with each. The growth of the empire by conquest brought a flood of money into Rome. For example, in the century from 157 BC, the volume of silver coins in circulation around Rome probably grew more than tenfold.[75] Much of the profits of empire remitted to Italy were free-floating resources, free-floating in the sense that they were not bespoken for traditional objectives. Their owners had unprecedented discretion in applying their new-found wealth to whatever they wanted to buy. It was a period of political and social upheaval. As we have seen, standards of living among the aristocracy and the costs of political competition rose considerably. Marriage was traditionally an instrument of political alliance. Dowries also rose in price, so that they became a substantial item in a family's budget (see note 60 above). But in the new form of marriage (*sine manu*), the daughter remained attached to her family of origin, with her rights of inheritance from her father unimpaired. In so far as daughters received substantial sums as dowry or inherited further sums on their father's (and brother's or mother's) death, then it was impossible to keep property, especially landed property consistently within an agnatic kin group. For the daughter, when she had children, was likely to devolve her assets by will to them, or even to her husband after a long attachment, that is to another clan. Substantial dowries and female inheritance are important elements in what Goody has called diverging devolution, a system of property transfer which

century BC, some wealthy women had considerable control over the dispersion of their property, expecially when they were widows. Perhaps they could be allowed more rights, when they were no longer sexually and reproductively at risk.

[75] See K. Hopkins, 'Taxes and trade in the Roman empire (200 BC–AD 400)', *Journal of Roman Studies* 70 (1980) 109–111.

defeats unilineal kin groupings, or at least undermines their property base.[76] Paradoxically, therefore, the new form of marriage (*sine manu*) which had been forged, we suspect, to strengthen political alliances, in the long run contributed to the dissolution of clan ties.

A further change, the weakening of legal guardianship over women, was critical for the growth in women's status and power. Without this further change, female heirs could have remained mere ciphers of the men who controlled them, simply intermediaries for the transmission of wealth between men. Traditionally, Roman women of whatever age and status were under the control of a man. 'Our ancestors wished that no woman should conduct even private business without the authority of a guardian; they were to be under the control of parents, brothers or husbands' (Livy 34.2.11). Traditionally, when her father died, if he had not appointed a guardian in his will, a woman's brother, nearest agnate or clansmen became her guardian (*tutor*); or if she was married in the old style (*cum manu*), her husband or his father became her guardian; on his death, he appointed a guardian in his will or the guardianship fell to his nearest male relative.[77] Without her guardian's authority, a woman could not enter contracts, contract debts, pursue legal actions or make a will. Guardians, therefore, could ensure that a woman's actions never went against the interests of her kinsfolk. What matters to us here is that this traditional legal control by men over women slackened, albeit gradually, during the last two centuries BC and the first century AD.

This development in law and custom provides us with a striking index of Roman women's increased status and freedom. But before we go further, two qualifications must be made: first, we are discussing only women of property; secondly, law provides only a shadowy reflection of reality. Yet changes in legal practice probably reflected widespread changes in social attitudes, whereas individual instances, however striking, may be simply exceptional, reported by ancient sources, and by us, because they were striking. That said,

[76] See J. Goody, *Production and Reproduction* (Cambridge, 1976) *passim*, but especially 7 and 89–90. The title of this book and the overall conception of social renewal is derived from Goody's discussion.

[77] On guardians, see best Gaius 1.144ff, Kaser 1971: 85ff and 367ff and Watson 1967: 102ff. Gaius' opinion is worth quoting: 'But hardly any valid argument seems to exist in favour of women of full age being in guardianship. It is popularly believed that they are liable to be deceived because of their frivolous minds and therefore it is right that they should be governed by the authority of a guardian. That is more specious than true. For women of adult age can conduct their own affairs; the guardian's approval in some cases is merely a matter of form…' (1.190).

there is one incident, reported incidentally by Livy, which seems generally indicative. In 186 BC, the consuls proposed rewarding an ex-slave, Hispala, for revealing the secrets of Bacchanalian rites to the authorities, *inter alia* by 'giving her a choice of guardian (*tutor*), just as if her husband had given it her by will' (Livy 39.19). We do not know how often husbands or fathers gave women this right in their wills at any period. But the mere existence of an institution (*optio tutoris*) allowing the woman a choice of guardian, and the capacity to change her choice, suggests a willingness to delegate real authority to women.[78] Livy's casual mention of the practice and the existence of a term to describe it suggests that the appointment of a 'guardian at will' (*tutor optivus*) was quite common, at least by Livy's time. It was a corrosion of ancient practice: 'Our ancestors required all women, because of their unstable judgement, to be under the control of guardians; but these lawyers have invented types of guardian who are controlled by the power of women' (Cicero, *In Defence of Murena* 27). The trend was strengthened by Augustus' laws on marriage, which allowed freeborn Roman women, who had borne three children, to dispense with the necessity of having a guardian (Gaius 1.145). It seems probable that this right was claimed and exercised (cf. P. Oxy. 1467 and 1475). In the reign of Claudius, the claims of the nearest agnate to become a woman's guardian, when none was appointed by will, were declared void (Gaius 1.157). There was a parallel trend in the rules of intestacy; the residual claim of distant clansmen to an inheritance under intestacy had still been recognised as a possibility in the middle of the last century BC, but by the middle of the second century AD (our earliest legal source on the matter), the practice was long dead (Gaius 3.17, cf. note 64 in Chapter 4 below). In sum, Romans whittled away the legal rights of male relatives over their kinswomen. Whatever the risk to tradition and to morals, they preferred to leave control over fortunes directly to their daughters, wives and widows, rather than to more distant kinsmen. The sphere of effective kinship became narrower.

One result was the increased wealth and social power of aristocratic women. In the beginning, attempts were made to stem the tide. In the course of the second war against Carthage, a law (the lex Oppia of 215 BC) had been passed restricting the display of wealth by women. In 195 BC, its repeal was proposed. Livy (34.1ff) made this

---

[78] On choice of guardian, see Gaius 1.150ff. A husband or father could restrict the choice of guardian to particular purposes, or to a particular number of choices: 'I give my wife Titia the choice of guardian "not more than once" or "not more than twice"' (1.152). Cf Kaser 1971: 368 and Watson 1967: 148.

the occasion for one of his grand set pieces: a powerful if invented speech by Cato the Censor against the recent growth in female freedom and influence and against the general growth in luxury. In spite of his eloquence, the law was repealed. Then in 169 BC, the Voconian law prohibited women of the top census class by wealth from being instituted as principal heir (*heres*), and slightly curtailed their rights under intestacy.[79] But the law was evaded. Whatever the mechanism, the result was clearly visible. Many aristocratic women became the effective controllers of their own property, displayed their wealth ostentatiously, controlled its use during their lives and disposed of it as they chose, when they died. To be sure, we should not exaggerate. As we have seen, there were many instances in which women continued to be treated as mere puppets in marriages between political allies. But we also get the contrasting impression repeatedly from our sources that some women in the last century of the Republic acted as independent personages, in control of their social lives and exercising political influence.

One dramatic example of political involvement by women is recounted by Sallust in his description of Catiline's failed *coup d'état*. Sallust's account is highly coloured, but beneath the rhetoric we can glimpse a world in which women were certainly not mere ciphers.

At that time, Catiline is said to have secured the support of many men of all types and of a number of women, who in their earlier days had lived sumptuously by selling their bodies, but later when advancing age reduced their incomes but not their extravagance, they fell hugely into debt. With their help, Catiline believed that he could win over the city slaves, set fire to Rome and either attract their husbands or kill them.

Among these women was Sempronia, who had often committed crimes of masculine daring. This woman had been favoured by fortune in birth and beauty, in husband and children. She was learned in Greek and Latin

---

[79] The law prohibited women of the first property class in the census from being instituted as principal heir, although according to Gaius (2.74) that could be avoided by creating a trust (*fideicommissum*). On the later enforceability of trusts see Chapter 4, note 72. Women were also prohibited from receiving by legacy more than the principal heir received (Gaius 2.226). Under the rules of intestacy, they could still inherit from a father or brother, and if married *cum manu*, from a husband; but by an extension of the Voconian law, women could no longer receive under intestacy from more distant relatives (Paul, *Opinions* 4.8.20 but cf. Gaius 3.26). The Voconian law was long-forgotten by the mid-second century AD (Aulus Gellius, *Attic Nights* 20.1.23); it probably dropped into disuse when the census was carried out less frequently. And in any case, like the Furian law on Wills (see p. 237 below), it was probably evaded by legalistic interpretations. For the terms of the law, see Kaser 1971: 684, 695 and 756; for a discussion, see Watson 1971: 167ff. The purpose of the law was presumably to stop women being sole heiresses to large estates.

literature; she could play the lyre and dance more elegantly than a modest woman needed, and had many other accomplishments which abet dissipation. But she liked everything better than modesty and chastity. It was difficult to tell whether she was more careless of her money or her reputation. She was so passionate, that she more often made advances to men than they did to her. Before this, she had often broken her word, defaulted on debts, and had been party to murder. High living and lack of money had driven her to the depths of depravity. But her abilities were not to be despised. She could write poetry, crack jokes, and in her language could be modest, earthy or tender. In short, she was a woman of wit and charm. (Sallust, *Catiline* 24–5)

We can see in her both sexual freedom and readiness for political involvement. Her husband was clearly not in control of her, nor was her father. If she were an isolated example, we could dismiss her as idiosyncratic, no more typical than an empress or one of the women who decorate Herodotus' history as lynch-pins of causation, women like Helen of Troy for men to fight over.

But other women were also engaged in politics. For example, after the assassination of Julius Caesar, a special tax was imposed in 42 BC on the 1,400 richest women. The women objected strongly and publicly; their leader, Hortensia, daughter of the orator Q. Hortensius, made a powerful speech in the Forum, and to some effect. The tax was reduced (Appian, *Civil Wars* 4.32ff). In the same period, Cicero described several anxious meetings held by Caesar's assassins and their supporters. Brutus' mother, Servilia, was sometimes present; she too was a powerful force. Once she stopped Cicero in his tracks, and then undertook to get a troublesome clause removed from a decree of the senate (*Letters to Atticus* 15.11–12). There is no indication that Cicero thought her role or influence inappropriate for a woman. Similarly, we get the impression from other parts of his correspondence with Atticus that his wife Terentia and his daughter Tullia were capable of managing, and sometimes managed, their own financial and marital affairs. Indeed, they arranged Tullia's third marriage during Cicero's absence in an overseas province. Rather to his embarrassment, the marriage was with the political opponent of an aristocrat whom he was buttering up.[80] Our conclusion is that a

---

[80] On hearing of his daughter's betrothal, Cicero complained to Atticus: 'Here I am in my province paying Appius all manner of compliments, when out of the blue I find his prosecutor becoming my son-in-law' (*Letters to Atticus* 6.6, cf. *Letters to Friends* 3.12, 8.6 and 13). Cicero himself had favoured another proposal, but his advice arrived after the engagement. There is no reason to think of this case as exceptional, although obviously the women's activity was aided by Cicero's absence in Cilicia. What matters principally here for us is that women could and did take important matters of family business into their own hands.

significant minority of wealthy Roman women exercised sexual, social and financial freedom in the last century BC.

We are thinking here of trends, not of a simple uniformity of practice. The four main trends which we have been discussing, increased competition and ostentation, greater individuation, secularisation and the higher status of women, were mutually reinforcing. They also led, we think, to lower fertility in the Roman upper classes, at least from the last century BC onwards. To be sure, much traditional practice was left undisturbed. Many or most Roman upper class girls were still married when they were only twelve to sixteen years old. The prime motive behind their early first marriages was political, and the social advantage which the marriage would bring to the family collective. Individual desires were subordinated or suppressed. But even in this seemingly hostile environment, some women, as they grew older, whether still married, widowed or divorced, were courted, often with a view to love affairs or to remarriage. Some remarried for love or pleasure. Seneca in the first century AD, wrote with witty malice:

Is there any woman who blushes at divorce, now that certain distinguished and aristocratic women reckon their years, not by consuls but by the number of their husbands? They leave home in order to marry, and marry in order to divorce. As long as it was rare, they feared the scandal. But now every gazette carries the news of divorce; they have learnt to do what they have often heard about. Is there any shame about adultery, when matters have come to such a pass, that no one has a husband, except to provoke her lover? Chastity is simply proof of ugliness. (Seneca, *On Benefits* 3.16)

Men competed for women, and women competed with each other in wit, beauty and the pursuit of pleasure.[81]

This movement towards competitive sexuality and emancipated pleasure-seeking was intertwined with a reluctance on the part of women to bear children. 'She who wants to appear beautiful, aborts', wrote a poet (? Ovid, *Nux* 23). Fashionable women were reluctant to spoil their figures with a large number of children. Of course, by

Similarly, when Cicero was in exile in 58/57 BC, he begged his wife not to spend her own money in helping him out (*Letters to Friends* 14.1); yet it is clear that she was a free agent in the matter. There is no indication that her activities were constrained by a guardian, even if formally her sale of property required a guardian's authorisation.

[81] The social power of rich Roman women to initiate divorce, to choose second and subsequent husbands, and to control their own wealth were exceptional by the standards of most 'high' cultures. The Heian culture in Japan in the tenth century offers suggestive parallels; see *The Pillow Book of Sei Shonagon* (translated by I. Morris (Oxford, 1967)) and I. Morris, *The World of the Shining Prince* (Oxford, 1964).

Mortality and fertility

no means all women even in the upper classes, succumbed to fashion. Seneca again in his letter of condolence to his mother Helvia contrasted her behaviour (she had had three children) with that of other Roman women.

Shamelessness, the greatest evil of our age has never attracted you, as it has the majority of women... You have never been ashamed about the number of your children, as if they taunted you with your age; unlike other women whose beauty is their only recommendation, you have never tried to conceal your pregnancy as though it were an indecent burden; nor have you crushed the hope of children already conceived inside you. (*To Helvia* 16)

Both fashions co-existed. Some upper class women had children; others restricted their fertility.

Once again our evidence is fragmentary and tangential. Indeed, the best evidence for the decline in fertility in the Roman upper classes during the last century BC is the Augustan laws on marriage of 18 BC and AD 9. The ostensible objective of the laws was to encourage marriage and fertility. They were part of Augustus' personal programme of moral regeneration. But they were more than that. After all, the marriage laws stayed in force and were elaborated over the next three centuries.[82] The problem of low fertility in the Roman aristocracy persisted. Indeed, even in the mid-fifth century AD, the western emperor Majorian was still concerned with encouraging aristocratic fertility (*Novel* 6 – AD 458).

For our present purposes, what is interesting is that Romans were given fiscal and political advantages, when they had begotten or borne only three children. But a target of only three children ever-born was well below the level of biological replacement. In order to keep the Roman population stationary, *average* fertility should have been between five and six live births per woman of completed fertility (the range depends upon one's estimate of mortality). In Augustus' opinion apparently, and he was not the first to hold this view, many Romans, particularly in the upper classes (at whom these laws were primarily aimed), were not achieving these targets. In 131 BC, the censor Q. Metellus Macedonicus in a famous speech complained about Romans' reluctance to marry (Aulus Gellius, *Attic Nights* 1.6).

---

[82] Only in AD 320 did Constantine, probably in response to Christian pressures, abolish most of the penalties attached to celibacy and childlessness (*C. Th.* 8.16). Then in AD 410 the remaining disabilities restricting inheritances between spouses with less than three children were removed (*CJ* 8.57.2, cf. Ulpian, *Rules* 15–16). On the fiscal interest of the Augustan marriage laws, see A. Wallace-Hadrill, 'Family and inheritance in the Augustan marriage laws', *Proceedings of the Cambridge Philological Society* 207 (1981) 58ff.

Augustus read out this old speech to the senate (Suetonius, *Augustus* 89); and he also upbraided the assembled knights on the same topic, confronting them with their own anti-social behaviour by separating the married sheep from the larger band of unmarried goats (Dio 56.1ff). In spite of these efforts, Tacitus tells us, the laws were unsuccessful (*Annals* 3.25); Pliny wrote of his own times as 'an age when the advantages of childlessness make many people feel that one child is too much' (*Letters* 4.15).

We should stress that Augustus' perception was probably focused on a narrow social circle. Even so we should be cautious. It is extremely difficult for any one individual, without synoptic statistics, to perceive the total demographic behaviour of several thousand people over time. Accuracy gets overruled by stereotypes. Perception may not correspond with reality.[83] We can well imagine a gathering of knights in Rome, which contained a high proportion of young unmarried men and widowers without a surviving child, whose total fertility before death could still be quite high. In short, we suspect that actual demographic behaviour in the Roman upper classes may have been more varied than a single stereotype of low fertility allows. That said, it would be cavalier to reject the repeated imputations of our sources that Roman upper class fertility had fallen by the end of the Republic; Augustus legislated to encourage higher fertility; his laws failed. But that is not the end of the story. Lower fertility itself has to be explained.

At this point, other sources can help in illustrating how some Romans perceived the problem. For example, the Stoic philosopher, Musonius Rufus, in the first century AD, wrote:

What appears terrible to me is that some people, not even having the excuse of poverty, but being well-off (*euporoi chrēmatōn*) and some even rich, nevertheless presume not to nurture their children, so that the children born previously may be better off. They impiously contrive the prosperity of their children by the murder of their siblings; that is, they destroy their brothers and sisters, so that the earlier children may have a greater share of the inheritance. (Frag.15b ed. O. Hense (Leipzig, 1905))

The conscious motive for restricting fertility, according to Musonius Rufus, was the need to conserve wealth for a few children, rather than dissipate it among all the children who could be born and who might survive. Explicit recognition of this motive is extremely rare in our

[83] See, for example, the arguments of Dr Richard Price, *Essay on the Population of England and Wales* (London, 1780), that the population had been falling in the eighteenth century, seemingly based on objective evidence, discussed by D. V. Glass, *Numbering the People* (Farnborough, Hants. 1973) 11ff.

surviving sources. We have found only two similar statements, and they are very much later.[84] Yet the same view was implicit in Plutarch's account of Hortensius' proposal to Cato, which we discussed above (pp. 87–8). A young woman was confronted with a dilemma, either to restrict her fertility or to 'burden and impoverish her household by having more children than was enough' (*Cato the Younger* 25). We simply do not know how many Roman aristocratic men and women saw the problem that way, nor to what extent they effectively restricted fertility and limited their family size by a combination of contraception, abortion and infanticide. A study of the techniques available would take us far afield. But two points should be made. First, the effectiveness of the contraception available depended to a great extent on how strong the motivation was of the actors involved. And secondly, although some women may have aborted to preserve their beauty, and although it was mostly women who executed the decision to restrict fertility, at least by contraception and abortion, and were then blamed by moralists for their behaviour, yet these women were acting partly in response to male pressures and social pressures. They acted to help maintain their own social status and the social status of their few surviving children. They acted in the collective interest of the small family. As individuals they, unlike the emperors, had no pressing interest in the biological reproduction of the Roman upper classes as a whole.

The interaction of social and demographic factors had important political implications. We can see this best by contrasting the effects of high and low fertility. High fertility, partible inheritance and competitive expenditure together encouraged downward mobility, by splitting family fortunes in each generation into pieces which were too small to support the social standing of marginal families. For such families, the costs of political life were perhaps so high that it was advisable for sons to withdraw and live off their estates, where the costs, risks and rewards were lower. Their places in the senate were taken by new men, and by more remote descendants of senators. In

---

[84] Ambrose, bishop of Milan in the fourth century AD, wrote: 'Poorer people get rid of their infants and expose them...The rich also try to avoid the division of their estates among several children, and get rid of their own embryos in the womb, and abort with parricidal poisons' (*Easter Sermons* 5.58). And Caesarius, bishop of Arles in the fifth century, wrote: 'Is it not, brethren, clearly the deceit of the devil, when he persuades some women, when they have borne one or two children, to kill the rest, either when they have just been born, or to take a drink which procures an abortion. They do this through fear that, if they had more children, the children would not be rich' (*Sermons* 5.2.4; ed. G. Morin, Turnholt[2], 1953). On contraception, see K. Hopkins, 'Contraception in the Roman empire', *Comparative Studies in Society and History* 8 (1965) 124ff.

97

conditions of high mortality, there was always, for example, a smallish pool of grandsons of consuls and praetors available, whose fathers had died too early to take high office and who were anxious to recoup their family's status. Thus, demographic factors, the uneven incidence of births and deaths, and of sons and daughters, created considerably fluidity within the apparently fixed political *structure* of the late Republic. Add the uneven receipt of dowries and of inheritances, the uneven access to and greed for provincial profits, and subtract the cost of lavish displays and lost elections. The senate as a body remained rich and powerful, but the rich and powerful families within it fluctuated and changed.

Low fertility, by contrast, produced two quite contradictory trends: first, many noble families died out and the rate of upward mobility correspondingly increased. Secondly, many of the noble families which did survive, had only one heir. This was one factor (the economic integration of the Mediterranean basin into the Roman political system was another), which led to the accumulation of huge wealth into fewer hands. We wonder whether perception of this trend underlay Augustus' encouragement of higher fertility in the elite, and his subvention of poor nobles. Higher fertility would break up large concentrations of wealth among several heirs, and yet would still provide a modest flow of empty places in the senate to be filled with 'worthy' new men. It is easy to surmise that from an emperor's point of view, low fertility concentrated too much wealth in the hands of noble social rivals, and at the same time produced an unwelcome flood of new men.

We have outlined a complex series of inter-related and mutually reinforcing changes. A recapitulation may be helpful. The greater the costs of competition, the harder it was to finance the political careers of several sons. The greater the freedom from communal pressures, the more uninhibitedly individuals pursued their own ambitions. The less respect for traditional rites, the less obligation men felt to provide for family continuity. The more complex the society, the greater the conflicting demands of the different social roles which each person was called upon to play, but at the same time, the more social space in which individuals could exercise discretion between conflicting demands. The lower the fertility, the greater the chance that a daughter would be sole heiress to an estate. The greater the fortunes which women controlled, the lower their fertility, partly because they were more seductively courted by men, who stressed their beauty and the emotional content of lust. The lower the fertility, the greater the concentration of wealth in a few hands, and the more likely that fertility would enter the political arena.

V HIGH AND LOW FERTILITY – THREE MODELS

Up to now we have used the terms high fertility and low fertility, without specifying any exact difference between them. We can now do this by constructing three model populations: the first with high fertility, the second with low fertility, the third with intermediate fertility. We shall then discuss the implications of different levels of fertility for succession in Roman conditions of high mortality. We shall set what we know about succession rates among consuls against the model populations; in short, we shall once again compare what we have observed with what we might expect.

Our main problem is that we want to know how many children Roman aristocrats had. More specifically, we want to know what proportions of consuls and praetors had 0, 1, 2, 3 or more children, ever-born and surviving to a given age. When death-rates are high, some families with many sons ever-born have no survivors; in other families, the only son ever-born may survive. Such information is not available directly. So it seemed sensible to try to get it from other comparable populations, and then to use the comparable evidence as a bench-mark for the Roman political elite. There are two major difficulties. First, there is no single universal pattern of family sizes, and historical demographers have not yet made a handy compilation of those patterns which are known. Secondly, the initial distribution of children ever-born is not enough; we want to know the distribution of survivors to age forty years, which was roughly the minimum age of entry to the political elite. But historical demographic data are often not presented in such a way that the fertility of men surviving to age forty can be isolated. It is an important age threshold for our study of Roman politics, but elsewhere it had little social significance.[85]

[85] Historical demographers have calculated the probability of fathers having an heir surviving them at death. Wrigley 1978: 138ff showed that the proportion with (a) no heir, (b) a female but no male heir, and (c) with more than one male heir surviving at father's death was roughly stable in a stationary population at different levels of mortality. J. Goody, *Production and Reproduction* (Cambridge, 1976) 133–4 came to similar conclusions, after allowing for 5% infertile adult males. All these results are approximate, since the calculations embody simplifying assumptions. Our own results (see Table 2.11 and note 47) are slightly different, (a) because we are dealing with survivors to age 40 years, who probably, other things being equal, had higher fertility than the average for all fathers; and (b) we are dealing with model populations, which are not stationary. The high fertility model has a small element of growth built into it; the low fertility model, at Roman death-rates, has fast population decline built into it. Finally, please note that we are using survival to age 40 as a simplification, which approximates the minimum legal age for praetors (39) and for consuls (42 years) in the Republic (see note 24). By age 42, 4% of survivors

In this situation, reasonable men would perhaps give up in despair. But then scholarship can sometimes be defined as spending an unreasonable amount of time on problems which others have given up. We decided to present three model populations, each with a different level of fertility (high, low and intermediate). They illustrate the range of possibilities, without being in a strict sense representative. We think that they can be properly used to show up inconsistencies in the known data on Roman fertility, and to point the direction in which the incomplete Roman data should be understood. We must stress that the three models (Figure 2.2) are constructs. They are built on good evidence of the number of live births per family from historical Geneva, France and Britain. But then, when the sources did not provide the necessary information, we deduced the number of sons and daughters in each family by probability (binomially). The live-born sons were then bombarded, casino style, with the probability of death, as though they had been living in Roman times.[86] We thus get the number of sons ever-born per family, and the number of sons surviving to age forty per family. The results are plausible, but hypothetical and they should be used with cautious scepticism.

Our high fertility model was derived from Henry's classic study of Genevese bourgeois, born about 1700, who were of sufficient social

to age forty would have died. For convenience, Wrigley's and Goody's figures are tabulated below:

At father's death:	$e_0 = 18$	$e_0 = 30$	High fertility, high mortality (Goody)
		(per cent)	
No heir	20	21	17
Only daughter(s)	20	20	21
One son	60 }	32	35
Two or more sons		28	27

[86] Our sources listed below (notes 87–9) gave us the distribution of family sizes. We distinguished sons from daughters binomially, by giving them each the chance (0.5) of being either male or female. For example, if 20% of families had two children ever-born, we reckoned that 1/4 (5%) had no son, 1/2 (10%) had one son, and 1/4 (5%) had two sons. This gave us the first distribution in Figure 2.2. All sons were then binomially subjected to the chance (0.4) of surviving to the age of 40 years. The probability of survival was taken from the UN model life tables ($e_0 = 30$). The same method was apparently used by J. Goody with G. A. Harrison for their calculations cited above (note 85) which first appeared in 'Strategies of heirship', *Comparative Studies in Society and History* 15 (1973) 16–18.

High fertility and low fertility

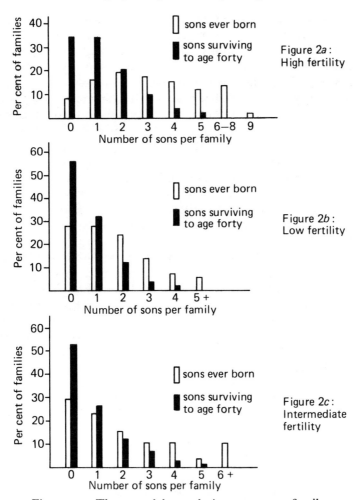

Figure 2.2. Three model populations: sons per family.

standing to have left full genealogical records. Their average expectation of life at birth ($e_o = 35$) was roughly comparable with what we have posited for the Roman elite; and their average fertility, adjusted so that the population was growing slightly, was 5.7 children ever-born.[87] The low fertility model was derived from two populations combined: Genevese bourgeois born after about 1740 and a small

---

[87] L. Henry, *Anciennes familles genèvoises* (Paris, 1956) especially 70ff. For technical reasons, Henry was particularly interested in the fertility of women surviving to age 45. We thought that these women could serve as excellent proxies, demographically speaking, for Roman consuls and praetors. Death rates were

French village in about 1800.[88] In both of these, the average number of children ever-born per woman of completed fertility was 3.2, low enough in Roman conditions to halve the population in just over one generation. Low fertility was achieved partly by an increase in the proportion of families which remained childless (13%, 14% as against only 2% in the high fertility model), and partly by a decrease in the number of large families. Other populations could, of course, achieve the same result by a different mix of childlessness and restricted fertility. But in the absence of reliable synoptic information, it seems reasonable to assume that lower fertility in the Roman elite was due to both of these processes in roughly this mix. Finally, we looked at the families associated with British peers in about 1600. They had on average 4.1 children ever-born, and 19% of their marriages were childless. They form the basis for our intermediate model.[89]

Figure 2.2 (cf. Tables 2.11 and 2.12 in the Appendix to this Chapter) shows the proportion of families in each model population with 0, 1, 2, 3 and more sons ever-born. It also shows the proportion of families with sons surviving to age forty years. Thus in Figure 2.2a, that is in a self-reproducing population with a slow rate of growth and a Roman level of mortality, less than 10% of families had no son ever-born, but about one third of families had no son surviving to age forty. The qualification, surviving to the age of forty is

comparable ($e_0 = 35$); the average age of women at the birth of their last child was 34 years, so that the early death of consuls, typically much older than their wives, would not have reduced fertility greatly. Childlessness at only 2% was exceptionally low; at this period, the Genevese population was growing rapidly. In order to construct a near stationary population, albeit with a slow rate of population growth, we reduced the average number of children born, binomially by 10%, from 6.3 to 5.7, so that 100 women surviving to age 45 produced 114 sons surviving to age 40, but 101 survivors to age 45. For details, see Table 2.11.

[88] The sources of this model are again Henry 1956 and Y. Blayo, 'Name variations in a village in Brie, 1750–1860', in E. A. Wrigley, ed., *Identifying People in the Past* (London, 1973) 59. The two populations were quite different in social class and in demographic composition. Henry analysed bourgeois women who survived to age 45 with marriage intact, and who married men born after 1700. Blayo's population is from a single French village and includes all married women, no matter what their age at death. Since our interest is exclusively in the pattern of family sizes, the social origins do not matter much. In any case, the initial differences between Genevese bourgeois and French villagers were much ironed out by deaths which occurred before the age of 40. For details, see Table 2.12.

[89] Our source for this model population is Stone 1965: 768 and 166ff. Note that these figures relate to first marriage only, and that childlessness at 19% was especially high among younger sons. Again, we think that this does not matter much, since we are not particularly intersted in the final fertility of British peers, but rather in a probable pattern of family size at a given level of fertility.

important. Other things being equal, non-survivors to forty would have had lower fertility, on average. In the total population, the proportion without a surviving male heir would have been larger than one third (see note 85).

What do these models show? They give us a standard against which we can judge the known rate of succession among Roman consuls. For example, they suggest that the fertility of Roman consuls was quite high, at least up to and including the cohort of 139–80 BC; secondly, they corroborate what we have already argued, namely that the number of politically successful brothers was less in all periods than we should expect from the levels of known fertility. Finally, it is convenient to foreshadow now what we shall show in the next chapter: the succession rate of supplementary (suffect) consuls in the Principate, *known* from their politically successful sons, was significantly lower than the biological succession rates implied in our low fertility model. We shall argue that this was more the result of political and social pressures than of low fertility, although lower fertility contributed. Moreover, as we have argued, low fertility was itself a response to social pressures.

Let us now take a closer look at the models and at our data on rates of succession among consuls. In Table 2.9, we have juxtaposed the succession rates derived from each of our three model populations and from our study of consuls; for the sake of simplicity, the data on

Table 2.9. *Succession rates of consuls compared with model populations*

| | Model populations | | | Inner elite | Other consuls | *Ordinary* consuls | Suffect consuls |
| | High | Low fertility | Inter mediate | 249–80 BC | | AD 18–235 | 70–235 |
	a	*b*	*c*	*d*	*e*	*f*	*g*
			(per cent)				
A FSM*	**65**	45	48	**61**	45	34	17
B SRP*	101	63	**83**	**84**	53	39	17
C B/A†	1·6	**1·4**	1·7	**1·4**	1·2	1·1	1·0

* FSM is the Rate of Family Status Maintenance; FSM answers the question: What proportion of consuls had a consular or praetorian son?

SRP is the Rate of Social Reproduction in Politics; SRP answers the question: How many sons of a given cohort of consuls reached the consulship or praetorship?

† B/A = the average number of politically successful surviving sons in families with at least one son.

Table 2.10. *How many consuls had one or more consular or Republican praetorian sons? How many such sons did they have?**

	249–195 *a*	194–140 *b*	139–80 *c*	79– AD 50 BC *d*	18–36 *e*	70–96 *f*	131–160 *g*	193–235 *h*	Less certain date *j*
Inner elite			(per cent)						
A FSM†	83‡	61	52						
B SRP†	125‡	83	63						
C	*Ordinary*		FSM	34	33	28	47	24§	0
D	consuls		SRP	36	42	28	53	30	0
Other consuls									
E FSM	53	43	39						
F SRP	65	50	48						
G		.		Suffect FSM	22	17	14	13	
				consuls SRP	22	17	14	13	
Praetors-never-consul (218–198 BC)									
J FSM	40								
K SRP	54								

* Data derived from Tables 2.6, 2.7, 3.7 and 3.9.
† For FSM and SRP see note on Table 2.9.
‡ Based on only 12 cases.
§ *Ordinary* consuls 1 only.

consuls are rather crudely aggregated into long periods (e.g. 249–80 BC). In Table 2.10, the compressed data are unscrambled to allow some necessary qualifications. We are sorry it looks so complicated; it contains a lot of data. For the Republic, read from the left; for the Principate, read from the right.

First, Family Status Maintenance (FSM), that is the proportion of consuls with consular or praetorian sons. Table 2.9 (row A: 65 % and 61 %) shows that the inner elite of consuls approximated our high fertility model and never (Table 2.10, row A: 52 %) got down as low as the intermediate model (Table 2.9, row A: 48 %). This implies that for the period 249–80 BC these consuls on average had significantly more than 4.1 children ever-born, which was the average fertility in the intermediate population. We assume that other consuls outside the inner elite, praetors-never-consul and mere senators surviving to the age of forty years all had, on average, similar fertility to inner elite consuls. But they had a lower proportion of politically successful sons.

We can trace the bias against a second son of the same father attaining high political office in the late Republic, by considering Table 2.9, col. *d*. As we have seen, the rate of Family Status Maintenance (FSM) in the inner elite approximated our high fertility model (61% as against 65%), but the rate of Social Reproduction in Politics (SRP – which answers the question: how many sons of a given cohort of consuls reached the consulship or, in the Republic, the praetorship) approximated only the intermediate model (83%–84%). Our second measure of how many families had more than one politically successful son (Table 2.9, row c) again shows a low level of social reproduction; by this measure, even the inner elite (row c, col. *d*) approximated only the low fertility model. Put another way, only one quarter (25%) of inner elite consuls 249–80 BC had more than one consular or known praetorian son, against an expected level of 50% in the high fertility model.[90] Of course, a complete list of praetors-never-consul and of mere senators would probably increase the number of known brothers of the politically successful sons of consuls. It would also demonstrate that the actual fertility of consuls was higher than their known fertility.

Let us now turn to the Principate. Under the emperors, second sons (not necessarily second in birth order) fared even worse. In only 8 cases out of the 160 cases which we sampled, did more than one son of an *ordinary* consul receive the consulship.[91] And not a single suffect (i.e. supplementary) consul, out of the 233 suffect consuls in our sample, is known to have had more than one consular son. Neither the deficiencies in our data nor low fertility can reasonably explain such a low demographic profile, since high death rates, uneven in their incidence, left a significant number of families with two or more surviving sons (see Figure 2.2).

[90] Put another way, in the high fertility model 66%, and in the low fertility model 50% of the surviving sons of consuls would have had brothers surviving to the age of 40. In the Republic 249–50 BC, the corresponding figures were 43% for the inner elite (with consular or known praetorian brothers), 35% for other consuls; in the Principate, for *ordinary* consuls (AD 18–160) 25%, and for *suffect* consuls (AD 70–235) 0%. These figures refer to sons of consuls, who were themselves consuls or praetors in the Republic, and are known to have had brothers of the same rank. Given our earlier estimates of the fertility of consuls, it looks as though there were a considerable number of sons of consuls, who had consular brothers who did not themselves become consuls or praetors:
$$\frac{(66-43)}{66} = 35\%; \frac{(66-35)}{66} = 47\%; \frac{(50-25)}{50} = 50\%.$$

[91] All *ordinary* consuls, except emperors, their heirs and consuls for the second time, in the periods AD 18–36, 70–96, 131–160 are included, as are *ordinary* consuls who had not previously been suffect consuls in the period AD 193–235. For details of this research, see the next chapter.

Finally, let us for a moment suppose that fertility in the Principate fell, so that the recorded level of Family Status Maintenance actually reflected the number of consular families with sons surviving to age forty. In accord with Table 2.9, col. *f*, let us suppose that only 34 % of *ordinary consuls* AD 18–235 had sons surviving to consular age. What would that imply? First, we should have to imagine that emperors chose one consul from every *ordinary* consul's family, which was able to provide a surviving son. But the fluctuations visible in shorter periods (see Table 2.10, row c) make that seem improbable. Besides, since at least half the sons of suffect consuls failed to become consul (Table 2.9, cols. *f* minus *g*), we might expect some drop-outs also among sons of *ordinary* consuls. This speculation is confirmed by rough calculation (see Figure 2.2b). Even at the low level of fertility implied by the known succession rates of *ordinary* consuls, some fathers would have had more than one son surviving to age forty; indeed, we estimate that there were many more such second sons of *ordinary* consuls than are known to have become consul. And did emperors choose a single surviving son of each consul who had one, and then systematically neglect their brothers? It seems highly probable that fertility was higher than is suggested by the known rate of status succession, certainly among suffect consuls, and probably among *ordinary* consuls as well.

One last point: we should stress how exceptional the fertility of the aristocracy was, in Roman conditions of high mortality, even if it was only as low as our intermediate model population. In the population at large, the average social reproduction rate was very near to 100 %; a consistent deviation of 2 % per year would have halved or doubled the total population of the empire every thirty-five years. That did not happen. Therefore the average deviation must have been consistently less than 2 % per year. Put another way, men and women surviving to the age of forty years in the population at large, according to our calculations, had on average about 5.7 children, as in our high fertility model population (Figure 2.2a); indeed, their average fertility was probably even higher than that over long periods, because their mortality was probably higher than aristocrats' mortality. If aristocrats had an average fertility of only 4.1 or 3.2 children ever-born, equal to our intermediate and low fertility models, then we have to inquire how they managed to restrict their fertility so effectively, what their conscious motives were, what social pressures they were responding to, and what were the consequences of their behaviour. We have already argued that low fertility would probably concentrate the ownership of wealth, and increase the recruitment of new men into the political elite, not least because its size was roughly fixed. If senators did not restrict their fertility to that extent, then we should ask what happened to their unknown sons.

In the last two sections, we have set out a social and demographic framework within which our complex figures on the succession rates of consuls and praetors can be better understood. Two major problems have emerged. First, up to about 140 BC, the known succession rates of inner elite consuls suggest a high or intermediate level of fertility. Even so, because of high mortality, many consular families died out in the male line. And some consuls also had, we think, politically unsuccessful sons; sheer probability and the shortage of brothers are two touchstones in this assertion. *A fortiori*, praetors and mere senators, whose status was lower than consuls, had even higher drop-out rates. Secondly, in the last century BC, and as we shall see, in the Principate, rates of succession were significantly lower. Lower fertility was probably responsible in part. But it was not, we think, completely responsible. Our comparison of the succession rates of *ordinary* and suffect consuls suggests very strongly that suffect consuls had many politically unsuccessful sons surviving to consular age. In sum, this demographic analysis provides an important supplement to the succession rates themselves. It provides bench-marks against which we can test the significance of the ancient data. It helps pose problems, without providing adequate explanations. For those, we must look to the political culture of the Republic and Principate.

VI   A COMPETITIVE CULTURE – SOME IMPLICATIONS OF
THE FINDINGS

Publius Scipio Nasica was a famous and powerful figure in ruling circles... who took a pride in being leader of the senate for many years. As a young man, when he was seeking election to the curule aedileship [the third ranking political office], he shook the hand of a certain peasant somewhat assiduously, as candidates do. He noticed that the man's hand was hardened by his country work, and to make a joke asked him if he normally walked on his hands. The bystanders took exception to his jibe, which spread among the country people and led to Scipio losing the election. All the country tribes thought that he was casting a slur on their poverty and so turned their anger against his offensive superciliousness. (Valerius Maximus 7.5)

History is usually and understandably the history of the successful. The story just quoted survives because of, indeed it takes its point from, the fact that an aristocrat who later became leader of the senate lost an election. In this chapter, we have tried to resurrect the sons of senators who were never successful in politics. We have argued that there were lots of them and that they have been ignored by the surviving sources, and by historians who are source-dominated. For example, probably over one third of the surviving sons of praetors-never-consul who held office 218–198 BC did not themselves become praetor or consul; this was our minimum estimate; the actual proportion was higher. In a political elite of fixed size, one son's failure provided someone else's son with the chance of success. Both success and failure were built into the Roman political system, and helped it adapt to the demands of acquiring and defending an empire.

This is not the place to start a full discussion of the nature of the Roman political elite and its place in the overall political structure. But a brief sketch, albeit partial, will help tease out some of the implications of our findings, that the Roman senate, both in the late Republic (249–50 BC) and in the Principate, was highly permeable to outsiders, to an extent probably unparalleled in post-feudal European aristocracies (cf. note 17 above).

One reason for the permeability of the senate was the close interdependence in Roman society between high political office and high social status; for example, all Romans elected consul became nobles. The contrast with post-feudal England may be helpful. The Dukes of Somerset and Northumberland, for example, were marked off from common men by titles which they had inherited. Personal achievement was unnecessary, though nobles had access to political office and royal favour through which they might increase their power, wealth and status. But basically, their wealth, power and status were centred on the ownership of land and control of districts in which their *fiat* had once been stronger than the king's. Even in sixteenth-century England, great nobles kept sizeable bands of armed and liveried retainers.[92] The power of the central government grew only by the suppression of these nobles, whose castles and country palaces survive to remind us of the power which they once wielded away from the capital. They preserved their wealth by primogeniture, and by marriages arranged with well-endowed daughters, as well as by chance, hard graft and political opportunism. To be sure, some families died out; others fell foul of the king or of political opponents; and new families were ennobled. But to a considerable extent, high social status was independent of, although it could be enhanced by, political success. Indeed, we suspect that such a system of automatic

---

[92] On the status and power of the English nobility, see Stone 1965: 201ff.

inheritance of title and high status by the eldest son could survive, only because it was not tied to the necessary exercise of political power.

So in comparing Roman senators or consuls with European aristocrats, we are not comparing like with like. The Roman senate was a political body of past and present state officers: generals, judges, administrators. European aristocracies each formed a hereditary estate, in which political achievement was unnecessary. That then is our first point. The two systems were different, and the differences partly account for the high rate of mobility into and out of the Roman political elite. But there is another problem. The meaning of the concepts, aristocracy or nobility, which we use to describe positions of high status and power in preindustrial societies, is inevitably fixed by our own cultural experience. By using them to describe the Roman political elite, we may unconsciously imply or assume that the Roman aristocracy was cast in the same mould.

Indeed, the Roman senate is conventionally described as though it were part of an archetypal estate system, in which the social orders (*ordines*; German: *Stände*) were distinguished from each other by law, wealth and dress. For example, senators (and their sons) were legally debarred from engaging in large scale sea-trade and in tax-farming. Their social status was made visible by their dress. Only senators were entitled to wear the toga and tunic with a broad purple border, while senior senators wore red shoes, visible symbols of their common membership of a club. Immediately below them came the knights. They were eligible for membership of the juries which tried senatorial provincial governors for extortion; they had to own property worth at least 400,000 HS, they had special seats in the theatre and wore

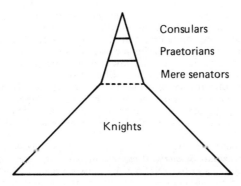

Figure 2.3. The Roman status pyramid: the conventional view.

tunics and togas with a narrow purple border.[93] These differences
lend credence to the conventional perception of Roman stratification,
in which consulars, praetorians, senators and knights form the top
segments of a status pyramid (see Figure 2.3).

In a formal analysis of Roman stratification, this pyramid model
is probably correct; yet its assumptions and limitations are worth
examining. It follows our politicocentric histories, both ancient and
modern, in assuming the primacy of the political elite. It also assumes
that political status was the single dominant dimension of social
status. It therefore assumes the congruence of all criteria of high
status: birth, wealth, education, ability, achievement, life-style. In
other words, it assumes that people who rated highly on one criterion,
rated highly on all.[94]. We doubt if this simplification does justice to
the diversity of Roman upper class life.

In social class terms, that is in relation to the means of production,
and in terms of life-style, senators and knights belonged to the same
upper class. Whatever differentiation there was within this class, they
had more in common with each other than with lower classes.[95]
During the Republic, the minimum property qualification was the
same for knights and senators. Sons of knights and sons of senators
wore tunic and toga with a narrow purple border; only when they
gained entry to the senate could they lay claim to the broad stripe.
Ten years' military service, at least in theory, was prerequisite for
all candidates for political office (Polybius 6.19). Sons of senators
served in the cavalry or as junior officers alongside other rich young

[93] See C. Nicolet, 'Le cens sénatorial sous la république et sous Auguste', *Journal
of Roman Studies* 66 (1976) 20ff who argued, in our view convincingly, against
previous scholarship, that senators were legally obliged to own the minimum
census qualification for knights. *De facto*, of course, they were mostly wealthy.
Wiseman 1971: 65–8 gives a useful account of the development of senatorial
symbols. On the status symbols of knights, see A. Stein, *Der römische Ritterstand*
(Munich, 1927) 21–49. In 218 BC, a law was passed prohibiting senators and
their sons from owning ships of more than seven tonnes burden; this limit
allowed them to carry most crops from estate to city (Livy 21.63). In the
beginning of the last century BC, the law was said to have become a dead letter
(Cicero, *Verrines* 5.45), but a similar law was re-enacted by Julius Caesar (D.
50.5.3 – Scaevola); we do not know to what effect.
[94] For a discussion of status congruence and dissonance, see K. Hopkins, 'Elite
mobility in the Roman empire', in M. I. Finley, ed., *Studies in Ancient Society*
(London, 1974) 103ff. Several statements in that article, which seemed plausible
at the time are disproved, we think, by the evidence analysed in this chapter
and the next.
[95] This is the view of C. Nicolet, *L'ordre équestre à l'époque républicaine* (Paris, 1966)
255 and of I. Shatzman, *Senatorial Wealth and Roman Politics* (Brussels, 1975) 177ff,
who gives details of extensive relationships between senators and knights. They
intermarried, often co-operated in business arrangements, notably in the
provinces, for their private enrichment.

men from equestrian families. The connections forged by shared experience were later supplemented by frequent intermarriages between senatorial and equestrian families. In famous instances, M. Vipsanius Agrippa, senator and leading general of Octavian Caesar, married the daughter of Atticus, a wealthy knight and friend of Cicero (Nepos, *Atticus* 12.1; 19.4); Quintus Pedius, a knight, married Julius Caesar's sister; their son was consul in 43 BC (Cicero, *In Defence of Plancius* 17; Suetonius, *Julis Caesar* 83). We know about these cases because of the actors' social connections, not because intermarriage was in any sense memorable.

The single upper class of senators and knights was cross-cut along many dimensions; it was internally stratified (e.g. rich, consulars); it contained different social groups (litterateurs, epicures) and different factions (friends, tax-farmers). For many social purposes, the dimension of political power, or membership of the senate, was merely one important factor among several. The persuasiveness of the pyramid model, which has influenced most discussions of Roman social and political life, lies in its simplicity and in its correspondence to legal status and to social ideals; after all, Roman writers did identify men by their status as knight, senator or consular. The obvious weakness of the model is that it oversimplifies a complex reality. Social status had many dimensions, not just one.

Another limitation of the pyramid model is its static quality. Within its limits it is true at any one time; and since the Roman political *structure* was stable for long periods, the model may tempt us to suppose that status was transmitted by fathers to sons from one generation to the next. That indeed was the Roman ideal, the desired pattern. At one period, young sons of senators attended meetings of the senate so that they could learn by observation. Sons of senators, like their fathers, were for a long period excluded from service on juries trying provincial governors for extortion. It was thus assumed that many sons would succeed to their father's status.[96] And it

---

[96] This assumption was enshrined in myth. The story was told that in the fourth century BC, a young boy who had attended the senate with his father, was questioned persistently by his mother. She wanted to know what the senate had debated. In desperation, he eventually told her that the senate had debated whether it was more beneficial to the state for a man to have two wives or for a wife to have two husbands. Next day, crowds of women surrounded the senate house, pressing for the second proposal. The boy was rewarded for his reticence by being allowed to continue attending the senate. But from that time onwards, other boys were excluded (Aulus Gellius, *Attic Nights* 1.23). Some ancient writers disbelieved both the story and the practice (Polybius 3.20 and Valerius Maximus 2.1.9), but the myth was apparently so strong that Augustus revived the custom, so that senators' sons would learn about politics (Suetonius, *Augustus* 38).

Political succession in the late Republic

happened: for example, over two fifths (46% – see Table 2.6) of consuls (249–50 BC) had a consular or known praetorian son(s). But succession to high status was by no means the only pattern. The succession rate among mere senators, who never became praetor, was as we have argued probably very much lower. Because status was multi-dimensional, that is because a family's status depended upon a variety of factors, such as wealth, ownership of land, style of life and on its general prestige as well as on political success, the loss of political status by some sons could be tolerated by fathers and by the sons themselves.

The very persistence of a family's reputation over several generations meant that every generation did not have to be successful. Apolitical sons did not necessarily lose membership of the upper class, but often just moved to a different set within the upper class. Formally, sons of senators who did not enter the senate remained knights, but their sons and grandsons who embarked on a political career stood a much greater chance than mere newcomers. To be sure, some of this argument is speculative, because our sources do not describe the status or life-style, or even the existence of apolitical sons of praetors and consuls. But we think that we have shown that they existed, probably in considerable numbers. Therefore a convincing model of the Roman elite has to take into account both a stable structure and a high turnover of political families in power.

In our view, a model of a circulating elite with only a very small hereditary core fits the known facts better than the assumption of automatic status inheritance. We have seen that about two fifths of the Republican consuls were the sons and grandsons of consuls; we called them the inner elite. We argued that other consuls, praetors-never-consul and mere senators were in that order increasingly varied in their origins; for example, well over three quarters (83%) of inner elite consuls, over half (53%) of other consuls (249–195 BC), and only 40% of praetors-never-consul (218–198 BC) had a consular or praetorian son(s). Who filled the vacancies which they created? The newcomers to the senate in each generation during the late Republic were probably often other near descendants (nephews, cousins, grandsons) or distant descendants of sometime senators and consuls. But there were also many outsiders, the representatives of Italian families, who owned large estates in Italian towns, which had recently been assimilated to Rome. Still others were simply men who had achieved wealth or fame in an expanding economy in a period of rapid growth.[97] After all, the prerequisite of senatorial status was

[97] On the rise of new men into the senate, see Wiseman 1971.

112

citizen birth and the ownership of substantial property, not noble blood.

The Roman political system both allowed, and as we think, encouraged mobility into and out of the political elite. It was a system in which achievement complemented ascription, in which choice supplemented preselection.[98] The Roman constitution developed as a power-sharing oligarchy, limited by an electorate of citizen soldiers, and led by annual magistrates whose plenary powers were limited by colleagues and by the shortness of their tenure. For our present purposes, three features of this system seem exceptional and important: first, the plebeian electorate was repeatedly the arbiter of Roman aristocrats' status and political power. Secondly, the system of successive election through a series of offices produced a large number of candidates each year and a highly competitive political culture. For example, over eighty elite officials, ranging from military tribunes to quaestors and consuls were elected each year. Most consuls would have won at least three, and often five elections in fifteen years.[99] Thirdly, among high officials, responsible jobs, including the command of armies which had to fight vital battles against Rome's enemies, were allocated by lot. Both fierce competition and considerable responsibility precluded the automatic inheritance of status.

Certainly, sons of consuls had the electoral scales heavily weighted in their favour. Honours given to past generations reflected glory upon their descendants. They were nobles (*nobiles*). Such men, said Cicero enviously, got all the honours of the Roman people bestowed on them while they slept (2 *Verrines* 5.180). And the electorate was organised in such a way that prosperous voters had disproportionate strength, while candidates with money and connections could influence or bribe the voters. No legislation could stop it.

Yet as the story about Scipio Nasica (quoted above, p. 107) showed, even the noblest had to tread warily. The system forced them repeatedly to adopt a posture of humbly soliciting support from their

[98] On achievement and ascription, and other so-called pattern variables, see H. C. Bredemeier and R. M. Stephenson, *The Analysis of Social Systems* (New York, 1962) 15ff. For a contemporary account of the Roman constitution, see Polybius 6.11ff. K. von Fritz, *The Theory of the Mixed Constitution in Antiquity* (New York, 1954) 155ff discusses Polybius' analysis and the checks imposed on the various officers of state in the Republic.

[99] In ascending order of status, there were elected each year: 24 military tribunes, 26 minor magistrates (mint masters, minor judges etc.), 20 quaestors (from 81 BC; before then, the number elected is uncertain), 10 tribunes of the people, 4 aediles, 8 praetors (from 81 BC), 2 consuls. For brief periods, election to the lower posts was replaced by nomination.

social inferiors, just in order to attain the same status as their fathers, in order to get positions in which they could win glory, wealth and power, and in order to confirm the political importance of their families. And although the electorate was probably biased in favour of nobles, the outcome of elections was often uncertain. Noble candidates were sometimes defeated by commoners; besides, nobles often competed with each other. As Cicero commented (*In Defence of Plancius* 15), if elections were decided by father's status, they could be abolished.

Rome was in no sense a democracy; but there was apparently a strong ideological tradition of citizens' rights, backed by the armed force of citizen soldiers, and expressed in popular elections and in legislation by popular assemblies.

This is the privilege of free peoples, and particularly of this great people, whose conquests have given it dominion over the whole world, that by its votes it can bestow or take away what it wishes from whom it wishes. Those of us who are tossed around in the waves and storms of popular favour must content ourselves with the people's wishes, win it over when estranged, keep it when it is won, calm it when it is disturbed. If we do not rate its honours highly, we need not put ourselves at the people's service, but if we set our hearts on those rewards, we should never grow weary of begging its favour. (Cicero, *In Defence of Plancius* 11)

This is the rhetoric of ideology, but it reflected a political force which could not be ignored. Occasionally, for example, when the Gracchi (133 and 123/2 BC) and Sulpicius Rufus (88 BC) were tribunes of the people, this political force took a populist, or even an anti-aristocratic turn. It may seem convenient to consider such events as isolated outbursts against the dominant oligarchy, instigated by the personal ambitions of demagogues, or to consider land distributions, colonies and wheat doles as bribes used by leaders to control the electorate. But they should also be considered as benefits wrested by the initiative of the poor citizen peasantry and the free urban populace, who expressed their wishes through the tribal assembly and the tribunes of the people. With all due allowance made for manipulation by the elite and for hereditary power, the element of popular power at Rome remained significant. The political myths of England and Rome are instructively different: contrast Magna Carta, in which barons forced rights from the king, with the Secessions of the Plebs, in which the armed people forced concessions from the nobles. Each member of the Roman political elite repeatedly put his status at risk in a competitive political culture to a degree seldom experienced by European aristocrats.

A competitive culture

In *Conquerors and Slaves* (Chapter I), we stressed the intense militarism of the Roman elite, the competitive urge to succeed, the desire of nobles to win glory which would enhance their family line. Two excerpts from our sources will suffice to evoke this achievement-oriented, competitive, aristocratic culture. A monument of the second century BC, for example, preserves an inscription carved to commemorate the achievements of Cn. Cornelius Scipio, the son and grandson of consuls:

Cn. Cornelius Scipio [conqueror] of Spain (*Hispanus*), son of Cnaeus, praetor, curule aedile, quaestor, tribune of the soldiers twice, one of the ten in charge of the judgement of cases, and one of the ten in charge of the performance of sacrifices.

By my life, I have added to the noble deeds of my clan (*genus*); I have begotten children; I have emulated the achievements of my father, won the praise of my ancestors, so that they may rejoice that I was born one of them; my honour has made my family noble. (*ILS* 6)

Ambitious young men, whether noble or not, had to establish themselves in the eyes of the electorate:

When Lucullus was a youth [*c*. 90 BC] before he had entered political life or stood for public office, the first task he set himself was to impeach the man who had accused his father... The Romans thought this is a brilliant stroke and the case was in everybody's mouth, like a deed of prowess. They did not consider impeachment without provocation ignoble, but wanted to see their young men fasten on malefactors like high bred whelps on wild beasts. (Plutarch, *Lucullus* 1)

Such dramatic encounters were a political blooding, reminiscent of mediaeval knightly jousts, but fought in a court of law. They served as a prelude to the serious business of winning public offices by popular election, and helped establish the reputation of the probable winners.

The emphasis on competitive achievement precluded a complete reliance on automatically inherited status. The same factors which moved some people out of the elite helped others in. The competition between aristocrats was conducted by criteria such as ability, achievement, wit, learning, which outsiders could occasionally match; all the more so since the formal prerequisite of political success was money, not noble birth. Some sons of consuls and senators had different ambitions and inclinations from their fathers or had different abilities, and so opted for, or were pushed into a quiet life. Opportunities for glory by which young men could publicise themselves and improve their chances of winning elections must have varied; they depended on the wars of the moment, on who else was competing and on a volatile electorate. The high costs of political life and the ostentatious expenditure associated with it may have induced some senators' sons to abstain from politics, or to retire early; some may well have been forced to sink below equestrian status. In a period of economic growth, by no means all old families kept pace with the rising standards of living in the elite; some new families became rich. The uneven incidence of death left some families with too many heirs, others with none. The division of estates between all surviving children would have fragmented the fortunes of some families, just as it concentrated the wealth of other families in the hands of a single heir or heiress; either case probably created vacancies in the elite, to be filled by newcomers. Fluidity in membership was thus compatible with the stability of structure.

As we see it, the fluidity of the Roman elite, or rather its fine balance of fluidity and ossification, was a response to two factors; first, the constitutional interpenetration of political office and social status; and secondly, the immensity of the military and administrative tasks performed in the course of Rome's territorial expansion. Post-feudal European aristocracies could be much more hereditary, because automatic heirs were divorced from the necessary exercise of political power in high offices of state. Other societies have achieved greater short-term stability by investing particular leaders with supreme power (prime ministers, chiefs, presidents, kings). The Romans managed to preserve a stable political structure in a period of considerable social change and economic flexibility drawing a rapid succession of leaders from a large set of families. This system allowed the hereditary principle to persist, without demanding adherence to it in every case in each generation.

The cost of the system, implicit in selectivity, was an extremely competitive political culture, focused externally on military achievement. Internally, the risk of the system, as Polybius saw (6.57), was that the competitiveness would get out of hand. The shame and fear of defeat would drive competitors to use unconstitutional methods of violence and corruption. The main weapons to hand were long-term military commands, which grew out of the needs of conquests overseas, the accumulation of massive resources in the hands of individual generals, and a professional army increasingly divorced from the ownership of Italian land. Hence the fall of the power-sharing oligarchy, which we call the Republic.

During the last two centuries of the Republic, the senatorial aristocracy was the political arm, first of the Roman and then later of the Italian ruling classes. It never developed, either in law or in fact, into a hereditary Estate. The oligarchic structure of government was stable, yet sufficiently flexible to allow a gradual but continuous turnover in the membership of the senate. Several interlocking factors – demographic, economic, political – stimulated these changes. Demographically, many families failed to have a male heir, and those with more than two surviving heirs, because of partible inheritance, risked falling in both wealth and status. Election to office was highly competitive and expensive. Both the expense and the competition militated against high rates of succession, especially in the last century of the Republic. Profits from empire increased the value of political prizes, such as provincial governorships, but they also escalated competition. And the incorporation of Italy into the Roman citizen state meant that many more wealthy land-owners were qualified to compete for high office.

In the second century BC, the Roman political elite consisted of a small inner core, which had relatively high rates of succession, and a broader band of the politically successful, drawn from the same social class of rich land-owners, but with lower rates of succession. Many members of this outer band of senators were the sole representatives of their families to enter politics for generations. This proposition is difficult to prove, but it is compatible with the surviving evidence. In the last century BC, political competition deteriorated into civil war. Death in war, judicial murder and confiscation wiped out many wealthy families within and just outside the senate. Yet however drastic the effect of civil war on individual familes, the basic social and economic domination of Italy by wealthy land- and slave-owners persisted, and was if anything strengthened by the accumulation of wealth into fewer hands.

The most obvious change to result from these protracted civil wars was political. Octavian Augustus effectively established both the monarchy and the Roman peace. The institution of monarchy implied a redistribution of political authority in the Roman state, a redefinition of the political role of the senate, a watchful eye on the political careers of senators, and radical changes in Roman political culture and rhetoric. In the next chapter, we turn to the social history of senators under the emperors.

APPENDIX

Table 2.11*. *In conditions of high mortality, many families have no surviving heir, even when fertility is high and a population slowly growing*

Number of children/sons per family	Children both sexes at birth	Sons at birth $(a/2)$	Sons surviving age forty $(40\% \text{ of } b)$	Sons surviving to age forty in slowly growing population $(90\% \text{ of } c)$
		(per cent)		
	a	b	c	d
0	2	8	31	35
1	4	16	33	34
2	8	18	21	20
3	10	17	10	9
4	10	15	4	3
5	10	12	1	1
6–8	25	14	—	—
9–11	28	1	—	—
12+	3	0	—	—
TOTAL	100	101	100	102
Average per family	6·3	3·17	1·27	1·14

* Derived from L. Henry, *Anciennes Familles Genèvoises* (Paris, 1956) 81–94, based on 58 women surviving to age forty-five with marriage intact, married before the age of twenty-five to husbands born 1650–1699; see also notes 86–7.

Table 2.12. *Low fertility and high mortality – Genevese bourgeois and French villagers compared*

No. of children sons per family	Children both sexes at birth		Sons at birth $(a/2)$		Sons surviving to age forty (40% of b)	
	Genevese bourgeois a_1	French villagers a_2	Genevese bourgeois b_1	French villagers b_2	Genevese bourgeois c_1	French villagers c_2
	(per cent)					
0	14	13	25	28	54	56
1	6	15	26	28	32	29
2	16	20	25	20	11	10
3	19	15	15	11	3	3
4	22	10	6	6	1	1
5	13	9	2	3	—	—
6–8	9	13	1	2	—	—
9+	1	4	—	1	—	—
12+	—	1	—	—	—	—
TOTAL	100	100	100	100	100	100
Average per family	3.15	3.2	1.56	1.6	0.646	0.62

3

AMBITION AND WITHDRAWAL: THE SENATORIAL ARISTOCRACY UNDER THE EMPERORS

by Keith Hopkins and Graham Burton

I INTRODUCTION

The imposition of monarchy changed Roman political culture but to a remarkable extent preserved the existing political structure. The first emperor, Augustus (31 BC–AD 14), boasted that he had restored the Republic. This was partly propaganda designed to legitimate his reign, and to obscure his innovations.[1] There was also some truth in it. But why did a monarch restore the Republican constitution? One partial answer is that the oligarchic system of power-sharing had significant advantages for a monarch who wanted the support of aristocrats, but who also wanted to fragment the power of each so that it did not constitute a danger for himself. The maxim, divide and rule, was applied to senators as well as to barbarians. The persistence of the Republican constitutional forms was in the emperors' interest.

But the emperors' self-interest is not a sufficient explanation. Emperors were also constrained by tradition and by the lack of alternatives. Emperors had to delegate power. In choosing generals, judges and provincial governors, they had little choice but to rely in the first instance on aristocrats, and to reward the new men to whom they gave elite positions with the traditional marks of aristocratic status. They also used knights and ex-slaves of the imperial household in a wide range of supervisory positions, but more as checks on senatorial governors than as their replacements. After all, the emperors were conservative not revolutionaries; too much change would have undermined their own legitimacy. They also relied on aristocrats because they themselves were aristocrats and identified

---

[1] Augustus' strategy was remarkably similar to that of the first emperor of unified China, Ch'in Shi-Huang-ti, who *inter alia* took a new title similar in meaning to Augustus, split the empire into provinces, and separated civil from military government. See D. Bodde, *China's First Unifier* (Hong Kong², 1967) 77–8, 123–35.

with the traditional system. As Catherine the Great said: 'Je suis aristocrate, c'est mon métier.'[2]

But aristocrats were those whose social power most threatened the emperors' supremacy and survival. Many of the tragedies of the early Principate arose out of its founding myth, that the emperor was only first among equals (*princeps*). Although this myth helped make the new order palatable by obscuring the unpalatable realities of monarchical power, it also elevated aristocrats so that they were the emperor's rivals. Some nobles thought, or were suspected of thinking, themselves well qualified to replace or succeed the reigning emperor. The founding ideology of the Principate thus fostered struggles which threatened its stability. This was particularly a problem at the moment of accession when the legitimacy of the emperors was weakest.[3] Those with imperial blood in their veins were most at risk. For example, on Nero's accession a great-great grandson of Augustus, M. Junius Silanus, was popularly regarded as a rival. 'Popular gossip suggested that he, a man of maturity, innocent of any crime, a noble descendant of the Caesars, should be preferred to Nero, who had scarcely reached manhood, and had obtained power by a crime' (Tacitus, *Annals* 13.1). Silanus was poisoned. Emperors could not tolerate rival aristocrats.

Hence the leitmotifs of Tacitus' history: the conflict between emperors and nobles, the conspiracies real or imagined, the persecution and execution of aristocrats, the activities of informers, the fawning hypocritical flattery of those who survived and prospered. Those were only some of the ingredients of change in Roman political culture. In addition, the establishment of monarchy curtailed the power and status of Roman aristocrats as individuals, and the initiative of the senate as a legislative body. The mere existence of a powerful emperor lessened the power and prestige of consuls. Their exercise of authority, their pursuit of military glory and of profit in the provinces were all restricted. Victory, as Tacitus perceived, was an achievement proper only for emperors.

[2] It is difficult to corroborate the statement that early Roman emperors identified themselves as Roman aristocrats. One indication may be that emperors entertained, and were entertained by other aristocrats at dinner and at literary recitals. For example, Augustus 'gave constant formal dinner parties with great regard for rank'; Valerius Messala records that he never invited an ex-slave to dinner (Suetonius, *Augustus* 74). In the second century AD, because several emperors died without a direct male descendant, the new emperors had been aristocrats before their elevation.

[3] R. Burling, *The Passage of Power, Studies in Political Succession* (New York, 1974) gives an interesting account of succession problems in several societies.

The senatorial aristocracy under the emperors

Emperors shut aristocrats off from their traditional access to the citizens of Rome. Popular elections to the highest offices were superseded in Augustus' reign and early in the first century were transferred to the senate. There too senators continued to compete for the traditional marks of honour. Divisive competition was to the emperor's advantage. And the emperor himself held the key to the most prestigious and profitable appointments in the provinces. By the middle of the first century AD, the emperor also nominated the consuls, from among whom senior provincial governors were chosen. But the concentration of power in the hands of the emperor did not necessarily lessen competition between senators; it merely changed the character and the location of competition, from senate to Court.

The tension between emperor and the political elite persisted. The emperor Claudius had thirty-five senators and more than three hundred knights put to death (Suetonius, *Claudius* 29).[4] The emperor Tiberius was lampooned for his cruelty; he starved two of his grandsons to death; he asked for twenty advisers from among the leading men and then had most of them killed; some senators were so sure of execution that they opened their veins at home or drank poison in full view of the senate (*id. Tiberius* 54ff). The emperor Caligula made senators kiss his feet (Dio 59.27), had senators who asked his advice run alongside his chariot for several miles, or wait on him at table (Suetonius, *Caligula* 26). The fact that he was mad did not make him easier to tolerate or to survive. Each emperor in turn in a different way by dramatic exercise of arbitrary power created terror and destruction, havoc and faction in the elite. Rich senators were murdered for their wealth, exiled for corruption or depravity, killed because they were planning rebellion or were suspected of it.

Humiliation and fear supplemented murder as weapons of disruption and demoralisation. It is reported that the emperor Domitian once invited leading senators and knights to dinner; he prepared a room with black walls, ceiling and floor, with bare couches on an uncovered floor; he had them come in alone, without their slave attendants. Each was given a place beside a gravestone, inscribed with the guest's name dimly lit by a small burial lamp. They were served the ritual meal of the dead by naked boys also painted black; all the guests thought that their last moment had come, since the

---

[4] The figures given by another contemporary source are slightly different: 35 senators and 221 knights killed (Seneca, *Pumpkinification (Apocolocyntosis) of Claudius* 14.1). On this savage satire by Seneca and Claudius' relations with the senate, see the pungent comments by A. Momigliano, *Claudius* (Cambridge², 1961) 74–9.

emperor, who was the only one to talk, kept to topics relating to death and slaughter. At last they were sent away, in carriages or litters which did not belong to them; nor did they know where they were going. No sooner had they got home than a messenger arrived from the emperor; this was the normal way in which a senator was given a choice in the way he killed himself – but instead the messenger delivered rich gifts, including the gravestone made of silver (Dio 67.9).

Such behaviour by emperors helped destroy the traditional aristocracy. Noble lineage, especially when combined with ability or success, apparently invited destruction (Tacitus, *Histories* 1.2). 'Whatever is high, let it fall', Nero is made to say in a historical tragedy written soon after his death; '...it is madness to keep on men who are puffed with pride in their famous families, a danger to prince and country' (Ps.Seneca, *Octavia* lines 471 and 493ff). Throughout the first century AD, many aristocrats were executed and their property was confiscated. If their sons survived them, they may not have had the means, or the will, to enter politics. Even the sons who survived with adequate funds may have been understandably reluctant to risk their lives in the pursuit of high offices. Withdrawal would have been a rational response to danger. As a consequence many aristocratic families disappeared from the central political stage or died out. The rate of political succession in the upper echelons of the senate fell even lower than it had been in the late Republic (see Chapter 2). But persecution is not a sufficient explanation of this fall. Even in the second century AD, when relations between 'good' emperors and the senatorial aristocracy were more cordial, the rate at which sons succeeded fathers in the upper levels of the senate was still strikingly low. Persecutions alone therefore cannot explain the very low succession rates found in the Roman political elite under the emperors.

The problem

Aristocrats in other monarchies have normally used their influence collectively and systematically in favour of their own sons. Our findings indicate that the great majority of Roman consuls and senators, in the first three centuries AD, either did not try to secure or did not succeed in securing for their sons a political status similar to their own. During these centuries, senators from established Roman and Italian families were increasingly replaced by successive waves, first of new Italian, then of western provincial and finally of eastern provincial senators. The Roman senatorial aristocracy in the course of two centuries was transformed from a conquering elite to include the elite of the conquered. That is well known, but it has never been explained; indeed, it is rarely seen as problematic. But we might have expected each new set of senators to resist further intrusions by entrenching the senatorial order as an entity against newcomers. Yet the Roman senatorial order during the Principate never became entrenched in defence of its collective privilege. Instead it was continuously replaced from outside. This weakness of the Roman aristocracy probably contributed to the stability of the Roman monarchy, just as the low rate of hereditary succession in the Chinese elite contributed to the stability of the Chinese monarchy.[5] But the problem remains: Why was the Roman aristocracy not hereditary?

Our first major problem in this chapter is to show what the succession rates among consuls were during the first three centuries AD. In much of this period, about half of all senators surviving to consular age became consuls, so we are talking about the politically more successful half of the senate. Even casual observation suggests that the succession rates of consuls under the emperors were lower than they had been in the political elite during the late Republic.[6] But the surviving evidence has never been thoroughly studied statistically. Our sample studies indicate that the drop in succession rates in the political elite was dramatic; three quarters of all consuls who held office AD 18–235 are not known to have had a single consular direct descendant in the next three generations.[7] As in the Republic, succession rates varied with status. First-rank consuls (technically called *ordinary* consuls) had a significantly higher succession rate than second-rank consuls (called *suffect*, that is supplementary) consuls. Only one sixth of these supplementary consuls appointed AD 70–235 is known to have had a consular son. As in the last chapter, we exploit the differences in rates of succession

---

[5] See R. Bendix, *Max Weber, An Intellectual Portrait* (London, 1960) 117–57; S. van der Sprenkel, *Legal Institutions in Manchu China* (London, 1962); J. M. Menzel, *The Chinese Civil Service* (Boston, 1963). On conflicts in other aristocracies, see G. Mosca, *The Ruling Class* (trans. New York, 1939).

[6] Direct comparison between late Republic and Principate might be misleading, but the relevant numbers are comparable. Out of an entry each year of 20 quaestors from 81 BC, typically 8 became praetor, and of these 2 then became consul. In the Principate, out of a similar entry to the senate, a gradually increasing number became consul (see Table 3.1). The status of the title consul diminished, compared with the Republic, but a study of imperial consuls is a study of a prominent part of the Roman political elite.

[7] These conclusions are based on systematic samples of incomplete evidence. For the methods and the limits within which our conclusions should be trusted see below, pp. 127ff.

by status to show that low fertility is by itself an inadequate explanation of the phenomenon. Moreover, in the dominant modern scholarly opinion, the Roman senate is considered hereditary. We document this tradition in a moment. Our analysis suggests that the common opinion is fundamentally wrong. To be sure, sons of senators automatically inherited certain privileges, but membership of the senate was not, we think, among them.

As in the last chapter, we begin by outlining traditional scholarly opinion. In the next section (II), we describe the methods which we have used to analyse succession rates among consuls; these include systematic sampling, which is an intellectually economical alternative to analysing all the evidence, and an estimate of the probability of being wrong when making estimates from incomplete evidence. These are standard procedures in social science, which are as yet rarely used by ancient historians. In section III, we present our findings, once again in the form of statistical tables, with running summaries of the main points of the argument and detailed commentary for the devotee. Some readers, we suspect, may prefer to skim (or even to skip) these pages.

In the following two sections of the chapter (sections IV–V), we search for a broad explanation of the weakness of the Roman senatorial aristocracy. We analyse some of the changes in the form of competition for political office, and a typical aristocratic reaction to such competition, namely withdrawal. Then in section V, we discuss the growth of alternative centres of power and influence within the political structure, principally the emergence of a patrimonial administration centred on the imperial palace – a development which weakened the corporate influence of the senate, and we suspect, senators' individual self-esteem. Finally, we suggest that the cultural integration of the elites of the conquered into an empire-wide elite of *literati* militated against hereditary succession for senators, in two ways. First, the pool of potential candidates, qualified by wealth, status and education from all over the empire grew enormously relative to a senate of more or less fixed size; consequently the competition for high status in the central Roman hierarchy also stiffened. Secondly, we suggest, though we cannot prove, that sons of senators whose chief estates were in the provinces, often preferred to return to their home province, their status enhanced with hereditary privileges, rather than try to compete at Rome for further glory in the emperor's service, all the more so since such ambition was expensive, uncertain and often even fatal.

The senatorial aristocracy under the emperors

The traditional view

In the traditional view (associated with such names as Mommsen, Friedländer and A. Stein), Augustus transformed the senatorial order into a legally hereditary body. A cornerstone of this change was the grant of senatorial privileges to descendants of senators down to the third generation in the male line. The Roman senatorial order thus became, they argued, and for a long time remained, a hereditary aristocracy (*Erbadel*). The son (or sons) of a senator had not only the right, but also the obligation to follow in his father's footsteps into the senate, provided he had at least the legally prescribed wealth.[8]

This view is still dominant and is found in standard works by respected modern scholars.[9] They too assume that in the Principate a senator's son or sons normally followed his father into the senate. Of course, there were a number of exceptions, and some individual cases are well known to us through the sources. Some senatorial families were impoverished by over-expenditure, others fells into

---

[8] The influence of these classic works is still strong, see T. Mommsen, *Römisches Staatsrecht* (Leipzig³, 1887) vol. 3, 466ff: 'The nobility became a legally circumscribed senatorial estate, it became a hereditary peerage' (p. 466) and: '...young men of senatorial origin were obliged to enter a senatorial career, in the Republican period by custom, in the Principate by law' (p. 507). L. Friedländer, *Sittengeschichte Roms* (Leipzig¹⁰, 1922) vol. 1, 115; A. Stein, *Der römische Ritterstand* (Munich, 1927) 74 and 81, who also (189ff) gives examples of exceptions: senators with equestrian sons and equestrians with senatorial sons. On the legal inheritance of senatorial privileges, see D. 23.2.44 *pr.* and 50.1.22.5 (Paul) and note 95 below.

[9] See, for example, F. Millar *et al. The Roman Empire and its Neighbours* (London, 1967) 28 and 52: (If they had the requisite fortune), '...sons of existing senators assumed...senatorial status at about sixteen or seventeen...the senate was fundamentally a hereditary body, heavily supplemented by imperial patronage'. E. Meyer, *Römischen Staat und Staatsgedanke* (Zurich³, 1964) 377: '...nicht nur tatsächlich, sondern auch rechtlich erblich...'; similarly A. Chastagnol, 'La naissance de l'*ordo senatorius*', *Mélanges de l'école française à Rome* 85 (1973) 583–607. These scholars seem to think that all senator's sons normally entered the senate; any shortfall was filled by the emperor's recommendation. Perhaps the clearest and strongest extension of the conventional view is made by G. Alföldy, 'Consuls and consulars under the Antonines,' *Ancient Society* 7 (1976) 288–9: 'As to the descendants of consuls, the following rather surprising statement may be made, as far as I know not yet stated explicitly for the imperial period: the consulate was, as in the Republic, hereditary; that means, the son of a consular, in the event that he reached the requisite age, could in principle automatically count on the consulship.' He cites in confirmation 76 known consular sons of consuls, and attributes their small number to the combined effect of low fertility and high mortality (p. 290). His recent book, *Konsulat and Senatorenstand unter den Antoninen* (Bonn, 1977) especially 84–94 re-emphasises this view. The clarity of Alföldy's expression is welcome, but his method of analysis is inadequate (see the kind review by Burton, *Journal of Roman Studies* 70 (1980) 204–5), and his conclusions are wrong. One problem is that our sources tell us disproportionately about politically successful sons, but Alfödy ignores such bias.

political disfavour, or were eliminated; still other senatorial families had no surviving sons. In so far as a reason has been sought for the existence of vacancies in the senate, the total answer has been purportedly found in low fertility among aristocrats and in imperial persecutions.

We try to show that these opinions are wrong on two counts. First, sons of consuls and senators surviving to consular age often did not enter the senate. The legal testimony is compatible with this view: the inheritance of senatorial privileges in the male line over three generations may have exonerated some sons of senators from the burden of pursuing a senatorial career. Secondly, lower fertility and the heightened mortality of senators under the emperors may have contributed to the drop in consular succession rates. But they cannot constitute a complete explanation. The difference in succession rates between *ordinary* (top) consuls and *suffect* (supplementary) consuls is marked. Social and political pressures on aristocrats seem much more likely to have been the main cause of their sons' withdrawal from politics than assumed differences in fertility within the political elite. In sum, explanations for low succession rates among consuls and senators in the first three centuries AD should be sought in the changes in Roman political culture, which were brought about under the emperors. Finally, we should stress that low fertility is not so much an explanation, as a phenomenon to be explained.

II METHODS

Our main objective is to find out how far Roman consuls were chosen from among the descendants of consuls or themselves had consular descendants. But first a discussion of methods. In many respects, the scope and limitations of the research design are similar to those outlined in the previous chapter, but there are also some important differences. As before, we covered seven generations, three generations before and three after the consuls investigated. The quality of the data available was far worse than for the Republic.[10] Patronyms

---

[10] We followed A. Degrassi, *I fasti consolari dell' impero romano* (Rome, 1952). For genealogies, we relied on *PIR*[1] (1897–8) and *PIR*[2] (1933–70), plus G. Alföldy, 'Septimius Severus and und der Senat', *Bonner Jahrbücher* 168 (1968) 112ff.; G. Barbieri, *L'albo senatorio da Settimio Severo a Carino* (Rome, 1952); W. Eck, *Senatoren von Vespasian bis Hadrian* (Munich, 1970); A H M Jones *et al.*, *The Prosopography of the Later Roman Empire* I (Cambridge, 1971); J. Morris, 'The Roman senate A.D. 69–193' (unpublished Ph.D. thesis, University of London, 1953); and R. Syme, *The Roman Revolution* (Oxford, 1939) and *Tacitus* (Oxford, 1958). We confined ourselves to senators and consuls for whom there is definite

are often not known. Consequently, the constructed genealogies which we used risk treating men who were really nephews as sons, cousins as brothers, and uncles as fathers. In cases of doubt, we have systematically erred on the side of assuming that similarly named consuls were directly related to each other. This tendency served to strengthen our conclusion that the rate of status inheritance was low. The direct inheritance of status from father to son was in fact probably even less than shown in our results.

The number of consuls appointed in the Principate was several times larger than in the last two centuries of the Republic. Over 1,800 held office between 30 BC and AD 235.[11] We know the names of about 1,400. The sheer number is a symptom of their diminished importance. But selection as consul remained a high honour. Besides, the expansion in the number of consuls means that the analysis of their origins and descent has broader implications. Be that as it may, we are faced with two new problems: a very large number of consuls, and incomplete information about them. Let us deal with each problem in turn.

In Table 3.1, we summarise our conclusions about the numbers of consuls known and appointed. For known and dated consuls, we simply followed the lists compiled by Degrassi (1952; see note 10); recent discoveries and more accurate datings have not materially altered the total picture. We have a full list of the two *ordinary* consuls appointed each year; but roughly one third of these prestigious appointments were filled by emperors, by their prospective heirs or by men who had already held consulship. We excluded these from all our tables and calculations.

Our information on suffect consuls is patchy, derived from lists inscribed on stone and surviving in fragments from Ostia and Potentia, from literary sources and from the known exercise of consular posts recorded in honorary or tombstone inscriptions. The problem is that we often do not know how many supplementary consuls were appointed. As Mommsen wrote: 'The number of

extant evidence, so that our number of known consuls is less than that reckoned by Morris in *Listy Filologické* 87 (1964) 324. It seemed better to follow standard lists rather than to try to incorporate all the detailed improvements of prosopography and dating made by several scholars in recent years. We do not think that recent changes would materially have altered the general conclusions. Our work on consuls unfortunately was finished before the appearance of Alföldy (1977) who provides a full list of consuls AD 138–180. His dating of suffect consuls is more accurate than Degrassi's, but his improvements do not, we think, materially alter our conclusions.

[11] Consulships held by emperors and their prospective heirs and by those who had already been consul are excluded from calculations throughout this chapter.

Table 3.1. *Numbers of consuls known and appointed in the Principate**

	Known dated consuls (Number)	Known but uncertainly dated consuls (Allocated number)	Total known consuls $(a+b)$ (Number)	Consuls probably appointed (Number)	Proportion known c/d (per cent)	Total known consuls (per year)	Consuls probably appointed (per year)
	a	b	c	d	e	f	g
30 BC–AD 17	121	0	121	122	99	2·6	2·6
18–54	146	9	155	210	74	4·2	6
55–69	88	3	91	98	93	6·1	7
70–96	166	12	178	203	88	6·6	8
97–130	203	24	227	273	83	6·7	8
131–160	178	33	211	261	81	7·0	9
161–192	143	35	178	311	57	5·6	10
193–235	156	101	257	394	65	6·0	9
TOTAL	1,201	217	1,418	1,872	76	5·4	7

* As listed by Degrassi (1952); emperors, their prospective heirs and second and further consulships are excluded, fragmentary names also excluded from cols. *a*, *b*, and *c*. On the distribution of consuls of uncertain date to periods, see notes 12–13.

[supplementary] pairs and the period for which they held office were extraordinarily unequal, and the latter hardly ever seems to have been regularised, although we can trace certain patterns which were followed for a while.'[12] We can make educated guesses from the data available; the probable margin of error is greater towards the end of the period (AD 161–235) when the evidence is at its thinnest.

In Table 3.1, we present the total number of consuls known and the total probably appointed in successive periods between 30 BC and AD 235.[13] The number of consuls appointed increased from under

[12] Mommsen 1887: vol. 2, 84. Mommsen's caution warned us against an easy acceptance of the idea that there were twelve consuls regularly appointed every year from the middle of the second century. Often there were, but apparently not always. There seems no way of being sure about the exact number. Several of the figures given and deductions made by J. Morris, 'Leges Annales under the Principate', *Listy Filologické* 88 (1965) 24 seem false or improbable. For example, he claimed that the number of known consuls 'demand an average of not much less than 12' consuls per year, and the consulate was 'large enough to absorb *almost* all senators who *desired the magistracy*' (my italics). The logical gap between lists of consuls and their desires is wide.
[13] We allocated consuls known by name but of uncertain date to our sub-periods as follows: Degrassi (1952) listed 354 consuls of less certain date. We excluded 81 either because their names were fragmentary, or because they had already

three per year on average in the beginning of the period, to eight per year by the end of the first century AD, to nine or ten per year by the end of the second century AD (emperors, their prospective heirs and repeated consulships excluded). Overall, we know the names of about 70 % of all suffect consuls, and of 75 % of all consuls. The early data are best (90 % known); the late data are worst (col. *e*: 57 %–65 % known). The overall figures are probably of the right order of magnitude. However, we should stress that there is probably a smallish margin of error, and because of that we have shown the average number of consuls appointed per year in round numbers, not to a decimal point.

The problem of too much evidence

It is a cardinal principle in ancient history that scholars should examine all the relevant ancient evidence. Ideally, before they publish any results from their researches, they should also have covered all the relevant secondary literature.[14] In this part of our research, we have adopted a different principle: the systematic selection of only part of the evidence. Our reason for sampling was simple; there was too much evidence. The names are known of over 1,400 consuls who held office between 30 BC and AD 235. The effort of investigating them all would have been disproportionate to the rewards. Some intellectual economy was necessary. We calculate below the margins of error probably implicit in our selection. They were small.

We selected four periods for investigation: AD 18–54, 70–96,

been included in the list of dated consuls (*doublets*), and some others because they seemed fictions of fourth-century historical fabricators (SHA). For Table 3.1 (col. *b*), we were left with 273; this was reduced to 217 by excluding the consuls assigned by Degrassi to the mid-third century and later, and by excluding a proportion *pro rata* of those allocated to periods (e.g. the third century) extending beyond AD 235, which was the limit of our research period. For two thirds of these 217 consuls, Degrassi allocated a date precise enough to fit inside one of our sub-periods. The remaining third was only roughly allocated. For example, we split those whom he allocated to 'the second century' between our sub-periods (96–130, 131–160, 161–192), *pro rata*. This was crudely mechanical and may be a source of slight error.

[14] Omission is seen as a sin in itself; reviewers often point out omissions from ancient sources or modern commentators without stating whether inclusion would have made any difference to the argument. But in order to avoid this criticism, scholars often persuade themselves to narrow the focus of their research. And learned journals publish many articles of almost unbelievable narrowness. The huge expansion in the number of periodicals in the last thirty years makes complete coverage of the secondary literature impracticable. The tradition must collapse. What will take its place?

Methods

131–160, 193–235. These were chosen on purpose, not at random. The Augustan period had already been well studied.[15] It seemed important to cover the establishment of the Flavian and Severan dynasties, and worthwhile taking two other periods to cover times when dynasties were well established. The four periods together account for just about half the total period (30 BC–AD 235). The analysis of consular ascendants and descendants spreads over the whole period and beyond.

Within each period, we selected every fourth dated consul listed by Degrassi (1952), excluding emperors, their prospective heirs and former consuls (see Table 3.1, col. *a*). We also took a one in five sample of Degrassi's less certainly dated consuls. We thought that if we confined our research to these sampling fractions (1/4, 1/5), our results would not be trusted. We doubled the size of our sample in three periods which seemed specially important for our analysis: AD 70–96, 131–160, 193–235.

Given our limited objectives, this was statistically irrational. In theory, it is obvious that there must be a stage when the usefulness or marginal utility of looking at each extra case diminishes. This may not hold for all research; but it does for some.[16] Investigating a complete population (of data or of people) brings certainty, but it can be very expensive and time-consuming. On the other hand, each random sample drawn is likely to produce a different response. Statisticians have developed techniques for estimating the probable error which results from choosing a sample of any given size. A brief discussion will be useful for the interpretation of our findings and an understanding of their limitations.

We can work out the limits within which most samples (normally 19 out of 20 or 99 out of 100 possible samples) are likely to produce results similar to those produced by any one sample. Surprisingly, the sampling fraction (e.g. 1/2, 1/4, or 1/1,000 of the population) is of minor importance. Put crudely, the probable error is dependent to a far greater degree on the absolute size of the sample (not the

---

[15] P. A. Brunt, 'The Lex Valeria Cornelia', *Journal of Roman Studies* 51 (1961) 71ff; M. W. Hoffman Lewis, 'The official priests of Rome under the Julio-Claudians', *American Academy in Rome, Papers* 16 (1955); G. Tibiletti, *Principe e magistrati repubblicani* (Rome, 1953) 245–6, 263–6. Cf. E. Groag, 'Zum Konsulat in der Kaiserzeit', *Wiener Studien* 47 (1929) 144–5.

[16] Even in Roman history, if data are standardised (as funeral inscriptions are), it is worth taking a sample, if only as a pilot study to see if further investigation might be worthwhile. Sampling theory is complex; our own experience is that we would have saved ourselves trouble if we had sought statistical advice in the earliest, planning stages of our research. W. G. Cochran, *Sampling Techniques* (New York², 1963) is good, but not light reading.

The senatorial aristocracy under the emperors

Table 3.2. *Too much research is a waste of time. A comparison of results from samples of one-quarter and one-half of dated consuls*

Consuls with:	Consuls AD 70–96		Consuls AD 131–160	
Sample size:	42	84	45	90
Sampling fraction:	one-quarter	one-half	one-quarter	one-half
	a	b	c	d
	(per cent)			
A any known consular ascendant or descendant in male line*	55	52	56	57
B in same generation	19	15	16	16
C in father's generation	19	18	27	27
D in son's generation	26	25	31	29
E in grandfather's generation	7	10	18	13
F in grandson's generation	17	17	16	14
G in great-grandson's generation	7	7	4	8

* We included relatives in the direct male line only (e.g. father, son, grandfather, etc.) except that we also included brother, and father's brother's son.
In no case did the extra research significantly change our interpretation of the response.

sampling fraction), and on the frequency with which the behaviour investigated is found. The larger the sample and the more common the behaviour investigated within that sample, the smaller the probable error.[17] These points may help reassure Roman historians, who sometimes express doubt about the value of their data, simply because they constitute only a small fraction in comparison with what has been lost.

In Table 3.2, we have tabulated the impact of doubling the size of our sample on the responses central to the analysis of succession. A casual glance shows that the differences within each pair of columns (a:b, c:d) are negligible.[18] In no case did all that extra work

[17] This is called the coefficient of the variation of the estimate; a formula for its calculation is given in Cochran 1963: 49–58. Examples of the variations within which our estimates probably hold true are given in the next paragraph.

[18] The sceptical reader may wish to compare our figures with Alfoldy's (1977: 303–6). He analysed all known consuls AD 138–180 (N = 292) excluding emperors and second consulships; of these, 26% were known to be sons of consuls; cf. our figure based on a sample from a substantial section but not all of this period: 27%.

132

significantly change the results: for example, 55% became 52%, 56% became 57% (top row). Yet a little caution is needed. By common statistical standards, all the samples taken were absolutely small. The similarity in the responses was partly a product of chance. Theoretically other samples drawn from the same total population could have divergent results. Doubling the size of the sample reduced the probable divergence, but the statistically probable error is still quite large especially when the response rate was low. For example, in Table 3.2 col. *b*, the responses should read 52% plus or minus 8%, 25% ± 7%, 7% ± 4% (estimated for 19 out of 20 samples, and see note 17). All this does not matter, provided we accept the figures as estimates: 52% and 57% should be read as meaning about half; 7% as less than a tenth. Minor differences should be ignored, except perhaps when several figures all point in one direction. Given our purposes and the other sources of error in the data, we considered these limitations acceptable. The extra work which we did by doubling our samples was wasteful. *A fortiori*, investigating all the consuls would have been self-indulgent.

Gaps in the data

There is one gap in our data, to which we should draw particular attention. It may affect all our conclusions about succession to consular status in the Principate. Overall, we do not know the names of about one quarter of all consuls. This deficiency is obviously serious. It means that we may wrongly attribute the status of newcomer to consuls who were in fact the sons of unknown consuls; or we may underestimate the extent to which known consuls had consular heirs, if their sons were unknown consuls.

There are two defences against error of this kind, the statistical and the practical. Statistically, we can correct our figures, based on known consuls, if we assume that unknown consuls had proportionately as many consular children as known consuls (this avenue is explored in Appendix 3.1). This assumption about unknown consuls seems improbable, since the best-known consuls (e.g. *ordinary* consuls) certainly had more consular sons than known suffect consuls. Nevertheless the assumption allows us to glimpse the maximum probable error in our conclusions. For example, at the end of the first century AD, this assumption would lead us to add onto the proportion of consuls known to have had a consular son (25%), an estimated correction factor of 5%, to allow for unknown sons of known and unknown consular fathers (total 30%). Towards the end of the second century, the deficiencies of our data increase; the correction

Table 3.3. *The political elite in the principate did not reproduce itself*

Ordinary and suffect consuls with any consular:	AD 18– 54 *a*	70– 96 *b*	131– 160 *c*	193– 235 *d*	Suffects of less certain date *e*	All consuls AD 18– 235 *f*
				(per cent)		
A Father	46	18	27	32	9	**27**
B Other ascendant*	8	6	6	5	7	**6**
C SUB-TOTAL†	54	24	32	37	16	**33**
D Son	32	25	29	19	13	**24**
E Other descendant*	8	7	7	6	4	**7**
F SUB-TOTAL†	40	32	36	26	18	**31**
G n =	37	84	90	78	44	333

* Grandfather, great-grandfather, grandson and great-grandson in the male line only.
† Sub-totals are recalculated from base figures; there are therefore minor discrepancies in the addition A + B = C.

factor becomes very much larger. The practical argument is simpler. In spite of the gaps in our data, it is worth analysing the evidence on consuls which we have. It is really very good. Much analysis of Roman society is unavoidably based on worse.

III   ANALYSIS OF FINDINGS

Consuls appointed AD 18–235 had a remarkably low rate of succession. Table 3.3 (col. *f*) shows that only one quarter (27%) of all the consuls (AD 18–235) in our sample had a consular father.[19] And even if we

[19] Most subsequent figures are based only on what is known; instead of repeating 'is known to have had' we write 'had'. Calculating a single percentage figure for all known consuls AD 18–235 is, of course, based on samples which leave intermediate periods out. This matters greatly only if the omitted periods were different from the periods included. We should stress that our conclusions are rough, not accurate. We prefer to write 'about a quarter' to the spurious precision of, say: 26.644%. For those who want to calculate for themselves, the easiest procedure because of different sampling fractions ($\frac{1}{5}$, $\frac{1}{4}$, $\frac{1}{2}$) is to work from

go back and include grandfathers and great-grandfathers, only one third (33%) of all consuls had any direct consular ancestor in the previous three generations. Similarly, only one quarter (24%) of these consuls had a consular son, and only one third (31%) had any direct consular descendant in the following three generations. The long period covered before and after each set of consuls investigated should make up for some of the gaps in our data; in any one generation, a consular relative might by chance be unrecorded in our surviving sources, but over six generations the chances are very much less.[20]

Even if we include in our reckoning mere senators, that is those who never became consul (or those who are not known to have become consul), the picture stays substantially the same. We know the names of about 3,000 of these mere senators-never-consul, which is perhaps about half the total number of senators who never became consul between 31 BC and AD 270. But only 4% of all consuls (AD 18–235) in our sample, who had no known direct consular descendant, had a known mere senatorial descendant in three generations after their consulship.[21] Once again the length of time covered helps make up for the serious inadequacies of our evidence. In sum, the evidence

Table 3.1 cols. *a* and *b*. Between AD 18 and 235, there were 1,080 dated known consuls and 217 less certainly dated consuls. The proportion having any given characteristic for the whole period is calculated by:

$$\left(\frac{N_1p + N_2p + N_3p + N_4p}{N_{1-4}} \times 1{,}080\right) + N_5p \Big/ (1{,}080 + 217),$$

where N_{1-4} are the number of consuls in each period from which the samples were drawn (Table 3.1, col. *a*) and N_5 is the number of uncertainly dated consuls (217) and p is the proportion having characteristic x. E.g. for Table 3.3, row A, calculate:

$$\{[(146 \times 46\%) + (166 \times 18\%) + (178 \times 27\%) + (156 \times 32\%)/646] \times 1{,}080\}$$
$$+ (217 \times 9\%) \div 1{,}297 = 27\%.$$

[20] Altogether, one half (54%) of all the consuls in our sample (AD 70–235) had no direct consular ascendant nor a direct consular descendant in the three generations before or after the consulship (Table 3.10, col. *h*).

[21] W. Eck, 'Sozialstruktur des römischen Senatorenstandes in der hohen Kaiserzeit und statistische Methode', *Chiron* 3 (1973) 375–94, especially 383–5, gives the total number of known senators 31 BC–AD 270 as *c.* 4,500. The total number of senators ever appointed in this period was *c.* 8,000. The reckoning should be an initial number of *c.* 800 senators in 31 BC + 301 years × 20 entrants, plus an unknown number of co-options. From these two totals, we must subtract consuls.

The number of known consuls in this period is 1,418; the number of consuls ever-appointed is 1,872 (see Table 3.1). Therefore, there are *c.* 3,100 known senators-never-consul (4,500 − 1,418) and *c.* 6,100 ever appointed senators-never-consul (*c.* 8,000 − 1,872). Altogether 8% of all consuls (AD 18–235) in our sample, who had no known direct consular descendant or ascendant, had a known senatorial-never-consul ascendant or descendant in the three generations before or after the consulship.

Table 3.4. *Consuls without consular ancestors under the early emperors*

Consuls without consular ancestors:	44–29 a	22–17 BC b	16 BC–AD 4 c	AD 5–22 d	23–37 e	38–54 f
			(per cent)			
A Ordinary consuls	—	58	15	7	28	30
B Suffect consuls	—	—	48	75	52	60
c All consuls	58	54	27	40	39	52
Numbers of consuls:						
D Ordinary	26	12	34	30	29	20
E Suffect	29	1	21	28	27	55

we have just discussed suggests that two thirds (65%) of all consuls (AD 18–235) are not known to have had a consular or a senatorial direct descendant for three generations after they held the consulship.[22] The Roman senate in the first three centuries AD was not a hereditary status group.

Succession rates among consuls under the emperors were lower than those of consuls and praetors in the late Republic (see Table 2.6, row D), though there are some difficulties in making this comparison.[23] The reign of Augustus marked the transition between two systems. Table 3.4 shows gradual evolution of a two-tier system.[24]

[22] This figure, 65%, is arrived at by subtracting consuls with a direct consular descendant (31% – Table 3.3, col. *f*) from 100%, = 69%, and then by subtracting those with a known senatorial descendant (4%), to arrive at 65%. It is worth noting also that of all the suffect consuls (AD 70–235) only 8% had a known senatorial-never-consul direct ascendant or descendant within three generations of the consulship, and no known consular ascendant or descendant. In sum, there is very little corroborative evidence that descendants of consuls became senators-never-consul.

[23] The large gaps in the Republican evidence on praetors and on senators-never-praetor favour the view that succession rates within the Republican senate were higher than our evidence shows (see above, p. 63). The persistent discrepancy between the succession rates of consuls and of praetors in the Republic, and between those of *ordinary* consuls and of suffect consuls in the Principate, is suggestive.

[24] Table 3.4 is derived from the figures given by Brunt, Hoffman Lewis and Tibiletti, in the works cited in note 15 above. Emperors and their prospective

Analysis of findings

Table 3.5. *The consular ascendants of* ordinary *consuls in the Principate*

Ordinary consuls with:	AD 18–36 *a*	70–96 *b*	131–160 *c*	193–235 *d**
	(per cent)			
A Ordinary consular father	48	12	26	49
B Suffect consular father	21	40	26	16
C Any consular grandfather and/or great-grandfather only†	8	25	4	0
D TOTAL	**77**	**77**	**57**	65
N =	33	25	53	49
n =	24	12	26	26

* Col. *d* contains *ordinary* consuls I only, i.e. those whose first consulship was an *ordinary* consulship. There were in this period also 21 *ordinary* consuls II, who had previously been suffect consuls. Only 4/21 had a consular father, and 5/21 had 5 *ordinary* and 1 suffect consular son. In cols. *b* and *c*, such *ordinary* II consuls are included in the figures given (N = 3 and 2 respectively).

† Figures in row C are derived from sample data, which in col. *a* covers AD 18–54. Please note that the number of *ordinary* consuls sampled in col. *b* is very small.

During the civil war period (44–29 BC), and in the early part of Augustus' reign, over half (58%, 54%) of all consuls came from non-consular families. But then, in a period of retrenchment (16 BC–AD 22), Augustus and his successor Tiberius sought the support of the old aristocracy, and effectively reserved the *ordinary* consulship for them; only a handful of *ordinary* consuls (15%, 7% – Table 3.4, row A) in this period came from non-consular families. But in the same period, there was a steady growth in the number of suffect consuls, and a substantial proportion (48%, 75%) of them came from

heirs and repeated consulships are excluded. Numbers of consuls are based on Degrassi (1952) from whom Hoffman Lewis slightly diverges for the period after AD 37, because of the difficulty of dating some consuls exactly. However, it is worth noting that Hoffman Lewis (1955: 173) reckoned that 47% (83/176) of consuls AD 14–54 were without consular ancestry, while our sample (Table 3.3, col. *a*, row C) produced 46% without consular ancestry for the period AD 18–54.

non-consular families. We thus have a two-tier system, a small inner-core of *ordinary* consuls, most of whom had consular origins, and a larger, outer band of suffect consuls, many of whom came from non-consular families.[25]

Ordinary consuls – origins. For two centuries, the inner core of *ordinary* consuls continued to be heavily recruited from senators with consular ancestry. Table 3.5 (row D) shows that well over half (57%), and in two of our sample periods three quarters (77%, 77%) of *ordinary* consuls were directly descended from consuls. Two factors help account for this preservation of the *ordinary* consulship for the descendants of consuls. First, the *ordinary* consulship was principally an honorary position, divorced from important executive responsibilities; secondly, a significant proportion (over a fifth, row B) of *ordinary* consuls were sons of suffect consuls. In other words, lumping together consuls of consular origin disguises the gradual advancement of families over two generations, culminating in an *ordinary* consulship.[26]

Ordinary consuls – fertility. Only a minority of *ordinary* consuls had a consular son. Table 3.6 (row A) shows that overall only about a quarter (20%–38%; average 28%) of the *ordinary* consuls surveyed had an *ordinary* consular son, and that it was exceptional (row B: 12% or less) for an *ordinary* consul to have a son who became suffect consul. The inclusion of grandsons and great-grandsons (row C) does not swell the proportion of *ordinary* consuls with consular descendants greatly. But the final result is somewhat strange. *Ordinary* consuls in two of our periods (AD 18–36 and 131–160) had overall succession rates, including consular grandsons and great-grandsons, of about 50% (Table 3.6, row D: 45% and 59%). But in the two other periods (AD 70–96, 193–235), the same overall political succession rates were substantially lower (28% and 32%). Political changes, rather than

---

[25] E. Groag 1929: 144–5 calculated that only 28% of all *ordinary* consuls AD 70–235 (N = 176) came from non-consular families (excluding emperors and their relatives). In the period AD 54–69 (Hoffman Lewis 1955: 173), 64% of all consuls came from non-consular families, an increase over the previous period (AD 3–54: 52%). We think that the increase reflected both the growth in the number of suffect consuls and the increased openness of the consulship to outsiders.

[26] Another index of the decline of the old nobility is the fall in the proportion of consuls who were patricians in successive Julio-Claudian reigns: 53% (Augustus), 37% (Tiberius), 19% (Caligula), 30% (Claudius), 18% (Nero); so Hoffman Lewis (1955: 171). This fall occurred in spite of the elevation of new families to patrician status. The increase in the number of consuls appointed also eroded the significance of the status of *nobilis*, once reserved in certain circles for descendants of consuls.

Analysis of findings

Table 3.6. *The consular descendants of* ordinary *consuls in the Principate*

	AD 18–36	70–96	131–160	193–235
Ordinary consuls with:	*a*	*b*	*c*	*d**
	(per cent)			
A *Ordinary* consular son	24	24	38	20
B Suffect consular son	12†	4	9	6†
C Any consular grandson or great grandson only	12	0	12	8
D TOTAL	45	28	59	32

* See notes to Table 3.5.
† Includes one suffect consular son of a father with an *ordinary* consular son as well; double-counting has been avoided in the total, which answers the question: what proportion of consuls had a known consular son, grandson or great-grandson?

violent swings in fertility (or in the availability of evidence), seem the most probable explanation of these differences.

We shall now exploit the same tactics which we used in the previous chapter. We need to distinguish between two questions: first, how many consuls had a consular son (whether *ordinary* or suffect)? The answer gives us the rate of Family Status Maintenance (FSM). Secondly, how many consular sons did each successive cohort of consuls have? The answer to this question gives us the rate of Social Reproduction in Politics (SRP). Put another way, the answer to the first question indicates how many consular families lost consular status. The answer to the second question tells us how many places became vacant at the top. And the difference between the two rates is a measure of consuls' success in placing more than one son successfully in politics.

Table 3.7 (row A) shows that the overall rate of Family Status Maintenance (FSM) among the *ordinary* consuls examined ranged from a low of 24% (AD 193–235) to a high of 47% (AD 131–160). The rate of Social Reproduction in Politics (SRP) was only slightly higher (row D: 42%, 28%, 59%, 90% in successive periods). Two conclusions came to mind. First, if the large variations in rates of replacement were due mostly to political changes, then *ordinary* consuls in periods of low replacement (e.g. AD 70–96) had many more

139

Table 3.7. *Self-replacement of* ordinary *consuls in the Principate*

		AD 18–36 *a*	70–96 *b*	131–160 *c*	193–235 *d*
		(per cent)			
A	FSM*	33	28	47	24
B	*Ordinary* consular sons	30	24	42	24
C	Suffect consular sons	12	4	11	6
D	B + C = SRP*	42	28	53	30
E	B/C†	2.5	6.0	3.7	4.0
F	N =	33	25	53	70‡

* FSM is the Rate of Family Status Maintenance; FSM answers the question: What proportion of *ordinary* consuls had an *ordinary* or suffect son? SRP is the Rate of Social Reproduction in Politics; SRP answers the question: how many sons of a given cohort of consuls reached the *ordinary* or suffect consulship?

† B/C shows the ratio of *ordinary* to suffect consular sons.

‡ Includes those who achieved the *ordinary* consulship as a second consulship (21 out of 70).

sons than succeeded them in politics. The second point is similar: we argued in the last chapter (pp. 64ff) that in Roman conditions of high mortality, it was difficult to achieve respectable rates of succession, without a significant number of families having more than one son surviving to adult age. *Ordinary* consuls of AD 131–160 achieved an FSM of 47%, yet very few of these consuls placed more than one son successfully in politics. Given that few known sons of *ordinary* consuls became suffect consuls, it is surely unlikely that many of their sons became mere senators-never-consul. Sons of successive cohorts of *ordinary* consuls left many positions at the top unfilled. Their fathers' low fertility is an insufficient explanation of the sons' failure in or withdrawal from politics.

Suffect consuls – origins. Table 3.8 shows that only a fifth (21% – average of row D) of all the suffect consuls sampled is known to have had consular ancestry in the previous three generations.[27] If we start

[27] We omitted suffect consuls of AD 18–54, because there were only 13 of them in our small sample (n = 37); only 5 of these thirteen had any consular ascendants and only 4 had any consular descendants. In Table 3.8, row C we counted as a consular grandfather the only case of a known consular great-grandfather.

Analysis of findings

Table 3.8. *The consular origins of suffect consuls in the Principate*

Suffect consuls with:	AD 70– 96 *a*	131– 160 *b*	193– 235 *c*	less certain date *d*
	(per cent)			
A Consular father and grandfather	4	19	2	0
B Consular father only	11	3	12	9
C Consular grandfather only	1	6	6	7
D TOTAL*	17	28	21	16
n =	72	64	52	44

* Totals are derived from raw numbers and may therefore diverge slightly from the sum of percentages.

from a preconception of a hereditary aristocracy, this is amazing. Four fifths had no consular ancestry over the previous three generations, and three quarters (75%) had no known consular or senatorial direct ascendant in the previous three generations. The turn-over in suffect consular families was very rapid.

Suffect consuls – fertility. Table 3.9 has important implications. It is remarkable that only a small minority of suffect consuls had consular sons (whether *ordinary* or suffect). The figures read: 22% for AD 70–96, then 17% for AD 131–160, 14% for AD 193–235, and 13% for suffect consuls of uncertain date (Table 3.9, rows A plus B). And not a single suffect consul in our total sample of 245 suffect consuls (AD 18–235) is known to have had more than one consular son. To be sure, a few examples of suffect consuls with politically successful sons may be found (they were by chance not in our sample). But neither these exceptions, nor the incomplete nature of our evidence can alter the general shape of our conclusions. Very few suffect consuls had consular sons, and almost none had more than one such son.

Was their fertility low? Our first tactic here is to compare the known succession rates of *ordinary* consuls with those of suffect consuls. If we assume that both *ordinary* and suffect consuls had on average a similar number of sons surviving to consular age, then the results

Table 3.9. *Few suffect consuls had consular sons*

Suffect consuls with:	AD 70–96 *a*	131–160 *b*	193–235 *c*	less certain date *d*
	(per cent)			
A Consular son only	15	8	12	11
B Consular son and grandson	7	9	2	2
C Consular grandson and/or great-grandson only	8	5	6	4
TOTAL*	31	22	19	18
n =	72	64	52	44

* Totals are derived from raw numbers and may therefore diverge slightly from the sum of percentages.

are striking. In the second and early third centuries AD, over half (68 %, 53 %) of the sons of suffect consuls who survived to consular age, did not become suffect consul.[28] Secondly, this is a minimum estimate, since *ordinary* consuls themselves probably had more surviving sons than were successful in politics. We do not know whether sons of suffect, and of *ordinary* consuls chose not to enter political life, or whether some of them were systematically disfavoured by emperors, who preferred to encourage and promote men without consular antecedents.

Ordinary and suffect consuls compared. Table 3.10 shows up yet

[28] We are doing here what we did in our comparison of inner elite consuls, other consuls and praetors in the Republic (see above, p. 62). We subtract the known succession rate of suffect consuls from the known succession rate (SRP – Table 3.7, row D) of *ordinary* consuls, and express it as a proportion of *ordinary* consuls' succession rate (SRP). The figure for *ordinary* consuls' succession in AD 70–96 (28 %) was very low, for political reasons.

AD 70–96: $\frac{28-22}{28} = 21\%$; AD 131–160: $\frac{53-17}{53} = 68\%$; AD 193–235: $\frac{30-14}{30} = 53\%$.

That is, in the last calculation (to base 100): 100 *ordinary* consuls had 30 consular sons; 100 suffect consuls had 14 consular sons and presumably 16 politically unsuccessful sons: at least 16/30 = 53 % of suffect consuls' sons surviving to consular age did not become consul.

Table 3.10. *The depth of consular generations in the Principate.*
Ordinary *and suffect consuls compared**

How many generations of consuls† (out of seven)?	Ordinary consuls		Suffect consuls				All consuls	
	AD 18–54	131–160 193–235‡	70–96	131–160	193–235	less certain date	18–54	70–235
	a	*b*	*c*	*d*	*e*	*f*	*g*	*h*
				(per cent)				
A one only	8	13	61	63	63	71	22	54
B two adjacent	25	29	15	13	19	13	24	17
C two not adjacent	13	8	7	8	6	7	8	7
D three	29	17	7	8	8	7	24	10
E four	17	23	8	6	2	2	16	8
F five or six	8	10	1	3	2	0	5	3
G TOTAL	100	100	99	101	100	100	99	99
n =	24	52	72	64	52	44	37	297

* The data cover great-grandfather, grandfather and father of consuls, their sons, grandsons and great-grandsons in the male line only. Our research thus covered seven generations *tuvwxyz*. Consuls were investigated from generation *w*; i.e. those known in one generation only are known in *w* only; those known in two adjacent generations only are known in *vw* or *wx*.
† Either *ordinary* or suffect consuls.
‡ There was no significant difference between the figures from each of these periods; the cohort of AD 70–96 of *ordinary* consuls was omitted, since there were only 12 *ordinary* consuls in our sample.

again the striking difference between *ordinary* and suffect consuls. At least half the *ordinary* consuls reviewed (cols. *a* and *b*) came from families which had at least three consuls in seven generations. By contrast, over three fifths of all the suffect consuls sampled (row A) had no traceable direct ascendant or descendant within a century before or after holding office. Their families, like those of Seneca, Tacitus and Pliny, made a single appearance on the political stage and then disappeared. Several qualifications need to be made. A significant minority of *ordinary* consuls were sons of suffect consuls ('Table 3.5); the extra number of consulships available in the Principate obviously made it statistically easier for some families to have consuls in successive generations than it had been in the

Republic. In each of our sample periods, more than half of all *ordinary* consuls were sons of consuls; yet by and large, in spite of their increased statistical opportunity to become consul, in most periods only a modest proportion of *ordinary* consuls had a consular son (Table 3.6). There was a disjunction between consular ascent and consular descent. Yet we should not exaggerate; Table 3.10 shows considerable persistence by some aristocratic families in the political elite over several generations under the emperors. Well-known individual cases (such as the Brutii Praesentes) may have helped preserve the image of a hereditary aristocracy. Finally, the apparently brief appearance of suffect consuls on the political stage may be exaggerated, simply because we do not know enough about senators-never-consul.[29]

Senators-never-consul. We know the names of perhaps about half of all the senators-never-consul appointed during the Principate (31 BC–AD 270). We have already noted that their inclusion in the analysis of the direct ascendants and descendants of consuls makes very little difference to our results (see note 21). In short, there is very little corroborative testimony for the proposition that sons of consuls became senators-never-consul.

This conclusion is implicit in two well-known pieces of research, by Hammond and Lambrechts. Hammond reported the origin by region of known senators, including consuls, AD 69–235 (see Table 3.15 in the appendix to this chapter). His precise conclusions depend on the reliability of the attributions of origin, which are often debatable, and on the assumption that the unknown origins of known and unknown senators were similar to those whose origins were known.[30] But his general picture seems valid and clear. The proportion of senators of provincial origin grew steadily from the beginning of the first century AD to the beginning of the third century. At the beginning of the Principate there had been no provincial senators. In AD 69–79, 17% of known senators whose origins are also known were of provincial origin, and came chiefly (70%) from the western provinces. In AD 193–212, over half (57%) of known senators whose origins are also known came from the provinces; almost three

---

[29] In the Appendix to this chapter we try to estimate the effect of missing evidence on our deductions about consuls, on the extreme and improbable assumption that unknown consuls were as likely to have had consular sons as known consuls. It seems significant that succession rates of consuls of uncertain date were lower than those whose date is known. But that too could be a trick of the evidence.

[30] M. Hammond, 'Composition of the senate A.D. 68–235', *Journal of Roman Studies* 47 (1957) 77. Hammond reported the known origins by region of 47% of known senators including consuls (N = 4,462); his numbers are higher than Eck's (note 21 above), because of considerable double-counting, which arose from attributing senators to more than one period over their probable life-span in the senate.

fifths of these (58%) were from eastern provinces, and over a fifth (23%) came from north Africa. These results show vividly how the composition of the senate changed. Yet Hammond's proffered explanation, 'biological failure' or as we would call it low fertility, seems doubtful in the light of the evidence which we have presented; and it is insufficient to explain why places at the top of the political elite were taken by successive waves of provincials from different regions.

Lambrechts' register of senators AD 117–192 including consuls, yields similar results.[31] We reanalysed his data to compare senators at the beginning of his period (AD 117–138, N = 322) with those at the end of the period (AD 180–192, N = 238). Only a quarter (26%) of those living at the end of the period had known senatorial ascendants living two generations earlier; seen the other way, only one fifth of those senators known in the first period had senatorial descendants two generations later. Once again the register is seriously incomplete. But the rate of disappearance was about twice that found over similar stretches of time in the English peerage 1325–1640.[32]

What is the likelihood that the data missing from our surviving lists of senators-never-consul would radically contradict our central proposition, that the Roman senate was to a considerable extent non-hereditary? Briefly we must return to three arguments which we used in the last chapter. First, the evidence from the Principate also confirms the unsurprising principle, that succession rates were highest among those with the highest status (*ordinary* consuls). Secondly, the corollary of this is that those with lower status, suffect consuls, had lower succession rates. By extension, senators-never-consul presumably had even lower rates of succession. Our third argument is that there was more marginal than long-range upward mobility; that is, in normal circumstances, sons of non-senators stood a greater chance of becoming senator-never-consul than of becoming consul.[33] These three arguments taken together (and the evidence

[31] P. Lambrechts, *La composition du sénat romain (117–192)* (Antwerp, 1936), nos. 2–323, 1019–1256. We doubt if recent modifications or additions would substantially change our conclusions.

[32] 44% of English peers survived in the direct line (father–son) over a 65-year period; that is our calculation from data given by Stone 1965: 769. Other comparisons are difficult, since English titles survived if necessary through brothers; but then we often do not know if Roman senators of the same name descended from each other only in a direct line. Among English barons, over two 75-year periods 1325–1400, 1425–1500, 47% and 49% survived in the male line against 22% among Roman senators AD 117–192. With all due adjustments, the difference seems significant. Cf. K. B. Macfarlane, *The Nobility of Later Mediaeval England* (Oxford, 1973) 173–5.

[33] For a similar argument, see Chapter 2, p. 67 above.

collated by Hammond – see Table 3.15 in the appendix to this chapter) should prevent us from thinking that the lower levels of the Roman senate were filled by politically unsuccessful sons of consuls or of senators-never-consul, or by their grandsons and great-grandsons.[34]

That is enough of figures. We must start searching for explanations. What made succession rates in the Roman aristocracy so low? But before we embark on that, we want briefly to turn aside and estimate senators' average expectation of life.

EXCURSUS

How long did senators live?

At several stages in our discussion, we need to know how many Roman senators survived to compete for the consulship. Surprisingly, we have three co-ordinates which allow us to estimate senators' average expectation of life. First, entry into the senate during the Principate was normally restricted to twenty men elected as quaestors at a minimum age of twenty-five years. It was apparently common to hold offices (quaestorship, praetorship and consulship) at the minimum age.[35] We may reasonably leave the co-option (*adlectio*) of mature men out of account; it was used occasionally to top up the senate, especially by the emperors Vespasian, Marcus Aurelius and Septimius Severus; but it was not a major method of normal recruitment.[36]

---

[34] At this stage more speculative arithmetic seems unnecessary. The rate of Social Reproduction in Politics (SRP) of *ordinary* consuls reached a peak of 53% for the cohort of AD 131–160 (Table 3.7, row D) and for suffect consuls a peak of 22% for the cohort of AD 70–96 (Table 3.9, rows A + B). We should raise these figures a little to allow for consuls' sons becoming senators-never-consul, but not so much as to leave fewer vacancies at that level than higher up (argument 3). We should bear in mind also the low proportion of sons of *ordinary* consuls who became suffect consul (Table 3.7, row C).

[35] There was probably more variation in the age of appointment than this sentence implies. See the cautionary remarks and well-chosen examples of Syme 1958: vol. 2, 652–6. The evidence is set out by J. Morris 1964: 316ff. He listed the age of or time-gap between offices held by 180 consuls. He assumed that all lower offices were reached at the minimum age, which prejudices the worth of his conclusions. In fact, between AD 18 and 235, we know the ages at consulship of only 34 consuls (excluding emperors and their heirs), and those whose ages we know are unlikely to form an unbiased sample. That said, a minority of consuls, probably predominantly patricians, reached the consulship at ages 32/4. Patricians comprised less than 14% of our sample of dated consuls. It is reasonable to deduce from Morris' data that a large group of consuls reached office at the end of the minimum interval between offices, that is at age 40, *if* they held their first office at the minimum age. On the normal age of quaestors: Dio 52.20; D. 50.4.8 – Ulpian.

[36] Festus (*sv adlecti*): '[senators] are said to be co-opted (*adlecti*) among the Romans, if they are taken into the senate from the equestrian order, because of a shortage'. A. Chastagnol, 'Latus clavus et adlectio; l'accès des hommes nouveaux au sénat

146

Secondly, twenty quaestors were elected each year. Thirdly, it is normally reckoned that the senate comprised six hundred members.

These three co-ordinates, taken together, imply an average expectation of life at age 25 of a further 30 years (20 entrants × 30 years = 600 members). Is an average expectation of life of 30 years at age 25 (e_{25} = 30) demographically probable? According to the UN model life tables, which set out standard patterns of mortality, an expectation of life of 30 more years at age 25 implies an average expectation of life at birth of about 30 years (e_0 = 30)[37] A similar expectation of life at birth prevailed among European ruling families and British ducal families in the sixteenth and seventeenth centuries. In families closely associated with the British peerage as a whole, life expectancy at birth was slightly higher; it was 36 years for those born in the late sixteenth century, and 32 years for those born in the seventeenth century.[38] In spite of the differences and the fluctuations, Roman senators seem demographically comparable with these later groups. But for the moment, it is sufficient that the three co-ordinates produce demographically reasonable results, and corroborate what is normally assumed about the size of the senate (see Table 3.11).[39]

We can go further and use the model life tables to estimate the number of senators in each age group and the survivors to exact ages (see Table 3.11). Of course, such estimates can serve only as a rough guide; sudden outbreaks of disease or persecution would have reduced the size of the senate; so too would any policy of admitting *quaestors* at significantly later ages. From Table 3.12 (col. *a*), we can see that only 15 out of 20 quaestors (77%) would on average have survived to the age of 40, which was probably the most common age for the consulship in the Principate (see note 35). Some

romain sous le haut-empire', *Revue historique de droit français et étranger* 53 (1975) 375ff cites 35 known co-opted senators from the period AD 96–192. On the size of the senate, see Dio 54.13.

[37] Average expectation of life at birth is a conventional summary statistic. It may be confusing, because in pre-industrial populations, infant mortality is so high that median expectancy of life at age 1 is 42 years (e_1 = 42), when e_0 = 30. For UN Model Life Tables, see 'Methods of population projections by age and sex', *UN Population Studies* 26 (New York, 1956) or more recently A. J. Coale and P. Demeny *Regional Model Life Tables and Stable Populations* (Princeton, 1966).

[38] For references, see Chapter 2 note 52. In the eighteenth and nineteenth centuries, average expectation of life at birth gradually rose in north-western Europe and the USA to levels never reached in ancient Rome.

[39] G. Barbieri *L'albo senatorio da Settimio Severo a Carino* (Rome, 1952) 415–31 reckoned that the size of the senate under the Severans (AD 193–217) had increased, because the number of known senators totals more than 900. This is not necessarily so. First, the knowable universe of senators for AD 193–217 is 600 (existing senators) + entrants per year (20) × length of period of years (24) = 1,080 without adlections. Barbieri may be right, but he has insufficient evidence. Similarly, F. Vittinghoff (*Gnomon* 29 (1957) 110–11) wrongly assumed an existing senate of *c.* 800 members in AD 190 with an annual entry of 20, plus adlections. Secondly, some of these men thought to be senators may not have been full active members of the senate, but members of the senatorial order (see below, p. 192).

Table 3.11. *Probable age composition of the senate in the Principate**

Age (in years)	If average expectation of life at birth was:	
	30 years† *a*	32.5 years† *b*
	Number of senators	
25–29	96	97
30–39	171	173
40–49	137	142
50–59	97	105
60+	81	93
TOTAL	582	610

* On the assumption that 20 men entered the senate each year aged 25 years.
† Derived from UN model life tables.

Table 3.12. *How many senators survived?*

Survivors to exact age (in years)	If average expectation of life at birth was 30 years			
	25 yr olds *a*	30 yr olds *b*	40 yr olds *c*	50 yr olds *d*
	(per cent)			
25 (quaestors)	100			
30 (available for praetorship)	93	100		
40 (available for consulship)	77	83	100	
50	59	63	76	100
60	38	41	49	65

favoured aristocrats (especially patricians) were selected earlier, but they were a small minority. Complementarily, some senators fell out of favour and reached the consulship late. We do not have enough evidence to know the average age of consuls. But if 40 is acceptable as the most common age for the consulship, then after about AD 70, at least half of the surviving senators and over half the surviving ex-praetors reached the consulship (Table 3.1, col. *g*).

IV THE CAREER PYRAMID – AMBITION AND WITHDRAWAL

Honours and magistracies

Augustus and his successors secured political stability partly by supervising the old oligarchic system of power-sharing so that it worked to their advantage. They enforced the rules of minimum age for office and the orderly procession of senators' careers. Occasional waivers in favour of special candidates (putative heirs to the throne, patricians or favourites) were merely another symptom of emperors' power, a mechanism of control also used today in complex organisations.[40] The consulship was still sought after both as an honour in itself and as a step towards important positions. Modern historians sometimes belittle the consulships of the Principate, both *ordinary* and suffect, as being in no way equal to the senior magistracies of the Republic. Although the form remained, the power and prestige of the office had changed.

True, consuls' access to popular favour, to immense provincial profits and to military glory were all sharply curtailed. Popular elections were abolished at the end of Augustus' reign and transferred to the senate; the heart had been taken out of them before then; from the reign of Nero onwards, consuls were formally appointed by the emperor. But most quaestors, tribunes, aediles and praetors continued to be elected by the senate and elections were still being vigorously contested at the beginning of the second century AD.[41] Governors continued to receive bribes and to make money out of the exercise of office; witness their willingness to pay for the privilege of appointment. For example, Vespasian's mistress is reported to have made a lot of money from the sale of 'magistracies, procuratorships and army commands...' (Dio 65.14). Imperial agents (*procurators*) and

[40] On this and other functions of rules, see A. Gouldner, *Patterns of Industrial Bureaucracy* (London, 1955) 157–80, 237ff.
[41] See A. H. M. Jones, *Studies in Roman Government and Law* (Oxford, 1960) 29ff. Electoral bribery would have been pointless unless there was both competition and a chance of swaying the electors.

provincial embassies reported 'bad' governors to the emperor and senate; knowledge of this doubtless served as a brake on extortion; but corruption and profiteering in the provinces persisted; we know of forty prosecutions of goverors for extortion in the first century, and our list is certainly incomplete.[42] Generals could still earn the insignia of a triumph, though the defensive policies of the emperors restricted opportunities for military glory; besides, they fought in the emperor's name. The general Corbulo, stopped from further victories against Germans beyond the Rhine, lest his reputation endanger the emperor's, pined for the freedom which generals had in the Republic (Tacitus, *Annals* 11.20).

Roman aristocrats must have been bitterly aware of how much power and prestige they had lost, now that they had to subserve an emperor. In AD 41, after the murder of Caligula, seventy years after the establishment of monarchy, the senate debated the restoration of the old Republic. While they bickered, the palace guard acted and saluted Claudius as emperor. Yet for all their memories of the past, most senators lived in the present and vigorously pursued the honours which were available.

The pyramidal structure of careers kept many senators in competition with each other for fifteen years, throughout the prime of their manhood, from the age of twenty-five to forty. Throughout these years, for many senators there remained doubt about the highest status which they would achieve, and doubt about the age at which they would achieve it, and the posts which they would attain. In the meantime, many spent a fortune on an ostentatious life-style commensurate with their social position and with their ambitions, in the pursuit of prestige, honours and royal favour. Divisive ambition thus supplemented terror as a mechanism of control.

All this can perhaps be best understood, if we put ourselves in the shoes of the young men who were candidates for the office of quaestor, and so for entry into the senate. Typically, a candidate who was a son of a senator had already served as a junior official (one of twenty *vigintiviri*) in the city of Rome, and had spent some time as an army officer (one of six tribunes in a legion) in a distant frontier province.[43]

---

[42] For a complete discussion of the evidence on extortion in the first century, see P. A. Brunt, 'Charges of provincial maladministration', *Historia* 10 (1961) 189–227. As in the Republic, one of the functions of such cases must have been to fix a rough norm of condonable corruption – a norm which was broken by both governors and accusers.

[43] This was the formal structure. But not all sons of senators who became senators had served as junior officials (*vigintiviri*) in Rome; and there is some dispute

The Roman elite remained, at least notionally, true to its military traditions. But the figures which we have already presented suggest that only a minority, even if it was a substantial minority of the successful candidates were sons of senators. The other competitors to enter the senate were young men from wealthy families of high social status, who had received formal permission from the emperor to stand as candidate for office, which they often signified by wearing a tunic with a broad purple stripe (*latus clavus*); permission to wear this was also by grant of the emperor, usually secured through the good offices of the candidates' relatives, friends or patron.[44] Both sets of candidates, sons of senators and outsiders, had themselves chosen to compete (self-selection) and had been selected from a much wider circle of potential candidates. And at each successive stage of their careers, quaestorship, praetorship, consulship, if they got that far, they had to compete both with their co-evals and with those who had been

among scholars as to how seriously military service was taken, or whether it was a normal step in a senator's career. Mommsen 1887: vol. 1, 513 thought that the tribunate was compulsory for senators and therefore lost its military character. E. Birley, 'Senators in the emperors' service', *Proceedings of the British Academy* 29 (1953) 197–214, argued from the gaps in known careers that many senators did no military service. Pliny, in his *Panegyric* (15) of Trajan implied that many senators, in contrast to Trajan, took a quick look at a camp or served only briefly and half-heartedly. But a panegyric may provide poor testimony. Sons of senators who wanted to opt out of politics may have done so before holding any junior office; others presumably held office and decided such a life was not for them.

44 On the mode of entry into the senate during the Principate, see Chastagnol 1975: 375ff. He argues that from Caligula's reign onwards all young entrants to the senate who were not sons of senators had first been marked out by receiving from the emperor the right to wear a tunic with a broad purple stripe. Known individual cases show that some young men were given this right, as the terms *lato clavo exornatus* (*ILS* 4715) and *laticlavus* show; but it is not at all certain that all candidates received this grant before they were elected quaestor. Chastagnol puts more weight on a single passage of Dio than it can properly bear; Dio described Caligula's reaction to a crisis in AD 38, not the sudden birth of a permanent change in practice: 'Since the equestrian order was short of men, he (the emperor) summoned the leading men in birth and wealth from the whole empire, even from outside Italy, and enrolled them. And he even allowed some of them to wear senatorial dress, before they had held any public office which gives us entry to the senate, on the strength of their prospects. Previously, only sons of senators were allowed to do this, so it seems' (59.9). Even so, the extension of senatorial dress to non-senators is an interesting symptom of an early disjunction between status symbols and full membership of the senate (cf. p. 192 below). The trouble is that we know very little about how young men chose to become candidates and which candidates emperors allowed to stand for election. There is no adequate modern discussion of the subject, partly because it is generally assumed that all sons of senators proceeded automatically into the senate, and partly because the phrase 'permission was granted by the emperor' is wrongly considered as a solution to the problem of selection. How did emperors know which young men to select?

passed over in recent years, but were still in the race. We now have the benefit of hindsight and know who was successful; but we should temporarily set aside that knowledge and try to see their world as they saw it, enter their doubts and fears, and avoid treating their success as inevitable.

Unfortunately we know very little of the criteria of selection, although it is easy to imagine the canvassing by candidates themselves and by their patrons. The following extract from a letter by a senior senator on behalf of a young man, the son of a dead senator, who was seeking election to the office of quaestorship at the beginning of the second century AD, gives us several insights.

Pliny to Fundanus greetings
More than ever I wish you were here in Rome now. Please come. I need a friend to share my prayers, my efforts and my anxiety. Julius Naso is standing for office; he is one of many candidates, and they are good men, who will be difficult to beat. A triumph if he does. So I am on tenterhooks, torn between hope and fear. I don't feel that I am an ex-consul; instead it feels as if I'm running again as a candidate for all those offices.

Naso deserves this hard work of mine, because of the affection which he has long shown me. To be sure, I was not a friend of his father's – the difference between our ages made that impossible. But when I was quite young, his father was pointed out to me as someone to admire...He was a man of distinction and character; the memory of his reputation should help his son. But many of today's senators did not know him; many knew him, but save their respect for the living. And so Naso, proud as he is of his father's achievements, cannot depend on them in the elections; he must fight his own fight and rely on his own exertions.

This is what he has been doing all along, as if he foresaw the present need. He has carefully made friends, and then taken care of the friendships. He chose me as his special friend and model...When I am speaking in court, he stands at my side, full of concern; when I give readings, he sits next to me. As soon as my little writings are published, immediately he shows the greatest interest...And now his brother has recently died, I must take his place and do what he would have done...since he is deprived of the help of a brother, he is left only with his friends.

I insist, therefore, that you come to Rome and add your vote to mine. It will be a great help to show you off, and to go around canvassing with you...In sum, if Naso gets elected, the credit will be his; but if he fails, the defeat is mine. (Pliny, *Letters* 6.6; cf. 2.9 and Cicero, *In Defence of Caelius* 72)

Clearly young men may have been favoured for various virtues or vices besides ability: flattery, charm, reliability, dullness, honesty, lack of ambition, to name but a few. We should be cautious not to fill the gaps in our knowledge about selection with meritocratic assumptions drawn from the ideals of modern societies. Sometimes 'idle' and 'disreputable' men of distinguished birth were preferred to industrious new men, and, wrote Seneca, 'not without reason' (*On Benefits* 4.30). There is no evidence that emperors systematically set about choosing men 'of the highest ability' to govern the empire 'efficiently'.[45] Pliny (*Letters* 10.12) pleaded with the emperor Trajan for the promotion of Attius Sura to a praetorship on the grounds that there was a vacancy, that it would be a favour to him (Pliny) and that the man was of good birth, and had behaved with integrity when he was poor. We do not know if he was successful, but clearly merit and achievement were not the only reasons worth pressing. To be sure, there was a difference between honorary office and important provincial governorships.

We should beware of arguing that men were promoted because they were able, when the only testimony which survives consists of men's names and their posts. We are not asserting that ability and achievement were disregarded or that they were unimportant, but rather that other criteria were also important and that mostly we just do not know why some people were promoted and others passed over. Efficiency, for which there is no word in Latin, was not the prime objective of Roman rule; innovations were a threat to the established order.

Nor were all senators hell-bent on promotion to top jobs. Some might not want a life of administration spent outside Rome and Italy, in the provinces. Indeed the competitiveness of some may have helped induce a compensatory retreatism in others, especially among those who had already lost an election, or feared that they would lose, or feared that success would expose them to risk. In a way, this retreatism may have been encouraged by emperors. We get the impression that some sons of nobles, scions of distinguished families, were given early marks of high status; for example, they might be the candidates nominated by the emperor and therefore elected without contest. But they were also typically kept away from provinces in which legions were stationed. We have not tested this proposition statistically, but patricians provide us with an illumi-

---

[45] This is the basic and unwarranted assumption of most career analysts, such as, for example, E. Birley (1953) and W. Eck, 'Beförderungskriterien innerhalb den senatorischen Laufbahn', *ANRW* (Berlin, 1974) vol. 2.1, 158ff. The recent discussion by B. Campbell, 'Who were the Viri Militares?' *Journal of Roman Studies* 65 (1975) 11–31 is much more balanced; see also the remarks by P. A. Brunt on the equestrian governors of Egypt (*ibid.* 124ff).

nating extreme case. Patricians were descendants of a small set of noble families, periodically added to by emperors. It seems that patrician senators were often appointed consul at the early age of about 32/33 years, that is before they were old enough to have gained military experience as commander of a legion.[46] And without that military experience, in the normal course of events, men were not made governors of important military provinces. Patricians were apparently 'kicked upstairs', given preferential promotion but prevented from being powerful.

But most senators faced competition at each successive stage of their careers. There were always more senators qualified to be candidates for office, than there were posts to be filled. In Pliny's time (*c.* AD 100), as we have seen, elections in the senate were hotly contested. Candidates gave dinner-parties, gifts and money (Pliny, *Letters* 6.19). We have shown that consular origin was neither a necessary nor a sufficient condition for achieving the consulship. Many sons of consuls did not become consul; many men without consular antecedents became consul. The field was wide open. Competition inevitably fostered channels of selection and criteria of judgement. A man's success must have depended upon his social origins, the status of his family, on his life-style, his reputation, his connections and on his achievements. We do not know the relative weight attached to each factor. But the political elite living in the city of Rome was small. Most members of the elite, men and women, must have known, or known about, each other. Gossip doubtless helped establish or ruin reputations. The extract we have just quoted from a letter by Pliny showed how hard some candidates worked for political success. The following extract, although it idealises the past, reveals the conflict between what passed as 'merit' and patronage.

There are some old men still alive who have often told me about that electoral procedure: the candidate's name was read out amid total silence; he then made a speech on his own behalf, detailing his career and naming referees who would vouch for him, such as the commanding officer under whom he served in the army or the governor whose quaestor he had been, and both if possible. Then he called on some of the voters, who said a few sensible words in his support, which were more useful than entreaties. Occasionally, the candidate would raise objections to an opponent's birth, age or way of life; the senate listened with judicious attention. And so merit prevailed more often than popularity. But now all this has been ruined by unbridled favouritism, and the senate has taken refuge in the secret ballot, as though it will be a remedy... (Pliny, *Letters* 3.20)

[46] This is the argument of J. Morris (1953). It is repeated, for example, by Alföldy 1976: 274ff and 1977: 37ff.

The transfer of the selection of consuls from election by popular assembly to appointment by the emperor did not stifle competition; it merely changed its locus and style. It left more to influence behind doors. So also with the appointment of governors to imperial provinces. The emperor himself had the final say, and probably had his personal impressions about many senators from seeing them at receptions, in the senate and at banquets. But the emperor must also have depended upon informants, on pressures from candidates' patrons, and on his palace officials (knights, ex-slaves and slaves); and some emperors no doubt responded to the persuasions of a wife or mistress, and to the hints of gossiping chamberlains.[47] One story illustrates how the emperor could be the victim of his sources. The emperor Claudius was holding court; a group of provincials were noisily accusing a governor of taking unreasonable bribes (the man was in fact an equesterian procurator who had taken over from the senatorial governor who had himself been convicted of extortion; but that makes no difference to our present point); because of the uproar, Claudius could not understand what the provincials were saying, and asked those near him; his trusted confidant, the ex-slave Narcissus said that they were thanking the governor. Claudius believed him and said: 'let him govern for two more years' (Dio 60.33). The emperor was trying to use rational criteria related to achievement, but as so often in pre-industrial societies, personal interest and the fear of despotic power obstructed the free flow of information.[48]

So far, we have concentrated on the consulship and the other traditional landmarks of a senatorial career, the quaestorship and praetorship. These were important, because they gave access to the additional offices allotted by the senate or granted by the emperor: the governorship of a province, the command of a legion, administrative posts in Italy, each one of which gave the incumbent limited

[47] We want to stress here the irrational, personal influences on the emperor's information and judgement. Apart from the well-known remarks about the manipulation of Claudius by his wives and ex-slaves (Suetonius, *Claudius* 29), there are several other known examples of influential wives and mistresses of emperors. For example, the future emperor Hadrian is said to have obtained a governorship and a second consulship through the influence of Trajan's wife, Plotina (SHA, *Hadrian* 4); and the concubine of Antoninus Pius reportedly procured the prefecture of the praetorian guard for Fabius Cornelius Repentinus (SHA, *Antoninus Pius* 8). See Friedländer 1922: vol. 1, 35ff and 65ff; cf. the influence of eunuchs at court, Hopkins, *Conquerors and Slaves* 172ff.

[48] In some contemporary under-developed states, rulers have tried to improve the flow of information upwards, by becoming more autocratic; but this tactic often proves counter-productive. See D. E. Apter, 'System, process and politics in economic development', in B. F. Hoselitz and W. E. Moore, edd., *Industrialisation and Society* (Paris, 1963) 135–58.

opportunity for profit and glory, and marked a man's progress up the steps of a senatorial career (*cursus honorum*). For many senators, the praetorship was important only because it opened the door to several profitable positions; the consulship was at once an enhancement of status and an opportunity for further advancement. The system entailed ambitious senators in working for several years under surveillance, on trial and at risk. The rewards in wealth and status were often considerable. But that political success took time and effort to achieve.

At this stage, some analysis of senatorial careers is essential. We need to know what was typical and what was exceptional. The task is difficult, for at least two reasons. First, there is a mass of testimony over which scholars have long laboured. But this testimony, which represents only a small proportion of all careers, is irremediably biased towards the successful, since it was the successful who were most likely to be commemorated in the honorary inscriptions which provide so much of our evidence.[49] Secondly, when we find a career recorded, we cannot tell whether the list of recorded honours was final, or whether the man went on to hold further offices, or soon died, or whether some posts in his career were for whatever reason omitted. It is necessary to stress these points, because modern scholars have sometimes rearranged the recorded order of Roman career positions to fit in with modern ideas of what was normal for Roman senators; and they have often unwarily analysed what we know about senatorial careers, as though what is known were representative of the unknown; similarly modern criminologists once used incautiously to assume that recorded crimes were similar to unrecorded crimes, and that convicted criminals were representative of law-breakers who escaped punishment.

In order to illustrate the testimony available, we have arbitrarily chosen four apparently complete careers of successful senators. They are set out on pages 158–9. These four careers illustrate what we can

---

[49] Prosopographers might find two steps in normal statistical research procedures helpful: (1) see how representative a sample is of the universe from which it is drawn; (2) look for disproof of each proposition advanced. It follows that one should not base a conclusion solely on corroborative illustrations, even when culled from ancient sources. The statement most sons of consuls became consuls cannot be proved correct from illustrations (e.g. C. Iulius Erucius Clarus Vibianus, *ordinary* consul of AD 193 and son of a consul) any more than the statement that all/most Bulgarians are blind could be proved by illustrating the point with 1, 2 or even 1,000 corroborative examples. This point would not be worth making, but for the fact that many widely accepted 'conclusions' from prosopographical studies have been arrived at by similarly weak arguments. But see Campbell 1975:12ff for trenchant criticisms of one such conclusion.

deduce from known careers. Politically successful Romans identified themselves by the official posts which they had held; and others identified them in large honorary inscriptions, publicly displayed, by the same criteria. Very successful senators spent many years, often more than ten years, at work outside Rome and Italy, in the provinces. But how typical was that? Did senators who became consul have different civil or military careers from those who did not become consul?[50] We can approach an answer schematically by setting the number of praetors available each year against the number of posts which were available for each set or cohort of ex-praetors.

In Table 3.13, we set out all the official positions regularly available for senators in the provinces and in the city of Rome in the mid-second century AD. By that period, there were often eighteen praetors each year, though the numbers appointed may have fluctuated.[51] There were (see Table 3.13 and Figure 3.1) about 18 jobs for ex-praetors, each lasting one year in the senatorial provinces (Table 3.13: B), and on average about 12 jobs, each lasting three years, in the imperial provinces (Table 3.13: c + D) plus 2 important jobs, also lasting about three years, held in the city of Rome (the prefectures of the treasuries). There were also perhaps up to 10 lesser jobs held by ex-praetors, normally perhaps lasting one year, concerned with the care of Italian roads, and with the city of Rome's food supply (Table 3.13: $J_{1, 2, 4}$), and an unknown number of jobs

---

[50] This was a question posed by Alföldy 1976: 277ff; cf. 1977: 54ff. His question was better than his answer, which is spoilt by a false assumption. 'Thus there can be no doubt that access to the consulate was possible only by a patrician career or by a praetorian career with offices in the emperor's service, and that a plebeian senator at the end of his career, as a rule had to be governor of an imperial province [D] or prefect of the treasury [J_{5-6}], or curator of an Italian main road [J_4] in order to be consul' (p. 278, cf. our Table 3.13). For the period AD 138–161, he reckoned there were 210–215 consuls, and that there were between 200 and 225 candidates qualified either by patrician origins or by having held one of the high administrative offices (listed above). But Alföldy did not take into account that a significant proportion of such men in known careers held more than one of his qualifying offices (e.g. *ILS* 1005, 1020, 1024, 1041, 2927). Therefore his conclusion, like several in this article, was too sweeping. Even so, it seems probable that most, although by no means all, consuls had filled one or more of these important posts, or were patricians..

[51] Before AD 42, the number of praetors per year fluctuated; that is clear from Dio (58.20; 59.20; 60.10). After that, we cannot be certain. Some think the number of praetors was fixed at 18 per year. But that is incompatible with the known competition at elections; because of death, on average only 18 candidates would have survived to compete for the praetorship. The number of consulships fluctuated, and the number of praetors may have varied also, at least throughout the first century AD, even if later it stabilised at 18 per year. For a general discussion, see Mommsen 1887: vol. 2, 202ff.

The senatorial aristocracy under the emperors

Four Careers of Consuls – typical of surviving recorded careers

(A) Cn. Julius Agricola, son of
Lucius. (Consul in 77)
one of the twenty officials
tribune of a legion (in
Britain)
quaestor in the senatorial
province of Asia
tribune of the people
praetor
chosen to check the gifts in
temples
sent to recruit soldiers
commander of the 20th
legion (in Britain)
governor of the imperial
province of Aquitania (in
Gaul)
consul, priest, appointed one
of the patricians
governor of the imperial
province of Britain

(B) Q. Lollius Urbicus, son of
Marcus. (Consul by 138)
one of the four men in
charge of roads
tribune of the 22nd legion
(in Mainz, Germany)
quaestor of the city – in
Rome
legate to the governor of the
senatorial province of Asia
tribune of the people, the
candidate commended by
the emperor
praetor, the candidate
commended by the emperor
commander of the 10th
legion (in Vienna, Austria)
legate of the emperor
Hadrian in the Jewish
expedition for which he
was decorated with the
spear (*hasta pura*) and a
golden crown

consul, fetial priest
governor of the imperial
province of Lower
Germany (with two
legions)
governor of the imperial
province of Britain
prefect of the city of Rome

(C) L. Burbuleius Optatus
Ligarianus. (Consul before
138)
one of the three men in
charge of capital cases
tribune of the 9th Spanish
legion (probably in Britain)
quaestor in the senatorial
province of Pontus and
Bithynia (Turkey)
aedile of the people
praetor
curator of the roads Clodia,
Cassia and Ciminia
(minor Italian roads)
curator of the cities of Narbo
(southern Gaul), Ancona
(eastern Italy) and
Tarracina (south of
Rome)
commander of the 16th
legion (in Samosata, Syria)
logistes (curator/supervisor)
(in Syria)
governor of the senatorial
province of Sicily
prefect of the treasury of
Saturn in Rome
consul
curator of public works and
places
governor of the imperial
province of Cappadocia
under the emperors
Hadrian and Antoninus
Pius

governor of the imperial
province of Syria, in
which he died
(D) L. Julius Marinus Caecilius
Simplex. (Consul 101/2)
one of the four men in
charge of roads
tribune of the 4th legion (in
Syria)
quaestor in the senatorial
province of Macedonia
aedile of the people
praetor
legate to the governor of the
senatorial province of
Cyprus
legate to his father, governor

of the senatorial province of
Pontus-Bithynia (Turkey)
curator of the road to Tibur
(in Italy)
Arval brother – a priesthood
commander of the 11th
legion (in Germany)
governor of the imperial
province of
Lycia-Pamphylia
(Turkey) under the
emperor Trajan
governor of the senatorial
province of Achaea
(Greece)
consul

Sources: A. R. Birley, *The Fasti of Roman Britain* (Oxford, 1981) 73ff and 112ff; *ILS* 1026, 1065–1066.

as curators or financial supervisors of provincial and Italian cities.[52] If these praetorian posts had been shared out equally, each praetor would have held 2.3 posts (excluding curatorships: B_2, J_3) and would have served less than four years in them.

We can now see how exceptional consuls' careers were, by comparing the number of official posts which they held with this notional average. Recent analyses of the known careers of (*a*) consuls and (*b*) consuls who went on to govern the so-called imperial provinces in which legions were stationed show that both of these sets had served in significantly more than their fair share of praetorian posts. Once again we should be cautious. These known careers cover less than 10% of (*a*) consuls and just less than 15% of (*b*) consular governors of imperial provinces; their known careers may be incomplete; and most important, the careers which are known may be biased towards particularly successful or hard-working consuls, whose chances of receiving honorary inscriptions setting out their careers in detail were increased with each successive post. For the

[52] See G. P. Burton, 'Curator rei publicae, towards a reappraisal', *Chiron* 9 (1979) 465ff. On the doubtful number of curators of roads, see Eck 1974: 191–2. In general, on minor senatorial offices: Mommsen 1887: vol. 2, 1077ff. The list given in Table 3.13 is schematic, and not accurate for all periods.

Table 3.13. *Senatorial administrators in the provinces about the year* AD 140

Rank and post	Tenure (years)	No. of posts	Place
	EX-QUAESTORS		
A Provincial quaestor	1	10	Africa, Asia, Achaea, Crete–Cyrene, Cyprus, Macedonia, Narbonensis, Pontus–Bithynia, Sicily, Spain–Baetica
	EX-PRAETORS		
B_1 Legate to governor of senatorial province	1	10 (out of 14)	As in A, except Africa 3, Asia 3, Sicily 1 (about 4 out of 14 were ex-quaestors)
B_2 Curators of towns	Ind.†	Varied	Especially Achaea and Asia Minor – often tied to legateship (B_1)
B_3 Governor of senatorial province	1	8	As in A, except Africa and Asia
C_1 Legal legate to governor of imperial province	3	2	Britain, Nearer Spain
C_2 Commander of a legion in an imperial province with a consular governor	3	23	Britain, Lower Moesia, Upper Pannonia, Syria (three legions each)
			Cappadocia, Lower Germany, Upper Germany, Upper Moesia, Syria–Palestine (two legions each)
			Nearer Spain (one legion)
D_1 Governor of an imperial province without legion	3	8	Aquitania, Belgica, Cilicia, Galatia, Lugdunensis, Lusitania, Lycia–Pamphylia, Thrace
D_2 Governor of an imperial province and commander of one legion	3	4	Arabia, Dacia, (Numidia),* Lower Pannonia
	EX-CONSULS		
Governor of imperial province with:			
E_1 no legion	3	1	Dalmatia
E_2 one legion	3	1	Nearer Spain
E_3 two legions	3	5	Cappadocia, Lower Germany, Upper Germany, Upper Moesia, Syria–Palestine
E_4 three legions	3	4	Britain, Lower Moesia, Upper Pannonia, Syria
F Governor of senatorial province	1	2	Africa, Asia

* In effect, though not formally, separately administered.
† Ind., indeterminate.

The career pyramid

Table 3.13a. *Senatorial administrative posts in the city of Rome and Italy*

		Tenure (years)	No. of posts
G	**BEFORE THE QUAESTORSHIP**		
	20 Junior officers: 3 moneyers, 4 in charge of streets in the city of Rome; 10 for judging cases; 3 for capital cases	1	20
	For quaestors in the year of office: 2 quaestors of the emperor; 4 quaestors for the consuls, 2 urban quaestors	1	8
H	Tribunes of the People	1	10
	Aediles	1	6
	Praetors in the year of office	1	(18)
J	**EX-PRAETORS**		
J₁	Prefect of the food distribution (usually a junior post)	1	2?
J₂	Curators of lesser roads Aurelia, Cassia–Clodia, Ciminia, Labicana–Latinae, Salaria, Valeria–Tiburtina	1	?5 variable
J₃	Curators of Italian towns	Ind.†	Sporadic
J₄	Curators of the major roads Aemilia, Appia, Flaminia	1	3?
J₅	Prefects of the military treasury	3	3
J₆	Prefects of the treasure of Saturn	2–3	2
K	**EX-CONSULS**		
	Curator of the water supply		1
	Curator of the Tiber's channel		1
	Curator of public works and sacred buildings		2
	(Italian judges (*iuridici*))*		4
	Prefect of the City		1

See also W. Eck, 'Beförderungskriterien innerhalb der senatorischen Laufbahn', in *ANRW* vol. 2.1 (Berlin 1974) 227–8.
* Abolished by AD 140; after AD 165 held by ex-praetors.
† Ind., indeterminate.

moment, let us leave such doubts on one side, and see where it leads us.

Table 3.14 sets out the number of official posts held by praetors who subsequently became consuls and consular governors of the imperial provinces in which legions were stationed. It is based on the known careers of 59 consuls (AD 69–138) and of 72 consular governors of these imperial provinces (AD 70–235),[53] Three conclusions may be

[53] Table 3.14 (cols *a* and *b*) is derived from Campbell 1975: 28–31, and (col. *c*) from Eck 1974:184ff. A considerable number of the consuls counted by Eck (col. *c*) became consular governors of imperial provinces (cols. *a + b*); in short, there

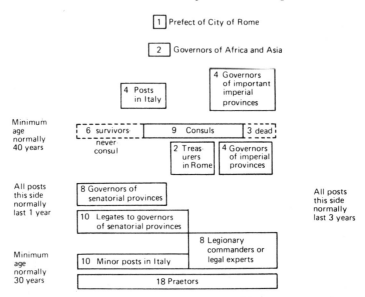

Figure 3.1. Schema of administrative offices held by ex-praetors (*c.* AD 140). This schema shows the average number of jobs available for each cohort of praetors. Vertical position implies sequence, but the normal order was often broken. Men moved from left to right and from right to left.

drawn. First, we should compare what we find with what we should expect by chance. The future consular governors of these imperial provinces on average served in praetorian posts much longer (6.5 years) than could be expected by chance (4.2 years). We calculated chance here by dividing the number and duration of posts available to ex-praetors by the number of ex-praetors.[54] These consular governors' occupancy of three-year posts (as legionary commanders, governors of lesser imperial provinces and as treasurers in the city of Rome) was also much higher (2.5 times higher) than chance. But

is overlap between the two samples. We excluded one of Campbell's cases (no. 73), because of its uncertain date. We also excluded the few extraordinary military commands which were not normal posts in an ex-praetor's career; we imagine that Eck did the same.

54 This comparison of what is observed and what is expected is a standard statistical procedure. For posts available to ex-praetors, see Table 3.13; only one third of the 42 three-year posts were available each year. We concluded that 28 one-year posts and 14 three-year posts were available for each cohort of praetors; we assumed that the number of praetors in the mid-second century AD was 18 per year, reduced to 15 on an average by death before the normal consular age of forty (see Table 3.12). We therefore divided 70 years of available praetorian service $(28 + (14 \times 3))$ by 16.5 praetors, to allow for this mortality; if all of these praetorian jobs were distributed equally, the length of each service would have been 4.2 years.

Table 3.14. *How many praetorian posts did politically successful praetors hold before their consulship?*

Number of praetorian posts held	Consular governors of imperial provinces (AD 70–235) Core posts only* *a*	Consular governors of imperial provinces (AD 70–235) All posts† *b*	Consuls (AD 69–138) All posts† *c*
0	4	2	Not given
1	10	8	Not given
2	23	19	13
3	16	20	19
4	12	11	15
5	3	5	6
6	4	4	5
7	0	1	1
8	0	2	0
A TOTAL (Number of holders)	72	72	59
B TOTAL (Number of posts held)	190	224	180
C Average number of praetorian posts held	2.8	3.1 (3.5)‡	(3.6)
D Average length of service in years	6.5	—	—

* Core posts include all posts listed in Table 3.13: BCDJ except curatorships of towns (B₂J₃) whose number and period of tenure are uncertain.

† All posts include core posts plus curatorships and other minor regular posts, but exclude extraordinary military commands.

‡ This figure in brackets is the average number of posts per person excluding those with one or no known posts; it is thus comparable with the figure in column *c*.

their occupancy of less important, single-year praetorian posts in senatorial provinces and in Italy was much lower (less than half) than chance.

This first conclusion leads to a second: the pattern of praetorian service in official posts was bi-polar. Some ex-praetors served in several posts; a significant proportion of consuls and consular governors of imperial provinces, whose careers are known, as we saw in Table 3.14, served in three or more praetorian posts.[55] But the number of official posts available to all praetors was limited. If some praetors served in several posts, other praetors served in none. Or if they did anything official, they served only in single-year posts in the senatorial provinces or in Italy.[56] Praetorian posts were not distributed equally among all praetors.

Thirdly, there was no single path to the top. The old view that senators were chosen early for specifically military careers is without foundation. But it does seem true that most future consuls later chosen to be governors of imperial provinces in which legions were stationed had served in the early part of their senatorial career as the commander of a legion.[57] But some praetorians served in only one, others in several posts; even among these future consular governors of imperial provinces, there was considerable variation: if we assume for the purposes of discussion that all three-year posts were held for a full term of three years, then one quarter of these future consular governors of imperial provinces (see Table 3.14) served for less than four years in praetorian posts; another quarter served nine years or more in praetorian posts. This variation must have reflected changing needs and circumstances, intrigue at court, and varying reports about a man's success and aptitudes.

Above all, we have to be wary because what we know about careers is very formal, fragmented and seriously biased towards the successful. Moreover, we should avoid conflating such patterns as we can now impose on the evidence with the historical actors' perceptions and expectations. To cite but one example of many, it has been claimed

[55] Eck (1974: 184ff) unfortunately did not list the number of consuls known to have held no or only one praetorian post. We cannot easily tell how complete such careers are. Does absence of information mean that a man held no posts, or only that the posts which he held were not listed in the surviving record? Alföldy (1977: 33ff and 327–45) listed 69 known careers of consuls AD 138–180. Of these, 57 out of 69 held two or more praetorian posts, and all 7 consuls who held no praetorian posts were patricians.

[56] Campbell (1975: 23ff; cf. Alföldy 1977: 53ff) came to a similar conclusion, but in a sharper form. Campbell reckoned that consular legates (AD 70–235) constituted a quarter (27%) of praetors but held half of the praetorian posts, and then extrapolated to the suggestion that half of all praetors filled all the praetorian posts. However, he seems to have omitted from his reckoning the (?) 10 annual legates to proconsular governors (Table 3.13: B_1); this omission somewhat undermines his first calculation and extrapolation; there were more praetorian posts available than he thought. But we agree with his basic point.

[57] Campbell (1975) demolished the old view about senatorial military specialists, but surely underestimated the importance of his own figure that 82% of known consular legates had been commanders of a legion.

that 'Every senator who was sent by the emperor to [govern] a praetorian [imperial] province could expect on the completion of his service to achieve the consulship in Rome.' This is doubly misleading: we know almost nothing of governors' subjective expectations, and the evidence cited to prove this proposition shows that only 76% of the known praetorian governors (N = 125 out of a universe of over 250, AD 69–138) are known to have become consuls.[58] The stated chances (at 76%) do seem high. But we must stress again that we are more likely to know the careers of those who later became consul. And besides, we really should preserve the distinction between what was probable and what was universal, between what people expected and what happened.

The separation of subjective expectation from what happened introduces a new dimension to our problem of understanding the impact of competitive struggle for honours and offices in the Roman aristocracy. How much do the patterns which we can now deduce from difficult data allow us to think that praetors, legionary commanders and provincial governors in senatorial and imperial provinces all perceived the same patterns? Did they perceive them with sufficient accuracy that once they had reached a certain post – whether as legionary commander or provincial governor – their anxieties were quietened, their prospects assured? We do not know; but there is a piece of testimony worth citing.

In the reign of Tiberius, it was proposed in the senate that the emperor should designate consuls five years ahead, giving automatic promotion to those appointed as commanders of legions. Tiberius and Tacitus (*Annals* 2.36) rightly saw that this threatened the emperor's power; it replaced divisive hope with certainty. The scheme was rejected. But the proposal itself shows how anxious praetors were about their chances. Soon afterwards their number was increased as was the number of consuls. This increase in the number of praetors must have satisfied most senators' ambitions to become praetor, but it also meant that many more senators were qualified to compete, over a longer period, for official praetorian posts in Italy and the provinces and for the consulship. The variety of career

---

[58] The quotation is from Eck 1974: 199, cf. 196. Eck similarly claimed, on the basis of 17 known cases of prefects of the treasury of Saturn (AD 69–138) of whom 14 became consul, that such prefects 'almost inevitably' became consuls. But what of the 30-odd prefects of the treasury in this period, about whom we know nothing? Are those who are known, disproportionately known just because they became consul? See similarly illicit deductions and confusions of 'all' with 'those known' in Alföldy 1976: 268ff and 1977: 33ff and 95ff. Such errors are unfortunately typical of their school.

The senatorial aristocracy under the emperors

patterns available, the very lack of certainty about future promotion served the emperors as a method of controlling ambitious senators.

Withdrawal

Some senators were not ambitious, or dropped their ambitions in the course of their careers. The defensive ideology of failure was retreatism or philosophical scepticism (Stoic, Cynic, or Epicurean), which infected others besides failures.[59] Epictetus' comments are cutting: '...a man becomes a slave when he enters the senate; there he serves the finest and sleekest slavery...' You can see him cringing, flattering, not for the sake of a meal, but for a governorship, or a consulship. He is a slave on a grand-scale (*megalodoulos*), a slave in a magistrate's toga, a slave to ambition. 'That is why in the senate, he cannot say what he thinks, even though his opinion shouts at him from inside' (*Discourses* 4.1.40 and 139ff).

Such criticism can undermine political orthodoxy; the emperors Nero and Domitian (Dio 67.13) both had senators executed for ostentatious withdrawal, which they interpreted reasonably enough as a symbol of rebellion. 'If many did that, there would be war' the prosecutor of Thrasea said in the senate in AD 66; 'he absented himself when divine honors were voted to Poppaea [the emperor's wife]...he scorns religion, and abrogates the law; the daily gazette of the Roman people is eagerly read in the provinces and by the army to find out what Thrasea has not done.' The senate decreed his death; he committed suicide, and as he opened his veins said: 'we are making a libation to Jove the Liberator' (Tacitus, *Annals* 16.22ff).

Other senators were more passive, and knew or hoped that bad rulers would be followed by good. As a provincial governor said to rebellious Gauls, 'you endure bad years, storms, and other natural evils, so endure the extravagance and greed of emperors; there will be vices as long as there are men, but they do not last forever; better times intervene and compensate' (Tacitus, *Histories* 4.74; cf. 4.8). All one had to do was wait. Some senators were 'well known for nothing except leisure' (Seneca, *Moral Letters* 55.3) or extravagance; other senators filled their voting papers with jokes and obscenities (Pliny, *Letters* 4.25), or ritually chanted a litany of praise to the emperor. The senate had lost its executive power; did it matter what they voted for?

[59] See the good account by C. G. Starr, *Civilisation and the Caesars* (Ithaca, NY. 1954) 134–63; with more colour Syme 1958: 572ff.

The career pyramid

A fragment of papyrus preserves an interesting attempt by Claudius to elicit debate in the senate:

If you agree with these proposals, conscript fathers, I will make them known... If, however, you disagree, find an alternative solution, but do so here and now... If you wish to take time to think it over, do so, but remember that you must be ready to give your opinions when you are summoned to meet... The consul designate should not repeat the phrases of the consul as though they were his own, nor should the rest say simply, 'I agree' and then 'We have debated'. (*Berliner griechische Urkunden* 611)[60]

This is all very well. At best emperors' persecutions and senators' lack of power provide circumstantial evidence as to why sons of consuls and of senators might not have wanted to succeed in politics. But it is only circumstantial evidence. It neither confirms nor refutes our hypothesis, based on statistics, that many surviving sons of consuls (and of senators) did not enter the senate. Of course, the hypothesis is to some extent novel, precisely because there is no obvious evidence to support it; but there is little comfort in that. To be sure, we know the names of a few men, who were qualified by birth and wealth for senatorial careers, and who refused the honour and preferred to make their way as knights. They were lured, as Tacitus wrote of Seneca's brother, by the ambition of remaining a knight and equalling a consular's power; 'he also believed that he could amass money more quickly by becoming a procurator and administering the emperor's business' (Tacitus, *Annals* 16.17). It did not help much; both he and his two senatorial brothers, one of whom had also become extremely rich, were forced by the emperor Nero to commit suicide.[61] Interesting as such cases are, they are obviously exceptional.

The withdrawal from politics by some sons of senators contributed to a shortage of qualified men willing to enter the senate. The best attested case occurred in 13 and 12 B.C. Dio wrote of 13 BC:

---

[60] Compare this with Tiberius' scathing condemnation of the senate: 'Men trained for slavery' (*O homines ad servitutem paratos* in Tacitus, *Annals* 3.65). The atrophy of senatorial debate is clearly seen in the prologue to the Theodosian code. Similar ritual repetition of laudatory clichés became established much earlier (cf. Chapter 1 above, note 23).

[61] Stein 1927: 189ff gave full details of the known cases of senatorial families' decline and of knights' rise into the senatorial order. In his opinion, senators' sons were generally obliged to become senators, if they had enough money. He also claimed that the senatorial order was increasingly, by the third century exclusively (p. 359), recruited from knights' sons! He also incautiously generalised from the known cases that it was normal, 'in der überwiegend befolgten Regel' (p. 323), for procurators' sons to become senators. The number of known cases is insufficient to justify these statements. The above criticisms are meant only to qualify, not to discredit Stein's classic work.

No one would willingly become a senator any more; moreover, sons and grandsons of senators, some of whom were really poor and others of whom had been reduced to poverty by their ancestors' misfortunes, would not claim senatorial dignity, or even if they were already on the list, swore that they were ineligible. (54.26)

Two factors were said to have caused the shortage of senators: the impoverishment of senators in the civil wars and the recent increase in the minimum fortune required of senators (from 400,000 to 1,000,000 HS). But these reasons were specific to this period, so that we cannot generalise from them. Previously and in 12 BC, there was also a shortage of men willing to serve in the normally senatorial office of tribune of the people. The post had formerly been prestigious, but then tribunes lost all power. Augustus tried to solve this problem by having wealthy knights nominated as candidates for the tribunate and by giving them an option, if they were elected, of pursuing a senatorial career, or of remaining knights (Dio 54.30). Knights were also at this time recruited as junior officials (*vigintiviri*) in the city of Rome, an office which was now normally held prior to entering the senate. In sum, there seems to have been a shortage at this time of recruits to the senate, who were of senatorial origin; to make up the numbers, knights were tempted into taking their place. In an effort to solve these problems, Augustus reviewed the composition of the whole senate, and is reported to have forced all those of senatorial descent under thirty-five years of age (he is said not to have bothered with those who were older) with the requisite fortune to become senators, unless they were physically disabled.[62] Augustus' action confirms our view that there were descendants of senators, some impoverished, others not, who were outside the senate.

The shortage of senators seems to have persisted. In AD 38, according to Dio (59.9), an attempt was made to attract knights into the senate by allowing some of them to wear the senatorial tunic, which had a broad purple stripe, even before they had entered the senate, on the strength of their prospects. Afterwards some young men, who were sons of knights, seem to have been granted the right to wear the senatorial tunic, as a visible token of their candidacy for

[62] All this is reported by Dio 54.26.8–9. But the meaning of this passage is disputed; see A. Astin, 'Augustus and "censoria potestas"', *Latomus* 22 (1963) 226–35. According to Suetonius (*Augustus* 38), Augustus encouraged all sons of senators to undertake senatorial obligations. With that end in view, he allowed sons of senators to wear senatorial dress and to attend meetings of the senate. The problems of 13–12 BC reflect the difficulties surrounding that policy.

the quaestorship and for membership of the senate.[63] But by no means all young knights wanted to become senators. Some refused the honour when it was offered, and one even cautiously boasted about his refusal.[64]

We know almost nothing of those who tried to enter the senate but failed to get elected. Perhaps they just reverted to a narrow-bordered tunic. The poet Ovid described his own experience: 'The senate passed me by; the border of my toga was narrowed. It was a burden greater than my powers. My body was not strong enough nor my mind attuned to such labours. I wanted to escape anxious ambitions' (*Tristia* 4.10.35–9). Once again our evidence is fragmentary and circumstantial. Yet the emperors' difficulty in filling all the places in the senate is striking. It seems reasonable to suppose that the same factors which turned away some young sons of knights disaffected some sons of senators as well. The decision in AD 38 to grant senatorial dress to knights and so mark them out as potential future senators is explicit admission of the need to recruit senators from outside the ranks of senators' direct descendants. The emperor Claudius' well-known elevation of provincial senators (about which more later) signified the formal abandonment of the desire to recruit senators only from senators' sons.

Let us sum up our arguments so far and their implications. First,

[63] A single case is revealing: a young man, by origin a knight, served as a junior official (*vigintivir*) in the city of Rome, but was then forced to commit suicide after he had beaten up the emperor Nero in a street brawl. The emperor was incognito and might have let the matter pass, but the young man foolishly apologised and so publicly acknowledged that he knew that it was the emperor whom he had struck (Dio 61.9). He was called a *laticlavius* by Suetonius (*Nero* 26) and by Tacitus 'a member of the senatorial order, even though he had not yet gained senatorial office' (*Annals* 13.25). The grant of senatorial dress (*latus clavus*) to a young knight was symptomatic of broadening ideas about the senatorial order, to include potential members. The development is interesting. Two questions: What happened if the young knights failed in successive elections for the quaestorship? Secondly, evidence that some individuals received the right to wear senatorial dress is not proof (*pace* Chastagnol 1974: 380ff) that all candidates for membership of the senate had to secure the same grant. How widespread was the emperor's grant of the right to seek senatorial office? By how much did it exceed the number of places available? We do not know. Cf. note 44 and Chastagnol 1973: 595ff with whom we disagree substantially.

[64] A tombstone from southern Gaul recorded a man's quite modest local career, and then finished up with 'The godly Hadrian offered this man senatorial dress with a quaestorship, but at his special request accepted his excuses' (*CIL* 12.1783). Pliny (*Letters* 1.14.5) mentioned a prominent knight who apparently refused the emperor Vespasian's offer of praetorian rank. But the emperor Claudius forced a senator who tried to opt out of senatorial life by going to live in Carthage, to come back to Rome, and 'declared that he would bind him with golden chains' (Dio 60.29).

the early emperors confronted serious difficulties in securing acceptance by aristocrats of their monarchical position. They therefore attempted to cloak their pre-eminence with the myth that senators were their equals. One disadvantage of this foundation myth was that it legitimated senatorial nobles as rivals to the emperor; some nobles perceived themselves or were perceived by others as possible replacements for emperors or as their successors. This was one reason why emperors repeatedly persecuted leading nobles in a vicious circle of suspicion, fear and oppression. Ancient and modern commentators have often ascribed this syndrome to the personal pathologies of individual emperors such as Caligula or Nero; but its recurrence at Rome and in other pre-industrial monarchies, precludes this as a sufficient explanation. The whimsical and arbitrary exercise of despotic power was also structural; it arose out of emperors' rivalry with their aristocrats, and perhaps out of their frustration at the recurrent discrepancy between their imagined and their effective power to control events. Whatever the explanation, their attacks on senators seriously curtailed the recruitment of senators' sons into the senate.

Secondly, the Principate was built upon Republican foundations. The emperors' chief aides were members of the senate and were rewarded with high status within the traditional framework of senatorial careers. Emperors neutralised senators' collective and individual powers not only by promoting competition between senators for high status posts, but also by restoring the old Republican oligarchic system of power-sharing. It is paradoxical but true that the Republican constitution, properly enforced, helped preserve monarchical power. Three components of the traditional constitution and two changes deserve special mention. As in the Republic, the power of each aristocrat was restricted (1) by short tenure of offices, which prevented provincial governors from winning too much glory and from plotting rebellion from a secure base; (2) by the orderly succession of offices, with gaps in between, which allowed provincials to complain or prosecute the former governor for corruption or malpractice;[65] (3) by competition between senators for each set of offices; competition was restricted to specific cohorts (such as ex-

---

[65] We take it for granted that corruption, that is the acceptance of gifts, fees and bribes in excess of condonable norms was prevalent in Roman administration. Decisions to prosecute, whether justified or unfair, may have been the result of personal intrigues and rivalries, as well as of governor's excesses. See the excellent suggestive essay by C. K. Yang, 'Some characteristics of Chinese bureaucratic behaviour', in D. S. Nivison and A. F. Wright, *Confucianism in Action* (Stanford, 1959) 134ff.

praetors, ex-consuls) according to age and experience. In these circumstances, competition between senators could be encouraged, because it was controlled.

The grand set and the power set

It was the breaks with the Republican practice which most enhanced emperors' power. First, emperors cut off senators' access to a popular electorate. This restricted the arena of their political campaigns, and so limited their chances of getting broad political support. Secondly, emperors themselves appointed commanders of legions and governors of provinces in which legions were stationed. This control over appointments separated traditional marks of high status, such as the praetorship or consulship, from the effective exercise of political power in the provinces. The traditional marks of high status became only a necessary and were no longer a sufficient condition of wielding political power. This bifurcation of power and status enabled emperors to establish a second arena for competition among senators, but outside the senate; namely competition for posts in the imperial service. From among the competitors, emperors could then choose as generals in the provinces men whose activities they knew about from their performance in several posts over more than a decade. This supervision of provincial governors' power was patently crucial for the survival of the Principate as a political system; in the late Republic, governors' capacity to construct power-bases with their armies in the provinces had precipitated the disintegration of the Republican political structure.

The separation of high status and political power also tempts us, at the risk of considerable simplification, to identify two sets within the senatorial elite. These are the 'grand set' and the 'power set'.[66]

[66] This distinction between two separate hierarchies of grandeur and power is derived from the French court in the reign of Louis XIV. Louis XIV himself in his impressive memoirs (1661) wrote: '...I believed it was not in my interest to seek men of more eminent rank because it was above all necessary to establish my own reputation, and it was more important that the public should know by the rank of those whom I chose to serve me that I had no intention of sharing my power with them. And since they were conscious of who they were, they had no higher aspirations than those I chose to permit' (*Mémoires de Louis XIV* ed. C. Dreyss (Paris, 1860) vol. 2, 391ff). And see the excellent and suggestive book by F. L. Ford, *Robe and Sword* (New York, 1965). To be sure, the Roman court was different, but in some ways it can be understood better by seeing how different it was from European absolutist courts, and by explaining the differences. An idea similar to ours has now been put forward in one of his gnomic utterances by R. Syme: 'Between the useful and the decorative, the front ranks of the Senate divide sharply', 'An eccentric patrician', *Chiron* 10 (1980) 427.

The first set comprises the most noble, those who were closest in status to the emperors and were his most obvious rivals. Among these, patricians, as we have already noted, were normally as a privilege given fast promotion from quaestorship to consulship; they were thereby precluded from the military experience which was normally a necessary condition for the governorship of the provinces in which legions were stationed. Other aristocrats, sons of consuls but not necessarily of patrician status, may also have been passed over and not chosen as imperial provincial governors.[67] They were kept away from military power. Some of them probably comforted themselves with social influence and with an extravagant social life in the city of Rome, which both expressed and enhanced their status. Indeed some members of this grand set may not have been in the senate at all. They remained members of the grand set by virtue of their inherited wealth and social status; they did not follow their fathers into political office. Their existence follows logically from the evidence on differential rates of succession which we presented earlier.[68] The grand set thus spread beyond the senatorial elite. Other members of the grand set retreated into philosophy which either elevated the ideal of Liberty or scorned the slavishness of political ambition. Many might not have wanted to serve as governor in a distant province with a bad climate.[69] As one late orator declared of early imperial times: 'The hard work of military service was rejected by all the nobles as sordid and ungentlemanly' (Mamertinus, *Latin Panegyrics* 3(11).20).

In this grand set, patricians and nobles of Republican lineage (such as Licinius Crassus, Pompeius Magnus and Calpurnius Piso) were the prime targets of early emperors' persecutions. They were attacked partly because they were so rich and their property was worth confiscating, and partly because they did plot against the emperors, sometimes pre-emptively. In the second century AD, confiscation and

[67] This is hard to demonstrate convincingly from surviving evidence, although it is implied by the low rates of succession secured by consular governors of imperial provinces (see below, p. 173 *ad* note 70). So similarly, R. Syme, 'Governors of Pannonia Inferior), *Historia* 14 (1965) 361: 'The new nobility thus being created all the time prefers to enjoy status...and opulence...and the Caesars for their provincial governors pass over the sons of consuls, turning ever and again to newer families and a widening zone of recruitment.'

[68] We realise that scholars may be chary of accepting the existence of a significant number of non-senatorial grandees, for whom there is no explicit ancient testimony. But both in theory and practice, there would have been insuperable difficulties in securing an exact match between those who inherited wealth and those who succeeded to political office.

[69] According to Dio (77.11.6), the emperor Carracalla sent 'senators to uncongenial provinces whose climate was injurious to their health...while pretending to honour them greatly'. Cf. A. J. Graham, 'Prosopography in Roman imperial history', *ANRW* (Berlin, 1974) vol. 2.1, 145.

persecution was less pervasive. Some holders of the *ordinary* consulship, with their relatively high rate of succession between generations, can be identified as members of the grand set. For example, the Brutii Praesentes produced six *ordinary* consuls in just over a century (*cos* II AD 139; *cos* I 153 and *cos* II 180; *coss* 187; 217; 224; 246); but only the first of these is known to have governed a military province. Such men may have had influence as friends, dinner companions or advisers of emperors, and their prestige and marriage connections extended to the imperial family itself (a daughter of a Bruttius Praesens married the emperor Commodus), but their social status was not matched by the exercise of effective power in administrative positions, and certainly not in the frontier regions of the empire. It is for these reasons that we call this set, the grand set.

Our second set, the power set, embraces senators who governed the major military provinces. These men competed for success and fame mostly by serving the emperor for long years as commanders of legions and as governors of frontier provinces. These were the men to whom the emperors delegated most power and these were the men who in a crisis of succession led rebellious armies against unpopular monarchs and against each other. Only a few of these men had consular or even apparently senatorial fathers; for example, of all known consular legates (i.e. governors of important imperial provinces – Table 3.13, E_{1-4}) from the period, AD 96–138 (N = 49), five out of six did not have a consular father.[70] Most must have come from families new to the political elite, and were descended from rich and respectable Italian or provincial gentry. Only a few are known to have been fast social risers, who made their way up from less respectable social milieux by personal prowess usually through military service. For example, Curtius Rufus, reportedly the son of a gladiator, was appointed governor of Upper Germany under Claudius (Tacitus, *Annals* 11.20–1), and the future emperor Pertinax was said to be the son of an ex-slave timber merchant (SHA, *Pertinax* 1.).[71]

The grand set and the power set are analytically distinct; but in

---

[70] Our analysis is based on the lists of known governors of the regular consular provinces of Britain, Cappadocia, Dalmatia, Germania Inferior, Germania Superior, Hispania Citerior, Moesia Inferior, Moesia Superior, Pannonia Superior and Syria, on all of which see Eck 1970: 233ff. Alföldy 1977: 105ff provides figures similar to ours for the period AD 138–80; of all known consular legates (N = 77), only 29% are known to be sons of consuls.

[71] Also Verginius Rufus 'from an equestrian family, with an undistinguished father' was appointed to be a governor in Germany (Tacitus, *Histories* 1.52). But examples can only illustrate, not prove, general statements about social origins. For similar views, see D. McAlindon, 'Senatorial appointments in the age of Claudius', *Latomus* 16 (1957) 252ff.

practice there may have been some overlap between them. Ties of patronage and intermarriage doubtless linked individual members, while some powerful governors, having skilfully increased their fortunes in the provinces, returned to the city of Rome to live in ostentatious luxury as members of the grand set. It seems likely that many sons of consuls in the power set were elevated to the grand set, either inside or outside the senate; other sons dropped out of the metropolitan elite altogether. These are the implications of the evidence which we presented earlier on succession rates. Few sons of suffect consuls had successful careers in provincial administration. And sons of *ordinary* consuls, if they entered politics, tended to have brilliant rather than powerful careers; they rarely finished as suffect consuls, in contrast to Republican practice, in which sons of consuls quite often finished their careers as praetors (cf. Tables 3.6 and 2.5).

Perhaps we should tentatively suggest the existence of a third senatorial set: those who never became consuls, and about whom we know very little, often not even their names. They form an ill-illuminated background to the consuls whose succession rates we have examined. Our brief discussion of senatorial careers showed that some of these senators probably served in no official posts after they had become praetor. There were simply not enough posts for them. Others served in one or two civil or military posts in the provinces. But then perhaps several factors, the lack of administrative ambition or competence, a desire to stay in Rome and lead a life of leisured luxury, the demise of a patron or the rise of an enemy at court, a change of ruler, mere chance, fashion or whim, or the loss of a fortune, curtailed their chances of being selected for further posts. So they were prevented from becoming full members of the power set and of the grand set as well.[72]

By establishing different though linked ladders for promotion to honours (praetor, consul) and to offices (governor, legate), the emperors also created, consciously or unconsciously, a system which prevented the formation of a powerful hereditary elite. Circulation in the elite was enlivened by three complementary techniques: (1) the promotion of outsiders to positions of power; (2) the expectation of ostentatious expenditure by aristocrats, supplemented by occasional confiscations; (3) the elevation of sons of the politically

---

[72] This does not mean that such senators were unimportant. They acted as electors and as supporters of their more active peers, and sometimes as informants against successful senators; an activity for which they were richly rewarded (Tacitus, *Annals* 16.33). For some characteristically insightful and arcane thoughts, see R. Syme, 'Pliny's less successful friends', *Historia* 9 (1960) 362ff.

successful to positions of higher status without power, in which aristocrats had to maintain their status by competitive ostentation without recompense from public office. Unlike the old British system of offices, for example, Roman imperial politics offered almost no offices of profit at court in the metropolis.[73] To be sure, some of the emperors' favourites were richly rewarded; but there was no regular system of supporting aristocrats at court out of state funds.

Staying at court in Rome cost money. In order to make large fortunes, or even in some cases in order to support their extravagance, ambitious senators had to go away from the capital to govern provinces, and make money there. Even then, they ran the risk of being prosecuted by outraged provincials or by political rivals in Rome. The inability or reluctance of many nobles and other senators to serve for long periods in the provinces must have drained the family wealth, and even endangered some families' social standing. In effect, by leading a life of ostentatious luxury in Rome, aristocrats were colluding in their own social suicide. Some could avoid falling out of the political elite only by securing imperial favour and generosity, or by securing a large inheritance from a distant relative or from a friend without heirs, or by marriage to an heiress, or by skilful management of their estates. But a change of ruler cut old lines of patronage and favour; exceptional wealth tempted attacks and confiscation; and parsimony, if they tried that, lowered their social prestige. In some cases, restricted fertility by chance or design concentrated resources in the hands of a single surviving heir or heiress; but in other cases, restricted fertility endangered the biological survival of the family. Some senators could choose between political activity or withdrawal, between relatively high or low fertility. But each course of action involved risk. And the overall effect was that vacancies were continually left free in the senate for outsiders. Our main point here is that the Roman aristocracy under the emperors never banded together effectively to minimise the risks to their individual or collective status. That was both symptom and cause of the weakness of the senatorial aristocracy during the Principate.

---

[73] On the English system, see G. E. Aylmer, *The King's Servants* (London[2], 1974) perhaps especially 253ff and 439ff; cf. L. Stone, *The Crisis of the Aristocracy 1558–1641* (Oxford, 1965) 385ff. It is very difficult to tell how much the great differences apparent between English and Roman government are due to differences in available information. Only John Lydus, *On Magistracies* written in the sixth century AD, gives glimpses into Roman bureaucracy which makes it seem recognisably similar to later office-holding and office-selling.

V   TOWARDS AN ARISTOCRACY OF STATUS NOT OFFICE

The continuous renewal of the Roman political elite depended more on outsiders than on the sons of insiders. We have discussed some of the social pressures which underlay and reinforced this process. Let us now briefly discuss two other factors which also contributed to low succession rates in the elite and to its incapacity to create strong hereditary privileges. First, under the emperors, there developed a palace administration, staffed by non-senators, which provided emperors with an alternative channel of effective control, both in the capital and in the provinces. Emperors could both by-pass senators and keep a check on them. Secondly, we have to reconsider the large numbers of provincial gentry who entered the Roman senate (cf. p. 184 below), and who were gradually integrated socially and culturally into the political elite of their erstwhile conquerors. These provincials were the chief source of the continuous flow of new senatorial families. Their recruitment reflected a significant political development, and contributed, so we shall argue, to changes in the location and function of the senatorial elite within the political system of the Roman empire.

The loss of status respect and the growth of imperial administration

The growth of an imperial administration staffed on the one hand by slaves and ex-slaves of the emperor's household, and on the other hand by knights, probably worsened aristocrats' self-image, just as it limited their power. The original status pyramid of Roman stratification – consulars, senators, knights, citizens, allies, free subjects, slaves – was significantly modified in the Principate to incorporate power-holders from outside the senate. They held their power by virtue of their personal closeness to the emperor, or as his personal nominees. They were not elected. They did not come from the highest strata of society; at best, they were knights; at worst, in the aristocratic view, they were slaves and ex-slaves.[74]

---

[74]   See the detailed work of G. Boulvert, *Esclaves et affranchis impériaux sous le haut-empire romain* (Naples, 1970) especially 334–57; the short account of A. M. Duff, *Freedmen in the Early Roman Empire* (Cambridge, repr. 1958) 143–86 is still valuable, as is P. R. C. Weaver, *Familia Caesaris* (Cambridge, 1972) especially 267ff. F. Millar, *The Emperor in the Roman World* (London, 1977) 69ff gives a detailed review of the sources. On Roman administration, the classic work by O. Hirschfeld, *Die kaiserlichen Verwaltungsbeamten* (Berlin², 1963) has not yet been superseded.

Towards an aristocracy of status not office

During the Republic, Roman senators had been masters of the world. Now they had to subserve an emperor; and in order to acquire favours from him, they often had to fawn on his slaves and ex-slaves:

...for the sake of these great and glorious offices and honours, you kiss the hands of other men's slaves, so as to be the slave of ex-slaves. And then you strut around solemnly once you've become praetor or consul. Don't I know how you got your praetorship and your consulship? Who gave it to you? I should not even want to live, if I had to live by Felicio's [an ex-slave of Nero's] favour and suffer his slavish insolence and arrogance. (Epictectus, *Discourses* 4.1.148ff; *ibid.* 1.26.11–12)

At the turn of the second century, the senator Pliny was appalled to find an inscription set up by the senate to Pallas, an ex-slave of Claudius, some fifty years earlier; on it, the senate had publicly thanked Pallas for his services, and had offered him the insignia of a praetor and the gift of 15,000,000 HS, that is fifteen times the minimum fortune of a senator. Pallas refused the money. Pliny cringed at the humiliating flattery of the senate's decree and commented:

I say nothing of this offer of the praetorian insignia to a slave, for they were slaves who made the offer... How glad I am that I did not live in those times for which I feel ashamed as if I had lived in them. (*Letters* 8.6; cf. Tacitus, *Annals* 12.53)

These excerpts illustrate senators' feelings of hostility and humiliation at repeatedly having to court their social inferiors for favours and access to the emperor.[75]

Throughout the first century of the Principate, emperors used ex-slaves as powerful functionaries in the central administration of the government. Ex-slaves of the imperial household acted as financial administrators (*procurators*) in the provinces, and as heads of administrative bureaux in the imperial household at Rome; they were in charge of judicial petitions, the emperor's correspondence and of his finances. Like the court eunuchs of the Later Roman empire, (see *Conquerors and Slaves*, Chapter IV), these ex-slaves wielded huge influence and power, in spite of their low social origins and their stigmatised social status. There is something incongruous about the use of freed slaves, members of a legally repressed stratum, as chief administrators in a society which was ostensibly elitist and

---

[75] Similar flatteries of important imperial ex-slaves can be found in Statius, *Silvae* 3.3.85ff: 'Now to you alone is given the control of our sacred ruler's wealth; in your sole charge are the riches which all the provinces render and the whole world's tribute...', and in Seneca, *To Polybius, On Consolation* 6.5.

aristocratic. It was as though bourgeois capitalists were appointed to key government posts in a modern communist state.

Surprise is no substitute for explanation, which is elusive. But three factors seem important. First, the central administration developed out of the emperor's own household; his household slaves were the only regular long-term aides available. The only possible exceptions were the senatorial officers of state (whose tenure was short term), and regular officers from the army, who were used increasingly as administrators. Secondly, the low status of the ex-slaves made them particularly dependent upon the emperor, and accountable to him; the ex-slaves did not belong to a collectivity or stratum to which the emperor had to pay political regard. They could be punished for misdemeanors, and sacrificed to popular indignation or imperial whimsy without risk of serious repercussions.[76] By the same token, because ex-slaves did not represent a political force in the society at large, they could be safely used by emperors to check the activities of aristocrats, both in the city of Rome and in the provinces. In the provinces, they were particularly useful, because their roles, for example as supervisors of imperial estates or of indirect taxation, were distinct from those of senatorial governors. In formal terms, their competence restricted the provincial governors' powers; informally, the emperor's ex-slaves could report back on aristocratic governors' abilities and indiscretions.[77]

Thirdly, emperors may have relied so much on ex-slaves, because free, high-status educated Romans were reluctant to serve as long-term dependants, even of the emperor. This may be difficult for us to credit, since in our culture we take paid employment for granted; indeed what a person 'does' has become a prime element in his or her social identity. The difference between modern and Roman assumptions is mirrored in the lengthy apology, composed in the second century AD by the litterateur Lucian, in defence of his own

---

[76] Augustus, for example, had the legs of his ex-slave secretary broken for taking a bribe (Suetonius, *Augustus* 67); his procurator in Gaul, the ex-slave Licinus, apparently bought himself off punishment for his extortions by turning over his profits to the emperor (Dio 54.21). Vespasian reportedly turned his aides' extortion to his own benefit by '…deliberately promoting the most avaricious of his procurators to higher offices, so that they would be all richer when he condemned them…he used them like sponges, soaking them when dry and squeezing them when wet' (Suetonius, *Vespasian* 16). Indications, if such were needed, that profiteering from office was rampant.

[77] The classic example is the report sent by the equestrian procurator of Britain, claiming that the war of conquest there would never be finished unless the existing senatorial governor was replaced. The emperor responded by sending one of the palace ex-slaves to investigate (Tacitus, *Annals* 14.38–9).

entry into the imperial civil service; he had previously written with considerable vigour advising a learned friend against entering the service of a great nobleman:

there is a very great difference between entering a rich man's household as a hireling, where one is a slave and endures what my essay [*On Salaried Posts in Great Houses*] describes, and entering public service, where one administers affairs as well as possible and is paid by the emperor for doing it... you are paid in both cases and are under a master's orders, but there is a world of difference... those who handle public business and make themselves of service to towns and whole provinces cannot rightly be criticised merely because they are paid... In short, I did not say that all wage-earners lived a mean and petty existence; no, it was those in private households who endured slavery under the pretext of education that I pitied. My own situation is different; my private standing is not reduced... (Lucian, *Apology* 11–12; translation from the Loeb Classical Library)

However justified Lucian's defence of becoming a civil servant, the mere fact that he considered it worth making argues the huge difference between our world and his.

Right from the beginning of the Principate, some of the emperor's trusted aides were educated free men, knights not ex-slaves. They served, for example, as governors of Egypt, from which senators were barred, because Egypt was considered too rich, too important and too easily controlled to be entrusted to a senator (Dio 51.17; Tacitus, *Annals* 2.59); they served as admirals and as governors of minor provinces, and as the senior fiscal administrators (procurators) of the provinces.[78] By origin, many of these knights belonged to the upper social classes, and possessed the minimum property (400,000 HS) which qualified them for equestrian status. As young men, they had served as responsible officers in the army, before becoming imperial administrators. The army was initially the only institution in which it was honourable for high status Romans to be regular employees. In addition, a significant minority of higher imperial administrators had acquired equestrian status as a reward for long military service.

[78] The best study is still that of H. G. Pflaum, *Les procurateurs équestres sous le haut-empire romain* (Paris, 1950), in spite of his conflation of first attestation of posts with their creation and his over-systematisation of knights' careers. For convincing arguments and evidence that there was very little specialisation in knights' careers, see P. A. Brunt, 'The administrators of Roman Egypt', *Journal of Roman Studies* 65 (1975) 124ff and R. P. Saller, 'Promotion and patronage in equestrian careers', *Journal of Roman Studies* 70 (1980) 44ff. Knights in about AD 140 regularly governed Egypt, and the following eleven provinces: Cottian Alps, Graian Alps, Maritime Alps, Corsica, Dacia Porolissensis, Epirus, Mauretania Caesariensis, Mauretania Tingitana, Noricum, Rhaetia, Sardinia.

Gradually, for both sets of knights, the progression from army officer to imperial administrator became an established step in an administrative career; and patterns of careers both within the upper echelons of the army and within the administration of the state gradually emerged.

Once again, we have to be cautious. First, most equestrian administrators seem to have served in only one or two administrative posts after their retirement from the army. Especially for those who had acquired knightly status by long service in the army, an administrative position must have seemed as much a retirement bounty as the start of a new life in the 'imperial service'. Secondly, the numbers of equestrian civil administrators were extremely modest, given the size of the empire; at the end of the first century AD, there were much less than one hundred attested posts, and by the end of the second century less than two hundred attested posts.[79] Finally, like senatorial posts, these posts were typically held only for short periods, perhaps on average for three years. Some knights clearly acquired considerable experience and expertise in their various jobs; yet, as it has recently been shown, there is little evidence that careers were planned with such expertise, or with administrative efficiency, uppermost in mind.[80]

Not all the emperors' administrative aides were ex-army officers. From the beginning of the Principate, some courtiers were intellectuals and litterateurs, especially Greeks. At first, in so far as these courtiers advised the emperor, they probably did so *ad hoc*; for example, they may have advised him on what answers to give to embassies from Greek cities. Two of the earliest attested imperial advisers holding regular positions, a doctor and a litterateur, are also known to have filled military posts; it seems improbable that they were competent, so it is likely that the military titles which they

---

[79] H. G. Pflaum, *Abrégé des procurateurs équestres* (Paris, 1974) 16 and 33. Pflaum reckoned that there were 64 equestrian posts in Italy and the provinces in the reign of Domitian and 173 in the reign of Septimius Severus. These figures may understate the actual levels due to the scarcity of data.

[80] Brunt 1975 showed that few Roman governors of Egypt had had previous experience of administration in Egypt. This constitutes a test case, since in Egypt there was opportunity for knights to gain administrative experience in several posts below the level of governor. Similarly Saller 1980 shows the lack of obvious pattern in equestrian careers, and like Brunt criticizes those who think they can deduce the character and ability of known officials from the list of posts which they held. That said, some equestrian officials did gain significant administrative experience in a variety of important posts; and when they were appointed, the emperor in a formal letter apparently stressed general virtues, such as integrity (*innocentia*), diligence and experience (*experientia*), as well as loyalty (*devotissima fides*) and respect for authority (*pietas*) – see *AE* 1962: 183 and *CPL* 238.

received were a convenient fiction.[81] The use of this tactic seems to confirm our point that originally the only long-term posts available for high-status freeborn officials were in the army. But before the end of the first century AD, it had become acceptable for litterateurs, with the status of knights, to replace ex-slaves in the top civil positions of the palace administration, for example, as Secretary of State for Correspondence (*ab epistulis*). Similarly, and especially in the second century, a significant minority of knights with a civilian, perhaps especially with a legal background, but without military experience, gained senior posts in the imperial service. For example, they served as treasury advocates and as superintendents of taxation, transport and of wheat supplies. To a limited extent, the civil administration had widened out from its military origins. But even so the bulk of equestrian administrators at all levels had a military background.[82]

In sum, from the middle of the first century AD onwards, knights increasingly replaced ex-slaves as heads of chancellery (Secretaries of State for Appeals, or Finance, or Correspondence). Ex-slaves did not disappear from the palace administration, nor did they lose their informal influence as the emperor's close confidants; far from it. But they were displaced in the upper reaches of the administration. The appointment of knights with a military, literary or legal background to top administrative jobs significantly diminished the incongruities between status and power, which had made powerful ex-slaves so hateful to aristocrats.

The importance of the knights in the imperial service sprang from their control of the collection and disbursement of taxes at a provincial level, from their command of navies, from the governorship of provinces in which significant bodies of auxiliary troops were stationed, and from their headship of central administrative bureaux. In effect, the equestrian administrators constituted a power set, supplementary to the power set located in the senatorial elite. And

---

[81] So Millar 1977: 86; the two men were Xenophon and Balbillus, who both held posts as military tribune and as quartermaster (*praefectus fabrum*); Xenophon became *inter alia* the emperor's chief doctor while Balbillus was in charge of receiving embassies and of writing replies to petitions written in Greek, both under Claudius.

[82] Pflaum 1950: 174ff stated that, from the data then available to him, five sixths of the known equestrian careers dated AD 70–117 and analysed by him began in the army (N = 60); the proportion of military careers diminished in the second century (AD 117–192) to 65%; one fifth (19%) of his analysed careers were definitely civil in origin, with 16% too fragmentary to be ascertainable (N = 26). One drawback to the careers analysed by Pflaum was that he excluded all those equestrians known to have occupied only one administrative post. In our view, many of these were also held by former soldiers.

the equestrian power set gradually increased in number and importance; more equestrians got paid higher salaries (130, 215 and 430 times the minimum subsistence level of peasant families), and were rewarded with corresponding honorific titles (*egregius, perfectissimus*).[83] There was no clear social gap between many knights and most senators; they belonged to the same social class of large landowners.

At the peak of equestrian power stood the praetorian prefect, who was originally commander of the palace guard. This was the most powerful body of regular troops stationed in the city of Rome, indeed in the whole of Italy, at the heart of the empire. The praetorian prefect was the Grand Vizier of the Roman empire. From the middle of the first century AD, praetorian prefects were regularly awarded the ornaments of a consul; they ranked as senior in status to consulars in the emperor's council (*consilium*), in that they entered the emperor's presence first, in precedence over all others, even the consuls. In short, their high power was recognised in traditional terms.[84] But in spite of their power and status, praetorian prefects were always (with minor exceptions) equestrian in origin. Marcus Aurelius is said to have expressed regret publicly that a very able man, the future emperor Pertinax, could not be appointed praetorian prefect, because he was a senator (SHA, *Pertinax* 2).

It seems likely that praetorian prefects' power was tolerated by emperors, exactly because in principle their origins excluded them from being rivals to the throne. The first praetorian prefect to be made emperor was Macrinus in AD 217; and his elevation, when knight not senator, caused considerable resentment, at least among senators. According to his contemporary, the historian Dio, who was a senator: 'He [Macrinus] might have been praised above all men, if he had not set his heart on becoming emperor himself, and had chosen instead some senator to head the Roman state, and had

---

[83] The salaries of equestrian administrators were fixed by the end of the first century AD at HS 60,000, 100,000 and 200,000 per year. The value of these salaries are worked out on the crude assumption that wheat cost 3 HS per *modius* of 6.5 kg, and that the average family needed 1,000 kg of wheat equivalent per year to live at the level of minimum subsistence. As from the middle of the second century AD, a higher salary level of 300,000 HS per year was introduced for top equestrian administrators. On equestrian titles, numbers and salaries, see Pflaum 1974: 43ff.

[84] On consular ornaments for praetorian prefects, see A. Stein 1927: 245ff and B. Rémy, 'Ornati et ornamenta...', *Revue des Etudes Anciennes* 78/9 (1976/7) 160ff. Praetorian prefects were also given the title *eminentissimus*; see the answers given by the emperor Hadrian, recorded in the *Corpus Glossariorum Latinorum*, ed. G. Goetz (Amsterdam, 1965) vol. 3, 388. On precedence, see J. A. Crook, *Consilium Principis* (Cambridge, 1955) 82–3; commenting on *CJ* 9.51.1 and *SEG* 17.759.

declared him emperor...But he grasped at monarchy himself, without even having the title of senator...' (Dio 78.41).

In the crisis of the mid-third century AD, Roman legions and armies were commanded almost exclusively by knights. Knights also, most of them with a background as professional soldiers, governed all the important provinces. The great soldier emperors of the late third century, Claudius, Aurelian, Probus, Diocletian, were drawn from professional military circles. Senators, in practice and by formal decree (of the emperor Gallienus AD 253–68), were excluded from the command of legions, and from decisive positions of power in the Roman state.[85] There had long been straws in the wind. Recurrent military crises showed the need to use experienced soldiers in top positions. Marcus Aurelius (AD 161–80) formally preserved senatorial exclusiveness, by co-opting equestrian military officers (by *adlectio*) into the senate. But the emperor Septimius Severus (AD 193–211), when he raised three new legions, handed them over to equestrian commanders, and so breached what once had been a senatorial preserve; his new important province of Mesopotamia, the new frontier against Persia, was also entrusted to a knight (Dio 75.3.2). And towards the middle of the third century AD, knights frequently took over temporary command of both legions and whole provinces from senators.[86] The edict of Gallienus on the exclusion of senators from military commands merely codified and regularised what had gradually become common practice. The protracted civil wars and foreign invasions of the period placed a premium on military professionalism and on experience of warfare and of hardship, which latter-day senators did not possess. No other development better illustrates the rise of power centres, alternative to the senate. By the end of the third century AD, the senate collectively and most senators individually were cut off from the exercise of political power on behalf of the state.

[85] On the reforms of Gallienus, see H. G. Pflaum, 'Zur Reform des Kaisers Gallienus', *Historia* 25 (1976) 109ff. Pflaum showed that after this decree senators no longer served as military tribunes or as legionary commanders. Moreover, the new mobile field armies were commanded by equestrian army officers, who were independent of any provincial governor. After AD 261/2, some important frontier provinces, such as Arabia, were governed only by equestrians, even though substantial bodies of troops were stationed there. Some other important provinces, such as Syria Coele, still had senatorial governors, but they no longer had serious military duties to perform.

[86] For example, from about AD 220 onwards, the forces stationed at Dura Europus, a focal point of the empire's eastern frontier, were commanded by a knight (called *dux ripae*, the duke of the bank), who was independent of the senatorial governor of Syria Coele. See Pflaum 1976: 113.

The senatorial aristocracy under the emperors

In sum, the growth of the imperial administration, headed first by ex-slaves and later by knights, significantly restricted senatorial power. The administrative service increasingly constituted an important locus of power, both at Rome and in the provinces, which was an alternative to the senate. The allocation of power to social inferiors, especially to ex-slaves and slaves in the early Principate, produced a dissonance between status and power, which was much resented by aristocrats, and probably by many free born Romans. But it allowed emperors to increase their control over the empire without delegating yet more power to senators. Even when the positions of the chief administrative aides to the emperor became established, the top administrative posts were filled by men of high social origin, but not by sons of senators. The separation of knights' financial and administrative roles from the gubernatorial roles of senators, and perhaps the diversity of knights' and senators' experience set equestrian administrators slightly apart from senators; but it would be misleading to suggest any identifiable difference between them in 'class' interests. Their roles and functions within the political system were different. And it seems reasonable to suggest that in the first three centuries AD, equestrian administrators were used increasingly, so that they restricted and controlled the power of senators in the provinces, and in the city of Rome.[87]

Provincial senators

The recruitment of provincial notables into the senate is an outstanding characteristic of the Roman senatorial aristocracy in the Principate. They came in increasing numbers from Gaul, Spain, Africa, Greece, Asia Minor, Syria and Egypt. Even by itself this process is an important index of the high turnover in senatorial families. Yet we still need to ask why provincials were recruited into the senate in such large numbers, and what were the consequences. Of course, this expansion in the provincial recruitment of senators

[87] We never know how consciously Roman emperors separated powers. Surely many of them were not naive, and saw the advantages to themselves of competition between aristocrats, short tenure and split responsibility. Such arguments are well set out in the speech to the future emperor Augustus attributed by Dio to Maecenas in 29 BC (see especially 52.19ff). He urged (*inter alia*) that knights should be in charge of revenues and tax-collection, because it would be wrong to have the same men in charge of both soldiers and money (Dio 52.25). Whether perceived or not, knights' administration of taxes in provinces governed by senators and of important affairs in the city of Rome seriously circumscribed senators' influence and power.

184

from the provinces is well known (see Table 3.15 in the appendix to this chapter for the proportions of known senators whose origins are known). Most modern accounts seem to concentrate on the identification of rival or allied groups of Italian or Spanish or African senators, either as a prelude to or in the wake of the elevation of a particular Spanish or African emperor. And it does seem that recruitment from some provinces occurred in waves, as influential men extended patronage to others with whom they had ties in their home province. But there seems little evidence that these provincial senators saw themselves as specifically 'Spanish' or 'African', as distinct from Roman; indeed, several so-called provincial senators were recognisably of Italian extraction, descended from Roman colonists.[88]

This identification of provincial large land-owners with Rome may have been a precondition of their integration into the conquering elite, but it does not explain their adoption. One landmark in our understanding of provincial recruitment is a speech made by the emperor Claudius in AD 46 in the senate at Rome, welcoming Gallic leaders as senators. It was thought sufficiently important to be set up on a bronze tablet which was discovered at Lyon; the speech was also reported by Tacitus. Much of the emperor's speech was devoted to rebutting the view that entry to the senate should be confined to the Italian aristocracy:

Augustus, my great-uncle, and Tiberius Caesar, my uncle, made an innovation. They wanted to see the flower of the colonies and cities everywhere, or at least of the worthy and wealthy, in this House. Is your objection that an Italian senator is better than a provincial? I can justify my censorship in words, but I shall show you my feelings by my actions. Provincials should not be rejected if they can be ornaments to the senate...(*ILS* 212 col. 2)

Senators objected that Italy could still fill the senate from its own resources.

...Is it not enough that Venetians and Insubrians have forced their way into the senate? Must hordes of foreigners be imported like slave gangs? What openings will be left for surviving nobles or for a poor senator from Latium? Every post will be filled by those rich men, whose grandfathers and great-grandfathers were leaders of hostile tribes, who attacked our armies with swords and violence, and besieged divine Julius at Alesia...Let

---

[88] See C. Habicht, 'Zwei neue Inschriften aus Pergamon', *Istanbuler Mitteilungen* 9/10 (1959–60) 121ff. On the so-called 'Punic' emperor, Septimius Severus, see A. R. Birley, *Septimius Severus* (London, 1971) 20ff with bibliography.

them, by all means, have the citizenship, but do not let them cheapen the insignia of the senate and the glory of office... (Tacitus, *Annals* 11.23)

Unfortunately, these excerpts from surviving testimony still do not explain why provincials replaced Italians.

The trouble is that a satisfactory explanation is difficult to find. However, four factors deserve special attention. First, the central government employed only a very small number of high-status administrators in the provinces. For example, in the middle of the second century, there were about one hundred and sixty senatorial and equestrian officials regularly appointed to administrative posts outside Italy to control and cater for a population (excluding Italy) of perhaps forty-five to fifty-five million; this meant one elite official for about every 300,000 provincials. By contrast, in southern China in the twelfth century, with a population of similar size, there were 4,000 gentry officials working in about 1,000 administrative areas outside the capital (compared with forty-five Roman provinces). That means that there was one gentry official outside the capital for every 15,000 Chinese people.[89] Moreover, many of the Roman officials in the provinces were concerned primarily with the command of troops rather than with the administration of justice, the collection of taxes or the preservation of internal peace. And they were concentrated in the frontier regions. As a consequence, the central government relied heavily on local notables, town-councillors (*decurions*). These local notables were the prime agents and supporters of the Roman government in the provinces. It was they who allocated the tax-burden among peasants, supervised tax-collection at the town-district level, organised ceremonies honouring the governor and the emperor and maintained order in the towns; it was their job to make sure that the streets were cleaned and that the scales used in the market place were equipped with standard weights; they tried to suppress banditry in the countryside and looked after the repair of the main roads. In sum, local notables helped the provincial governor in the exercise of his duties, since the governor's own staff was completely inadequate to administer a province, except in a rudimentary and supervisory style.

Of course, what we have just described was the ideal. Practice

[89] Certainly, such crude comparisons are difficult. But the scale of difference should outweigh any quibbles. These Chinese gentry officials were high status *litterati*, who had passed metropolitan examinations. See B. E. McKnight, *Village and Bureaucracy in Southern Sung China* (Chicago, 1971) 7; for similar results from seventh-century China, see D. Twitchett, *Financial Administration under the T'ang* (Cambridge², 1963) 11 and 217.

diverged. Local notables probably greased their own palms when they collected taxes; they honoured themselves under guise of honouring the emperor; willy-nilly they condoned disorder in the towns and banditry in the countryside; and they neglected to repair the main roads. Reality was an oscillating balance between the central government's ideal, the governors' self-interest and the varied self-interests of the local notables.

The conflicts of interest were disguised by rhetoric; and local leaders were rewarded with Roman citizenship for aiding and abetting their own subordination. The following extract is from the speech, *To Rome*, by the second-century rhetorician Aelius Aristides, who came from Asia Minor:

Vast and comprehensive as is the size of your empire, its perfection is greater even than the area which its boundaries encircle...The whole civilised world prays all together for the eternal duration of this empire...so beautifully is it harmonised by the leader in command...Of all who have ever gained empire, you alone rule over men who are free...But there is that which very decidedly deserves as much attention and admiration now as all the rest together. I mean your magnificent citizenship with its grand conception, because there is nothing like it in the records of all mankind. You have divided all those in your empire into two groups...in the entire civilised world, you have everywhere appointed to your citizenship...the better part of the world's talent, courage and leadership...(Aelius Aristides, *One Rome* 29, 36 and 59; adapted from the translation by J. H. Oliver, *Transactions of the American Philosophical Society* 43 (1953) 985ff)

The greatest provincials, or the most ambitious, progressed from the hierarchy of their own cities to the hierarchy of the provincial council. Some became Priests or High Priests of the imperial cult of the province; and for their pains and in return for their generosity to the provincial metropolis or to the festivities surrounding the cult, they were rewarded with the governor's favour and patronage. Others went on embassies to the capital, to the emperor's court. Through their connections and because of their wealth, some provincials became Roman knights or were given membership of the senatorial order.[90] Our first point, then, is that members of the provincial elite were elevated into the central elite of the empire, that is into the senate at Rome, because of their importance to the Roman government. Roman government in the provinces succeeded so well,

---

[90] Millar 1977: 85ff, 275ff and 491ff; G. W. Bowersock, *Augustus and the Greek World* (Oxford, 1965) 140ff; A. N. Sherwin-White, *The Roman Citizenship* (Oxford², 1973) 251ff.

partly because leading provincial land-owners consented in, profited from, and identified with the Roman peace.

Secondly, there was no formal barrier against the entrance of outsiders into the Roman senate. The prerequisites of senatorial status were wealth, connections and social acceptability, not noble descent. Provincials could qualify in the same way that Italians, as distinct from Romans, had been able to qualify in the late Republic. Leading provincials rivalled and sometimes even surpassed, some Italian senators in wealth; Herodes Atticus is an outstanding example. Thirdly, educated provincials belonged to the same upper-class culture as the Romans. They had friends among Roman aristocrats and emperors. And future Roman emperors, before their elevation to the throne, often had provincial friends. Especially when dynasties changed, some of these old friends, the new emperor's supporters, were elevated to the senatorial elite.[91] The openness of the Roman senate to outsiders was complemented by the homogeneity of aristocratic culture throughout the empire. The barbaric Romans, as the Greeks considered them, had conquered a superior culture, which the leading Romans admired and also sought to imitate and absorb. This integration of Roman with Greek literary culture allowed the acceptance of upper class alien provincials into the senate, because educated provincials conversed in a similar elevated and allusive language.[92]

Finally, the emperors had no particular interest in keeping the elite exclusively Italian. It was only a tradition; of course in some other societies, that would have been enough. But as the emperor Claudius pointed out in his speech which we cited above, the Romans also had a tradition of absorbing selected outsiders into the senate. And it was that tradition to which Claudius appealed when he promoted romanised Gauls. Indeed, it can be argued that emperors had a distinct interest in widening representation in the senate to include

[91] Millar 1977: 110ff. Herod Agrippa, king of Judaea, who made friends with the future emperor Caligula in the last years of Tiberius, profited considerably from this friendship (see Josephus, *Jewish Antiquities* 18.143ff).

[92] Claudius reportedly regarded these cultural affinities as very important: 'now they are imbued with our customs and culture, and have married into our families' (Tacitus, *Annals* 11.24); and see the lively tableau of cultural integration portrayed by G. W. Bowersock, *Greek Sophists in the Roman Empire* (Oxford, 1969). The earliest known Greek senator, Pompeius Macer, was the son of a friend of Tiberius (Strabo 13.2.3) who had been entrusted by Augustus with the organisation of his libraries (Suetonius, *Julius Caesar* 56); long attachment to the emperors brought promotion for the son, but did not save him eventually from suicide in lieu of execution (Tacitus, *Annals* 6.18).

provincial land-owners. Long-established Roman aristocrats could be more easily controlled by making them compete with selected outsiders. The power of Roman provincial governors could be balanced by the presence of other senatorial residents in the provinces which they governed.

We do not know whether or how far emperors consciously encouraged the recruitment of provincials into the Roman senate in order to control the senatorial aristocracy. But we think that successive Roman emperors were aware that there was a conflict of interests between aristocrats and themselves. They used such mechanisms as were available, which would help them control both senators and powerful provincial land-owners at the same time. To be sure, the recruitment of provincials into the senate probably had many causes. But among the multiple causes, these four factors, the dependence of the central government on local notables in the provinces, the tradition of using objective criteria of wealth besides birth for entry to the senate, the cultural homogeneity of the upper-classes, and the emperors' lack of interest in preserving the Italian monopoly of the senate, all help explain the steadily increasing recruitment of provincials into the Roman senate and its elite.

Once in Rome, provincials were as subject as their Roman and Italian predecessors to the extrusive demographic, social and political pressures which prevented many aristocratic sons from succeeding to the status of their fathers. Provincials were subject to an additional pressure; according to two known regulations of the second century AD, they had to have one third, later one quarter of their patrimony invested in Italian land.[93] It was said that they should be Italian landowners, not just house-guests in Italy. The first regulation produced a flurry of land purchases in Italy and correspondingly probably involved sales in the provinces. Yet the regulations also imply that provincial senators kept the bulk of their property outside Italy. If they took their senatorial careers seriously, senators spent most of their adult lives at court in the city of Rome or governing provinces, far away from their native province. They were prohibited from leaving Italy without the emperor's permission. The active administration of their estates at home must therefore have been entrusted to slave agents (*vilici*), or to ex-slaves, or to relatives. It seems reasonable to conclude therefore that court life significantly increased provincial senators' living expenses, and at the same time

[93] Pliny, *Letters* 6.19; SHA, *Marcus Aurelius* 11. The reduction in the required proportion implies that it was difficult to secure compliance.

endangered their major source of regular income, the revenues and rents from the estates at home.[94]

There was a solution. A law of Augustus provided that sons of senators and their descendants in the male line down to the great-grandson kept some of the privileges associated with senatorial status. This law was apparently kept in force and elaborated in the following centuries. Mommsen interpreted these rulings as conclusive evidence that the senatorial order from the time of Augustus became an hereditary estate. And so in a sense it did, providing we distinguish between full members of the senate, senators, and their privileged descendants, many of whom (we have argued) did not enter the senate. The Augustan law in effect excused three generations from the risk and trouble of serving in the senate, while preserving some of their senatorial privileges.[95]

For provincial senators and consuls, there were obvious attractions in returning in middle age to their home towns and estates and to a provincial milieu, in which they could continue to reap the advantages of their wealth and status, now newly embellished with senatorial rank. Their senatorial dignity formally freed them from some local municipal obligations and burdens (*munera*), because by a convenient legal fiction, all senators were considered to be residents of the city of Rome and not of their native towns (*origo*). Senators were also exempt from what were occasionally oppressive impositions by the central government; they and their lands were not liable to lodge and feed passing soldiers (*hospitium*), nor to provide horses or draught animals for the state post.[96] And although their provincial estates were liable for payments of direct tax (*tributum*), senators'

[94] For example, Pliny requested the emperor to give him thirty days' leave from his administrative duties in Rome in order to visit his estates some 220 km away, in order to let farms and to review rents. He claimed that his personal attendance was vital. Yet these were by no means the most distant of his Italian estates from Rome (see R. P. Duncan-Jones, *The Economy of the Roman Empire* (Cambridge, 1974) 19). If Pliny had difficulty with the management of scattered Italian estates, then imagine the difficulties of provincial senators with estates in various provinces, as well as Italy. To take two late but illustrative examples, Melania had estates in Italy, Sicily, north Africa, Britain and Spain (*Life* 11; ed. D. Gorce (Paris, 1962); Paulinus of Pella had estates in south-west France and in northern Greece (*Poem of Thanksgiving* 414–15 and 570ff).

[95] See note 8 above. Note also that the title *clarissimus* (in Greek *lamprotatos*) was applied to members of senatorial families (*clarissimus puer, clarissima femina*); cf. Friedländer 1922: vol. 4, 77ff.

[96] For the material and fiscal privileges of senators and their descendants, see the interesting discussion by Eck in T. Drew-Bear, P. Herrman and W. Eck, 'Sacrae litterae', *Chiron* 7 (1977) 365. The continued voluntary generosity of senators to their cities of origin enhanced their local prestige. See also W. Eck in W. Eck *et al.* edd., *Studien zur antiken Sozialgeschichte* (Cologne, 1980) 283ff.

status and influence may well have lessened their total liability, because they could bring pressure to bear on the process of allocating and collecting taxes. Former consuls and their families were in a strong position in their provincial milieu to use their social prestige and metropolitan connections to defer tax-payments, to win concessions, to confer patronage. The elevation of one member of the family cast a senatorial lustre on the family as a whole.[97] Their sons and grandsons may often have considered wealth, influence and prestige enjoyed without danger at home, preferable to cut-throat competition at court in the city of Rome. Some may simply have preferred hunting to politics.

Many sons of senators stayed in the provinces without ever enrolling in the senate at Rome. That is our proposition. But there are difficulties. First, there is a dearth of testimony providing evidence of their existence. To be sure, a few inscriptions exist honouring senators' sons or grandsons who occupied middling or merely provincial honorific positions. For example, in Aphrodisias in south-western Asia Minor, P. Aelius Hilarianus was a knight, the son of a top centurion (*primuspilaris*) and the grandson of an ex-consul (*PIR*² 190); apparently his brother and nephew were senators.[98] Yet the rarity of explicit testimony is not so worrying. Those who did not achieve high official positions were less likely to have been honoured

---

[97] One convenient collection of inscriptions from the eastern provinces contains well over a hundred examples in which men and women were described as being of 'senatorial rank' (*sunklētikos*) or as a 'relative of senators' or of 'consulars' (*sungenos sunklētikōn/hupatikōn*; e.g. *IGRR* vol. 3, 69 and vol. 4, 280, 858 and 910). But the exact relationship of these people to senators or consuls is often unknown, because it is at least possible that some of the men commemorated as 'of senatorial rank' had never themselves been full members of the senate. Cf. P. Lambrechts, *La composition du sénat romain de Septime Sévère à Dioclétian* (Budapest, 1937) 94–5, for similar views; he noted that many such men are not known to have held senatorial office. But our evidence on some senatorial offices is so incomplete that not much can be made of that. Our general view fits in with, but does not coincide with, that of Chastagnol. He also considered (1973: 583ff) that the senatorial order could be understood in a broader sense to include at least sons of senators and knights who had been awarded the *latus clavus* as well as senators. But he tried to find a birth-date for the change, a search which misconceives how these institutions changed and exaggerates the trustworthiness of our sources (see note 44 above). In our view, the grant of privileges to senators' descendants grew in importance as more came from the provinces. The exercise of privilege, even if fixed by law, depended for its significance on the social context in which it was claimed, so that the inheritance of senatorial privilege probably mattered more in the provinces than in Rome.

[98] So A. Stein 1927: 192 based on P. Le Bas and W. H. Waddington, *Inscriptions receuillies en Asie Mineure* (Hildesheim, repr. 1972) 595 and 1617 = 2792–3. P. Aelius Hiliarinus' mother was called mother and grandmother of senators on these inscriptions. Stein (*ibid.*) cites two or three similar cases.

in a commemorative (as distinct from a tombstone) inscription. And besides, some of those recorded in tombstone inscriptions as having senatorial status (*vir clarissimus, sugkletikos*) may have had their status inflated by local deference; they may not have been full members of the senate, but rather politically inactive members of the senatorial order. This distinction between full senators and the senatorial order is obviously important, and we shall return to it in a moment. A second problem is to know what politically unsuccessful sons of senators did. The problem is partly misconceived. In modern, industrial societies, a man's identity is largely given by what he 'does'. But in Roman society, the son of a wealthy senator or landowner could easily slip into the life of a country gentleman, even if the family fortunes were declining from metropolitan levels. If the family fortunes were unimpaired, he could, without being a senator, live the luxurious life of a grandee, partly in the provinces or in Italy, partly in the capital. There was more to Roman upper class life than serving the emperor.

One further piece of evidence seems suggestive. In the fourth century AD, senatorial status became largely divorced from active membership of the senate. Most men of senatorial status lived in the provinces away from the capitals of the empire, and never attended meetings of the senate in Rome or Constantinople. Indeed, in the fifth century, men of only routine senatorial status (*clarissimi*) had to send a request for written permission from the emperor, before they were allowed to visit the capital city (*CJ* 12.2.1 – AD 450). Senatorial status had become largely hereditary.[99] Senatorial descent still gave advantages to those starting a political career, but it was neither a prerequisite nor a guarantee of success. Routine senatorial status had become far removed from the peaks of political power. No one knows the precise sources of these developments. We tentatively suggest that they were anchored in the history of the senatorial order from the first and second centuries onwards. Provincial senators returning to their home province, at first informally, then in the long run formally,

---

[99] The two senates of the eastern and western halves of the empire both grew enormously during the fourth century AD (see, for example, Ausonius, *Professors of Bordeaux* 5.1). One of the main channels of growth was legalised infiltration by knights and town-councillors. Once they had gained senatorial status, it often became hereditary; cf. the following ruling: 'Since it is not right for sons to envy their father's rank, a son acknowledged by a senator...will stay in the senatorial rank' (*CJ* 12.1.2 – AD 377). For a brief analysis of the complex developments in the senatorial order from the fourth century onwards, see Jones 1964: 525ff. We disagree somewhat with his views on the senate in the third century AD, which was not a detailed analysis but merely an extrapolation of the then conventional picture of the senate in the Principate (see notes 8–9 above).

preserved their senatorial rank. But they did so at the cost of splitting senatorial rank away from the exercise of political power in the central government of the empire.

At this point, we should return to the distinction which we made between the senate (*senatus*) and the senatorial order (*ordo senatorius*). During the Republic, the two terms were interchangeable or they referred to different aspects of the same body of men. Then, under the emperors, the term senatorial order came to include senators' immediate family and descendants, though exactly whom it included probably varied over time and according to context. Some privileges allowed to senators and to their descendants were determined informally and socially: for example, wives of senators were increasingly called *femina clarissima* to match their husbands' title of *vir clarissimus*. Other privileges were defined legally: for example, sons, grandsons and great-grandsons of senators in the male line were excused from liability to some local, municipal taxes (*munera*); but a wide range of descendants (including grandsons and great-grandsons in the female line) were prohibited by a senatorial decree of AD 19 from acting on the stage, or fighting as a gladiator, or from marrying an ex-slave girl.[100] In other words, there was a distinction between full active membership of the senate, which involved holding senatorial office (at least the quaestorship, and for most senators the praetorship as well) and elements of senatorial privilege and status which devolved on members of the senatorial order. These elements of senatorial privilege were hereditary by right, while full membership of the senate was not hereditary by right, and in historical times never had been.

In sum, the sons of senators inherited elements of their father's status, and that alone diminished their need to become full active members of the senate in Rome. Provincial senators, we imagine, had particular reason not to want to live permanently in the city of Rome. But Italians may also have demurred from dedicating themselves to an anxious life of competitive ambition. A Roman geographer in his guide to the Mediterranean, written originally in Greek in the fourth century, AD, described the city of Rome as follows:

(Rome) has a great senate of rich men; if you were to check through each one of them, you would find all the present and future provincial governors, or those who could be, but do not want to, because they want to enjoy their fortunes without risk. (Anon., *Description of the Whole World and its Peoples* 55 (ed. J. Rougé, Paris, 1966)

[100] In this recently published decree, rights and disabilities were inherited by knights' descendants also; see M. Malavolta, *Sesta miscellanea greca e romana* (Rome 1978) 363.

VI   CONCLUSIONS

In this chapter, we have tried to show that during the first three centuries AD membership of the Roman senate was to a large extent not hereditary. Ideally, there may have been a presumption that sons should follow in their father's footsteps. But ideals and practice diverged. Although some senators' sons became senators, many more did not. The basis of this finding was a statistical study, over seven generations, of consuls appointed between AD 18 and 235. We were surprised at their very low rates of succession. The differences in succession rates between periods and between *ordinary* and suffect consuls showed that neither persecution by the early emperors nor low fertility was an adequate explanation. Although the evidence was mostly confined to consuls, the politically successful half of the senate, we considered that our results could also be applied to other senators, who never became consul. We cannot reasonably suppose that the top half of the Roman senate contained a large proportion of outsiders, while the bottom half was packed with successive waves of politically unsuccessful sons, grandsons and great-grandsons of consuls. The fragmentary evidence which we have on senators-never-consul bears this out. We deduced therefore that many sons of consuls and of other senators simply opted out of politics.

Why were succession rates so low? Any elite in a society suffering high mortality faces considerable problems in reproducing itself exactly. In Rome, the problems were exacerbated by the high age threshold past which senators' sons had to survive in order to succeed in politics. There was a wide gap between biological and social reproduction. Even if fertility was high, and the elite was replacing itself biologically, roughly one third of families would have had no son surviving to consular age (about forty years), and another third would have had two surviving sons. But a senatorial career was expensive, and the profits from it were uncertain. Launching more than one son into senatorial politics was apparently beyond most consular families' capacity or desires (see p. 141 above). Exact social reproduction assumes that one could divert the resources of senatorial families without a surviving son to senatorial families with more than one surviving son. Marriage to an only daughter, well-endowed and with prospects of a rich inheritance when her parents died, was one tactic. Legacy-hunting was another. But in both of these, single sons might also be competing. Another tactic was adoption; some childless senators may have accepted an adopted son from a family with more than one surviving son, but in other cases, kin-ties would have induced childless senators to adopt a brother's or a cousin's only surviving son. Adoption may have been quite common among the Roman aristocracy (but see p. 49 above), but it was not frequent enough to transfer massive resources from those without surviving sons to those who had too many. Succession rates were so low, partly because many senators had no son surviving into adult life, and partly because some senators with two or more surviving sons could not afford to launch them all into competitive politics.

When elite fertility fell below the level of biological reproduction, exact social reproduction was impossible. More senators had no surviving son. For a few, that may have been intentional; but for most, we suspect, it was the chance result of a delicate balancing act. Many senators, as we have already noted, had to choose on the one hand between biological continuity and the risk of social demise, and on the other hand social survival with the risk of having no direct surviving heir. If they tried to guarantee the biological survival of their family by having lots of children, and if by chance several survived, then each child inheriting an equal share of the family fortune ran the risk of falling in the social scale. A sub-divided estate might not support senatorial ambitions. But if they wanted to avoid splitting their patrimony between several children, they could try to restrict their fertility, by contraception and abortion, and if they failed, by infanticide and a refusal to remarry after divorce or widowhood. The risk they ran was that no heir survived them. The Augustan laws on marriage, childlessness and inheritance were designed to arrest this trend. The emperor had an understandable interest in the reproduction of the elite as a whole. But each family was interested primarily in its own advantage. That is one reason why the Augustan laws failed. But we should not exaggerate. It seems probable that elite fertility in the Principate fell below the level of biological replacement. It was lower than it had been among consuls in the early second century BC (see pp. 63 and 103). But known succession rates among *ordinary* consuls in the mid-second century AD approximated to what we have called intermediate fertility, implying an average of at least 4.1 children ever-born per woman of completed fertility. If *ordinary* consuls then also had politically unsuccessful sons, total fertility would have been higher. In sum, restricted fertility among aristocrats in the Principate contributed to low succession rates, and so did emperors' persecutions. But even together, they do not completely explain low succession rates.

Many of the vacancies left free in the senate were filled by provincial land-owners. Politically, it was in the emperors' interest to involve them, because Roman government in the provinces depended upon their support and co-operation. It was in the emperors' interest to foster competition among a growing pool of candidates qualified for entry into the senate. The competition took two forms: ostentatious expenditure aimed at maintaining status at court and in the capital city, and rivalry between senators for election to and selection for high offices of state. Competitive expenditure undercut some senatorial families' capacity to stay in the political centre for generations, all the more so because the emperors restricted, even though they did not suppress, senators' opportunities to make huge profits out of public office, both in the city of Rome and in the provinces. In short, for many senators, waiting for promotion to positions of honour as praetor and consul, and then for profitable positions as provincial governor was a huge drain on family resources. Nor was it a question of merely waiting. For long years, between the ages of twenty-five and forty, senators competing for the highest honours and for the most powerful jobs, had to subserve the emperor and his protégés. In the early years of the Principate, some aristocrats were suspected of planning rebellion instead. To be both powerful and noble was dangerous. So emperors systematically (though not completely) excluded the noblest Romans from positions of great power, and promoted men from relatively new senatorial families instead to those positions. That is why we identified two sets within the senate: the grand set of high status but with little political power, and the power set holding positions of great delegated responsibility in the city of Rome and in the provinces, but whose sons tended either to opt out of politics, or to be recruited into the grand set. This continuous circulation created successive vacancies in the elite. In our view, provincial senators and their sons, with a home base distant from the capital, were even more likely than Italians to drop out of politics. The increased recruitment of provincials therefore gradually lowered the rate of political succession.

In the late Republic, senators had an effective monopoly of positions of great power within the Roman state. Under the emperors, senators lost that monopoly. Senators not only failed to secure individual hereditary succession to all senatorial privileges, they failed as a body to protect the senate's previously undisputed primacy as a source of law-makers, judges, administrators and generals. They were partly replaced by knights. In the third century AD, senators even ceased to be generals and governors of the most important provinces. Although the formal status of senators remained high, their collective political power was undermined. The functions of the senate within Roman politics had changed completely, partly because the senate was subordinate to the emperors, and partly because the emperors created alternative channels of power which were more directly under their own control. For example, the palace administration, staffed by slaves, ex-slaves and knights, first supplemented and then even in some respects superseded senatorial control. Senators acquiesced in their own political demise, we imagine, partly because they were internally divided, in competition with each other for honours and positions bestowed only by the emperor, and partly because their wealth and their social status especially outside the capital did not depend upon their political power in the central government. Reciprocally, emperors found it all the easier to erode the political power of the senate as a corporate body, because senators had not formed themselves into a small, tightly closed group of hereditary peers.

At the risk of repeating ourselves, let us rapidly go over familiar ground again in order to highlight the chief elements in our analysis. In the last chapter, we have charted the social and political transformation of the Roman senate. Originally, the senate was the political arm of the Roman land-owning elite. It was Rome's chief political decision-making body. It comprised all the chief officers of state. Until the middle of the first century AD, the senate had been exclusively Italian in membership. Under the emperors, in the first three centuries AD, its character changed considerably and it lost much of its corporate political power. Successive emperors undermined the importance of the senatorial monopoly of powerful state offices. They used three main tactics. We do not know, although we may suspect, how conscious different emperors were of the probable results. First, they increased the pool of potential entrants to the senate by the admission of provincials; this tactic, among others which we have discussed, helped reduce hereditary succession to senatorial office. Secondly, emperors established an alternative ladder to political and military power. In the beginning, this ladder was surreptitiously climbed by ex-slave palace administrators. Later, it was mounted openly by knights, both soldiers and lawyers, who held crucially important offices of state. To be sure, appearances were preserved by awarding senatorial insignia to these power-holders. Thirdly, the senate's formal powers of political decision-making were overshadowed and often by-passed by the emperor's own activities, as judge, law-maker and chief executive. The crisis of the third century AD highlighted the senate's political demise. Power was concentrated at the emperor's court, and in the armies at the frontiers. During the fourth century, emperors rarely visited the city of Rome. As a decision-making body, the senate became little more than a prestigious local Italian assembly with a ceremonial history.

In spite of the senate's collective loss of legislative power, individual senators preserved their high status and prestige. In every period, many of the wealthiest and noblest Italians were senators. But from the middle of the first century AD, the senate (which for over two centuries remained more or less stable in size) accommodated successive waves of provincial land-owners. The reasons for their ambitions are obvious. Senatorial status lent an additional and long-lasting gloss to the reputation of each senator's family, and it lent lustre to senators' descendants. But, by and large, senators' sons did not follow in their fathers' footsteps. They did not enter the senate. That was partly, we have suggested, because politics in the capital were dangerous and expensive. It was also because senators' descendants, even if they did not enter Roman politics, could still profit from senatorial privileges; and in local politics, they could readily convert their high social status into effective power. On the metropolitan stage, being a mere senator may have counted for less under the emperors than it had in the Republic. But in provincial politics, a senator and his descendants could cut a fine figure. It was their wealth, their ownership of land, their ostentatious life-style, and perhaps their literary education which together mainly determined their social standing. Senatorial status was the cream on the cake. In the political system as a whole, the extension of senatorial privileges to senatorial descendants, even those who lived in the provinces, helped transform the senate from a small political elite into a broadly-based prestigious social stratum, consisting predominantly of provincial land-owners. The elite of the conquerors had been gradually fused with the elite of the conquered.

APPENDIX

Incomplete evidence – some implications

Analysing the social origins of Roman consuls in the Principate is complicated by the fact that we know the names of only about three quarters of all consuls. We are therefore in some doubt as to whether known consuls are:

    (i) sons of unknown consuls
OR (ii) others, whom we shall call new men.

The following calculations allow us to assess the probability of each.

Let us assume that from any one period of time we know the names of a% of consuls, while the names of b% are unknown.

From the next generation, we know the names of c% consuls, who by the similarity of their names can reasonably be assumed to be the sons of (a) known conuls.

We also know (d) consuls who may be:

EITHER (d_1) the sons of (b) consuls unknown in the fathers' generation

OR (d_2) they may be new men.

In the sons' generation there are also (e) unknown consuls who may be:

EITHER (e_1) sons of (a) known consuls

OR (e_2) new men

OR (e_3) sons of (b) unknown consuls

This can be expressed diagrammatically:

	(a)			(b)		
fathers' generation	known consuls			unknown consuls		
	(c)	(d_1)	(d_2)	(e_1)	(e_2)	(e_3)
sons' generation	sons of known consuls	sons of unknown consuls	new men	sons of known consuls	new men	sons of unknown consuls
	known consuls			unknown consuls		

If we assume that (a) known consuls, and (b) unknown consuls in one generation on average had proportionately the same number of consular children, we can estimate the probable size of (d) and (e) as follows:

$$d_1 = \frac{c}{a} \times b; \quad e_1 = \frac{c}{(c+d)} \times e; \quad e_3 = e_1 \times \frac{b}{a} = \frac{d_1}{c+d} \times e$$
$$d_2 = d - d_1; \quad e_2 = e - e_1 - e_3$$

This is obviously a complicated way of dealing with the problem. But the simpler method, used for example by J. Morris (1953), which assumes that all consuls not known to be sons of consuls were upwardly mobile, is clearly wrong.

It may be helpful to give an example to show how these formulae work. From Table 3.1 and for the period AD 70–96, we know the names of 88% of all consuls (a = 88, b = 12). The proportion of known consuls with consular son (Table 3.3) was 25%, therefore c = 22. The proportion of consuls known in the next generation is 83%; c+d = 83; e = 17; d = 100−c−e = 61. In Table 3.3, on the basis of incomplete data, we reported that 25% of known consuls had known consular sons; on the assumptions stated above, we should add in our estimate of their unknown sons ($e_1 = 5$%); the corrected figure is 30%. In the period AD 131–160, the discrepancy between the reported and the corrected figure would be larger because the gaps in the evidence are much larger (a = 81, c = 23, e = 43).

The senatorial aristocracy under the emperors

The 29% reported in Table 3.3 would, on the assumptions stated, be corrected to 47%.

We suspect that in fact known consuls were more likely to have had consular sons than unknown consuls, on the argument that the names of people of highest status and highest inheritance rates are more likely to be recorded. Obviously, the correctness either of the assumptions made in the above calculations or of our suspicion could qualify some of our arguments based on incomplete data. However, overall we think that our main propositions stand in spite of the gaps in our data.

Table 3.15. *Italian and provincial origins of known senators**

			AD 69– 79	81– 96	98– 117	117– 138	138– 161	161– 180	180– 192	193– 212	218– 235	Third century
			a	*b*	*c*	*d*	*e*	*f*	*g*	*h*	*j*	*k*
A	Senators known	N = 386	404	428	332	355	342	259	937	471	548
						(per cent)						
B	Origins known		46	40	36	47	47	53	44	51	51	48
C	Italian		83	77	66	56	58	54	55	43	47	44
D	Provincial		17	23	34	44	43	46	45	57	53	56
	Origins of provincials:											
E	Western		70	76	56	46	24	10	8	15	14	14
F	Eastern		17	16	35	37	47	54	61	57	58	58
G	African		10	5	6	16	27	31	31	26	26	23
H	Provincial senators known	N = 30	38	52	68	71	82	51	275	125	149

* The figures are taken from M. Hammond, 'Composition of the Senate A.D. 68–235', *Journal of Roman Studies* 47 (1957) 77. A small number of senators from Dalmatia have been omitted from rows EFG.

4

DEATH IN ROME

Written in collaboration with Melinda Letts

I INTRODUCTION

When a Roman noble died, his funeral cortège comprised relatives and friends, hired actors wearing waxen masks of the dead man's famous ancestors, professional mourners wailing loudly and shouting out his exploits, and by contrast troupes of boisterous satyr dancers, all accompanied by flutes and horns (Dionysius Halicarnassus, *Roman Antiquities* 7.72).[1] The corpse was carried to the forum, and was placed, usually upright but sometimes reclining, on the raised platform (*rostra*) from which public orations were delivered. The dead man's eldest son then gave a funeral speech, in which he praised his father's exploits and those of his ancestors. The historian Polybius, who lived in the second century BC, has given us a detailed description.

After the burial...they put the image of the dead man in a conspicuous position in the house, enclosed in a wooden shrine. This image takes the form of a mask, which recreates the dead man's features and colouring so that it seems astonishingly true to life. These masks are displayed, lavishly decorated, at public sacrifices. And when a prominent member of the family dies, they are taken to the funeral procession and are worn by men who bear a close resemblance in stature and gait to the original. (6.53)

These actors wore the robes and insignia of the highest office which each ancestor had gained, purple stripes for consul or praetor, full purple for a censor, gold embroidery for a general who had been awarded a triumph (cf. Diodorus 31.25). They all rode in chariots, preceded by rods, axes, and other marks of public office. 'And when

---

[1] The best modern accounts are by J. M. C. Toynbee, *Death and Burial in the Roman World* (London, 1971) and F. Cumont, *After Life in Roman Paganism* (repr. New York, 1959). R. Reece, ed., *Burial in the Roman World, Council for British Archaeology, Research Report* 22 (London, 1977) is useful for its archaeological coverage; and DS *sv Funus* is impressively packed with relevant references from classical literature.

they arrive at the *rostra*', Polybius continued, 'they all sit down in a row on ivory chairs. A young man who dreams of nobility and renown could not easily find a more inspiring sight. For who could fail to be moved by the sight of these images of men who were famous for their virtue, all together, all apparently alive and breathing?' (6.53).[2]

Polybius claimed that it was experiences such as these, and the repeated reminder of the glory to be won from success, which stimulated young men to suffer even death for the public welfare. Individual self-interest was subordinated to the common good, in the hope of bringing glory to a family line. The individual was merely one link in a long chain of succession. Of course, Polybius' account is idealised, but it shows how funerals were used in the Roman aristocracy to enhance a family's status by the public display of ancestors, and also to reaffirm core civic values.[3]

In this chapter, I shall discuss the social process surrounding death in Rome – the ways in which people reacted to and coped with death. Seven main topics have been chosen: the monuments erected for the rich in Rome and the mass graves of the poor; the burial clubs and collective tombs which catered particularly for those who wanted to escape the humiliation of a mass grave, but were not rich enough to buy an individual grave plot; funerals, grief and mourning; the subsequent commemoration of the dead, and some of the ways in which, in Roman society, the dead invaded the world of the living; the power of the dead to dispose of their property in wills and the much-criticised activities of legacy-hunters in the city of Rome; and finally, the vain attempts of men and women to secure everlasting commemoration by leaving substantial sums of money and property to so-called perpetual foundations.

It would require several books to treat all these topics exhaustively. That is not my present purpose. Instead, my overall objectives have

---

[2] Roman aristocrats customarily spent huge sums on funerals. One leading Roman noble, who died in 153/2 BC, instructed his sons to give him a relatively inexpensive funeral, costing 'no more than one million *asses*' (= 400,000 HS = enough to sustain > 800 peasant families at minimum subsistence for one year). He wanted to limit expenditure because 'the funerals of great men are properly enhanced not by expenditure, but by the parade of ancestral masks' (Livy, *Summary of Book* 48). Painted wax funeral masks (and from the late Republic, busts) were displayed in the central area (*atrium*) of a noble's house (Pliny, *Natural History* 35.6; Seneca, *On Benefits* 3.28). These too were said to have inspired Roman heroes to great deeds (Sallust, *War against Jugurtha* 4). Some families displayed genealogical trees in the hall-way of their houses (Seneca, *Letters* 44.5). There must have been great temptation to fake (cf. Pliny, *Natural History* 35.4ff).

[3] See the Appendix at the end of this chapter.

been: first, to evoke and recapture some of the feelings which Romans experienced in accommodating death. I wondered, and still wonder what it was like to be there. My second objective was to describe some of the customs and institutions which helped Romans cope with death. I wanted to understand, and that has been a primary concern of the whole volume, the effects of the frequent and unpredictable incidence of death on the social reproduction of society. For example, how did Romans secure the orderly transfer of wealth and social roles from the dead to the living? On this track, we can move from a study of feelings and attitudes to the more traditional and fundamental historical problems, such as the distribution of wealth and the exercise of political power.

Two major difficulties obstruct the achievement of this objective. One is a problem of evidence, the other a problem of analysis. First, there are no general ancient descriptions of Roman funerary practices or of beliefs in life after death. Modern accounts have to be pieced together from a miscellany of passing comments made by various authors in different periods, or from descriptions of specific events. From such evidence, how can we tell what was typical of the very different social strata in Roman society? How can we trace, let alone explain, detailed changes in practice, expression and belief among different groups of the Roman population over long periods of time? The simple answer is that we cannot, or not with any certainty. The best we can hope for is an impressionistic sketch, a collage. For better or for worse, we have to make do with an artificial, almost timeless composite, inset with illustrative vignettes.

The prime focus of this chapter is the city of Rome during the late Republic and the Principate (about 250 BC–AD 250). But Rome was at the heart of an expanding empire. To fill in the picture, I have also drawn on evidence from outside the city of Rome, from Roman Italy and from the conquered provinces. I have also occasionally discussed much later developments. The term Roman, therefore, sometimes refers to different sets of people. Mostly, it refers to the free inhabitants of the city of Rome, sometimes to the free inhabitants of Roman Italy, and seldom to the inhabitants of the whole empire. I see no easy and elegant way out of these ambiguities. Finally, because of its subject matter and the quality of the surviving evidence, this chapter is quite different from conventional political history, in which time is the main vector of analysis. It is also different from the two previous chapters of this book, each of which worked outwards from specific and circumscribed bodies of evidence.

Secondly, we face particular problems in analysing the emotions

aroused in Romans by death. Once again, this is partly a problem
of evidence. Most of our evidence comes from inscribed tombstones.
Over 100,000 published epitaphs survive from the western half of the
empire alone. Those once carved and now lost were surely numbered
in millions. In our own culture, we too have incised gravestones,
probably in imitation of the Romans. That may lead us, without
thinking, to underestimate the significance of ancient tombstones,
both as an index of literacy and as a guide to the emotions aroused
by death. To be sure, many epitaphs record no emotion; they merely
state the name of the deceased and his or her commemorator. Even
those which do record emotions may have been carved by
stonemasons working from a stock of conventions, or even from
hand-books; the eventual epitaph may have had only a tenuous
connection with the instructions or feelings of the bereaved. We
confront similar problems with sophisticated essays on grief or with
elaborate semi-philosophical letters of consolation to the bereaved;
beneath the rhetorical veneer and the conscious imitation of literary
predecessors, we never know where feelings lie.

That is the kernel of our problem. What were their feelings? What
is the connection between the experience of feelings and their
expression? Needless to say, I have no satisfactory answer to such
questions. But Romans had feelings, and it seems reasonable to ask
what they were. Conventionally, both historians and sociologists
have been reluctant to discuss feelings or emotions. The notorious
recent failures of psycho-history have not helped. They may even
have reinforced the conviction that the proper subjects of history are
politics, law, institutions, war, power and property – in short, public
life. Emotions, private emotions, have been to a large extent ignored.

In Roman history, at least, with some reason. Most ancient sources
record events; they describe them much more thoroughly, and more
credibly, than the motives of the human actors involved. Modern
historians try to reconstruct Roman history and, in the absence of
sound evidence, attempt to rediscover intentions (what made leading
Romans act in a given way?), by working backwards from events
to probable motives. They usually do this by unconsciously assuming
a common-sense rationality: we can understand the Romans, or a
particular Roman, better by putting ourselves in his place. This
empathetic understanding is an irreplaceable and fruitful tactic. But
it can also be a dangerous trap, blinding the historian to important
differences between the Roman world and our own.

We should not take for granted that our modern patterns and
habits of reasoning necessarily linked Roman motives with Roman

actions. Their rationality was probably different from ours. In addition, it is at least worth asking when and why important decisions and actions in the Roman world were governed, as ours sometimes are, by non-rational emotions. When we boldly imagine ourselves as a Roman legionary on a distant frontier, or as the empress Messalina, or even as Nero, we should not assume a universally constant set of thoughts and emotions. But posing this problem is not the same as finding a solution to it. The truth is that nobody knows the precise relationship between the enormous cross-cultural variation in the expression of feelings and the ways in which those feelings are experienced.

II THE RICH AND THE POOR – INDIVIDUAL AND MASS GRAVES

The first sights which a visitor saw, as he entered the city of Rome, were monuments to the dead. They provide some of our best evidence for the importance which the Romans attached to the care of the dead. Surviving tombs, catacombs and cemeteries were strung along the roads on the outskirts of the city of Rome and other Roman towns. Some were grandiose structures, towers, columns, truncated cones, tombs like castle keeps or like private houses, some built as though to house modern reflector telescopes, others of strangely geometric design, including even a pyramid on the outskirts of Rome. This pyramid was built for a Roman senator, Gaius Cestius, who is otherwise unknown, in accordance with instructions in his will, towards the end of the last century BC. It is faced with slabs of white marble and must have cost a fortune, since it is 27 m high and about 22 m square at its base; it took 330 days to build, as the inscription on it proclaims (*CIL* 6.1374b). This pyramid is still a landmark in Rome today, and must have been even more impressive in ancient times.[4] If it was the dead man's intention to create a long-lasting memorial to himself, he succeeded.

The architectural virtuosity of large Roman tombs reflected the unrestricted use of internal space, since these monuments were designed mostly to hold only a single coffin. It was apparently rare for tombs to contain the remains of family members over several generation. A well-known exception is the burial-chamber of the

[4] For details and photographs of the pyramid, see S. B. Platner and T. Ashby, *A Topographical Dictionary of Ancient Rome* (Oxford, 1929) 478, E. Nash, *Pictorial Dictionary of Ancient Rome* (London, 1962) vol. 2, 321ff, and F. Coarelli, *Guida archeologica di Roma* (Rome², 1975) 305.

Death in Rome

Cornelii Scipiones, in the city of Rome. It contained several family coffins (*sarcophagi*), datable from inscriptions to the early third and the second century BC (*CIL* 1.² 6–16). In addition, the sepulchre contained several burials which cannot now be identified, and two burial inscriptions dating from as late as the first century AD, and dedicated to distant relatives (see *CIL* 6.1439). There was apparently some, but only some, continuity in the use of this family burial-chamber over several centuries. Of course, other long-term family burial-chambers may have existed, both in Rome and elsewhere; but very few have been discovered. For example, in the extensive excavations at Aquileia in northern Italy, tombs rarely contained the remains of more than two generations of any one family. This absence of long-established family burial-chambers is important; it looks as though, in the period from which such evidence survives (i.e. after about 200 BC), the Roman and Italian family was a small, short-lived social unit. It also seems as though broader kinship units, such as clans or clan segments (*gentes*), at least from this period onwards, played an unimportant role in burials; in Chapter 2, we argued that they were similarly unimportant in politics.[5]

My general impression is that rich Romans spent huge amounts of money, relative to the wealth available in their society, in order to create an enduring and ostentatious shelter for their dead. Some, like Cestius, left exact specifications in their wills for the the tombs which they wanted built. Others, like the emperor Augustus, chose not to rely on their successor nor to wait until death. Instead, they had their own tombs built while they were still alive. Augustus' mausoleum was enormous (87 m in diameter), and, surprisingly, it was built in 28 BC (Suetonius, *Augustus* 100); Augustus died in AD 14. But most rich Romans had their tombs erected for them after they

[5] For a description and discussion of the burial-chamber of the Cornelii Scipiones, see Coarelli 1975: 325ff, and Toynbee 1971: 113. For the excavations at Aquileia, see A. Calderini, *Aquileia Romana* (Milan, 1930) 371. Another family burial-chamber, lasting several generations, has been found at Tibur in Latium; inscriptions recorded the death of Marcus Plautius Silvanus, consul in 2 BC, and some of his descendants (*CIL* 14.3605–8). On ancestral clan rites, neglected in the second century BC, see Cato frag. 74 (*ORF* 34) and P. Fraccaro, *Opuscula* (Pavia, 1957) vol. 2, 1ff. For passing references to clan tombs, see, for example, Cicero, *On Laws* 2.55, Velleius Paterculus 2.119 and *RE sv Gens* 1186–7. In the picturesque graveyard surviving near Ostia (Isola Sacra) described by R. Meiggs, *Roman Ostia* (Oxford², 1973), some modestly built tombs contain spaces for 80–100 ash urns. They may have been designed with the intention of providing for a family over several generations, but in the event there is no evidence that this happened. This graveyard contained house-like tombs, which are remarkably similar in design to modern tombs still to be seen, for example, in Sicily at Agrigento and Enna.

had died, by a close relative. Overall, these relatives gave much more attention to, and spent much more money on tombs than we do in modern British culture. They did this partly out of respect for the dead, partly in the hope of immortalising their memory, and partly to impress the living.[6]

Many Romans died abroad on military service, without a family memorial. During the last two centuries BC, tens of thousands of Roman and Italian soldiers were almost continuously engaged in wars of conquest overseas. And they were bloodthirsty wars. Polybius, for example, has left a startling account of Roman soldiers' behaviour when Scipio Africanus was capturing the Spanish town of New Carthage in 210 BC:

> When Scipio thought that enough of his men had entered the town, he sent most of them, as the Roman custom is, to set upon the inhabitants, with instructions to kill anyone they came across and to spare nobody, and not to start plundering until the signal was given. The reason why the Romans do this, in my opinion, is to inspire terror; and when they are capturing cities, slaughtered men are a common sight, as well as dogs which have been sliced in two, and other dismembered animals. And that is exactly how it was on this particular occasion, because of the huge number of people who were caught inside the city. (Polybius 10.15)

This wanton slaughter of non-combatants strikes us as shocking, but it was probably taken for granted by many people in the Roman world. There can be no doubt that the Romans conquered the Mediterranean basin with carnage. And in the process, Roman armies suffered significant losses particularly in civil wars. Romans grew up in this period in the knowledge that sons would become soldiers, and face the risk of killing or of being killed. The prospect of their dying must have loomed large in their minds and in those of their families: 'Think of all those years lost by mothers and of the anxiety imposed on them while their sons are in the army' (Seneca, *Letter of Condolence to Marcia* 24). Many a Roman family which sent a young son or husband as a soldier abroad never saw him again.

Most poor Romans left no memorial. Many of the urban poor in the late Republic had their corpses thrown unceremoniously into

---

[6] The term 'their memory' is deliberately ambiguous. Commemorators often wanted to commemorate themselves as well as the dead. Almost all the Latin tombstone inscriptions from the city of Rome feature the commemorator's name as well as the dead person's. In a small and arbitrarily drawn sample (n = 200), a significant minority (23%) put the commemorator's name more prominently, excluding those who commemorated themselves while still alive (8%). On Augustus' tomb, see Platner and Ashby 1929: 332ff, Nash 1962: vol. 2, 38ff and Coarelli 1975: 274ff.

collective pits outside the city. These pits were called *puticuli*, a word which the scholar Varro associated with *putescere* – to rot (*On the Latin Language* 5.25; cf. also *putor* – stench). Archaeological excavations in the late nineteenth century of a burial area on the Esquiline hill just outside the city of Rome dramatically confirmed Varro's associations, not etymologically but in everyday life. A considerable number of these Roman burial pits were found; their average size was 5 m by 4 m square, and about 10 m deep. In many of them, according to the excavator R. Lanciani, the contents 'were reduced to a uniform mass of black, viscid, pestilent, unctuous matter'.[7] In a few cases, bones could be extracted and identified; it seems that human corpses, dead animals and ordure had all been thrown together into these pits. This degrading mixture of human and animals corpses was a common fate for the very poor.

Conditions in death probably mirrored living conditions in the city of Rome. We know very little about how the Roman poor lived. It was not a question which upper class Roman historians tackled.[8] But we do know that the living conditions of the poor in London in the eighteenth and nineteenth centuries were often appalling, in spite of developments in public medicine and growth in state expenditure on public welfare. We can easily imagine that the rapid growth of the city of Rome's population during the last century BC, without effective medicine or significant concern for public welfare (except through distributions of free or subsidised wheat), led to a sharp deterioration in the living conditions of the Roman poor. Constitutionally, the mass of the Roman poor had almost no political power. But in the streets, and at the Games, they had ample opportunity for political protest. It is striking, but I suppose not surprising, that tens of thousands of Roman citizens, living packed

---

[7] R. Lanciani, *Ancient Rome in the Light of Recent Discoveries* (London, 1888) 65. This is an exciting book, written when massive archaeological discoveries were being made in Rome. See also his 'Le antichissime sepolture Esquiline', *Bulletino della commissione archeologica comunale di Roma* 3 (1875) 43 and E. Brizio, *Pitture e sepolcri scoperti sull' Esquilino* (Rome, 1876) which at the back of the book has interesting drawings of the various urns and tombs found. Ancient commentators (scholiasts) on Horace (*Satires* 1.8) and the grammarian Festus (*sv puticuli*) stated that the corpses of the poor and of cheap slaves were buried and left to rot in these pits; see F. Pauly, *Scholia Horatiana* (Prague, 1861) vol. 2, 186.

[8] The necropolis at Isola Sacra, near Ostia, may be instructive. Behind the main street which cut through the cemetery, there was unplanned chaos: very poor graves were haphazardly intermingled with the house-like tombs of the prosperous. See G. Calza, *La necropoli del Porto di Roma nell' Isola Sacra* (Rome, 1940) plate 3 *ad* p. 36. I suspect that the cities of the living were similarly disorganised.

together in a culture which set a high value on a proper burial, tolerated the dehumanisation of mass graves.

During epidemics, mortality soared. Several ancient writers have left us vivid descriptions of the spread of infection, the unpredictable incidence of death, the difficulty of burying all the dead quickly, the increasing neglect of traditional burial rites, the stench of dead bodies, their contamination of the water supply and then further infection.[9] In such circumstances, cremation was too costly, because it consumed expensive fuel. Mass death involved mass burial; and in a serious epidemic there was no practical alternative to mass graves, into which the human dead were thrown pell-mell. The same nineteenth-century excavation in Rome revealed a mass grave near the Esquiline cemeteries and the ancient fortification of the city, Servius Tullius' wall, which had been reinforced with a moat. At some time in the late Republic, a section of this moat had been filled literally to the brim with corpses.[10] In 1876, a builder digging deep foundations for a new house found to his dismay that part of these new foundations collapsed, because they had been built over the ancient moat, which had been:

filled up with thousands upon thousands of corpses, which, when brought in contact with the air after twenty centuries, had crumbled into dust or

[9] The best account is by Procopius (2.22–3), describing the plague at Constantinople in AD 542, but there are several others, giving varying degrees of detail: cf. Dionysius Halicarnassus, *Roman Antiquities* 10.53, Tacitus, *Annals* 16.13 and, of course, the classic account by Thucydides 2.47ff. Sometimes, figures are given: 30,000 people are said to have died in the city of Rome in the autumn of AD 65 (Suetonius, *Nero* 39); 'often about 2,000 people died each day in Rome' during the plague of AD 189 (Dio 73.14). This evidence implies that the authorities in the city of Rome attempted to count deaths, but figures given in ancient sources are notoriously unreliable. And the descriptions may owe a lot to literary imagination and convention as well as to reality. In spite of these qualifications, the ancient testimony gives us some inkling of the frequency and severity of pestilence in the Roman world. For a cautious appraisal of evidence and of legitimate deductions, see J. F. Gilliam, 'The plague under Marcus Aurelius', *American Journal of Philology* 82 (1961) 247ff; E. Patlagean, *Pauvreté économique et pauvreté sociale à Byzance, 4e–7e siècles* (Paris, 1977) 73ff goes through the late evidence with a fine toothcomb.

[10] Lanciani 1888: 65. So far as I know, this discovery was not reported in any of the voluminous archaeological journals of the day, presumably – and it is a remarkable point – because the excavators found no *objets d'art* or Latin inscriptions, only the dust of 24,000 corpses. H. Jordan, *Topographie der Stadt Rom im Alterthum* (Berlin, 1878) vol. 1.3, 270 remarked sceptically that these remains could date from a later period; my inclination is to trust Lanciani in gross, if not in all details. Lanciani's report of the smell is high-flown; at first, I was sceptical that smells could survive for 2,000 years. But Professor A. M. Snodgrass, from his archaeological experience in Greece, assures me that they can last even longer; see similarly M. I. Rostovtzeff et al., edd., *The Excavations at Dura-Europus* (New Haven, 1936) *Preliminary Report of Sixth Season* 195.

nothing, leaving open a huge chasm. According to measurements which I took at the time, this mass of human remains was, at least, one hundred and sixty feet long, one hundred wide, and thirty deep. (R. Lanciani, *Ancient Rome in the Light of Recent Discoveries* (London, 1888) 66)

Lanciani estimated that this part of the moat had been filled with 24,000 corpses, during a single epidemic.

Even in normal circumstances, a city the size of Rome (with a population close on a million by the end of the last century BC and suffering high mortality) faced considerable problems in disposing of thousands of bodies each year. We can get some idea of these problems from a large boundary stone (2.2 m high × 0·65 m wide) which Lanciani also discovered during his excavations a few years later. It dates from the early first century BC, and was inscribed with the following regulation:

> L. Sentius, son of Caius, Praetor,
> has made regulation,
> by Decree of the Senate, about the siting of graves.
> For the Public Good. No burning of
> corpses beyond this marker in the
> direction of the city. No dumping of
> ordure or of corpses.

And added below, not incised but written in red letters, was the message:

TAKE SHIT FURTHER ON, IF YOU WANT TO AVOID TROUBLE. (*CIL* 6.31615)[11]

Lanciani commented that when this boundary stone was found (in 1884) he had to let his diggers off work from time to time, because the smell from the excavation was unbearable (1888: 67). If it was tough on excavators even then, it must have been much worse for Romans, two thousand years earlier.

In the reign of Augustus, this particular burial ground outside the Esquiline Gate, which Horace had once seen strewn with whitened bones, where witches gathered to summon the spirits of the dead (*Manes*), was converted into pleasure gardens (*Satires* 1.8). For rich Romans this was an extra convenience, and it preserved the site for modern archaeologists. But it did not solve the problem of where or how the urban poor should be buried. Of that we know little, except

---

[11] The Latin text of his painted message reads: *Stercus longe aufer ne malum habeas.* Two similar pillars (one 3.1 m high) with the same inscription have been found nearby, but without the additional message. See *CIL* 6.31614 and R. Lanciani, *Bulletino del commissione archeologica comunale di Roma* 10 (1882) 159 and 12 (1884) 59, and A. E. Gordon, *Greece and Rome* 20 (1951) 77–9 for details of these finds.

that at the end of the first century AD, the new emperor Nerva, probably in an attempt to win popularity, instituted the payment of a
substantial burial allowance (*funeraticium*) to the *plebs* in the city of
Rome.[12] Unfortunately, there is only one slender reference to this
innovation; we do not know whether it persisted; but Nerva's action
reflected central government concern for the continuing problem and
cost of burying the poor in the city of Rome.

In between grand monuments and mass graves there were simple
graves in small plots of land, often marked by a stone slab or altar.
From the end of the last century BC, it became common to incise
gravestones with the name of the deceased and his or her
commemorator.[13] But we cannot tell what proportion of the Roman
dead went to a mass grave, or were commemorated with wooden or
painted inscriptions which have perished, or were given a nameless,
even if individual grave. For example, poor Romans were sometimes
buried in giant wine jars (*amphorae*) split in half to form a cheap
container and cover for the corpse; smaller wine jars were also used
as receptacles for the ashes, their necks projecting above the ground,
both to mark the grave and to serve as a funnel, down which the
bereaved could pour libations to the dead.[14]

III   BURIAL CLUBS AND COLLECTIVE TOMBS

As the population of the city of Rome grew, the price of land around
the city soared. Romans responded to the twin problems of mass

[12] The burial allowance was 250 HS, payable to the urban plebs, presumably those
who received the wheat dole. See the *Chronography of the Year 354* in T. Mommsen,
ed. *Chronica Minora* (Berlin, 1892) vol. 1, 146.

[13] The mass of surviving Roman tombstone inscriptions, indeed the mass of all
Roman inscriptions, date from the first few centuries AD. There are only a few
hundred Roman inscriptions from the Republican period (before 31 BC). The
expansion of the city of Rome probably destroyed many earlier monuments.
Even so, and in spite of noted exceptions (see note 5 above), the relative
quantities of surviving evidence indicate that it first became fashionable to
inscribe tombstones in Roman Italy only towards the end of the last century
BC.

[14] So Toynbee 1971: 101ff and Calza 1940: 44ff, an evocative description of the
cemetery near Ostia, with good colour illustrations which remind us that some
Roman tomb-chambers, put up by people of middling wealth, were very prettily
decorated inside (see especially his Plates 1, 5 and 7). It is worth stressing that
cremation was dominant at Rome from about the fourth century BC to the end
of the first century AD, and then was gradually displaced by inhumation.
However, the practices co-existed, and it has proved impossible to correlate
change of practice with religious beliefs or with particular social groups; see
Toynbee 1971: 39ff and A. D. Nock's famous sceptical essay 'Sarcophagi and
symbolism', in his *Essays on Religion and the Ancient World*, ed. Z. Stewart (Oxford,
1972) vol. 2, 606ff. On grave goods, see, briefly, note 35 below.

burial and the high price of land, institutionally by developing co-operative burial clubs, and architecturally by building collective burial chambers, shaped like dovecots and called by modern scholars *columbaria*. First, burial clubs. The Roman central government was recurrently hostile to voluntary associations since it feared that they might become centres of political dissension. But burial clubs were allowed.[15] Burial clubs became a widespread feature of Roman society. Evidence has been found of their activities from all over the empire. Lists of club members (mostly male) survive in part, and so do occasional commemorations of dead members and of club officers; archaeologists have also uncovered several of their common burial chambers. Burial clubs, like other associations of artisans and traders, were often centred on a temple under the protection of tutelary deity. Some burial clubs centred on work associates such as, for example, the cloth-dealers and timber merchants at Antinum (*CIL* 9.3837), or the smiths at Venafrum (*CIL* 10.4855). Others were associations of people who had just bought a share in a collective or entrepreneurial project to erect a tomb-chamber, in which individuals were then allocated a space.[16]

[15] The emperor Trajan, for example, refused a provincial governor's request to form a fire-brigade of 150 men in a provincial town, on the grounds that whatever the original purpose, they would soon turn it into a political pressure group (Pliny, *Letters* 10.33–4). The danger was that firemen or other club members would form an organised claque, capable of disrupting local elections, assemblies and public games, and available to the highest bidder – so Tertullian, *In Defence of Christianity* 38. I doubt that the Roman government's legal regulations: no fire-brigades and no more than one meeting per month, no one to belong to more than one club (D. 47.22.1 – Marcian) were effectively enforced. To be sure, some illegal clubs were shut down, especially after riots (e.g. Tacitus, *Annals* 14.17); but Christianity survived in spite of persecution. The best modern account of clubs and associations (*collegia*) is still J. P. Waltzing, *Étude historique sur les corporations professionelles chez les Romains* (Louvain, 1895–1900) vol. 1, 115ff; vol. 4 contains a useful, although now incomplete, list of known collegia; see also F. M. de Robertis, *Il fenomeno associativo nel mondo romano* (Naples, 1955). A. Cameron, *Circus Factions* (Oxford, 1976) gives an exciting account of the workings of popular associations in the political arena in the late Roman and early Byzantine empire.

[16] For example, an inscription gives the following details about one co-operative: 'M. Aemilius Crestus and M. Fabius Felix, Directors in charge of this Tomb for 36 associates who have contributed money for its construction, have (themselves) received the accounts...' (Rome, 6 BC – *CIL* 6.11034). Other inscriptions found nearby then show that contributors each received one or several spaces (*loci*) by lot. For example, the ex-slave C. Rabirius Faustus received 5 spaces in separate draws (spaces 6, 9, 28, 30 and 31) – *CIL* 6.11044–8. We have occasional testimony about the sale of burial places in collective tombs; one man, Pinarius Rufus, is known to have sold four spaces for urns in one tomb (*CIL* 6.4884, 4902, 4940, 5014a). Even in Christian catacombs, which were the spiritual descendants of Roman *columbaria*, burial places were bought and sold (e.g. *IG* 14.83 and 96 – Syracuse).

Burial clubs and collective tombs

The popularity of burial clubs reflected the general Roman concern for the proper care of the dead, and an anxiety that death was both unpredictable and expensive. When a wife with young children lost her husband, she lost her chief means of support; it was not the easiest time to lavish money on a funeral (paid mourners, sacrifices at the grave, a funeral banquet, a commemorative tomb). In our culture we can insure against the risk of premature death. In the Roman world, many men of modest means (*tenuiores*) – free, slave and ex-slave, joined a burial club. The social intermingling of slave and free, well known elsewhere from religious sects in Roman Italy, is interesting, because it undermines our familiar dichotomy slave/free. In important social contexts slave and free met together, and were buried next to each other.[17] Burial clubs were also, I think, symptomatic of an urban society, in which many people needed to rely on fellow club members, unrelated by blood or marriage, for help in performing traditional funeral rites. They helped men to cope with an anxiety that they would perhaps die without kin or cash with which to provide a proper burial.

By chance, we have the rules of one burial club from the Italian town of Lanuvium near Rome, dating from AD 136 (an extract is printed on page 215). This club was founded under the joint auspices of the goddess Diana and of Antinous, the prematurely deceased but deified homosexual favourite of the reigning emperor Hadrian. A benefactor had given the interest (800 HS per year) on a capital sum (15,000 HS) to be spent equally on the birthdays of Diana and Antinous. He instructed that the rules of the club be inscribed in the porch of the temple of Antinous. These rules were formal and sophisticated (as the extract illustrates). They began with a quotation from a senatorial decree legalising burial clubs, providing that they met only once a month, and proclaimed the prime purpose of the club: 'to provide decent obsequies at the departure of the dead'. Would-be members were advised to read the rules carefully, in order to avoid complaints later and law-suits by their heirs. Detailed regulations and conditions of membership were set out; for example, those who had not paid their dues or who had committed suicide forfeited their right to club benefits; special arrangements were made for slave members

---

[17] Slaves were legally allowed to join a burial club only with the permission of their owners (D. 47.22.3.2 – Marcian). But even when a burial club or collective tomb-chamber was filled predominantly with slave and ex-slave members of a single household, free outsiders seem to have penetrated; for example, free men and free women were buried among imperial ex-slaves in the Vigna Codini *columbarium* (*CIL* 6.5214 and 5240) and also in the *columbarium* of the empress Livia's household (e.g. *CIL* 6.4153).

whose owners refused to hand over their bodies for burial by the club; fines were imposed for rowdiness at meetings. The detailed legal formalism of these rules is impressive in itself, and somewhat surprising to find so low in the social scale, in a small-town burial club. The legal formalism also implies that the members did not feel able to rely on the informal bonding of kin and community to secure a decent burial. So they relied instead, or as well, on the formal regulations of a burial club.

These burial clubs also served as social clubs, with regular feasts and business meetings. Providing a large jar of good wine was part of the entry fee. The clubs held most of their meeting on holidays associated with the rites of the dead.[18] Perhaps commemoration of the dead was merely an excuse for a good party. But the feasts often took place in banqueting rooms built above or adjoining their collective tombs (e.g. *CIL* 10.2015). Members may have chosen to ignore the location, but they feasted in the shadow of their own, unpredictable deaths.

Burial clubs provided men of modest means with a decent burial. But in the city of Rome they did more than that. They saved men from the anonymity of mass graves, and guaranteed each man's individuality in death. The development of burial clubs as social institutions is to be understood against the huge growth in the population of the city of Rome; by the end of the last century BC, it was approaching one million, and so was roughly as large as London in 1800 (see *Conquerors and Slaves* 96ff). It was an embryonic mass society, which threatened to submerge men's individuality, in death as well as in life.

The architectural adaptation to mass living and mass death was the dovecot burial chamber. This idea was adopted not only by burial clubs, but also by rich families with large numbers of slaves and ex-slaves to bury, and by individuals who could not afford an expensive private grave, but who were anxious to avoid a pauper's end in a mass burial pit. Men, women and children living like the proverbial sardines as slaves and ex-slaves in great households, or as tenants in multi-storeyed apartment blocks (*insulae*) were also buried in their serried ranks, pigeonholed in death. One *columbarium*

---

[18] For example, the burial club of the healing gods Aesculapius and Hygeia in the city of Rome received a considerable gift (50,000 HS) from the wife of an imperial ex-slave in honour of her dead husband, who had been assistant-keeper of the emperor's picture galleries. By the terms of the gift, the club was to meet several times a year: on the emperor's (Antoninus Pius) birthday, on the anniversary of the club's foundation, and at three festivals associated with commemorating the dead, the *Parentalia*, the *dies Violaris* and the *Rosaria* (*CIL* 6.10234; AD 153).

Burial clubs and collective tombs

It was voted unanimously that whoever desired to enter this society shall pay an entry fee of 100 HS and an *amphora* of good wine and shall pay monthly dues of 5 *asses* (1 1/4 HS)...If anyone has not paid his dues for six consecutive months and the common lot of man befalls him, his claim to burial shall not be upheld...It was voted further that upon the death of a paid-up member of our club, there will be due to him from the treasury 300 HS [enough to feed a family of four at minimum subsistence for about eight months] from which will be deducted a funeral fee of 50 HS to be distributed at the pyre (to the mourners)...It was voted further that if we hear that any member has died (up to) 20 miles from Lanuvium, three men from our society will be chosen, with the task of seeing to his funeral, and rendering a true and honest account to the members...They shall be given his funeral due, and over and above, shall receive travel expenses, there and back, of 20 HS each. If the member dies more than 20 miles away...if the man who has buried him testifies to having done so on a document signed and sealed by seven Roman citizens, and if his case is proved, and if we are satisfied that no one else will make the claim, he shall be given the man's funeral due, after expenses and funeral dues have been deducted in accordance with the rules of our club...

It was voted that, when any slave who is a member of the club dies, if his master or mistress should unjustly refuse to hand over his body for burial, and if the slave has left no directions, proper funeral rites will be performed over his imaginary body.

It was voted that if any member commits suicide, for whatever reason, he shall forfeit his right to a funeral.

It was voted that if any slave who is a member of this club should be freed, he shall be bound to pay an *amphora* of good wine.

(There follow regulations about the dates and proper conduct of feasts; there were to be six each year on the birthdays of the founders and patrons. The four men chosen to be in charge of each feast)...must provide an *amphora* of good wine, as many 2-*as* loaves of bread as there are members in the club, four salt fish, covers for the table, couches, warm water and attendants...

It was resolved that if anyone has any complaint or wishes to discuss anything, he should bring it up at a meeting, so that we may feast on ceremonial days in peace and good cheer.

It was resolved that if any member moves from his place to another place in order to create a disturbance, he should be fined 4 HS. If any member insults another, or becomes rowdy, he should be fined 12 HS. If any member becomes insulting or abusive towards the president at feasts, he should be fined 20 HS.

It was resolved that each president, on the ceremonial days while he is in office, should make offerings of incense and wine, and should officiate, robed in white, at other ceremonies. And on the birthdays of Diana and Antinous, he should place oil at the public baths for members of the club, before the feast takes place. (*CIL* 14.2112)

discovered in 1726 but since left to decay is estimated to have held 3,000 burial urns in a chamber 10 × 6 m, and 7 m high.[19] The urns in this collective tomb belonged mostly but not exclusively to the slaves and ex-slaves of Livia, the wife of the emperor Augustus. Other excavated *columbaria* held 600 or 700 urns, but there were smaller ones. They all share similar characteristics. The general decoration fell to the entrepeneur or collective which built the tomb, but niches were decorated individually, by their occupants. The niches were bought or allocated by lot ('4th lot, 34th place' *CIL* 6.11042) and could be traded. Sometimes they were numbered (for example '4th wall, 2nd niche' *CIL* 6.10293; '3rd gate, 5th urn' *IG* 14.150). Cinerary urns were placed in rectangular or arched niches, usually two, but sometimes four or more per niche. There were steps and movable wooden platforms (the stone supports are still visible) which allowed relatives to visit and place offerings by the urns of the departed. Burial clubs ensured relatives access and space for cooking commemorative banquets and for drawing water, and nearby reserved places for burning corpses. Nowadays the *columbaria* are kept clean, in archaeological reservations: in some, their bare walls are bathed in electric light. In Roman times, they must have been prettier, decorated in painted stucco, but were dingily lit by distant sloping overhead windows.[20]

Collective tombs were an attempt to cope with burial in a mass society. What at first seems surprising is that many of the pigeon-holes in these collective tombs were marked by inscriptions giving the name and relationship of the commemorator. Even when buried together, people were concerned to preserve their individuality in death. And

[19] This fine collective tomb is beautifully drawn by G. B. Piranesi, *Le antichità romane* (Rome, 1756) vol. 3, Plate 26, imperfectly reproduced in DS *sv Columbarium* Fig. 1741, which also gives a ground plan and several interesting reconstructions; further details are usefully collected in *RE sv Columbarium*. Good pictures are reproduced in Nash 1961: vol. 2, 333ff.

[20] The original and very pretty moulded stucco in several Roman graves can be seen in the tombs excavated from 1939 onwards deep under St Peter's in Rome (J. M. C. Toynbee and J. Ward Perkins, *The Shrine of St Peter and the Vatican Excavations* (London, 1956) 80ff, reproduced, for example, in Toynbee 1971: Plate 42). The Romans used selenite as well as glass for windows; it gives a diffused but good light, as can still be seen in the church of St Sabina on the Aventine in Rome. Some collective tombs had two or three storeys, with only the bottom storey below ground; others like the Christian catacombs were deep and murky. Such murkiness tempted re-use: for example, the end of the third room of the Vigna Codini *columbarium* in Rome (see Coarelli 1975: 335ff) was in ancient times filled with corpses thrown in pell-mell, presumably when the original occupiers had been forgotten (see R. Lanciani, *The Ruins and Excavations of Ancient Rome* (Boston, 1897) 332). On Christian catacombs, see P. Styger, *Die römischen Katakomben* (Berlin, 1933).

in the same period, at the end of the last century BC, it became common, albeit somewhat expensive, to portray the dead man or woman, sometimes husband and wife together, in stone.[21] Paradoxically, Roman mass society helped boost this individualism in death. Commemorative inscriptions and collective tombs were relatively simple ways of avoiding the shameful anonymity of a mass grave. Individual funerary portraits were a further attempt to secure the social survival of the dead in the world of the living. These portraits are especially interesting to us, because they are so different in their realism from classical Athenian idealisations. Sculptors in Rome carved faces of men and women of middling means in the style created by the waxen images of aristocrats.[22]

IV   FUNERALS, GRIEF AND MOURNING

Death is a protracted social process. Commemorative inscriptions and funerary portraits are only the long-surviving residues of social rituals and personal experience. If we are to understand how the

---

[21] Originally, prosperous Romans kept waxen masks of ancestors in cupboards at home (Pliny, *Natural History* 35.6). By the end of the first century BC, portrait busts made perhaps of terracotta replaced waxen masks (we know of them from stone grave reliefs which depict busts in cupboards with open doors (A. N. Zadoks-Josephus Jitta, *Ancestral Portraiture in Rome* (Amsterdam, 1932): Plates 4–5). In the same period, some tombs had an inset stone portrait bust of the deceased. In the Augustan period, in the city of Rome, it became common (92 examples survive) for the dead person to be commemorated in a group relief, sometimes hand in hand with the commemorator. Surprisingly, all those whose status is known were ex-slaves. We do not know why, although we can speculate. For an interesting study, fully illustrated, see D. E. E. Kleiner, *Roman Group Portraiture* (New York, 1977). The origins of these new forms of Roman art are of course disputed – the best explanation seems to be that they arose from a combination of Roman native tradition, contemporary tastes and immigrant Greek artists. See O. Vessberg, *Studien zur Kunstgeschichte der römischen Republik* (Lund, 1941) 173ff – with excellent reproductions, and Zadoks-Josephus Jitta 1932: 4ff for arguments; on important details, these two disagree.

[22] Dr S. Walker of the British Museum kindly warns me that I should not exaggerate the realism of Roman sculpture of this period; it also followed conventions; some portraits look remarkably alike, even though each appears realistic, when viewed individually. A good point. But I stick by the idea that Roman sculptors were trying to express significant individual differences in their portraiture, as well as ideal virtues, and that their style descended from, though it was distinct from, that of death masks. Roman realism could be ghoulish. After the assassination of Julius Caesar, his body was brought to the Forum and displayed as was customary on a bier. But it could not easily be seen by all the crowd. So a waxen effigy was made and fixed above the bier, where it was revolved by some mechanism so that the crowd could clearly see the 23 wounds on all parts of Caesar's body – so Appian, *Civil Wars* 2.147; a display rivalling Madame Tussaud's.

Romans coped with death, we should be careful not to overrate the historical importance of monuments which were made of stone and have therefore survived. We have to try to understand what Romans felt, and that is very difficult. A few tombstones depict funeral cortèges and sorrowing survivors. According to ancient Roman ideals, men should be unmoved by personal loss, while women were allowed much greater licence, though in the Twelve Tables (10.4; traditional date 451 BC), they were prohibited from tearing their cheeks with their nails at funerals. Later philosophical essays advise readers of both sexes against grieving too loudly, too much or too long.[23] Such exhortations surely imply that uncontrolled or 'unseemly' mourning was widespread.

No detailed Roman account of a private funeral survives. But there is a vivid account of beliefs and funerary practices at well below the aristocratic level written by the satirist Lucian. He was born in Syria in the second century AD, lived in Greece, and travelled widely in the Roman empire, eventually becoming an administrator in the imperial service in Egypt. His writings are partly descriptions of contemporary life in different parts of the Roman empire, partly derived from literature, and partly sheer invention. We do not know whether this description of a funeral depicted any particular cultural circle.[24] But it coincides, as closely as words and pictures can, with

[23] Seneca, for example, exhorted Marcia, a Roman aristocrat who had lost a son, to follow the example of Livia, wife of the emperor Augustus. When she lost her son, she received and listened to the philosopher Areus, even 'during the first passion of grief, when sufferers are most impatient and violent' and gained much comfort from him. By contrast, Octavia, Augustus' sister, when she lost her son 'for all the rest of her life, set no bounds to her weeping and wailing, and refused to listen to anybody who offered helpful advice' (*Letter of Condolence to Marcia* 2.3ff, cf. his similar letter to Polybius). In both letters, the arguments are filled with commonplaces of Stoic philosophy. But educated Romans read such literature, however boring we find it. There was a tension between philosophical ideals and normal practice. This is clear from Cicero's reaction to his daughter Tullia's death, and in Plutarch's reaction to the death of an infant daughter. He wrote a long letter to his wife, when he heard the news. He told her to keep her grief under control. He would find extravagant expression of grief more painful than the loss itself; he was glad to hear that she was bearing the loss philosophically. He implied that her reaction was exceptional. Most people in a similar situation would yield to 'the insatiable appetite for wailing, which excites us until we are beside ourselves with noisy lamentation' (609B, cf. 114F).

[24] Besides the essay *On Grief* quoted below, two other essays, *Charon* (511ff) and *Conversations with the Dead* (363ff) are very amusing about death, especially the latter, in which the dead, before they can cross into Hades in Charon's small boat, must strip off their pretensions as well as their clothes. The philosopher, for example, has shed his cloak but is still overweight: 'Good God, what pretensions he carries, what humbug, competitiveness, conceit, unanswerable questions, thorny arguments and complicated concepts, not to mention wasted effort, a great deal of nonsense, a lot of fuss about nothing and split hairs...' (*Conversations with the Dead* 369). Not much changes in the world of scholarship.

the impression one gets from the detailed tableaux of the stages of mourning carved on the family tomb of the Haterii, now in the Vatican museum.[25] This correspondence gives us confidence that elements of Lucian's account are transposable to some sections of the Roman bourgeois population.

> Then the women begin to wail and shriek, and they all weep and beat their breasts, tear their hair and scratch their cheeks until they bleed. On some occasions they tear their clothes into strips and sprinkle dust on their heads. as a result, the living are more pitiable than the dead, as they roll repeatedly all over the ground and beat their heads against the floor, while the dead man, serene and handsome, elaborately garlanded, lies in lofty exalted state, decked out as though for a pageant.
>
> What happens next is that his mother or even his father comes forward from among the crowd of relatives and throws himself upon the corpse. To heighten the drama of the scene, let us imagine that the dead man was young and handsome. The father emits strange and foolish cries, which would provoke the corpse itself to answer, if it could. In a plaintive tone, protracting every word, he says: Sweetest child, you are gone from me, dead, snatched away before your time, leaving me behind all alone and grieving, before marriage, before having children, before serving in the army, before working the farm, before reaching old age! Never again will you join in a festival, or fall in love, or get drunk at parties with your young friends.
>
> This is the sort of thing he will say... But the old man who mourns in this way with all the melodramatic ranting which I have described, and more besides, probably does not do it on his son's account, nor for himself. After all he knows that his son will not hear him... it is on account of the others present that he talks this nonsense... (*On Grief* 12–15)

Lucian then makes the corpse reply, in an attempt to stop his father shrieking and making a fool of himself in front of so many witnesses. He makes the young corpse put forward the routine philosopher's case in favour of early death: 'What do you think I am suffering that is so terrible? Are you grieving because I did not get to be an old man like you, with your head bald, your face wrinkled, your back bent, and your knees trembling?' Lucian's praise of death over life falls a bit flat, but he picks up speed again in his attack on the old man's wailing, the extravagant conduct of the women in lamenting, and the uselessness of pouring wine on the grave: 'You don't think do you, that it will drip down... and get all the way to Hades?' (*ibid.* 19). Lucian's essay is entertaining, but it hardly does justice to the social pressures which drove the mourners to display their grief or to the real feelings of sorrow which relatives and friends experienced in bereavement.

[25] Conveniently reproduced by Toynbee 1971, Plate 9, cf. 10–11.

Death in Rome

Of this sorrow in bereavement, there is ample testimony on tombstones and in literature. Cicero's description of his grief at his daughter's death is very touching. He had just received a letter of sympathy from his friend Sulpicius, which took for granted that he was deeply distressed. Cicero replied: 'At times I feel overwhelmed and can hardly fight my grief' (*Letters to his Friends* 4.5–6). In his letters to Atticus of the same period, Cicero claimed that he had read 'everything that anyone has ever written on the topic of assuaging grief', but his sorrow could not be conquered. He could hardly work; his attempts to read were constantly interrupted by tears. It was a great struggle to appear composed, impossible to feel it. 'Even the idea of seeing you upsets me', he wrote, '...everything in me that you used to love has died' (*Letters to Atticus* 12.14–15).

To be sure, these letters are literary compositions, products of art as well as feeling, and difficult to interpret. But all that does not rule out the underlying fact, as I see it, that Cicero was suffering. Similarly, it is clear from Seneca's *Letter of Condolence* to Marcia, a close friend of the empress Livia, that she had been severely stricken by grief for her two dead sons; even three years after the death of the second son, she had not yet recovered.

Many Latin epitaphs are touching. But we have to be careful. Grief was expressed on tombstones from a limited stock of conventions.[26] But then feelings always are; the very act of transforming feelings into words automatically channels them along conventional lines. Language is a set of conventions. In order to interpret epitaphs, we have to resort to subjective judgement. To me, the emotions which inspired the following two epitaphs, from a father and from a husband, are immediately recognisable as grief:

---

[26] These conventional formulae are arranged by topic and interestingly discussed by R. B. Lattimore, *Themes in Greek and Latin Epitaphs* (Urbana, Ill. 1942). In spite of these conventional ingredients, many epitaphs leave an individual and even touching impression, although *en masse* the total impact is stupefying; at least that is my personal reaction. For collections, see F. Buecheler, *Carmina Latina Epigraphica* (Leipzig, 1895–1926) 3 vols.; and for Greek epitaphs, G. Kaibel, *Epigrammata graeca ex lapidibus conlecta* (Berlin, 1878), or the convenient selection edited with a German translation by W. Peek, *Griechische Grabgedichte* (Berlin, 1960). My untutored eye sees more conventionality in the pictorial decoration of Roman tombs (deriving probably from stonemasons not mourners) than in epitaphs. Unfortunately, there is no synoptic catalogue of Roman tomb art comparable with the magnificent work of E. Pfuhl and H. Möbius, *Die ostgriechischen Grabreliefs* (Mainz, 1977–9) 4 vols.; both authors died before their work was completed. And see the interesting articles on ancient tomb sculpture collected in *Archäologische Anzeiger* (1977) 327ff. On Roman tombs, W. Altmann, *Die römischen Grabaltäre der Kaiserzeit* (Berlin, 1905) is not yet superseded.

My baby Acerva was snatched away to live in Hades before she had had her fill of the sweet light of life. She was beautiful and charming, a little darling as if from heaven. Her father weeps for her, and because he is her father asks that the earth may rest lightly on her for ever. (*CIL* 14.1731 – Ostia)

And similarly:

I have lost my wife. Why should I stay longer now? If I had been fortunate, my Piste would have been alive. I am gripped by grief, alive when my wife is dead. Nothing is so miserable as to lose your whole life, (and yet to go on living). (*CIL* 6.15546)

The trouble with subjective judgement is that it is liable to error, all the more so since we are translating from one language to another; modern English may infuse Latin words with feelings which were not intended. And in any case, a poet writing odes, however evocative, is not necessarily heart-broken, while she who mourns silently or expresses her grief conventionally on a tombstone may nevertheless be truly grief-stricken. In spite of these difficulties, it is important to stress that Roman culture allowed, gave opportunities for, and at funerals even encouraged, the public expression of grief.

Understanding grief is difficult. The main problem lies in the gap between expression and experience. Each culture fosters different rituals, different ways of expressing grief; and so we get essays and books on Greek funeral rites, Roman funeral rites, and on funeral rites in Madagascar, China and the USA. We can correlate these rites with beliefs about life after death, with social organisation or with economic and demographic conditions. For example, Goody has suggested that funeral rites are more elaborate when death involves the redistribution of the dead person's wealth.[27] But can we go behind the rites, behind the forms of expression in order to understand the feelings experienced by those involved? Many historians and anthropologists may think that such a question is misconceived; at

---

[27] J. Goody, *Production and Reproduction* (Cambridge, 1976) 9; cf. his earlier fundamental monograph *Death, Property and the Ancestors* (London, 1962), a study of the mortuary customs of the Lodagaa in West Africa. M. Alexiou, *The Ritual Lament in Greek Tradition* (Cambridge, 1974) provides an excellent account of Greek lament through several centuries, and also points out (p. 20) the close connection between the right to mourn and the right to inherit. R. Huntington and P. Metcalf, *Celebrations of Death* (Cambridge, 1979) serves as a useful introduction to the anthropological literature on mortuary ritual, although it is more of a monograph than its title suggests. Among historical works, M. Vovelle, *Le piété baroque et déchristianisation* (Paris, 1973), a study of wills in which testators left money for perpetual masses to be said for their souls in Provence in the eighteenth century, is methodologically sophisticated.

the very least, rites are the cultural mirror in which feelings are reflected. Or in a stronger view, rites do not merely express, they also mould feelings; feelings therefore cannot be analysed apart from the rites or the language in which they are expressed, any more than dreams can be analysed apart from the words which dreamers use to describe them. Some psychologists, on the other hand, take it for granted that certain feelings are common elements in a universal human experience. Grief following bereavement is one such feeling. Cultural variety merely disguises this common experience. Rites provide a framework within which some human emotions can be expressed, others suppressed, only to surface later and in different social contexts. But grief cannot be evaded; it is part of the human condition.

The clash is between cultural relativism and human nature. Such issues are far too large for this chapter. And so I shall simplify discussion by the convenient tactic of polarising the argument into two opposing camps, occupied by cultural relativists and ethological humanists. Cultural relativists would argue, or simply assume, that culture and material conditions significantly change both the expression and the experience of grief. Historians and anthropologists, as I have already implied, tend to be cultural relativists. They are more interested in the variety of mortuary rites or in changes over time than in the cross-cultural similarity or constancy of underlying emotions. For example, Stone argued that in England during the sixteenth and seventeenth centuries, when mortality was high, frequent death and the expectation that death might at any time rupture close relationships prevented people from investing huge amounts of emotion in loving attachments or intimacy: 'to preserve their mental stability, parents were obliged to limit the degree of their psychological involvement with their infant children'.[28] Only when mortality fell could there be a revolutionary growth of 'affective individualism', that is, a growth in the emotional commitment made between husbands and wives and between parents and children; then too a growth occurred in the extent to which individuals pursued individual loves, without being deterred by collective family goals. Stone assumes that men and women's emotions are governed by their demographic and material conditions. By implication he advances

---

[28] L. Stone continued: 'Even when children were genuinely wanted, and not regarded as economically crippling nuisances, it was very rash for parents to get too emotionally concerned about creatures whose expectation of life was so very low' (*The Family, Sex and Marriage in England 1500–1800* (London, 1979) 57, cf. 80ff = 70 and 93ff in the larger 1977 edition).

a theory which should hold good, *mutatis mutandis*, in other cultures where mortality was high. Paradoxically, in Stone's view, one cost of modern emotional commitment is deep-felt grief at the death of loved ones. And yet, in modern industrial societies, where affective individualism is widely assumed to be a birth-right, a basic element in human nature, the display of grief is severely constrained. Depths of feelings about bereavement and opportunities for their open expression seem out of balance.[29]

The ethological humanist argument is that grief is common to apes and humans. Evolutionary development and culture may alter surface expressions of grief, but behind the astonishing variety of cultural expressions, much is constant. It is after all 'only natural' for a mother to mourn her baby's death. There is a normal process of grieving, with stages which go from numbness, through intense distress and anger, then pining and searching for the lost figure, through disorganisation and despair, to the gradual reformation of a new social identity. Bowlby is one of the most eloquent and persuasive members of this school. He cites evidence from modern British and American studies which show how widows and parents of dead children very often have vivid dreams of the dead, and hallucinatory meetings or conversations with them. Survivors yearn for reunion with the dead; intermittently, widows dream or hope that their husbands are not really dead; they keep visiting old haunts which previously they had both frequented together – all in order to preserve a continuing, though diminishing relationship with the dead loved one. Even after a year, a majority of widows interviewed in both British and American studies were still grieving a great deal, or were intermittently disturbed or distressed, and were not feeling wholly themselves again.[30] There is no necessary implication of a single, constant, cross-cultural human nature; but there are some constant human elements or drives. Without taking a specific position in this debate, I think that these modern observations

[29] The other side of the paradox is that open and dramatic expressions of grief are found particularly in those societies in which, according to Stone's theory, feelings of grief were constrained. Restrictions on expressions of grief in our own society are relevant here, because they shape our expectations about appropriate feelings. See G. Gorer, *Death, Grief and Mourning in Contemporary Britain* (London, 1965). Gorer regretted the decline of rituals which allowed the open display of grief, and the social isolation of the recently bereaved. See also C. M. Parkes, *Bereavement* (London, 1972) from which I have borrowed the phrase 'the cost of commitment' and the successive stages of grief, and P. Marris, *Loss and Change* (London, 1974), two good but very different studies of mourning.

[30] J. Bowlby, *Loss: Sadness and Depression* (London, 1980) 81ff – a most impressive work. It is volume three of *Attachment and Loss* (London, 1969–80).

suggest interpretations of Roman evidence. They suggest that Roman funeral customs, with their public and open expressions of grief, visits to the grave, feeding the dead, the recognition of anniversaries and prescribed periods of mourning, helped provide social support for mourners' basic psychic needs.

In both camps, the arguments are complex and sophisticated. My simplifications are in no way intended to suggest that there is a straight opposition between anthropologists or historians and psychologists or ethologists. For example, the noted anthropologist Malinowski sought to identify the problems which underlay all funeral rites in tribal societies. He argued that mourners are torn between 'love of the dead and loathing of the corpse'. Survivors want both to maintain the tie with the dead person, and yet to break the bond. They fluctuate between lingering attachment to the personality of the dead person, and fear of the gruesome corpse. In different societies, mortuary rituals of mummification at one extreme and of incineration at the other extreme reflect the competing objectives of preservations and rejection. The dramatised outbursts of grief which are so often expected at funerals in tribal societies, indeed the whole mortuary ritual 'compels man to overcome the repugnance, to conquer his fears, to make piety and attachment triumphant...'.[31]

Complementarily, some of the psychological studies of bereavement bring us closer to the cultural relativist camp. Modern clinical evidence shows that mothers bereaved of young children suffer immensely (see notes 29–30). But in some cases, the mother's loss deeply affects her emotional relationships with her other, surviving or subsequent children; for example they may be rejected, or be treated as idealised replacements of the dead person. It is an important part of Bowlby's thesis that such rejections or idealisations affect a child deeply, so that he or she in turn, when adult, will tend to react pathologically if similarly bereaved, often by denying that bereavement matters.

The relationship between individual pathology and broad cultural patterns of behaviour is almost uncharted territory. But this psychological research implies that repeated bereavements among parents and children might engender a façade of indifference, without providing immunity from grief. It raises the question once again as to how parents or children coped with frequent deaths in a society such as Rome or sixteenth-century England, which suffered from

---

[31] B. Malinowski also argued that attitudes to death 'among the most primitive peoples' were complex and 'more akin to our own than is commonly assumed'. See his *Magic, Science and Religion* (repr. New York, 1954) 47–8 and 50.

high mortality. Repeated individual psychological experiences must at some level or stage affect the dominant cultural mode of coping with grief.

Did repeated deaths inure Romans against deep and long-lasting grief at the loss of close relatives? There are many fewer tombstone inscriptions to infants and young children than we should expect. Demographic expectations, based on comparative evidence, indicate that more than a quarter (28%) of all live-born Roman babies died within their first year of life (I am assuming an average expectation of life at birth of 25 years). Let us now compare this expectation with what we can observe. On tombstones recording ages at death surviving from the city of Rome and Italy (N = 16,106), only 1.3% were set up to babies who died when they were less than one year old. Of these, many more were boys than girls (179m: 100f). Among infants who died aged one to four years old the level of under-recording on tombstones was much lower (expected: 21% of all deaths; observed: 13%), but again the recorded sex-ratio was unrealistically high (162:100). One obvious explanation is that dead babies and infants, especially if they were girls, did not have a social personality which justified individual commemoration. In strict law, they received no formal mourning.[32] As children grew older, they stood a greater chance of commemoration, but their deaths were still under-recorded compared with youths and young adults (I discuss these patterns of commemoration further in the next volume). Can we deduce from all this that Roman parents passively tolerated, or pretended not to care about the death of babies and young children? I do not think so. After all, many parents did commemorate their children's deaths, and some did so in touching individual epitaphs (e.g. pp. 221 and 227).

And yet nagging doubts remain. Even rich and educated Romans killed or exposed new-born babies. For example, the future emperor Claudius had a baby daughter exposed, reportedly because he thought she was not his own (Suetonius, *Claudius* 27). Several authors (Seneca, Musonius Rufus, Tacitus, Tertullian) implied that infanticide was common enough among the rich and powerful, without our being able to quantify it even very roughly. For present purposes,

---

[32] In very ancient Roman practice, according to Plutarch (*Numa* 12), children who died under the age of three were not to be mourned formally at all; for children who died over three but under ten years old, the mourning period was one month per year of life. In late Roman law, children who died under one year old were not to be mourned at all, and those who died less than three years old were to be half-mourned (*sublugetur* – *Frag. Vat.* 321 = *FIRA* vol. 2, 536). The persistence of these regulations is interesting; but their relation to practice is unknown.

that does not matter much. What matters is that Roman parents killed or exposed new-born infants, and no one objected effectively.[33] What did parents feel as they killed? There is almost no testimony, but Plutarch, who is on the whole a perceptive and sympathetic writer, claimed that deaths of infants and of young children could be borne with equanimity, even with indifference: 'Untimely death is an evil; the most untimely death is that of infants and children, and above all of the newly born. But those are the deaths which we can bear easily and cheerfully...' (*Moral Essays* 113D). There is no need to think that such sentiments were universal in the Roman world; doubtless many parents adored their children and were broken-hearted if they died (cf. Horace, *Epistles* 1.7.2ff). Plutarch's view is probably more of a philosopher's prescription than an acute observation of common practice. Even so, it seems remarkable to us that such views could be openly expressed, though we should take into account the ethological humanist argument that heart-felt grief can be masked by social or psychic pressures. Roman funeral rites had the advantage of cracking this façade of indifference by demanding open and dramatic expressions of grief, especially from women, in violation of the self-control which was conventionally expected of them.

V   THE COMMEMORATION OF THE DEAD AND LIFE
AFTER DEATH

The experience and expression of grief may also depend on the nature of beliefs about life after death. For example, some of the bereaved may have derived comfort from the idea that they would eventually meet the departed in the Lands of the Blessed. At this point, we face considerable difficulties. Roman religious beliefs were extraordinarily varied; there was no single dominant orthodoxy; polytheism was supplemented by inventive, philosophical speculation and by individual sects, such as Stoicism, Mithraism, Judaism and

---

[33] There is no satisfactory modern study of Roman infanticide, though see the useful collection of references in *RE sv Kinderaussetzung* and DS *sv Infanticidium*. The most striking passages on the subject are Musonius Rufus, ed. O. Hense (Leipzig, 1905) frag. 15b quoted above, p. 96, Tacitus, *Germania* 19 and Tertullian's counter-attack against pagan judges: 'How many of you, most just governors (*praesides*), who are so severe against us, should be struck in your consciences for having killed your own children, when they are already born?' (*In Defence of Christianity* 9). See also Seneca, *On Anger* 1.15, Hierocles quoted by Stobaeus, *Anthology* ed. C. Wachsmuth and O. Hense (Leipzig, 1889–1912) vol. 4, 603 and the frequent references to exposed children by the senator Firmicus Maternus, *Astrological Handbook* 7.2.

Christianity. To outline the doctrines on after-life of each sect would be a tremendous task, well beyond the scope of this chapter (and beyond my competence).[34] Nor would it be sufficient, since we are concerned here not only with what priests or philosophers taught, but also with what was believed by their adherents and by non-believers. My solution is simply to sketch the range of Roman beliefs about life after death, as conventionally understood, and to illustrate them from non-doctrinal literature and from tombstone epitaphs. For all their short-comings, these epitaphs provide the best available evidence for the penetration of philosophical and religious ideas about immortality beyond the narrow set of philosophers, theologians and litterateurs, whose writings survive.

Pagan beliefs ranged from the completely nihilistic denial of after-life, through a vague sense of souls' ghostly existence, to a concept of the individual soul's survival and of personal survival in a recognisable form. These individual surviving souls were sometimes subject to a purgation which reflected a moral judgement on the virtues and misdeeds of the life just lived. Most tombstones were dedicated to the *Manes*, the revered spirits of the dead (see p. 228 for an illustrative selection of epitaphs). Originally, these *Manes* were ghostly shadows, without personal or individual shape. They were transient beings which inhabited the underworld for the period between leaving one body and entering another (Servius, *Commentary on Virgil's Aeneid* 3.63). But from the last century BC, some Romans depicted individuals as having an individual existence after death. On tombstones, which survive mostly from the early centuries AD, commemorators often assumed that the dead person would survive as an individual in the world of the dead. For example, one father expressed bitter grief and longing for his nine-year old daughter, and hoped that he would one day be reunited with her in death:

> ... The cruel Fates have left me a sad old age.
> I shall always be searching for you, my darling Asiatica.
> Sadly shall I often imagine your face
> to comfort myself. My consolation will be that soon
> I shall see you, when my own life is done,
> and my shadow is joined with yours. (*CIL* 11.3771 cf. (*k*) on p. 228)

The specific expressions of his grief remind us of modern observations about bereavement: mourners often have a strong yearning for the

---

[34] The best discussion of Roman beliefs is still that by Cumont 1959; see also his *Recherches sur le symbolisme funéraire des Romains* (Paris, 1942), sceptically reviewed by Nock 1972: vol. 2, 606ff. On epitaphs, see Lattimore 1932.

Death in Rome

Some Illustrative Tombstone Inscriptions*

(a) To the revered Spirits of the Dead. To M. Annius Paulinus. He lived 17 years 2 months 2 days. Annia Smyrna to her most loved son (City of Rome)

(b) To the revered Spirits of the Dead. To M. Metilius Emineus. Valeria Prima set this up to her husband with whom she lived 15 years 3 months 20 days. He deserved well (Beneventum, Italy)

(c) Sacred to the revered Spirits of the Dead. Fatia Rogatina lived 55 years Ma...phius set it up to his dearest mother. May the earth lie lightly on you (Theveste, Tunisia)

(d) To Pollia Cominia Lucilius Artemidorus to an incomparable wife (Milan, Italy)

(e) To the revered Spirits of the Dead. To Tertius (Split, Yugoslavia)

(f) I Apphia lie here with my husband Menekles When we were alive together we had this privilege. We leave two children; the younger is Artemidorus: out of piety he built this tomb for the departed; Hail, passers-by, say a prayer for him (Apamea Cibotos, central Asia Minor)

(g) Parents to Innocentia who lived 5 years and 3 months and 18 days. She was buried 16 March. In Peace (City of Rome, Christian)

(h) In the year 250 [AD 166], on the 1st day of the month Loos, Alexandros with his children to his wife Valeria and to himself while he is alive *In Memoriam*. Whoever lays an envious hand (on his tomb), may he meet an untimely fate (Phrygia, Asia Minor)

(j) Tibur was my home; Flavius Agricola my name. Yes, I'm the one you see reclining here, just as I used to once at dinner, for all the years of life which Fate granted me, taking good care of myself. And I was never short of wine. Flavia Primitiva, my darling wife passed away before me. Chaste worshipper of Isis, attentive to my needs; and graced with every beauty. Thirty happy years we lived together. As a consolation, she left me the fruit of her body, Aurelius Primitivus, to tend my tomb with dutiful affection. Friends, who read this, listen to my advice: mix wine, tie the garlands around your head, drink deep. And do not deny pretty girls the sweets of love. When death comes, earth and fire consume everything (Rome)

(k) Valerius Philologus, ex-slave of Marcus, To Qutia Silvana his wife. I await my husband (Narbonne, France)

*The sources of these epitaphs are:
(a) *CIL* 6.11746; (b) 9.1882; (c) 8.10660; (d) 5.6070; (e) 3.2554; (f) Kaibel 1878: 386; (g) *ICUR* 13557; (h) Pfuhl and Möbius 1979: 1137; (j) *CIL* 6.17985a; (k) 12.5193.

dead loved one, they have a vivid image of his or her face, and imagine that, one day soon, they will meet again.

Individual survival after death was also reflected in grave-goods. In Rome, as in many other societies, tombs were often equipped with goods which would make the dead person's life after death more pleasant: toys for children, mirrors and cosmetics for women, dice and drinking cups for men.[35] It may sound idyllic. But slave-owners were also surrounded by lesser memorials to their freed slaves, tucked away in niches around the main tomb.[36] I wonder if the ex-slaves thought that they had served long enough in life, without an extension of their service into eternity. The idea of life after death occurred in poetry too; in part, that was merely literary convention, a commonplace borrowed from the Greek; but presumably what Roman poets wrote about also reflected the assumptions and beliefs of Roman readers. Propertius, for example, wrote of his dead lover Cynthia, who continued to live in recognisable form in the underworld. At night, she came to haunt him and to reproach him for forgetting their love so soon. The poem (4.7) begins with a defiant assertion of life after death: 'The *Manes* do exist. Death is not the end of everything. The pale ghost struggles free from the body's pyre.' Cynthia finished her admonition with the words: 'Let other women enjoy you now. Soon you will be with me, mine alone; our bones will intertwine and press together.' Finally, Lucretius' eloquently impassioned philosophical argument that nothing exists after death

[35] Such grave-goods can be seen in the Roman Life room in good museums, but it is worth remembering that each good exhibition has been culled from thousands of graves. For a detailed catalogue of the grave-goods found in each tomb in a large cemetery in central Italy, dating mostly from the first and second centuries AD, see M. Capitanio, 'La necropoli romana di Portorecanati,' *Notizie degli Scavi* 28 (1974) 142ff. Among the objects most commonly buried were bronze coins, lamps, pottery bowls and plates, and unguent jars; less common were: bronze rings, brooches and earrings. According to the lawyer Ulpian, 'Ornaments should not be buried with corpses, nor anything else of the kind, as happens among the simpler folk' (*simpliciores* – D. 11.7.14.5). Such legal advice was ineffective.

[36] Slaves seem often to have been excluded from small family tombs. Owners customarily dedicated these to themselves, their immediate relatives and collectively to their 'ex-slaves, male and female, and to their (ex-slaves') descendants' (*libertis libertabusque posterisque eorum*). Ex-slaves may have had a special obligation (*officium*) to care for their former owner's tomb. But that does not explain the repeated absence of the owner's own descendants from this common formula. In a few cases, slaves were explicitly admitted to the tomb; for example, 'M. Ennius Marcellus, son of Titus...built this (tomb) when he was alive with Patronia Fusca, ex-slave of Lucius, for his ex-slaves, male and female, and for his male and female slaves in common' (published by G. Brusin, *Nuovi monumenti sepolcrali di Aquileia* (Venice, 1941) 43). Ennius' care for his slaves may have been sharpened by his wife, who was herself a former slave.

(*On the Nature of Things* 3.830ff) presupposes the idea of survival. But that idea, the idea of survival after death and of immortality was at least as old as Homer and Plato.

Philosophical scepticism sometimes crumbled in the face of unexpected death. Mourners found consolation in the idea that there might, after all, be some life after death, some opportunity to continue a cherished relationship. In Roman conditions of high mortality, illness and death struck many people in their prime, without warning. It was the obvious arbitrariness of death's incidence and its pervasiveness which together encouraged Romans, educated and uneducated, to treat the question of immortality passionately. Several epitaphs reveal a tension between the acceptance of loss and hope. And sometimes the crisis of bereavement pierced the veneer of intellectual sophistication. One husband, for example, set up a tomb to his 'incomparable, sweetest, most seemly and pure wife, who died at the age of 32, after 13 years of the sweetest marriage'. He commended her 'to eternal sleep', commented that 'no one is immortal', and covered his ontological compromise 'though dead, yet will she live for me' with idealising sentiment: 'She will always be golden in my eyes' (*CIL* 6.11082). Other epitaphs display a more formal logic, yet underneath, hope still lurks uncomfortably:

> Loved by my family I lived, and lost my life, still a virgin.
> Here I lie dead, and am Ashes. Ashes are Earth.
> If Earth is a Goddess, then I am a Goddess,
> And I am not dead. (*CIL* 6.35887)

But many more epitaphs (by the standards of Christian culture, a surprising number) are thoroughgoing in their nihilism. 'If you want to know who I am, the answer is ash and burnt embers...' (*CIL* 9.1837) or

> We are nothing.
> See, reader, how quickly
> We mortals return
> From nothing to nothing. (*CIL* 6.26003)

Such sentiments were so common that they were sometimes expressed simply by the initials *nf f ns nc* (*non fui, fui, non sum, non curo*) meaning 'I didn't exist, I existed, I don't exist, I don't care' (*CIL* 5.2283, cf. 1813).

Christian attitudes were much more positive. Christians believed in Christ's death and resurrection; they hoped for life everlasting for themselves, and many of them believed in the resurrection of the body. That is evident from the formal statements of Christian belief, the Creeds, and from Christian literature written to convert pagans and to defend Christianity against pagan attacks.[37] The conquest of death was an important element in Christian belief.

There are some striking similarities in attitudes to death between Christianity, late philosophical schools (Stoicism, Neo-Pythagoreanism, Neo-Platonism) and the so-called 'Oriental' religions (such as the worship of Attis and Cybele, Isis, Mithras, Serapis). This is not surprising. Christianity borrowed and absorbed several elements from the varied cultures in which it developed. And so in other religions also we can find the final judgement by an infallible, all-seeing judge, or damnation to Hades, or the possibility of expiation, and Heaven and Paradise as the eternal dwelling-place for the souls of the virtuous, bathed in perpetual light and happiness. We can also find God's own death and resurrection in pagan cults; for example, worshippers of Isis mourned the death of the god Osiris; when his body was mutilated and the parts scattered all over Egypt, Isis collected the damaged parts together and reanimated him; the believers rejoiced regularly at his resuscitation. The life-cycle of death and rebirth were also important in the initiatory rites of Mithras and Attis. Participants symbolically experienced mystic union with their god in the course of the ritual by dramatically reliving the cycle from birth to death to resurrection (roughly as Christians do in the Holy Communion).

At this stage, we should distinguish between (*a*) rites which dramatised the life-cycle, (*b*) belief in the immortality and resurrection of the Godhead, and (*c*) belief in the immortality and redemption of all believers. The first two, (*a*) and (*b*), are both found in 'Oriental' religions. But Christianity put more stress than any ancient religion on the possible salvation of its followers. It is difficult to know how important this particular element of belief was in the eventual triumph of Christianity. We cannot weigh each item in the

---

[37] 'I believe in...the Resurrection of the Flesh' was a troublesome element in Christian doctrine, attacked by pagans and by Christian heretics, but defended by the orthodox. See best Tertullian, *On the Resurrection of the Dead* (*Corpus Christianorum* (Turnhout, 1954) vol. 2, 921ff) and the work *On the Resurrection* conventionally attributed to Athenagoras, ed. W. R. Schoedel (Oxford, 1972) 88ff, but dated to the fourth century by some scholars; cf. J. Daniélou, *The Origins of Latin Christianity* (London, 1977) 396. The nature of this belief can also be illustrated from the early Christian-Jewish *Odes of Solomon* (22.0ff). 'Thou hast chosen them from the graves and separated them from the dead. Thou hast taken dead bones and covered them with bodies. They became solid, and thou didst give them the energy of life.' Cf. J. N. D. Kelly, *Early Christian Creeds* (London³, 1972) 163ff.

total package of Christian values and practice.[38] Different aspects
would have appealed to different people. But Jesus' crucifixion and
resurrection were a central feature in Christianity's message. The
hope of eternal salvation was likely to appeal to Romans who, as we
have seen, honoured their dead, worried about their fate, and were
preoccupied by the prospect of their own imminent death. Nor were
pagan traditions completely lost. By a curious doctrinal twist, the
powerful dead, the martyred saints became valued intermediaries
between man and God. Pure monotheism was modified, or so it seems
to an agnostic, into polytheism. Saints became lesser gods and
goddesses. Martyrs' relics, their collected bones, became objects of
veneration.[39]

It is difficult to tell in what ways these changes in belief affected
the experience of grief. But Christianity certainly changed the routine
expressions of grief on tombstones. Death was seen as a release from
earthly troubles. 'She rests in peace' (*Requiescit in Pace* – R.I.P.) or
simply 'In Peace' became the predominant phrase on Christian
tombstones. In longer epitaphs, commemorators were keen to point
out that virtue would be rewarded by life everlasting. In the
representative quotation which follows, earthly virtue and heavenly
rewards were both enhanced by the contributions which the dead
priest had made to the church:

I am Tigrinus, a priest. I have lived out my life's allotted span and here
I place my bones. My mind is purified and my body is at peace, each in
its proper place: my body in the grave, my mind rejoicing in Heaven. I have
put aside my fears about my fate; for Christ, the one hope of salvation, is
with me, and where he leads, Death itself must die. Enthralled by the joys
of the kingdom of Heaven, I repaired the Houses of God in several places;
and here, where the roof-beams had collapsed, I renewed them and
renovated the whole building. The reward I have earned is to go in greater
bliss to the Dwelling place above. (*Inscriptiones Latinae Christianae Veteres* ed.
E. Diehl (Berlin, 1961) vol. 2, 3420)

[38] On the triumph of Christianity, see still A. von Harnack, *The Expansion of
Christianity in the First Three Centuries* (London, 1904) vol. 1, 25ff and 102ff. There
is a later revised edition *Die Mission und Ausbreitung des Christentums* (Leipzig[4],
1924). On the difficulty of finding ancient testimony to corroborate the views
often expressed that 'Oriental' religions offered their followers hope of
immortality, see R. MacMullen, *Paganism in the Roman Empire* (New Haven,
1981) 53ff – a sceptical antidote to the exaggerated claims made by Cumont
1959 *passim*. I should stress that many pagan writers expressed the hope of or
belief in life after death for some people, but for Christians it was an article of
faith, uniting all believers.
[39] See the brilliantly evocative work of P. R. L. Brown, *The Cult of the Saints*
(London, 1981) and *Relics and Social Status in the Age of Gregory of Tours* (Reading,
1977), reprinted in *Society and the Holy in Late Antiquity* (London, 1982).

Burial did away with the corpse, but not with the dead. Two major religious festivals, the *Parentalia* and the *Lemuria*, were set aside each year for the commemoration and care of the dead. During these festivals, the law-courts and temples were closed, and no public business was done, and special rituals were performed in honour of the dead (Ovid, *Fasti* 2.533ff and 5.419ff). At the *Parentalia* and on other days, relatives traditionally visited the graves of their kin and had a meal at the grave-side. Collective graves, as we have already noted, were often provided with adjacent banqueting rooms; elaborate private tombs often had a special area designed for feasting; in the graveyards at Pompeii and at Ostia, for example, there are modest family tombs with private courtyards, equipped with stone dining benches, an oven and a well. We have to imagine Roman families picnicking *al fresco* at the family tomb, where, according to Christian critics, they often got boisterously drunk, with their dead relatives around them.[40] Sometimes, the dead were thought of as being present at these feasts. For example, an inscription from the city of Rome expressed the hope that the couple whom it commemorated would 'come in good health to the funeral feast and enjoy themselves along with everybody else' (*CIL* 6.26554). The living and the dead were in close touch.

Some of the dead were unwilling to leave their after-care to chance and formally set money aside in their wills to be spent on libations, sacrifices and feasts at their tombs. For example, a ragman from a small Italian town provided enough money for twelve men from his guild to dine at his tomb once a year on a day of the *Parentalia* (*CIL* 11.5047); another left the usufruct of some flats to his ex-slaves on condition that out of the rents they paid for sacrifices in his memory at the *Parentalia*, on the anniversary of his birthday, and at two minor festivals when violets and rose petals were customarily scattered over tombs; in addition, they were required to place a lighted lamp filled with incense on his tomb three times a month (*CIL* 6.10248). Nothing

---

[40] See the photograph of a tomb courtyard in Calza 1940: plate 8 and cf. Meiggs 1973: 458–61. An inscription from the city of Rome recorded the transfer of rights in a tomb with 24 urns; the rights included access, use of a kitchen and of a well for drawing water (*CIL* 6.14614). St Augustine condemned Christians 'who drink excessively over the dead, and prepare feasts for corpses over the grave...and ascribe to religion their own greed and drunkenness' (*On the Morals of the Christian Church* 34 = *PL* 32.1342). Augustine recognised the similarity between traditional pagan practices at the graveside and popular Christian worship at martyrs' memorials (*Confessions* 6.2).

illustrates the continuing needs of the dead better than the fact that several surviving tombs were built with pipes in them, so that food and drink could be poured down to succour the dead.[41] Ovid recounted the myth that once the Romans in time of war neglected to celebrate the *Parentalia*. The spirits of the dead came up from the tombs as 'misshapen ghosts' and 'howled in the city streets and in the countryside at large' (*Fasti* 2.547ff). The message is clear. The dead had to be placated by offerings of food and drink. In popular belief, that is what they lived off. Other authors recorded similar fears (Apuleius, *The Golden Ass* 8.9; Porphyry on Horace, *Epistles* 2.2.209). If offended or deprived, the spirits of the dead could turn nasty.

In our world, the dead are safely locked away in cemeteries, or in photograph albums. Occasionally, they make excursions into ghost stories or horror movies, but we all know that those are fictions. Except in occasional nightmares, only the psychotic or the recently bereaved allow the dead to intrude effectively into consciousness. In the sleeping world of the Romans also, ghosts appeared in dreams and foretold the future. Pliny the younger, litterateur and consul, wrote that he was himself inclined to believe in spirits and ghosts; and he then told a classic ghost story.[42] It is worth citing because it illustrates how even educated, politically powerful Romans believed in the supernatural. It may therefore not be sensible to try to explain their actions by attributing motives which follow our canons of rationality. It is also interesting that ghost stories have such a long pedigree.

In Athens, there was a large and spacious mansion with the bad reputation of being dangerous to its occupants. At dead of night the clanking of iron and, if you listened carefully, the rattling of chains could be heard, some way off at first, and then close at hand. Then there appeared the spectre of an old man, emaciated and filthy, with long flowing beard...wearing fetters on his legs and shaking the chains on his wrists. The wretched occupants would spend fearful nights awake in terror; lack of sleep led to

[41] Examples from the city of Rome are described by Toynbee and Ward Perkins 1956: 61, 118–19 and 145–6. For other examples, see Mau 1899: 417ff and see especially R. E. M. Wheeler, 'A Roman pipe-burial from Caerleon, Monmouthshire', *Antiquaries Journal* 9 (1929) 1ff which is much more synoptic and generally useful than its title suggests. Such pipes were provided for both inhumed and cremated bodies.

[42] For another version of the same story, but set in Corinth, see Lucian, *The Lover of Lies* 30; in the same essay, Lucian tells other ghost stories (19ff). In the same letter (7.27), Pliny told another story about a man fated to become a provincial governor and die; also told by Tacitus (*Annals* 11.21). Modern historians of Rome usually underrate the importance of beliefs in the supernatural in Roman politics.

illness and then to death as their dread increased, for even during the day, when the apparition had vanished, the memory of it was in their mind's eye, so that their terror remained after the cause of it had gone. The house was therefore deserted... but it was advertised for let or sale, in case someone was found who knew nothing of its evil reputation. (*Letters* 7.27 Loeb Classical Library translation)

Enter the hero.

The philosopher Athenodorous came to Athens and read the notice of sale. His suspicions were aroused when he heard the low price, and on enquiry the whole story came out.

Armed with pen and books, our learned hero refused to be perturbed. He noted exactly where the ghost had disappeared and marked the spot. Next day, he advised the city magistrates to have the floor dug up at the spot which he had marked. 'There they found bones, twisted round with chains... The bones were collected up and given a public burial.' That ghost was heard of no more, except in stories, which keep most ghosts alive. But other ghosts, some beneficient, others hostile and feared, wandered in the night in the world of the living.[43]

VII WILLS AND LEGACY-HUNTERS

The individual dead also had power. We can see this in wills, by which the Roman dead, men and women, legally disposed of their property even to the disadvantage of their direct descendants. The fact that the dead in our own society have similar rights should not blind us to the amazing aspects of Roman social arrangements.[44] In

---

[43] For example, a beautiful young man died. He was an only son. He was cremated. His parents were grief-stricken. On the evening after his cremation, he appeared in all his beauty to his mother, and talked with her so long as it was dark. At dawn, he disappeared. Each night he came, so that the mother's grief at his loss was assuaged. But she did not tell her husband the reason; at last, she told him, so that he too could share in their dead son. He reacted with fear. He did not want his house haunted. He called in a wizard (*magus*), who sang chants at the tomb, and to imprison the ghost, shuttered the tomb with iron bars. The son stopped coming. The mother was desolate, and sued the father for wilful damage (Quintilian?, *Rhetorical Exercises* 10). It is interesting that it was the wife who wept most; mourning was the woman's concern (*ibid.* 10.10).

[44] I have relied heavily in the following paragraphs on the elegantly clear account given by H. F. Jolowicz and B. Nicholas, *Historical Introduction to the Study of Roman Law* (Cambridge³, 1972) 123ff and 242ff. M. Kaser, *Das römische Privatrecht* (Munich², 1971) 678ff provides a fuller account with many references to modern scholarly literature. H. S. Maine, *Ancient Law* (London⁹, 1833) 171ff is still well worth reading, not least because he placed Roman achievements in a wide comparative context. See also J. A. Crook, *Law and Life of Rome* (London, 1967) 118ff.

the distant past, before the fifth century BC, Romans had no right of testation. The children, sons and unmarried daughters, simply took over the land which previously they had worked together as a family. In later periods also, among peasants and families of modest means, this practice must have been common; parents did not make wills; children simply inherited the property and the social *persona* of their dead parents. 'Even during the lifetime of their father', wrote the lawyer Gaius, '[children] are regarded as in some sense owners' (2.157). That was the normal pattern. But among prosperous Romans, it became customary to make wills.[45]

Originally, wills had to be approved or witnessed by a public assembly (*comitia calata*), presided over by the chief priest (*pontifex maximus*). They were therefore the exception rather than the rule, and probably provided for men without direct descendants or for those who wished, for whatever reason, to divert inheritance away from direct descendants. Later another form of will became established – the testator went through a ritual sale of his estate (*per aes et libram*) to a trusted friend, who on the testator's death would act as the executor of the instructions first spoken, later written in his will. These rituals persisted for centuries, but the formal purchaser and erstwhile executor of the estate became a mere cipher. By the second century BC and perhaps much earlier, the written will was executed by the principal heir(s).[46] Well before the second century BC also, it had become possible to diminish the principal inheritance by leaving legacies to outsiders, that is to people who were not related to the

---

[45] I write this with some hesitation. First, in Roman Egypt, men and women of very modest means left wills, see K. Hopkins, 'Brother–sister marriage in Roman Egypt', *Comparative Studies in Society and History* 22 (1980) 338. Was Roman Italy so much less literate? Graffiti election slogans and other surviving fragments from Pompeii (for example, the price-list written on the wall of an inn – *CIL* 4.1679, cf. 9.2689) suggest a widespread capacity to read. But that is not adequate proof that many wills were written. On the frequency of wills among the prosperous and educated, see the convincing arguments of J. A. Crook, 'Intestacy in Roman society', *Proceedings of the Cambridge Philological Society* 19 (1973) 38–44 against the witty scepticism of D. Daube, 'The preponderance of intestacy at Rome', *Tulane Law Review* 39 (1965) 253ff. Finally, it is remarkable that testation was well established in Rome by the time of the Twelve Tables (traditional date: 451 BC) – see Table 5 in *FIRA* vol. 1, 37–8.

[46] In Roman law, there was a critical distinction between what I have called the principal heir (*heres*) and those who received legacies. The principal heir singly, or jointly with other principal heirs, inherited the total estate, including debts and the obligation to pay legacies. Legacies, were thus a diminution of the inherited estate (D. 30.116 pr). However, I should stress that the principal heir did not necessarily receive the greater part of any estate, although that was intended by the Voconian law of 169 BC. That law was evaded (Gaius 2.226). But the Falcidian law of 40 BC was effectively drafted to ensure that the principal heir received at least one quarter of the total estate.

testator. In sum, prosperous Romans had the power to leave their whole estate or parts of it in violation of kin ties.[47]

Two problems arise: first, to what extent did rich Romans leave substantial sums to persons unrelated by blood or marriage? Secondly, why? Neither question can be answered satisfactorily. The evidence is sparse and scattered over several centuries. Even so, the theme of large-scale distributions by the dead to non-relatives is recurrent in surviving Roman sources. For example, the Furian law on Wills (pre-169 BC) restricted the size of legacies to distant relatives and non-relatives to a small symbolic sum (1,000 *asses*). But the law was evaded with typically Roman legalistic ingenuity, by giving each legatee several bequests each worth less than this (Gaius 2.25). Cicero boasted that he had himself received 20 million HS in bequests from friends (*amici* and *necessarii*), while Antony had received inheritances (Cicero implies by skulduggery) in spite of the existence of close relatives to the testator (Cicero, *Philippics* 2.40). The emperor Augustus was reported to have received on average 70 million HS each year for the last twenty years of his life in the wills of admiring subjects (Suetonius, *Augustus* 101).[48] To be sure, making the emperor

---

[47] Roman legal terminology implied that immediate descendants, such as children, were expected to inherit; they were *sui heredes* – a man's own heirs. But a father had the right to disinherit any one or all of his children. He had to disinherit a son, and later even a grandson explicitly by name, else the will was void; indeed even if he missed a child's name out of the will, the child could bring an action for a share in his or her father's estate – he or she would be given a share 'contrary to the provisions of the will' (Gaius 2.123ff). But providing a father obeyed due form, he could disinherit any or all children. His will was paramount. Then perhaps at the end of the Republic, it became possible to upset a will on the grounds that the testator had not shown proper regard for his nearest relatives (*querela inofficiosi testamenti*), and so was in some sense 'of unsound mind', an ingenious extension of the incapacity which followed from actual madness (D. 5.2.2 – Marcian). Ulpian remarked that such suits were frequent (D. 5.2.1); according to Gaius, usually because of the malice of step-mothers (D. 5.2.4). Formally, it was not necessary to give grounds for disherison; but to ward off suits, it was probably wise either to give grounds or to give a child a pittance (one quarter of what he would have received on intestacy precluded suits of this kind D. 5.2.8.8. – Ulpian). Finally, the mere capacity to institute a non-family member as principal heir was an effective disherison of near agnatic kin and of distant relatives such as clansmen (*gentiles*) who would inherit in the last resort if a man or woman died intestate.

[48] This sum seems impossibly large, because it amounts almost to 10% of the total state revenues from the whole empire (cf. K. Hopkins, 'Taxes and trade in the Roman empire', *Journal of Roman Studies* 70 (1980) 101ff). And giving gifts to the emperor was something special. Even so, attitudes and customs revealed in the bequests made to emperors reflect current practice among Roman notables. Complementarily, Augustus' own will (Suetonius, *Augustus* 101) reflected contemporary practice. He named principal heirs in three grades, each successive grade in case the previously named heirs did not survive or did not wish to accept

Death in Rome

joint heir was partly tact, partly insurance that the rest of one's will would be respected, and partly a special death-duty for rich courtiers. But the practice grew out of and was itself an extension of the well established Roman custom of leaving legacies to friends.

Several Roman writers of the early Principate give the impression by casual remarks that prosperous Romans simply expected both to inherit and to testate substantial sums to their acquaintances and friends. This Roman custom is vividly illustrated by a popular joke. According to St Jerome, schoolboys laughingly recited a 'piglet's will', a caricature of a soldier's will. To be funny, it must have reflected common practice; it therefore constitutes much better testimony than individual examples.

Mr Grunter Squealer the piglet has made this will. As I cannot write myself, I have dictated it...As he saw that he was going to die, he asked for an hour's reprieve and petitioned the cook in order to be able to make a will. He called for his parents, in order to leave something to them from his provisions. To my father...I give and bequeath 30 *modii* of acorns, to my mother...and to my sister...And of my organs I shall give and donate to the cobblers my bristles...to the deaf my ears, to the lawyers my tongue,...to the women my loins, to the boys my bladder, to the girls my tail, to the sodomites my bum, to runners and hunters my heels, to thieves my claws...And I want a monument inscribed with golden letters: 'M. Grunnius Corocotta the piglet lived 999½ years...' (may) my name be honourably mentioned until eternity...(seven witnesses sign).[49]

For present purposes, I want to stress only that piglet distributed his worldly goods widely, and to note incidentally that his age at death was precise but not accurate.

Legacy-hunting

In more elevated social circles, according to Seneca, the hope of receiving a legacy threatened to undermine friendships (*On Benefits*

the inheritance. The third grade ('relatives and quite a lot of friends') was named out of courtesy rather than because there was a realistic chance that they would inherit. Hence the use of a will as a political or social instrument (see note 65 below). Some emperors after Augustus reportedly refused to take up inheritances if the deceased was not a personal friend (Tacitus, *Annals* 2.48), or if he had children of his own (Suetonius, *Domitian* 9); other emperors insisted on being included as heirs to the rich (Suetonius, *Tiberius* 49 and *Caligula* 38). R. S. Rogers, 'The Roman emperors as heirs and legatees', *Transactions of the American Philological Association* 78 (1947) 140ff assumes too consistent a policy by emperors; see better F. Millar, *The Emperor in the Roman World* (London, 1977) 153ff.

[49] The Latin text is to be found in F. Buecheler, *Petronii Saturae* (Berlin, 1958) 346-7, and in a recent edition *Testamentum Porcelli* by N. A. Bott (Zurich, 1972). Jerome's comment is in his *Commentary on Isaiah* 12 pr = *Corpus Christianorum* vol. 73a, 465. The translation is slightly changed from that of D. Daube, *Roman Law* (Edinburgh, 1969) 78-81. The date of composition is unknown.

4.20 and 6.38). The expectation of receiving bequests engendered a special breed of legacy-hunters, called *captatores*. The very existence of a special word for them in Latin is evidence enough that their activities became a well-established element in Roman life. Legacy-hunting was the social reciprocal of widespread bequests. In surviving literature, there are frequent suggestions that legacy-hunting had reached pathological levels, and that legacy-hunters were stereotypically considered as social villains.

Why were legacy-hunters so hated? Two reasons seem important. First, legacy-hunters were considered mercenary and self-seeking; they undermined the atmosphere of sincerity and trust which ideally prompted gift-giving among friends. They were pilloried, I suspect, for operating with motives which true friends had to suppress or hide. Secondly, legacy-hunters who courted successfully and so received large bequests from non-kin, whatever their formal status, whether senators or knights, were regarded as social adventurers. They lived at the margins of the rules of polite society. Their success violated overt ideals that status was ascribed by birth, not achieved, just as modern asset-strippers, by maximising profit, reveal the unacceptable face of capitalism. Legacy-hunters were operating in a social world where status depended upon competitive expenditure, but where there were only limited opportunites for making a fortune. Courtiers in the city of Rome, after the empire had ceased to expand, were caught in an especially vicious trap of restricted income and open-handed ostentation. Legacy-hunters had hit upon a transmission fault in the passage of wealth from one generation to the next. They had found a weak spot in the Roman system of social reproduction. They were pilloried for their success in exploiting it.

Even those with direct descendants often left considerable sums in legacies to acquaintances.[50] Attempts were made to restrict the

[50] In addition to the passages cited in the text, two further examples are worth quoting. In a letter to the historian Tacitus, Pliny wrote 'You must have noticed that in wills, unless someone has been a particular friend of one of us, we are left identical legacies' (*Letter* 7.20). By chance in the will of Dasumius, there are indeed legacies of (? one) Roman pound of gold left to both Tacitus and Pliny (the names are restored); but now see *AE* 1976:77. Dasumius had direct descendants and heirs, a daughter and a son adopted by his will, but he also left substantial legacies of gold and silver to at least fifty other people (*CIL* 6.10229). Secondly, a wealthy old man, the ex-consul Domitius Tullus had, according to Pliny (*Letters* 8.18), encouraged legacy-hunters. But then in his will he had made his adopted daughter his principal heir, with substantial legacies to his wife, his grandsons and great granddaughter; the popular saying 'a man's will is the mirror of his character' had been proved false, since in this case Domitius had behaved 'much better in death than in life'. Pliny's account is interesting, because it shows that legacy-hunters had hopes even when there were direct descendants available, and that the provisions of a will were matters of gossip 'all over the city' (*Letters* 8.18, cf. 7.24).

practice by legislation. The Furian law of 169 BC has just been mentioned. The Falcidian law of 40 BC prescribed that the principal heir (*heres*) should receive at least one quarter of the total estate. But why was it common, even in restricted social circles, to leave the principal heir less than or only one quarter of the total estate? To be sure, those without dependants, the unmarried, the widowed and the childless could best afford to disperse their estates widely. They were the prime targets of legacy-hunters, especially when they were old or sickly. Satirists and philosophers ridiculed the undignified extremes to which legacy-hunters sank; the ex-slave Epictetus drew attention to their money-grubbing subservience, their voluntary self-enslavement: 'Who could abide your passion for old women and for old men, wiping their noses, cleaning their faces, giving them presents, nursing them like a slave, while all along you are praying for their deaths, and interrogating the doctors about whether they are really dying? (*Discourses* 4.1.148 and similarly Cicero, *Stoic Paradoxes* 39).

Not that the traffic between hunters and hunted was all one way. Some old men pretended to be richer than they were, or enticed courtship by feigning to be at death's door. The trap could be baited, and the hunter caught. These two epigrams by Martial, wickedly malicious as ever, illustrate that the well-worn path could be travelled from two directions:

> Gemellus seeks marriage with Maronilla.
> He desires her; he insists; he implores her and sends her gifts.
> Is she so beautiful? No. She is disgusting.
> What then is the attraction? Where is her charm? She coughs, (1.10)

> Because Naevia wheezes and has a racking cough,
> And continually sends her spittle flying towards your chest,
> Do you imagine, Bithynicus, that you have attained your objective?
> You're wrong. She is having you on, not dying. (2.26)

That is obviously satire. But in Pliny's correspondence, we find actual cases of legacy-hunting by senators, as well as disputed wills and disherison.[51] Some people enlarged their following by repeatedly

---

[51] Pliny tells three stories of legacy-hunting by a senator and orator, M. Aquilius Regulus, who had reportedly enriched himself by worming his way into people's wills (*Letters* 2.20). The stories presuppose that legacies were customarily given even to slight acquaintances in return for favours, that the content of wills allegedly became public knowledge within informed social circles before a man or woman's death, although that knowledge was liable to upset in the final event. For a case of disputed dishersion, when an eighty year old remarried and then disinherited his daughter, see Pliny, *Letters* 6.3 (cf. 5.1).

changing their will, or by allegedly revealing its provisions (e.g. Martial 5.39). Whatever the truth of each jibe or rumour, the rumours existed and circulated. The prospect of getting an inheritance, or of hearing who had got one, widened and deepened Roman interest in sickness and in death.

The dead had the last laugh. Only when the will was opened, did those around know for certain whether they had been duped. Lucian invented an amusing dialogue between an old man who had just arrived in the underworld, after a marvellous old-age flirting with legacy-hunters:

> P. I kept telling each of them straight-out that I was leaving it all to him. They swallowed it every time, and just stepped up their flattery. But what I actually said in my will was rather different. I just told them all to go to hell.
> S. And who finally got it? Some relation of yours?
> P. Certainly not. I left it to a rather pretty Phrygian boy I'd recently bought. (*Conversations with the Dead* 362),[52]

I am not suggesting that such behaviour was universal, only that such humour had a sharp point because the behaviour which it laughed at – the legacy-hunting, the disappointment of relatives, the whimsical arbitrariness allowed to testators – actually occurred. Valerius Maximus, who wrote early in the first century AD, told several stories of disappointment or happy surprises revealed in wills: one Roman aristocrat, Q. Caecilius, was courted assiduously by another (L. Lucullus); on his death-bed Caecilius gave Lucullus rings, presumably as a token of his prospective heirship. But when the will was opened, it was found that Caecilius had left his whole estate to a third person (Cicero's friend, Atticus). As a result: 'the Roman people dragged the corpse of this deceitful and devious man through the streets by a rope tied around his neck. So the wicked man got the son and heir he wanted, and the funeral rites he deserved' (Valerius Maximus 7.8.5, cf 7.8.6–9). The story may well be apocryphal; it does not ring quite true.[53] But it assumes widespread interest, common knowledge and high feelings about wills.

---

[52] P. went on to say that although the boy spoke atrocious Greek, and was so young and a foreigner, nevertheless with the dead man's wealth he would be treated as an aristocrat and courted. S. replied: 'Oh well...he can become Governor of Greece, for all I care' (*ibid.* 362). So much for Roman senators – in Lucian's view, a matter of luck and vulgar wealth. Martial also poked fun (4.70) at a son's discovery that his father, whose death he had been longing for, had disinherited him in his will.

[53] Which section of the Roman people felt so outraged as to take revenge on a corpse at the funeral? Ancient comments on legacy-hunting are so shot through with

The Augustan marriage laws of 18 BC and AD 9 penalised the unmarried and the childless by restricting their capacity to inherit by will. Widowers and widows who delayed remarriage were also penalised.[54] The purpose of the laws was to encourage marriage and fertility, and failing that to short-circuit the testatory power of those who refused to comply. The implication was that the upper-class Romans (the laws were aimed primarily at them) remained unmarried or childless wilfully, just in order to increase their social power and prestige. Because they had an estate to bequeath, which was not bespoken, they would be courted. But even in a self-reproducing population, suffering Roman levels of mortality, at least one sixth of couples had no surviving heir (see Chapter 2, note 85). Writers of the period assumed that childlessness and legacy-hunting were common in upper social strata, and attacked legacy-hunting in particular as immoral, and as a symptom of Rome's moral degeneration.[55]

caricature, stereotypes and exaggeration, that it is difficult to know where reality lies behind this smokescreen, and to guess which emotions (?fear of disability in old age) prompted the moral outrage. On this particular incident see also Cornelius Nepos, *Life of Atticus* 5 and Cicero, *Letters to Atticus* 3.20.

54 One major motive for the maintenance and elaboration of these laws over the next three centuries was probably that the Roman state increased its revenue by confiscating illicit bequests. 'Inheritances left to unmarried or childless Roman women with property worth 50,000 HS are confiscated' *Regulations of the Chief Financial Administrator* (of Egypt) 30, cf. 24ff. That is a simplified version of the Roman law. Initially, the marriage law of 18 BC forbad the unmarried to be principal heirs or to accept legacies; the later law of AD 9 prohibited the married but childless (*orbi*) from accepting more than half of anything left to them by will (so Gaius 2.286). But that too is a simplification, since close relatives, the unmarried who had or had had three children or who were of an exempt age (see above, note 36) could all take inheritances; in sum, the law was complicated and its exact provisions are unclear and disputed. See best Kaser 1971: 724–5, *Epitome of Ulpian* 14–18, *Opinions of Paul* 4.9. For most of the first century, the penalties of the law could be evaded by setting up a trust (*fideicommissum*), but that loophole was closed to the advantage of the state treasury (Gaius 2.286). My impression is that the state increasingly benefited from successive revisions of the inheritance law (*Epitome of Ulpian* 17.2 and 24.12). I find still useful the long essay by A. Bouché-Leclercq, 'Les lois demographiques d'Auguste', *Revue Historique* 57 (1895) 241–92 and the discussion by V. Arangio-Ruiz in *Augustus: Studi in occasione del bimillenario Augusteo* (Rome, 1938) 101ff.

55 In modern literature, as in ancient comments (see note 51), legacy-hunting is viewed primarily as a moral problem. Pliny the Elder, for example, wrote: 'When senators began to be chosen for their wealth (*censu*), and judges too, when wealth became the crowning achievement of state-officials and generals, when childlessness came to wield the greatest influence and power, and when legacy-hunting yielded the fattest profits, when acquisition became the only source of pleasure, then the true rewards of living had been destroyed...' (*Natural History* 14.5). Legacy-hunting was wittily ridiculed by Horace (*Satires* 2.5) and by Petronius (*Satyricon* 116).

But were the sums at stake as enormous as the satirists assumed?
One important piece of evidence suggests that they were very large.
In AD 6, Augustus was searching for revenues with which to pay for
army provisions and retirement bounties, without paying for them
out of existing revenues. He thought that enough could be raised from
a 5% tax on inheritances and legacies, from which close relatives
and the poor were exempt (Dio 55.24–5).[56] Unfortunately, we do not
know how much this tax actually raised. But it remained an
important source of revenues for over two centuries. Its persistence
was a symptom of the large sums which Romans dispersed to distant
kin and to outsiders. The inheritance tax was a memorial to the
testatory power of the Roman dead.

The social development of the will as an instrument for the
dispersion of capital is difficult to explain. But four contributory
factors seem important: paternal power, the Roman concept of
property, increased monetisation and high mortality. First, paternal
power (*patria potestas*).[57] The Roman head of household was notorious,
even in Roman times, for his power (Gaius 1.55); he had the formal
right of life and death (*vitae necisque potestas*) over his new-born
children and even over his grown-up sons and daughters. To be sure,
by the late Republic, this right was qualified (perhaps it always had
been) by the need to consult with the family council, and to act with

---

[56] I doubt that a 5% tax on inheritances with these exemptions would have raised
enough money. I estimate the cost of retirement bounty in a legionary army of
140,000 men with retirement after 20 years service at about 67 million HS per
year. The crude assumptions behind the calculation are given in Hopkins 1980:
124. To meet this out of an inheritance tax implies an annual volume of
inheritances dispersed by Roman citizens outside the immediate family of over
1,300 million HS. It seems too high. But such calculations are fragile.

[57] See best J. A. Crook, 'Patria potestas', *Classical Quarterly* 17 (1967) 113–22; and
for clear technical discussion, Kaser 1971: 60–5, 341–50. On the probable
limitations on paternal powers by a family council see W. Kunkel, 'Das
Konsilium im Hausgericht', *Zeitschrift der Savigny-Stiftung* 83 (1966) 219ff.
Eventually, paternal power was limited by imperial power and by law. Three
examples illustrate this development. First, according to an early-third-century
legal elaboration of the Julian laws on marriage, children could appeal to
provincial governors against fathers who refused to let them marry (D. 23.2.19).
Secondly, the father's right to make his son or daughter divorce if the marriage
was happy (*bene concordans*) was restricted in the mid-second century AD (*Opinions
of Paul* 5.6.15 cf. D. 43.30.1.5); see A. Watson, *The Law of Persons in the later Roman
Republic* (Oxford, 1967) 52 and P. E. Corbett, *The Roman Law of Marriage*
(Oxford, 1930) 122ff. Thirdly, in relation to adultery, Ulpian declared 'A father
cannot kill his son unheard; he ought to accuse him before the prefect or the
provincial governor' (D. 40.0.2). In a famous case, an Egyptian father claimed
the right under Egyptian law to make his daughter divorce against her will, but
the Roman judge through an interpreter asked the woman her wishes, and
allowed the marriage to stand (P. Oxy. 237 – AD 186).

just cause. Even when a son or daughter was married (if she was married *sine manu*), a father could insist upon divorce, even against his or her wishes and those of the spouse. And he could kill his daughter and her lover if he caught them in the act of adultery, provided that he killed them both 'with a single blow and in a single attack' (D. 48.5.24.4. – Ulpian).[58]

My present point is less dramatic. Formally, a Roman head of household had complete control over his own property. His son, however old and even if he had held distinguished public office, had no right to independent mastery of his own estate. Like a slave, he had only his pocket money (*peculium*), held at his father's pleasure. He became head of his own household only when his father died. To be sure, a father could free (technically: 'emancipate') his son, but we know very little about how often this happened.

In Roman folk-lore, stories of conflict between father and son recur. For example, Dionysius Halicarnassus wrote of the 'harsh and implacable anger of fathers against offending sons' in early Rome, and illustrated his point with Titus Manlius Torquatus, consul in 340 BC, who had his son summarily executed for disobeying orders: 'he decorated him for his courage, but at the same time accused him of disobedience... and put him to death as a deserter' (*Roman Antiquities* 8.79). Livy tells the same story at greater length, and comments that the story became legendary, a sad example for later generations (8.7).[59] Morally, the conflict between fathers and sons was hidden

---

[58] The Roman law of adultery is more complicated than I have allowed; the adulteress had to be discovered in the father's or his son-in-law's house of residence; the father was to kill both – not just one, unless the daughter, without his connivance, escaped while the angry father was killing the adulterer (D. 48.5.21ff). The aggrieved husband had the right to kill the adulterer, but not his wife (D. 48.5.21 and 25). If the first set of laws was construed literally, as against Shylock, they would have constrained paternal power by imposing impracticable conditions, while preserving traditional rights in the letter of the law.

[59] Valerius Maximus, a historian of morals of the first century AD, wrote a section on 'Fathers' harshness towards their sons' (5.8). Some of the stories which he told were already legendary and perhaps even fictional. For example, Spurius Cassius, thrice consul, in 502, 493 and 486 BC, was flogged to death by his father after he laid down public office, because of his populist politics (5.8.2; cf. Dionysius Halicarnassus, *Roman Antiquities* 8.78; Livy 2.41 with commentary by R. M. Ogilvie (Oxford, 1965) 337ff); other stories were more recent and reliable; a senator, A. Fulvius, was famous for having killed his son in 63 BC, because he had left Rome to join the conspirator Catiline (5.8.5 and Sallust, *The Conspiracy of Catiline* 39). But in the first century AD, a knight called Tricho flogged his son to death; his behaviour provoked a violent reaction: a crowd in the Roman forum stabbed him with their writing-pens (Seneca, *On Mercy* 1.15). Both Valerius Maximus and Seneca added other stories about father's indulgence towards sons who had plotted against their lives. The truth of these tales matters less than their currency. They all imply that relations between Roman fathers and their sons were often strained.

by elevating filial respect (*pietas*) into a core Roman virtue, illustrated, as every school-boy used to know, by *pius* Aeneas who carried his aged father on his shoulders from burning Troy.[60] Veyne has acutely observed that Romans were divided into two distinct groups, the fortunate and the unfortunate. The fortunate comprised those whose fathers had died when they were still young, leaving their sons as masters of their estates. The unfortunate were those who remained long under the thumb of their fathers.[61] The reciprocal of paternal power was not only filial respect but also filial hostility. Of course, it would be unreasonable to suggest that fathers gave considerable sums in legacies simply out of hostility to their sons. But it is reasonable to suggest that sons may have greeted or awaited a father's death with some ambivalence, because at long last it gave them independence. And some sons must have blenched, when they heard, as the will was read out, that their father had given freedom to a hundred slaves or had distributed a substantial portion of his patrimony to his friends.

Secondly, dispersion of possessions by will to the disadvantage of direct descendants depended on a developed concept of property. The head of the household had the right to dispose of what was *his own*, as he wished. Once again, we may take this for granted, since by the laws current in our own society, we can if we are rich enough, own a lake (my lake!), a mountain or an island.[62] That is an extraordinary imposition of the social on the natural. The Roman creation of an absolute right in law to own land and goods, and to alienate them as one wished, especially when dead, was a significant social development, which seems to have been well-established early

---

[60] *Pius Aeneas*, warrior and dutiful son, famous from Virgil, was in the first two centuries AD commonly portrayed on Roman artefacts (coins, lamps and altars) carrying his father. His father was himself carrying the ancestral *sacra*, while Aeneas led his small son by the hand. A fresco discovered in Gragnano near Naples in 1760 is a vulgar caricature of the scene – each character is given a dog-head and a monkey-tail. Aeneas has yellow bootees, a jagged yellow skirt and a long, rather droopy penis. I assume that one gets caricatures only of easily recognisable scenes – see Colonel Fanin, *The Royal Museum at Naples*... (London, 1871) plate 31, and more conventionally G. K. Galinsky, *Aeneas, Sicily and Rome* (Princeton, 1969) Chapter One, with numerous illustrations. On father–son hostility, see the suggestive essay by M. Fortes, 'Pietas in ancestor worship', in his *Time and Social Structure* (London, 1970) 165ff; an eldest son in the Tallensi said to Fortes: 'My Destiny struggles that he shall not live... Don't you see, there sits my father and he has his ancestor shrines; if he were to die today it would be I who would own them. Thus it is that my Destiny strives for him to die so that I can take over his shrines...' (*ibid.* 171).

[61] P. Veyne, 'La famille et l'amour sous le haut-empire romain', *Annales* 33 (1978) 36 – an adventurous, stimulating but error-prone essay.

[62] I take this idea from V. G. Kiernan, 'Private property in history' in J. Goody *et al.*, edd., *Family and Inheritance* (Cambridge, 1976) 361.

in Rome's history, before the period of rapid imperial expansion.[63] Such an unfettered concept of property is by no means unknown in pre-industrial societies, but it is rare.

The two remaining factors which contributed to the Roman use of wills, increased monetisation and high mortality, can be dealt with briefly. The increased use and availability of money from the second century BC onwards helped people devise and pay legacies. For example, in the will of Dasumius (AD 108), more than fifty friends and dependants were paid, in some cases substantial sums (*CIL* 6.10229). High mortality left a significant minority of parents childless. To these we must add those who were by accident or by design infertile and those who never married. The childless were the prime targets of legacy-hunters. It may be worth speculating that the will was developed in response to the interests of the childless, who wished to control the dispersal of capital, rather than have it revert automatically to distant relatives or to the fading collective of the clan.[64]

The initial causes of the development of the Roman will predate our surviving sources. It is easier, though still speculative, to work out later implications. When the Roman political and social elite comprised a few hundred families, repeated gifts of legacies across kin boundaries must have created an elaborate network of social obligations, operating inside and between generations. It was a system of deferred reciprocities. What a donor gave (when it hurt him least) would, in due course, with luck be repaid to his heirs, in cash or in favours. Ideally, and in the long run, dispersion of capital by testation cost nothing. The political system had no unifying ideologies, but depended upon collaboration between families. Marriage, as we have seen, was one tactic employed to forge strong links, but its use was limited by the number of marriageable children. Legacies were a supplement to the bonds created by kinship and marriage, a flexible

[63] Jolowicz and Nicholas 1972: 137ff and Maine 1883: 244ff.
[64] If a man or woman did not leave a valid will, or if the will was not accepted by the heirs, under the ancient rules of intestacy, then his estate fell to those within his power, e.g. his children, grandchildren and his wife (if married *in manu*), or failing them to the nearest relative in the male line, and failing them to the clan. By the last century BC, it seems that individual clansmen rather than the collective inherited (inferred from Suetonius, *Julius Caesar* 1 – Caesar was punished by being deprived of his 'clan inheritances'); in the reign of Augustus, traces can also be seen of clan guardianship in the famous tombstone obituary: *The So-Called Laudatio Turae*, ed. E. Wistrand (Göteborg, 1976) 18 and 33. Indeed A. Watson, *The Law of Succession in the Later Roman Republic* (Oxford, 1971) 181 shows that succession by the clan was still practised in the early part of the last century BC. But by the second century AD, 'the whole law relating to clans had fallen into disuse' (Gaius 3.17). See Jolowicz and Nicholas 1972: 124–6.

adaptation of gift-giving to meet family needs in a changing political system, which became increasingly competitive as the empire grew. Legacies were symbolic reinforcements of political and social alliances. The significance was multiplied, by expectation and hope, before the will was opened, and afterwards, by gratitude or disappointment. Wills were weapons of social approval and rebuke, in which the dead nearly always had the last say. Among aristocrats, it was a matter of pride and status that one was mentioned or rewarded in a friend's will.[65] Deaths therefore stirred interest. The public funeral ceremonies which aristocrats attended provided participants not merely with a parade of public virtues, but also with an anticipation of private profit and the enhancement of individual status.

VIII PERMANENT MEMORIALS AND COMMEMORATIVE FOUNDATIONS

Some prosperous men and women left considerable sums, not to relatives and friends, but for the erection of monuments, or for the establishment of charitable foundations, which would ensure them a permanent memorial on earth.[66] In their wills, they gave detailed instructions for the construction and care of their tombs, and for the celebration of their memory. For example:

My wishes are that the memorial shrine which I have under construction should be completed to the specifications which I have given. The shrine is to contain a recess, in which there is to be set a seated statue of myself, made of the finest, imported marble, or else of the finest bronze, at least five (Roman) feet [1.5 m] in height. Just inside the recess there is to be a sedan chair, with two seats on either side of it, all made of imported marble. There are to be covers kept there, which are to be spread out on the days

---

[65] For example, in AD 22, Junia the widow of Cassius and the sister of the Brutus who helped assassinate Julius Caesar, died. 'Her will was the subject of much rumour among the populace, because in disposing of her great wealth, she named and honoured nearly all the leaders of society; but omitted the emperor. He took it well' (Tacitus, *Annals* 3.76).

[66] The modern literature on gifts and foundations is extensive; A. R. Hands, *Charities and Social Aid in Greece and Rome* (London, 1968), is a useful introduction; but B. Laum, *Stiftungen in der griechischen und römischen Antike* (Leipzig, 1914), with its invaluable collection of documents, has not been superseded. Both books stress the continuity in gift-giving and the establishment of charitable foundations from the Greek to the Roman world. P. Veyne, *Le pain et le cirque* (Paris, 1976), puts such generosity into a wider political and cultural context, while E. F. Bruck, *Über römisches Recht im Rahmen der Kulturgeschichte* (Berlin, 1954) 46–100, in an attractive essay discusses developments in Roman religion and law pertaining to foundations.

when the memorial shrine is opened, and there are to be two rugs, two dining cushions of equal size, two cloaks and a tunic. In front of this monument is to be placed an altar, carved in the finest style from the best Luna marble, and in this my bones are to be laid at rest. The shrine is to be closed with a slab of Luna marble, in such a way that it can be both opened and closed again without difficulty. (*CIL* 13.5708, from Langres, France)

In the following sections, the testator, probably called S. Julius Aquila, provided funds for repairs and for the upkeep of the gardens (three gardeners and their apprentices) in which the monument was situated. No one else was to be buried nearby, ever. The regulations were to apply 'in perpetuity'. Any violator was to be fined a huge sum (100,000 HS), payable to the local city. Every year, his ex-slaves and their descendants and Julius Aquila's own descendants were to provide money from which a feast was to be prepared at the tomb, '...and they are to consume the food and drink there, and to stay there while they consume it all'. Finally, Julius Aquila specified who was to be responsible for his funeral and burial rites (his grandson, two friends(?), and an ex-slave) and he directed that his hunting equipment, his rush-boat, his sedan-chairs, all his equipment for medical study and his medicines be cremated together with him (*CIL* 13.5708).

Several elements in these prescriptions are commonly found elsewhere. Testators wanted sacrifices or libations to be made at their tombs, and they wanted their birthdays commemorated. To secure this end, they laid obligations on their descendants and on their ex-slaves, who by custom and by law owed them certain services (*officia*). Testators also wanted to be remembered in a good light, as generous benefactors. That was one of the main reasons, I suppose, for the development of the Roman custom of freeing slaves by will, at the owner's death. But freed slaves were not the only audience whose applause was wanted. Testators also left money for public feasts, for public distributions of money or cakes and mead (*crustulum et mulsum*) to the entire local population or to local town councillors, usually to be given on the anniversary of their birthday.[67] Such gifts

---

[67] A dignitary of a small town (Ferentinum) in central Italy made elaborate arrangements for public donations to the local population both during his lifetime and after his death. A. Quinctilius Priscus bought a small estate for 70,000 HS from the town, and then gave it back as a gift, on condition that the annual income from the estate (reckoned at 6% = 4,200 HS) was spent as he directed: every year, food, drink and money were to be distributed on the anniversary of his birthday (10 May); cakes and mead were to be given to the townsmen (*municipibus*) and to others residing there (*incolis*), and to all their wives (they were explicitly included). Rewards were carefully graded. Town

had the added advantage of involving beneficiaries in ensuring that the legacy would continue to be used for its intended purpose.

Self-interest was not the only motive for generosity. There was a long tradition in the Graeco-Roman world of giving to the local community, partly out of local patriotism, or religious devotion, and partly from a sense of obligation felt by the rich and powerful that they had to enhance their status by giving; so they gave back some of what they had extracted from the poor in rent and low wages. Hence the large gifts (the actual size of the gift was prominently recorded) for the foundation of public baths and libraries, and for the endowment of schools and of distributions of food and money to local children.[68] The eternal commemoration of the founder's name played perhaps only a minor part in the total motivation, although it was sometimes explicitly, even flamboyantly recognised:

And I wish the gift which out of my generosity I have made to the gymnasium and to the city on the stated conditions to be inscribed on three stone pillars. One is to be set up in the market-place fixed to the front wall of my house; the second should be set up at the entrace of the temple to Caesar, next to the city gates; the third at the entrance to the gymnasium, so that my philanthropic generosity should be conspicuous and acknowledged both by citizens and by visitors to the city... My idea is that I shall

councillors and their sons got cakes and mead plus a small gift in cash (10 HS); lesser town officials (*seviri augustales*) got slightly less money. The children of the plebs both free and slave, were not forgotten; they got handfuls of nuts, 'without distinction of liberty'. But in pride of place in the inscription, Quinctilius had recorded the statue of himself which the local town-council had voted him in return for all this generosity. He insisted that every year a sum be spent, as the local officials directed, on the adornment of his statue and ancestral portraits (*imagines – CIL* 10.5853).

[68] For the sizes of gifts, see the annotated lists in R. P. Duncan-Jones, *The Economy of the Roman Empire* (Cambridge, 1974) 156ff. The first known private foundation (indeed the first known Roman foundation of any kind) for the support of children dates from the middle of the first century AD (*CIL* 10.5056 – Atina); from the end of the first century AD we know of over forty such foundations in Italy (conventionally called *alimenta*) set up with state aid. The method of their establishment is revealing. The state gave a capital sum, which was taken up by local landowners in the form of a loan against the security of their farms (roughly, one could borrow 8% of the declared value of the land) and in return the borrowers had to pay 5% each year to a fund for children (aged up to 18 years for boys and 14 for girls – D. 34.1.4.1), which was locally administered. The scheme is a mixture of crudity and sophistication. The central government paid out a huge capital sum and clearly had no mechanism available for dispensing annual funds throughout Italy for this purpose. On the other hand, the complicated procedure of burdening local land with debt in return for a perpetual obligation to pay annual interest was well established. And that was the institutional basis for most foundations, whatever their objective. See R. P. Duncan-Jones, 'The purpose and organization of the *alimenta*', *Papers of the British School at Rome* 32 (1964) 123ff.

be immortal by virtue of this just and kindly gift...(*IG* 5.1.1208, from Gytheion, southern Greece, AD 161–9; text partly restored)

The Christian writer Tertullian scoffed at pagans' search for immortality by statue and inscription instead of by service to the true God (*In Defence of Christianity* 50.11). But whatever the motives, two results are clear. First, donors testated sizeable sums away from family and friends for the wider benefit of the local community. Secondly, the social rituals of local communities often centred around the celebration of the generous dead.

The main problem was that permanent memorials demanded everlasting care. But would heirs or beneficiaries carry out testators' intentions in perpetuity? Greek and Roman donors attempted to secure the performance of their wishes with a whole battery of devices; their sheer variety underlines the legal and practical difficulties of binding future generations. Pliny wrote to an acquaintance outlining some of the difficulties:

You ask me what steps you can take to protect, even after your death, the money which you have offered our native town for an annual feast. I am honoured to be asked, but I have no ready opinion.

You could hand over the cash in full to the town, but it would run the risk of being dissipated. You could donate land; but it might be neglected, as tends to happen with public property. (*Letters* 7.18)

Pliny's own complicated solution was to give land to the town and then to lease it back to himself at a low rent, a tactic which he thought would prove durable since after his death a low rent would always attract a tenant. We do not know whether he was proved right.[69]

Other benefactors tried to safeguard their wishes by involving the local town-council, whether as curators or as beneficiaries. In one case, for example, the entire town-council was present when a donation for the upkeep of a temple dedicated to a long-dead empress was formally inscribed (*CIL* 14.2795 – Gabii). One donor setting up

[69] Evidence on the persistence of foundations is sparse. Neither their continuation nor their collapse required an inscription on stone. One case sometimes cited (Laum 1914: 222, based on P.Oxy.705 – AD 200 and P.Oxy.43 – AD 323) does not stand up to close examination; it shows the persistence of games, not of a specific foundation. But we do know of one elaborate foundation, set up by C. Vibius Salutaris in Ephesus in AD 104 with the normal declarations of eternity reinforced by decree of local council and people and by the provincial governor. Yet within 3–6 years, admittedly with the donor's agreement, a substantial sum was diverted from the foundation. See Laum 1914: 222–3; R. Heberdey, *Forschungen in Ephesos* (Vienna, 1912) vol. 2,150 and now H. Wankel, ed., *Die Inschriften von Ephesos* (Bonn, 1979) vol. 11.1, 27 and 36.

a foundation in honour of his dead son, provided sufficient funds (250,000 HS) for the town-councillors to have a lavish banquet every year on the anniversary of his son's birthday (*CIL* 11.4815–Spoletium). By the terms of another, relatively modest foundation, the beneficiaries had to abide by the conditions of the bequest or the funds of the foundation would be forfeit and would pass to a neighbouring and presumably rivalrous town, ten kilometres away (*CIL* 14.2793 – Gabii).[70] Some provincial donors sought approval for their donations from the Roman governor, or even from the emperor; they obviously hoped that such august sponsors would provide some protection for their trusts. Other bequests were protected by the threat of fines (sometimes hugely unrealistic), sometimes payable to the local town-council or to the Roman state treasury.[71]

Traditionally, it had been impossible in Roman law to bind an heir to use part or all of an inheritance for a particular purpose. One could not testate conditionally, nor could one bind future generations (technically, 'uncertain persons', i.e. those not named or not yet born). But in the first century AD, two developments made it easier legally to establish perpetual foundations. First, Romans invented legally enforceable trusts (*fideicommissa*), probably as a mechanism for evading the strict letter of some laws. It was an innovation of considerable importance in legal history. It meant that a testator could leave money by means of a trust to 'uncertain persons' or to corporate entities such as towns. If a principal heir failed to fulfil the conditions of a trust, the frustrated beneficiary could sue. Secondly, right at the end of the first century AD, corporate entities such as towns first acquired a legal personality, which enabled them to receive

---

[70] A similar set of conditions was specified at Pisa. A soldier in his will left 4,000 HS to the association of shipbuilders, on condition that out of the revenue from the gift, they celebrated two festivals of the dead each year at his tomb. If they did not, then the association of carpenters at Pisa were to get the money instead, but on the same conditions (*CIL* 11.1436, cf. 9.1618).

[71] Approval and protection of a foundation by the provincial governor or emperor are discussed by Laum 1914:219 and by J. H. Oliver, *The Ruling Power* (Philadelphia, 1953) 963ff with special reference to two cases (the foundation of Vibius Salutaris (see note 69) and *IG* 5.1.1147–Gytheion). For a fine payable to the state treasury, if the terms of the gift were not observed, see for example *CIL* 6.1925; or to the tutelary gods of a club, see *IG* 14.759 – Naples. Tombs also were frequently protected by the threat of fines. For example, M. Vocusius Crescens warned that anyone who attempted to buy or sell his family tomb or to chisel away the stone would be liable to a fine of 20,000 HS payable to the local town of Aquileia: and by way of incentive, the informer (*delator*) who brought the infraction to light should be rewarded with a quarter of the fine (*CIL* 5.952).

legacies in their own right (rather than though a trust). Again, the idea that a corporation could enjoy some of the legal rights of a human was an important development.[72]

Law was not everything. People established foundations, just as they drew up wills, without the benefit of lawyers, relying on custom and social pressures rather than on the strict letter of law.[73] We have examples of formal foundations, which in spite of the developments just outlined, prescribed legally unenforceable conditions for the continuous succession of an inheritance with its contingent responsibilities for the upkeep of the testator's tomb; these were designed to pass from freedmen to their descendants, and in turn to their descendants, in perpetuity.[74] Such a foundation binding successive generations could not be enforced legally or practically in the long

[72] On the detailed law of trusts, see F. Schulz, *Classical Roman Law* (Oxford, 1951) 312ff. On the development of the trust: '...in early times, trusts had no force, because no one could be forced to carry out a trust if he did not want to. If someone left an inheritance or legacies to someone else who could not legally inherit, he entrusted himself to the good faith of these who were entitled to inherit under the will. That is why they were called trusts (*fideicommissa*), because they were not based on legal obligation, but on the sense of honour (*pudor*) of those who were asked to execute them' (Justinian, *Institutes* 2.23). Augustus made trusts legally enforceable; the increased use of trusts can be gauged from the fact that the emperor Claudius assigned two praetors specifically to deal with the law of trusts in Italy; this was later reduced to one (D. 1.2.2.32; Gaius 2.278). On the Roman law relating to corporate entities, see P. W. Duff, *Personality in Roman Private Law* (Cambridge, 1938) esp. 88ff and 154ff. Towns could be instituted as principal heirs from the reign of Nerva (*Epitome of Ulpian* 24.28); clubs were allowed to receive legacies from the middle of the second century AD (D. 34.5.20 – Paul), see also Crook 1967: 121–2.

[73] For example, in the Digest, the following case was cited: 'I have written this my will without anyone learned in the law, following the reasoning of my mind rather than an excessive and pitiful exactitude. And if I have done anything not quite lawful or unskilful, nevertheless the wishes of a sane man should be considered valid in law' (D 31.88.17 – Marcian, who upheld the will). Cf. the Roman tombstone inscription: 'Away with fraud and lawyers. All my ex-slaves, male and female, are to have access and entry to this tomb. My heir shall give them the key to make sacrifices, however often and whenever there is need' (*CIL* 6.12133).

[74] The wealthy senator Dasumius, for example, in his will left his burial park and the farm in which it was sited to his ex-slaves 'for the purpose of cultivating my memory'. He directed that shares in the land and the accompanying obligations were to pass from one freed slave to another and to their descendants or successors; they were never to sell it, mortgage it or give it away (*CIL* 6.10229). In two other well-known foundations, the testator attempted to ensure perpetuity by placing an obligation on his legatees to bind their heirs in turn to perform exactly the same duties which he had imposed on them (*CIL* 6.10239 and 13.5708 – Langres). Finally, a tomb 'on the Vatican hill' carried the inscription: '...I ask you, my heirs, I order you and I rely upon your good faith to build me a tomb...at a cost of 6,000 HS...I charge my freed slaves, male and female, with the right and duty of maintaining my cult at that tomb. This applies to all (their) descendants...' (*L'Année épigraphique* 24 (1945) 136).

term. But in the social and political arena of a small town, a public foundation constituted a trust, with openly prescribed conditions and penalties, published on stone for all to read and act on. That is why these records have survived. Perhaps the status of the donor or of the beneficiaries under the trust helped ensure execution for a time. But neither we nor the Romans knew how to be absolutely certain that a trust would be fulfilled for ever.

The establishment of foundations for the commemoration of the dead from the first century AD onwards reflected an important change in Roman religious culture. We began this essay with a description of Roman aristocrats in the second century BC assembled in the Roman Forum before a popular audience to commemorate the death of a kinsman with due ceremony. Continuing commemoration was the responsibility of the family and the clan (*gens*). Traditionally, each family had its own rites (*sacra*), passed down from father to son in perpetuity (Cicero, *On Laws* 2.22). By the end of the Republic, according to Cicero, the chief priests (*pontifices maximi*) had evolved legalistic mechanisms by which the heavy financial burden of these traditional rites could be evaded (*ibid.* 2.48–53).[75] An inheritance without these sacral obligations (*sine sacris hereditas* – Festus *sv*) became a byword for a gift without strings. In the same period, as we have seen, there was a growth in beliefs about individual salvation. I do not want to exaggerate these changes, nor their coincidence in time. But it is plausible to link them together.

A decline in traditional family rites, a decline in the political power of collective kinsmen, a growth in beliefs about individual salvation, all helped promote commemorative foundations. Instead of entrusting the task of commemoration to their kin, or to their children and their descendants, many Romans, men and women, both those with wealth and those of moderate means, left bequests to ensure the

[75] See E. F. Bruck 1954: 24ff. Bruck warns against interpreting Cicero's testimony as evidence for the decline of traditional religious rites at the end of the Republic. The high priests were aiming at the preservation of the heir's obligations. He argues with some force that the byword *sine sacris hereditas* also implied that other people *were* performing family rites. But by the second century AD, these family rites (*sacra*) were obviously not practised widely. Gaius (2.55): '...ancient lawyers wished inheritances to be entered on promptly, in order that there should be persons to carry on the *sacra*, to which in those days great importance was attached...' – but clearly not in Gaius' own day; his contemporary Festus (370L) also indicated their disuse. One technical difficulty was that the right or obligation to perform family rites went with the inheritance of more than half the property, but sometimes the principal heir received less than the chief legatee. This conflict was recognised in the formula often found on Roman tombs: H M H N S – This Tomb Shall Not Follow the Principal Heir (e.g *CIL* 6.23838). See F. de Visscher, *Le droit des tombeaux romains* (Milan, 1963) 101.

survival of their memory. They left benefits and obligations to their ex-slaves, to fellow tradesmen and associates in a club (*collegium*), or to the local town-council.[76] And some did this, we know, even when they had surviving children (e.g. *CIL* 6.10229). This development may reflect a narrowing perception of who counted as belonging in the effective circle of kinship (see above, p. 206). For reasons which are not clear to me, many donors and testators apparently distrusted family members and their own descendants; they apparently thought that these descendants would not persist in honouring and commemorating them and in sacrificing at their tombs. Was it because their own ties with distant ancestors were tenuous, or was it because they perceived the considerable risk that their direct descendants would die out? In their own world, tombs were forgotten and neglected. Whatever the reason, many Romans entrusted their survival as individuals on earth to the strength of Roman law and to the institutions of property. They entrusted their life after death to an impersonal collectivity, a burial club, a trade association, or the local town-council. Private grief for the socially distinguished was at first supplemented and enhanced by public recognition, then it was displaced by municipal ceremonies purportedly in honour of the dead. Mourning was municipalised.

But in the end, all these attempts to create permanent memorials in honour of the dead proved in vain. Subsequent generations defalcated and diverted monies from their original objectives. Inflation lessened the purchasing power of fixed sums. Sudden crises, social changes, religious conversions, all undermined charitable foundations. Tombs and their ornamental gardens were sold or re-used in spite of legal prohibitions.[77] Rich graves were obvious

[76] Of course, our evidence could be biased. If one set up a memorial foundation, it was worthwhile having its regulations inscribed on the tomb, just to encourage their fulfilment. But if one left one's tomb to family care there was no need for such an elaborate inscription. That is a problem. But long-lasting family tombs have not often been found (see above, p. 206 and note 5). I need here to note a passage in the Digest: 'Ex-slaves can neither be buried, nor bury others, unless they have been instituted as principal heirs to their former masters, even if the masters have inscribed on the tomb that it is for themselves and their ex-slaves' (D. 11.7.6 pr – Ulpian; cf. *CJ* 3.44.6). This is not a general rule, but is limited by its context to the exceptional circumstances of disherison. For a detailed discussion, see de Visscher 1963: 74ff and 95.

[77] A famous Greek inscription, reportedly found in Nazareth in 1930, and dated to the early first century AD, contained the following imperial decree: 'It is my pleasure that graves and tombs set up for the cult of ancestors or children or relatives shall remain undisturbed in perpetuity...' (*SEG* 8 (1937) 13). The regulation goes on to threaten trial for anyone accused of removing the dead from a tomb or of taking away tombstones. There is very little chance that it relates directly to the resurrection of Christ; that was outside imperial control.

targets for robbers who wanted to strip corpses of their valuables, or who wanted to re-use the dressed stone of which even relatively simple graves were constructed. Indeed the municipal toilets in Ostia were made out of old gravestones.[78] And we owe the preservation of many Roman tombstone inscriptions to their incorporation in the walls of Christian churches. The very frequency of the curses against tomb violators bears witness to their inefficacy, at least in this world. That said, the fact that even now we can study so many Roman tombstones and epitaphs testifies to Roman success in securing a lasting commemoration for their dead.

APPENDIX

Doubts about restricted rights to display ancestral busts (*ius imaginum*)

The dominant scholarly view is that the right to display ancestral masks at home and in funeral processions (*ius imaginum*) was strictly limited to higher (curule) magistrates or to nobles (T. Mommsen, *Römisches Staatsrecht* (Leipzig³, 1887) vol. 1, 442ff). It is difficult to argue against Mommsen, but it is noteworthy that the phrase *ius imaginum* is first attested in the sixteenth century. *Ius imaginum* is a product of post-renaissance attempts to place all Roman custom and practice within a formal framework of Roman law. But is it really likely that commemorative practices, especially at home, were differentiated precisely along the boundaries between those families with or without praetorian ancestry? There is no evidence, and I see no reason why, the display of ancestral masks or busts at home, or even in funeral processions, was formally limited to higher magistrates. Nor can the point be proved by citing testimony which illustrates that nobles had ancestral masks. Emperors had the right to wear purple; but others wore purple too (see M. Reinhold, *History of Purple as a Status Symbol in Antiquity* (Brussels, 1970) 37ff and 48ff). That said, high office-holders in the late Roman

On the Roman law of tomb violation, see D. 47.12. Law was reinforced by private imprecation. For example, a tomb in Aquileia threatened a fine of 100,000 HS payable to the state treasury if anyone disturbed the founder's corpse or that of his wife, or tried to bury someone else there (*CIL* 5.1102, cf. 6.13785). But in excavated tombs, one can also find evidence of re-use. For example, in one of the fine late Republican tombs of the Villa Wolkonsky in Rome, built like city terraced houses, an original occupant's bones had been moved into a corner in antiquity to make way for a second corpse (so F. Fornari, *Notizie degli Scavi* 14 (1917) 175). For an illegal sale of a tomb garden, revoked by judgement of the Chief Financial Administrator (*idiologos*) in Egypt, see de Visscher 1963: 197ff.

[78] Meiggs 1973: 143; an evocative change of use, but foreshadowed in some tombstone inscriptions. As a variation on those which commonly greeted the passing traveller, and asked him to consider his fate, or to offer a thought for the dead (e.g. *CIL* 11.5357), one finely lettered marble tombstone from Rome (*CIL* 6.3413; cf. 3.1966) bears the subscription: 'Do not piss here.'

Republic did acquire some right to display their portaits (Cicero, *Against Verres* 2.5.36). Unfortunately, we do not know the exact extent or nature of this privilege. Finally, it is worth noting that sculpted funerary busts, artistically derived from death masks, were widespread by the last century of the Republic. For detailed arguments, see A. N. Zadoks-Josephus Jitta, *Ancestral Portraiture in Rome* (Amsterdam, 1932) 32ff and 97ff.

BIBLIOGRAPHY

MODERN WORKS CITED IN CHAPTERS I AND 4

Alexiou M. (1974) *The Ritual Lament in Greek Tradition*, Cambridge.
Altmann W. (1905) *Die römischen Grabaltäre der Kaiserzeit*, Berlin.
Arangio-Ruiz V. (1938) 'La legislazione' in *Augustus: Studi in occasione del bimillenario Agusteo*, Rome, 101ff.
Bean G. E. (1971) *Journeys in northern Lycia 1965–67*, Vienna.
Beard M. (1980) 'The sexual status of Vestal Virgins', *Journal of Roman Studies* 70, 12ff.
Bloch M. (1971) *Placing the Dead*, London.
Bollinger T. (1969) *Theatralis Licentia*, Winterthur.
Bott N. A. (1972) ed. *Testamentum Porcelli*, Zürich.
Bouché-Leclercq A. (1895) 'Les lois démographiques d'Auguste', *Revue Historique* 57, 241ff.
Bowlby J. (1980) *Loss: Sadness and Depression*, London (*Attachment and Loss*, London, 1969–80, vol. 3).
Brizio E. (1876) *Pitture e sepolcri scoperti sull' Esquilino*, Rome.
Brown, P. R. L. (1977) *Relics and Social Status in the Age of Gregory of Tours*, Reading.
Brown, P. R. L. (1981) *The Cult of the Saints*, London.
Bruck E. F. (1954) *Über römisches Recht im Rahmen der Kulturgeschichte*, Berlin.
Brusin G. (1941) *Nuovi monumenti sepolcrali di Aquileia*, Venice.
Brusin G. (1956) *Aquileia e Grado*, Padua.
Calderini A. (1930) *Aquileia Romana*, Milan.
Calza G. (1940) *La necropoli del porto di Roma nell' Isola Sacra*, Rome.
Cameron A. (1976) *Circus Factions*, Oxford.
Capitanio M. (1974) 'La necropoli romana di Portorecanati', *Notizie degli Scavi* 28, 142ff.
Carettoni G. (1956–8) 'Le gallerie ipogee del Foro romano', *Bulletino della commissione archeologica di Roma* 76, 23ff.
Coarelli F. (1975) *Guida archeologica di Roma*, Rome².
Colin J. (1965) *Les villes libres de l'orient gréco-romain et l'envoi au supplice par acclamations populaires*, Brussels.
Corbett P. E (1930) *The Roman Law of Marriage*, Oxford.
Crook J. A. (1967) *Law and Life of Rome*, London.

257

Crook J. A. (1967 *bis*) 'Patria Potestas', *Classical Quarterly* 17, 113ff.

Crook J. A. (1973) 'Intestacy in Roman society', *Proceedings of the Cambridge Philological Society* 19, 38ff.

Cumont F. (1942) *Recherches sur le symbolisme funéraire des Romains*, Paris.

Cumont F. (1959). *After Life in Roman Paganism*, repr. New York.

Daniélou J. (1977) *The Origins of Latin Christianity*, London.

Daube D. (1965) 'The preponderance of intestacy at Rome', *Tulane Law Review* 39, 253ff.

Daube D. (1969) *Roman Law*, Edinburgh.

Degrassi A. (1947 and 1963) ed. *Inscriptiones Italiae*, Rome, vol. 13, 1 and 2.

Duff P. W. (1938) *Personality in Roman Private Law*, Cambridge.

Duncan-Jones R. P. (1964) 'The purpose and organization of the *alimenta*', *Papers of the British School at Rome* 32, 123ff.

Duncan-Jones R. P. (1974) *The Economy of the Roman Empire*, Cambridge.

Enciclopedia dell'Arte antica classica e orientale.

Fanin (Colonel – ?pseudonym) (1871) *The Royal Museum at Naples, Erotic Paintings, Bronzes and Statues*, London, privately printed.

Finley M. I. (1960) ed. *Slavery in Classical Antiquity*, Cambridge.

Fortes M. (1970) *Time and Social Structure*, London.

Foucault M. (1979) *Discipline and Punish*, London.

Fraccaro P. (1956–7) *Opuscula*, Pavia, 3 vols.

Frend W. H. C. (1965) *Martyrdom and Persecution in the Early Church*, Oxford.

Friedländer L. (1922) *Sittengeschichte Roms*, Leipzig[10].

Galinsky G. K. (1969) *Aeneas, Sicily and Rome*, Princeton.

Garrucci R. (1856) *Graffiti di Pompeii*, Paris[2].

Geertz C. (1975) *Interpretations of Culture*, London.

Gilliam J. F. (1961) 'The plague under Marcus Aurelius', *American Journal of Philology* 82, 225ff.

Goffman E. (1961) *Encounters*, Indianapolis.

Goody J. (1962) *Death, Property and the Ancestors*, London.

Goody J. (1976) *Production and Reproduction*, Cambridge.

Goody J. *et al.* (1976) edd. *Family and Inheritance*, Cambridge.

Gorer G. (1965) *Death, Grief and Mourning in Contemporary Britain*, London.

Grant M. (1967) *Gladiators*, London.

Grant M. (1975) *Erotic Art in Pompeii*, London.

Hands A. R. (1968) *Charities and Social Aid in Greece and Rome*, London.

Harnack A. von (1904) *The Expansion of Christianity in the First Three Centuries*, London, 2 vols.

Harnack A. von (1924) *Die Mission und Ausbreitung des Christentums*, Leipzig[4], 2 vols.

Harris M. (1978) *Cannibals and Kings*, London.

Harris, W. V. (1979) *War and Imperialism in Republican Rome 327–70 B.C.*, Oxford.

Heberdey R. (1912) *Forschungen in Ephesos*, Vienna, vol. 2.

Hopkins, K. (1980) 'Taxes and trade in the Roman empire', *Journal of Roman Studies* 70, 101ff.

Hopkins, K. (1980 *bis*) 'Brother–sister marriage in Roman Egypt', *Comparative Studies in Society and History* 22, 303ff.

Humbert M. (1972) *Le remariage à Rome*, Milan.

Huntington R. and Metcalf P. (1979) *Celebrations of Death*, Cambridge.

Jolowicz H. F. and Nicholas B. (1972) *Historical Introduction to the Study of Roman Law*, Cambridge³.

Jordan H. (1871–1907) *Topographie der Stadt Rom im Alterthum*, Berlin, 2 vols.

Kaibel G. (1878) *Epigrammata graeca ex lapidibus conlecta*, Berlin.

Kaser M. (1968) *Roman Private Law*, London².

Kaser M. (1971) *Das römische Privatrecht*, Munich².

Kelly J. N. D. (1972) *Early Christian Creeds*, London³.

Kiernan V. G. (1976) 'Private property in history' in J. Goody *et al.* 1976.

Kleiner D. E. E. (1977) *Roman Group Portraiture*, New York.

Kunkel W. (1966) 'Das Konsilium im Hausgericht', *Zeitschrift der Savigny-Stiftung* 83, 219ff.

Lanciani R. (1888) *Ancient Rome in the Light of Recent Discoveries*, London.

Lanciani R. (1897) *The Ruins and Excavations of Ancient Rome*, Boston.

Lattimore R. B. (1942) *Themes in Greek and Latin Epitaphs*, Urbana, Illinois.

Laum B. (1914) *Stiftungen in der griechischen und römischen Antike*, Leipzig, 2 vols.

MacGeachy J. A. (1942) *Quintus Aurelius Symmachus and the Senatorial Aristocracy of the West*, Chicago.

MacMullen R. (1981) *Paganism in the Roman Empire*, New Haven.

Maine H. S. (1883) *Ancient Law*, London⁹.

Malavolta M. (1978) 'A proposito del nuovo s.c. da Larino', *Sesta Miscellanea greca e romana*, Rome.

Malinowski B. (1954) *Magic, Science and Religion*, repr. New York.

Marris P. (1974) *Loss and Change*, London.

Mau A. (1890) 'Iscrizioni gladiatorie di Pompei', *Römische Mitteilungen* 5, 25ff.

Mau A. (1899) *Pompeii, its Life and Art*, London.

Mazois F. (1824) *Les ruines de Pompeii*, Paris, 2 vols.

Meiggs R. (1973) *Roman Ostia*, Oxford².

Millar F. (1977) *The Emperor in the Roman World*, London.

Mommsen T. (1887) *Römisches Staatsrecht*, Leipzig³, 3 vols.

Musurillo H. (1972) ed. *The Acts of the Christian Martyrs*, Oxford.

Nash E. (1961–2) *Pictorial Dictionary of Ancient Rome*, London, 2 vols.

Nock A. D. (1972) *Essays on Religion and the Ancient World*, ed. Z. Stewart, Oxford, 2 vols.

Ogilvie R. M. (1965) *A Commentary on Livy*, Oxford.

Oliver J. H. (1953) *The Ruling Power*, Philadelphia.

Oliver J. H. and Palmer R. E. A. (1955) 'Minutes of an Act of the Roman Senate', *Hesperia* 24, 320ff.

Otto A. (1890) *Die Sprichwörter und Sprichwörtlichen Redensarten der Römer*, Leipzig.

Pace B. (1955) *I mosaici di Piazza Armerina*, Rome.

Parkes C. M. (1972) *Bereavement*, London.

Patlagean E. (1977) *Pauvreté économique et pauvreté sociale à Byzance, 4ᵉ–7ᵉ siècles*, Paris.

Pauly F. (1861) *Scholia Horatiana*, Prague.

Peek W. (1960) *Griechische Grabgedichte*, Berlin.

Pfuhl E. and Möbius H. (1977–9) *Die ostgriechischen Grabreliefs*, Mainz, 4 vols.

Piranesi G. B. (1756) *Le antichità romane*, Rome.

Platner S. B. and Ashby T. (1929) *A Topographical Dictionary of Ancient Rome*, Oxford.

Reece, R. (1977) ed. *Burial in the Roman World, Council for British Archaeology, Research Report* 22, London.

Reinhold M. (1970) *History of Purple as a Status Symbol in Antiquity*, Brussels.

Robert L. (1940) *Les gladiateurs dans l'Orient grec*, Paris.

Robertis F. M. de (1955) *Il fenomeno associativo nel mondo romano*, Naples.

Rogers R. S. (1947) 'The Roman emperors as heirs and legatees', *Transactions of the American Philological Association* 78, 140ff.

Rostovtzeff M. I. *et al.* (1936) edd. *The Excavations at Dura-Europus*, New Haven. *Preliminary Report of Sixth Season*.

Schulz F. (1951) *Classical Roman Law*, Oxford.

Stone L. (1977 and 1979) *The Family, Sex and Marriage in England 1500–1800*, London.

Styger P. (1933) *Die römischen Katakomben*, Berlin.

Toynbee J. M. C. (1971) *Death and Burial in the Roman World*, London.

Toynbee J. M. C. (1973) *Animals in Roman Life and Art*, London.

Toynbee J. M. C. and Ward Perkins J. (1956) *The Shrine of St Peter and the Vatican Excavations*, London.

Tumolesi P. S. (1980) *Gladiatorum Paria*, Rome.

Vessberg O. (1941) *Studien zur Kunstgeschichte der römischen Republik*, Lund, 2 vols.

Veyne P. (1976) *Le pain et le cirque*, Paris.

Veyne P. (1978) 'La famille et l'amour sous le haut-empire romain', *Annales* 33, 35ff.

Ville, G. (1981) *La gladiature en Occident*, Rome.

Visscher F. de (1963) *Le droit des tombeaux romains*, Milan.

Vovelle M. (1973) *Le piété baroque et déchristianisation*, Paris.

Waltzing J. P. (1895–1900) *Étude historique sur les corporations professionelles chez les Romains*, Louvain, 4 vols.

Wankel H. (1979) ed. *Die Inschriften von Ephesos*, Bonn, vol. 11.1.

Watson A. (1967) *The Law of Persons in the Later Roman Republic*, Oxford.

Watson A. (1971) *The Law of Succession in the Later Roman Republic*, Oxford.

Watson G. R. (1969) *The Roman Soldier*, London.

Wheeler R. E. M. (1929) 'A Roman pipe-burial from Caerleon, Monmouthshire', *The Antiquaries Journal* 9, 1ff.

Wistrand E. (1976) *The So-Called Laudatio Turiae*, Göteborg.

Zadoks-Josephus Jitta A. N. (1932) *Ancestral Portraiture in Rome*, Amsterdam.

Amelotti M. (1966) *Il testamento romano*, Florence.
Astin A. E. (1957 and 1958) 'The Lex Annalis before Sulla', *Latomus* 16, 588ff. and 17, 49ff.
Badian E. (1972) *Publicans and Sinners*, Oxford.
Balsdon J. P. V. D. (1962) *Roman Women*, London.
Bayet J. (1957) *Histoire politique et psychologique de la religion romaine*, Paris.
Bergues H. (1960) ed. *La prévention des naissances dans la famille*, Paris.
Biondi B. (1955) *Successione testamentaria e donazioni*, Milan[2].
Bleicken J. (1975) *Die Verfassung der römischen Republik*, Paderborn.
Bredemeier H. C. and Stephenson R. M. (1962) *The Analysis of Social Systems*, New York.
Broughton T. R. S. (1951–60) *The Magistrate of the Roman Republic*, New York.
Cassola F. (1962) *I gruppi politici romani nel III secolo a.c.*, Trieste.
Chastagnol A. (1973) 'La naissance de l'ordo senatorius', *Mélanges de l'école française à Rome* 85, 583ff.
Corbett P. E. (1930) *The Roman Law of Marriage*, Oxford.
Crook J. A. (1967) *Law and Life of Rome*, London.
De Sanctis G. (1967–9) *Storia dei Romani*, Florence[2], 6 vols.
Develin R. (1979) *Patterns in Office-Holding 366–49 BC*, Brussels.
Dixon S. (1982) 'The family feeling of Scipio Aemilianus', unpublished.
Fallers L. A. (1965) *Bantu Bureaucracy*, Chicago[2].
Finley M. I. (1974) ed. *Studies in Ancient Society*, London.
Fourastié J. (1959) 'De la vie traditionelle', *Population* 14, 417ff.
Fowler W. W. (1911) *The Religious Experience of the Roman People*, London.
Freedman M. (1958) *Lineage Organization in South-eastern China*, London.
Friedländer L. (1922) *Sittengeschichte Roms*, Leipzig[10], 4 vols.
Fritz K. von (1954) *The Theory of the Mixed Constitution in Antiquity*, New York.
Gellner E. (1964) *Thought and Change*, London.
Gelzer M. (1962) *Kleine Schriften*, Wiesbaden vol. 1.
Gelzer M. (1969) *The Roman Nobility*, Oxford.
Glass D. V. and Eversley D. E. C. (1965) edd. *Population in History*, London.
Glass D. V. (1973) *Numbering the People*, Farnborough, Hants.
Goodwin A. (1975) ed. *The European Nobility in the Eighteenth Century*, London.
Goody J. (1973) 'Strategies of heirship', *Comparative Studies in Society and History* 15, 1ff.
Goody J. (1976) *Production and Reproduction*, Cambridge.
Goody J. (1976 *bis*) ed. *Family and Inheritance*, Cambridge.
Groag E., Stein A. *et al.* (1933–70) *Prosopographia Imperii Romani*, Berlin[2].
Gruen E. S. (1974) *The Last Generation of the Roman Republic*, Berkeley.
Henry L. (1956) *Anciennes familles genèvoises*, Paris.
Hollingsworth T. H. (1964) *The Demography of the British Peerage, Population Studies Supplement* vol. 18.

Hopkins K. (1965) 'The age of Roman girls at marriage', *Population Studies* 18, 309ff.

Hopkins K. (1965 *bis*) 'Contraception in the Roman Empire', *Comparative Studies in Society and History* 8 124ff.

Hopkins K. (1978) 'Rules of evidence', *Journal of Roman Studies* 68, 178ff.

Hopkins K. (1980) 'Taxes and trade in the Roman empire (200 BC–AD 400)', *Journal of Roman Studies* 70, 101ff.

Humbert M. (1972) *Le remariage à Rome*, Milan.

Jolowicz H. F. and Nicholas B. (1972) *Historical Introduction to the Study of Roman Law*, Cambridge[3].

Kaser M. (1971) *Das römische Privatrecht*, Munich[2], vol. 1.

Latte K. (1960) *Römische Religionsgeschichte*, Munich.

Lyne R. O. A. M. (1980) *The Latin Love Poets*, Oxford.

MacMullen R. (1967) *Enemies of the Roman Order*, Harvard.

Martin D. A. (1969) *The Religious and the Secular*, London.

Martino F. de (1972–5) *Storia della costituzione romana*, Naples[2], 5 vols.

Mommsen T. (1887) *Römisches Staatsrecht*, Leipzig[3].

Morris I. (1964) *The World of the Shining Prince*, Oxford.

Morris I. (1967) translator of *The Pillow Book of Sei Shonagon*, Oxford.

Münzer F. (1920) *Römische Adelsparteien und Adelsfamilien*, Stuttgart.

Nicolet C. (1966) *L'ordre équestre à l'époque républicaine*, Paris.

Nicolet C. (1976) 'Le cens sénatorial sous la république et sous Auguste', *Journal of Roman Studies* 66, 20ff.

Nicolet C. (1977) 'Les classes dirigeantes romaines sous la république: ordre sénatorial et ordre équestre, *Annales* 32, 726ff.

Nicolet C. (1980) *The World of the Citizen in Republican Rome*, London.

North J. A. (1976) 'Conservatism and change in Roman religion, *Papers of the British School at Rome* 44, 1ff.

Scullard H. H. (1973) *Roman Politics 220–150 B.C.*, Oxford[2].

Shackleton Bailey D. R. (1960) 'The Roman nobility in the Second Civil War', *Classical Quarterly* 10, 253ff.

Shatzman I. (1975) *Senatorial Wealth and Roman Politics*, Brussels.

Stein A. (1927) *Der römische Ritterstand*, Munich.

Stone L. (1965) *The Crisis of the Aristocracy 1558–1641*, Oxford.

Stone L. (1979) *The Family, Sex and Marriage in England 1500–1800*, London.

Stroheker K. F. (1948) *Der senatorische Adel im spätantiken Gallien*, Tübingen.

Syme R. (1939) *The Roman Revolution*, Oxford.

Taylor L. R. (1949) *Party Politics in the Age of Caesar*, Berkeley.

Taylor L. R. (1960) *The Voting Districts of the Roman Republic*, Rome.

Taylor L. R. (1966) *Roman Voting Assemblies*, Ann Arbor.

Toynbee A. J. (1965) *Hannibal's Legacy*, Oxford.

Wallace-Hadrill A. (1981) 'Family and inheritance in the Augustan marriage laws', *Proceedings of the Cambridge Philological Society* 207, 58ff.

Watson A. (1967) *The Law of Persons in the Later Roman Republic*, Oxford.

Watson A. (1971) *The Law of Succession in the Later Roman Republic*, Oxford.

Modern works cited in chapter 3

Weber M. (1947) *The Theory of Social and Economic Organization*, Glencoe, Illinois.
Willems P. (1878) *Le sénat de la république romaine*, Louvain, 2 vols.
Williams G. (1958) 'Some aspects of Roman marriage ceremonies and ideals', *Journal of Roman Studies* 48, 16ff.
Williams G. (1962) 'Poetry in the moral climate of Augustan Rome', *Journal of Roman Studies* 52, 28ff.
Wiseman T. P. (1971) *New Men in the Roman Senate 139 B.C.–A.D. 14*, Oxford..
Wiseman, T. P. (1974) 'Legendary genealogies in late Republican Rome', *Greece and Rome* 21, 153ff.
Wiseman T. P. (1979) *Clio's Cosmetics*, Leicester.
Wrigley E. A. (1969) *Population and History*, London.
Wrigley E. A. (1973) ed. *Identifying People in the Past*, London.
Wrigley E. A. (1978) 'Fertility strategy for the individual and the group', in C. Tilly, ed., *Historical Studies of Changing Fertility*, Princeton.
Wrigley E. A. and Schofield R. S. (1981) *The Population History of England 1541–1871*, London.

MODERN WORKS CITED IN CHAPTER 3

Alföldy G. (1968) 'Septimius Severus und der Senat', *Bonner Jahrbücher* 168, 112ff.
Alföldy G. (1976) 'Consuls and consulars under the Antonines', *Ancient Society* 7, 263ff.
Alföldy G. (1977) *Konsulat und Senatorenstand unter den Antoninen*, Bonn.
Apter D. E. (1963) 'System, process and politics in economic development', in B. F. Hoselitz and W. E. Moore, edd., *Industrialisation and Society*, Paris.
Astin A. E. (1963) 'Augustus and "censoria potestas"', *Latomus* 22, 226ff.
Aylmer G. E. (1974) *The King's Servants*, London[2].
Barbieri G. (1952) *L'albo senatorio da Settimio Severo a Carino*, Rome.
Bendix R. (1960) *Max Weber, An Intellectual Portrait*, London.
Birley A. R. (1971) *Septimius Severus*, London.
Birley A. R. (1981) *The Fasti of Roman Britain*, Oxford.
Birley E. (1953) 'Senators in the emperor's service', *Proceedings of the British Academy* 29, 197ff.
Bodde D. (1967) *China's Great Unifier*, Hong Kong[2].
Boulvert G. (1970) *Esclaves et affranchis impériaux sous le haut-empire romain*, Naples.
Bowersock G. W. (1965) *Augustus and the Greek World*, Oxford.
Bowersock G. W. (1969) *Greek Sophists in the Roman Empire*, Oxford.
Brunt P. A. (1961) 'Charges of provincial maladministration', *Historia* 10, 189ff.
Brunt P. A. (1961 *bis*) 'The Lex Valeria Cornelia', *Journal of Roman Studies* 51, 71ff.

Modern works cited in chapter 3

Brunt P. A. (1975) 'The administrators of Roman Egypt', *Journal of Roman Studies* 65, 124ff.

Burling R. (1974) *The Passage of Power, Studies in Political Succession*, New York.

Burton G. P. (1979) 'Curator rei publicae, towards a reappraisal', *Chiron* 9, 465ff.

Campbell B. (1975) 'Who were the Viri Militares?' *Journal of Roman Studies* 65, 11ff.

Chastagnol A. (1973) 'La naissance de l'*ordo senatorius*', *Mélanges de l'école française à Rome* 85, 583ff.

Chastagnol A. (1975) 'Latus clavus et adlectio; l'accès des hommes nouveaux au sénat romain sous le haut-empire', *Revue historique de droit française et étranger* 53, 375ff.

Coale A. J. and Demeny P. (1966) *Regional Model Life Tables and Stable Populations*, Princeton.

Cochran W. G. (1963) *Sampling Techniques*, New York[2].

Crook J. A. (1955) *Consilium Principis*, Cambridge.

Degrassi A. (1952) *I fasti consolari dell'impero romano*, Rome.

Drew-Bear T. *et al.* (1977) 'Sacrae litterae', *Chiron* 7, 355ff.

Dreyss C. (1860) ed. *Mémoires de Louis XIV*, Paris.

Duff A. M. (1958) *Freedmen in the Early Roman Empire*, Cambridge (repr).

Duncan-Jones R. P. (1974) *The Economy of the Roman Empire*, Cambridge.

Eck W. (1970) *Senatoren von Vespasian bis Hadrian*, Munich.

Eck W. (1973) 'Sozialstruktur des römischen Senatorenstandes der hohen Kaiserzeit und statistische Methode', *Chiron* 3, 375ff.

Eck W. (1974) 'Beförderungskriterien innerhalb den senatorischen Laufbahn', *ANRW* vol. 2.1, 158ff.

Eck W. *et al.* (1980) *Studien zur antiken Sozialgeschichte*, Cologne.

Ford F. L. (1965) *Robe and Sword*, New York.

Friedländer L. (1922) *Sittengeschichte Roms*, Leipzig[10].

Gouldner A. (1955) *Patterns of Industrial Bureaucracy*, London.

Graham A. J. (1974) 'Prosopography in Roman imperial history', *ANRW* vol. 2.1, 145ff.

Groag E. (1929) 'Zum Konsulat in der Kaiserzeit', *Wiener Studient* 47, 143ff.

Habicht C. (1959–60) 'Zwei neue Inschriften aus Pergamon', *Istanbuler Mitteilungen* 9/10, 121ff.

Hammond M. (1957) 'Composition of the Roman senate A.D. 68–235', *Journal of Roman Studies* 47, 73ff.

Hirschfeld O. (1963) *Die kaiserlichen Verwaltungsbeamten*, Berlin[2].

Jones A. H. M. (1960) *Studies in Roman Government and Law*, Oxford.

Jones, A. H. M. (1964) *The Later Roman Empire*, Oxford, 3 vols.

Jones A. H. M. *et al.* (1971) *The Prosopography of the Later Roman Empire* vol. 1, Cambridge.

Lambrechts P. (1936) *La composition du sénat romain (117–192)*, Antwerp.

Lambrechts P. (1937) *La composition du sénat romain de Septime Sévère à Dioclétian*, Budapest.

Lewis M. W. Hoffman (1955) 'The Official priests of Rome under the Julio-Claudians', *American Academy in Rome, Papers* 16.

McAlindon D. (1957) 'Senatorial appointments in the age of Claudius', *Latomus* 16, 252ff.

MacFarlane K. B. (1973) *The Nobility of Later Mediaeval England*, Oxford.

McKnight B. E. (1971) *Village and Bureaucracy in Southern Sung China*, Chicago.

Malavolta, M. (1978) 'A proposito del nuovo S. C. da Larino', *Sesta Miscellanea greca e romana*, Rome.

Menzel J. M. (1963) *The Chinese Civil Service*, Boston.

Meyer E. (1964) *Römischer Staat und Staatsgedanke*, Zurich[3].

Millar F. *et al.* (1967) *The Roman Empire and Its Neighbours*, London.

Millar F. (1977) *The Emperor in the Roman World*, London.

Momigliano A. D. (1961) *Claudius*, Cambridge[2].

Mommsen T. (1887) *Römisches Staatsrecht*, Leipzig[3].

Morris, J. (1953) 'The Roman senate A.D. 69–193', unpubl. Ph.D. London.

Morris J. (1964) 'Leges Annales under the Principate', *Listy Filologické* 87, 316ff.

Morris J. (1965) 'Leges Annales under the Principate', *Listy Filologické* 88, 22ff.

Mosca G. (1939) *The Ruling Class*, New York.

Pflaum H. G. (1950) *Les procurateurs équestres sous le haut-empire romain*, Paris.

Pflaum H. G. (1974) *Abrégé des procurateurs équestres*, Paris.

Pflaum H. G. (1976) 'Zur Reform des Kaisers Gallienus', *Historia* 25, 109ff.

Rémy B. (1976–7) 'Ornati et Ornamenta quaestoria praetoria et consularia sous le haut empire romain', *Revue des Etudes Anciennes* 78/9, 160ff.

Saller R. P. (1980) 'Promotion and patronage in equestrian careers, *Journal of Roman Studies* 70, 44ff.

Sprenkel S. Van der (1962) *Legal Institutions in Manchu China*, London.

Starr C. G. (1954) *Civilization and the Caesars*, Ithaca, NY.

Stein A. (1927) *Der römische Ritterstand*, Munich.

Stone L. (1965) *The Crisis of the Aristocracy 1558–1641*, Oxford.

Syme R. (1939) *The Roman Revolution*, Oxford.

Syme R. (1958) *Tacitus*, Oxford.

Syme R. (1960) 'Pliny's less successful friends', *Historia* 9, 362ff.

Syme R. (1965) 'Governors of Pannonia Inferior', *Historia* 14, 342ff.

Syme R. (1980) 'An eccentric patrician', *Chiron* 10, 427ff.

Tibiletti G. (1953) *Principe e magistrati repubblicani*, Rome.

Twitchett D. (1963) *Financial Administration under the T'ang*, Cambridge[2].

UN (1956) 'Methods of population projection by age and sex', *UN Population Studies* 26, New York.

Weaver P. R. C. (1972) *Familia Caesaris*, Cambridge.

White A. N. Sherwin- (1973) *The Roman Citizenship*, Oxford[2].

Yang C. K. (1959) 'Some characteristics of Chinese bureaucratic behavior', in D. S. Nivison and A. F Wright, *Confucianism in Action*, Stanford.

INDEX OF SUBJECTS

Index of subjects

consuls: age of, 47, 146–7; appointed by
emperor, 122, 155; careers, 158–9,
161–4; clan membership of, 38, 53;
elected, 34; fertility of, 33, 63, 64, 65, 99,
103, 104, 140–2; inner core of, 62–3;
listed (249–50 BC), 45–6; minimum age,
47, 73, 146, 154; number, 45, 128–30;
ordinary, 128; origins 56–9, 134–5, 136,
137–8, 140–1; other, 62; power of, 121,
149; sampled, 130–1; sons' political
failure or success, 33, 55–7, 59–65, 103–7,
112–13, 124, 134–6, 138–40, 142, 145–6,
174, 195, 198–200; suffect
(supplementary), 128–9; *see also*
aristocrats; praetors; senators
contraception, 97
conventional views, 36, 81, 126–7
corruption, 38, 80, 149–50, 155, 254
courtesans, 85
criminals: as gladiators, 10–24; executed,
2–3; modern, 156
crowd: lacking coherence, 18; power, 14;
psychology, 27; relations with emperor,
9, 10–11, 16–18
cruelty, 1ff, 28–9

dead: and the living, 233ff; care of, 213,
233–4; love and loathing for, 224; spirits
of (*Manes*), 227–8
death, 201ff; of children, 218–26; façade of
indifference to, 224–6; fear of, 26–7, 29,
213; fights to, 27; incidence
unpredictable, 73; insurance against,
213; life after, 226ff; masks, 201, 217
death rates: of gladiators, 25; high, 72–3,
118–19, 210, 246; of senators, 47, 64, 69ff,
147–8; of senators' sons, 33
decimation practised, 1–2
demonstrations, in Circus, 16
deviants, punished, 11
dinner parties, gladiators fight at, 28
disherison, 77, 237; *see also* wills
divorce, 87, 94
dowry, 77–8, 86, 88–9

elections, 33, 34, 107–8, 113–15, 122, 149,
151–2, 154
elite: circulating, 112, 174; defined, 44–5;
permeability of, 36, 42–3, 69, 108, 113,
185; reproduction of, 69, 73
emperors: absent from Rome, 19; agents
(*procurators*) of, 149; appointed consuls,
122, 155; arbitrary power of, 10, 12, 16,
171, 197; at gladiatorial shows, 15–20;
delegate power, 120, 173; generosity to
aristocrats, 75–6; hostility to aristocrats,

121, 122–3, 166, 170, 172–3, 177;
household administration of, 176ff;
legitimacy of, 11, 16, 121; power of, 9,
12, 15, 165, 170; worship of, 13, 14
empire: administration of, 35, 157ff, 177ff;
expanded by conquest, 1, 35; increased
by wealth of aristocrats, 79
England, post-feudal, 108
epidemic, 209–10
epitaphs, 115, 220–1, 227–8, 230
estates, 109
expression and experience, 221–2, 226

family size, 99ff
feelings: about divorce, 87; of grief, 203–4,
218ff; of hostility, 177; and language,
85; of romantic love, 85; suppressed,
94
fertility, 73ff, 99ff, 194–5; actual higher
than known, 105; of aristocrats, 106–7;
of consuls and praetors, 63, 73–4, 103,
138ff; controlled, 84, 87, 94–5, 96–7, 175,
195; defined, 33; fall in, 69, 74, 78, 95–7,
127, 145; of senators, 33, 75, 127
findings, analysed, 55ff, 134ff
fire brigade, 212
FSM: consuls and praetors, 62–4, 103–6;
defined, 61; of *ordinary* consuls, 139–40;
of suffect consuls, 140–2
funeral: banquet, 213, 214; cortège, 31;
cost, 213, 214; games and gladiatorial
shows, 3–4, 6, 12; procession, 201–2;
rites, 219, 226; speech, 52, 201

ghosts, 229, 234–5
gladiatorial shows: advertisements for, 7,
25; associated with emperor worship, 13,
14; betting at, 26; cost of, 7ff, 14;
criticisms of, 2–3; distributions of meat
at, 5; given by emperor, 9; in Italy and
provinces, 12; itinerant, 13; origins of,
3ff, 10; as political theatre, 14ff; religious
component in, 4–5
gladiators, 2ff; contaminated, 23; emperors,
20; killed, 18, 25, 27; sex appeal of,
21–3; social origins of, 21–5; spared, 18,
25–6; victors rewarded, 20, 25
graves: banquets at, 216, 233; dove-cot,
212, 214, 216–17; emperor's, 206; family,
206; grave-goods, 229, 248; mass,
209–10, 214; for poor, 202, 207–8, 211;
for rich, 202, 205; soldiers', 207; *see also*
memorials
grief, 217ff; stages of, 223
guardians, 89, 90–1; women's choice of
(*tutor optivus*), 91

hereditary nobility, 32, 36–7
hereditary status, 31–2, 37–8, 40–1, 42–3,
  172; of consuls, 56ff, 134ff; difficulties of
  maintaining, 70, 73, 194; in England,
  108; as ideal, 43, 111, 126; in law, 190,
  192; lessened by elections, 114–15
historical demography, 70–1, 99–100, 147;
  see also method
history as weapon, 16, 39
human sacrifice, 3, 5, 29

ideal: of administration, 186–7; of citizen's
  rights, 114; of inherited status, 43, 111;
  of marriage, 86
individuation, 78, 79–81, 84; difficulty to
  know what it means, 80
infanticide, 225–6
inheritance: by women, 88–92; of wealth,
  33, 88, 172, 221, 239ff; outside agnatic
  group, 89; partible, 43, 69, 76, 78, 96–7;
  see also wills
intestacy, 76

judicial murder (*proscriptions*), 70, 80
justice, 10

knights: as army officers, 179–80, 183; as
  gladiators, 21; in imperial
  administration, 120, 167, 176, 179–84,
  186; power, 196; and senators, 110–11,
  167–8, 191; sentenced to death, 70;
  special dress and reserved seats for, 17,
  109; as tax-farmers, 35; wealth of, 35

law on: guardians, 90; hereditary status,
  190; inheritance, 76; marriage, 91, 95–6,
  242; mourning, 218, 225; trusts, 251–2;
  wills, 236, 237; women's display of
  wealth, 91–2; women's inheritance, 92
lawyers, 252
legacies, 237ff, 250–1; *see also* wills
legacy-hunting, 194, 238ff
legal language, 214–15
life expectancy, 72, 100–1, 146ff
lists: bias in, 45, 58, 128, 156, 164; of
  consuls, 45
living conditions, 208
local notables (*decurions*), 13, 186–7, 248ff
love, 85, 86

marriage: age at, 85–6, 94; dissoluble, 86;
  for political alliance, 48–9, 86–9; for
  transferring wealth, 74, 86; new form
  (*sine manu*), 86, 88, 89–90, 244;
  reluctance to enter, 95
memorials, 247ff

methods: authentication from fragmentary
  evidence, 8 and *passim*; comparative
  demography, 42, 70–1, 146–9, 225;
  corroboration by later evidence, 78;
  empathetic imagination, 152, 205;
  estimating probable error, 128, 131–3;
  evocation, 1ff, 199ff; filling gaps in
  evidence, 38, 42, 46, 65, 133, 198–200;
  observations over expectations, 62, 103;
  resuscitation of missing persons, 42, 133,
  199; sampling, 53, 125, 130–3;
  simplifying assumption, 47, 64;
  speculation, 66–9; statistical analysis,
  32–3, 38, 41–2, 45, 55ff, 72, 99ff, 130ff;
  subjective judgement, 220–1; tautology,
  38
military service, 110
mobility: downward, 43; marginal, 40; via
  marriage, 49; into political elite, 42, 45
monarchy, imposed, 120
money supply, rise in, 89, 246
mortality, *see* death rates
mourning, municipalised, 254

names, 45, 51
new man (*novus homo*): as consul, 39, 57; as
  senators, 97, 112, 196, 173, 198–200
nobilis, nobiles: defined, 31; died out, 98;
  difficulties of concept, 38–9; hereditary
  status of, 43–4; monopoly of consulship
  by, 36, 39; non-participation in politics,
  44; political power of, 37, 113

oligarchic system of power sharing, 120,
  149

palace administration, 125, 176–8, 181,
  197
palace guard (*praetorians*), in fight, 10
paternal conflict with sons, 244–5
paternal power, 28, 243–4
patrician privilege, 35, 153–4, 172
placards, 19
plebs, mass walk-out (*secessio*), 35, 38; *see
  also* tribunes of the people
political competition, *see* aristocrats
political theatre, 14ff; applause, 14, 15, 16,
  17; claques, 15; emperor's absence from,
  19
poor: little electoral power, 34; standing
  room in amphitheatre, 18
popular assemblies: elections by, 33–4, 122;
  at gladiatorial shows, 14; powers of, 34
popular power, 12, 14ff, 114, 208
power separated from status, 171
praetorian prefect, 182

Index of subjects

praetors: elected by senate, 149; ex-praetors, 160–5; fertility, 64; 107; listed in full (218–166 BC), 46; minimum age, 47, 73; number, 35, 157, 158–9, 165; number of potential candidates, 47–8; origins, 59; rates of political reproduction, FSM, 62–3, 104; rates of political reproduction, SRP, 62–3, 104; their sons' political failure/success, 32, 47, 57ff, 104–5, 108, 112
prisoners of war: execution of, 2, 3; suicide, 8
property, concept of, 245–6
prosopography, 41, 42, 46, 156
proverb, thumbs down, 7
provinces: imperial, 157, 159; military, 154, 159
punishment reinforced legitimacy, 11

quaestors: elected, 35, 47, 146, 149, 150, 158–9, 169; ex-quaestors, 34, 160

rationality, 204–5
realism, 217
religion: alleged decline of Roman traditional religion, 81ff.; beliefs in immortality, 226, 230–1, 234; religious component in gladiatorial shows, 4–5; libations to the dead, 211, 234; 'Oriental' religions, 81–2, 231; sects, 213
research design, 45ff, 127ff: concentrated on consuls, 55; limitations of, 48ff; over seven generations, 50, 127
rich, disproportionate electoral power of, 34
ritual acclamations, 15, 18
rostra, 201–2

sacrifice, in amphitheatre, 17
scepticism, 82–3, 230; recommended, 100
secularisation, 78, 81–4; a dangerous concept, 81
senate: age at entry – Republic, 47; an aristocracy of office, elected by people, 44, 109; candidates for, 167–9; composition, 146; debates, 167; decline in power, 196–7; decrees, 34; entrants, 12; expulsion, 75; loss of power, 116, 170, 197–8; membership, 34–5, 115–17; and monarchy, 117; open to outsiders, 40, 69, 108, 241; power in Republic, 34; recruitment, 32, 34, 40–1, 47, 197; size, 35, 39, 40, 147–8, before 81 BC, 47; after 81 BC, 48
senatorial decree, c. AD 177 to reduce cost of gladiatorial shows, 14
senatorial order, 44, 147, 151, 169, 192–3

senatorial status, 192
senators: absent from Rome, 157, 175, 190; active 192; careers of, 150, 152–3, 156ff, 170, 174, 196; dress, 17, 109; executed, 122, cf. 70, 80; expulsion of, 75; as gladiators, 21; and knights, 110; life expectancy, 71, 146ff; military experience of, 150–1, 153–4, 157, 165, 172, 183; minimum wealth of, 75; never-consul, 174; never-praetor (*pedarii*), 48, 60, 66; number known, 135, 144; owned Italian land, 189; provincial, 125, 144–5, 169, 176, 184ff, 195–6, 200; reserved seats for, 17; sons of, 67–8, 112, 116, 126–7, 144–5, 151, 167, 190–3, 194ff; sons of, ranked as knights, 44; tenure of office by, 170; withdrawal by, 166, 175, 193; *see also* aristocrats
shit, 210, cf. 255
slaves: brutalisation of, 27; captured in war, 1; crucified, 28; emancipation by will, 248; freed slaves as gladiators, 25; as gladiators, 23–4; killed, 28; in burial clubs, 213; of imperial household, 176, 178; rebellion crushed, 29; metaphorical slavery of aristocrats and grammarians, 166, 179; sold to gladiator school, 28; tombs of, 229
ex-slaves: in death, 229; in imperial household, 120, 176–9, 181, 184; obligations of, 248, 252; as powerful administrators, 197; as private bailiffs, 189
soldiers: decimation of, 1; discipline of, 1
sons: one cheaper than two, 79; and fathers, 54, 84; two, 74; younger, 74, 77
SRP: defined, 61–2; of consuls and praetors, 62–4, 67, 103–5; of *ordinary* consuls, 139–40
status: tied to office, 116; without office, 173, 176ff
status symbols, senatorial dress and reserved seats, 109, 151, 168–9, 201
stories, 29, 122–3
stratification, by rank, 17–18
structural differentiation, 84
suicide, 215

tax: from gladiatorial shows, 13, 14; on inheritance, 242–3
tax collection, 186
tax-farmers, 35
testators, gave freedom to slaves, 77
theatrical shows, 6
tombstones, 204, 211, 218, 225

SELECTED INDEX OF PROPER NAMES

Ancient authors are indexed by first or most important citations

Selected index of proper names

Caesar, C. Iulius, dictator: civil war with Pompey, 54; display of his corpse, 217; giver of games and gladiatorial shows, 4, 6; legislation of, 83; marriage alliance of, 48; other mentions, 31, 41, 81; wealth of, 80–1

Caesarius, bishop of Arles, 5th century AD, on restriction of fertility, 97

Caligula, emperor (AD 37–41): and games and gladiatorial shows, 8, 10, 16, 19, 20; and senatorial order, 76, 122, 151

Calpurnius Bibulus, M., consul 59 BC: marriage of, 87–8; obstructed legislation of Caesar, 83

Calpurnius Piso Caesoninus, L., consul 58 BC, 31

Calpurnius Siculus, poet,? 1st century AD, 18

Campbell, B., on senatorial careers, 156, 161–4

Caracalla, emperor (AD 211–17): and gladiatorial contests, 20; and senatorial order, 172

Cassius Longinus, C., noble, assassin of Caesar, 31

Cassius, Spurius, consul 502, 493 and 486 BC, flogged to death by father, 244

Catiline, L. Sergius, renegade aristocrat: ancestry, 38–9, 65; conspiracy of, 81, 92–3

Catullus, love poet, 1st century BC, 85

Cestius, C., senator, 1st century BC, his funerary pyramid, 205–6

Charon, ferryman in Hades, 4, 218

China, administration of, 170, 186

Ch'in Shi-Huang-ti, first emperor of China, 120

Cicero, M. Tullius, orator, consul 63 BC: bequest to, 237; his consulship, 36; dowry to daughter, 77; on elections and politics at Rome, 31, 38–40, 44, 50, 113–14; on faking of ancestry, 52; on familial religious rites, 253; on gladiatorial shows, 14; his grief at death of daughter, 218, 220; on guardians for women, 91; on political influence of women, 93

Claudius, emperor (AD 41–54): his accession, 150; his cruelty, 28; exposure of infant daughter, 225; and games and gladiatorial shows, 6, 10, 19–20; political influence on, 155; and senatorial order, 17, 76, 122, 167, 169, 185–6, 188; and law of trusts, 252

Claudii Pulchri, preeminent noble family of Republic, 55–6

Claudius Pulcher, Appius, consul 212 BC, his sons, 65

Claudius Pulcher, Appius, consul 54 BC, 14

Claudius Pulcher, P., consul 249 BC, on omens, 82

Colosseum, amphitheatre in Rome, 2, 9, 18

Commodus, emperor (AD 180–92): and games and gladiatorial shows, 11–12, 14, 15, 17, 20, 21; and senatorial order, 15, 17

Cornelii Cethegi, leading noble family, fluctuations of their political fortunes, 65

Cornelius Cinna, L., consul 87–84 BC, 81

Cornelius Lentulus Clodianus, P., as censor (70 BC), 54

Cornelius Lentulus Sura, P., consul 71 BC, expelled from senate, 54

Cornelius Repentinus, F., praetorian prefect, 2nd century AD, 155

Cornelii Scipiones, preeminent noble family of Republic, family burial chamber of, 205–6

Cornelius Scipio Aemilianus, P., consul 147 and 134 BC: destroyer of Carthage, 80; his inheritance, 88

Cornelius Scipio Africanus, P., consul 205 and 194 BC: captor of New Carthage (Spain), 207; dowry to daughters, 77

Cornelius Scipio Asiaticus, L., consul 83 BC, marriage of his daughter, 49

Cornelius Scipio Hispanus, Cn., praetor 139 BC, his achievements, 115

Cornelius Scipio Nasica, P., consul 162 BC, leader of senate, canvassed votes, 107, 113

Cornelius Sulla, L., consul 88 BC, dictator; his constitutional reforms, 39, 47; his funeral procession, 31; marriage alliances of, 87; as political general, 41, 51; proscriptions of, 70, 80

Corocotta, piglet, his will, 238

Curtius Rufus, consul c. AD 43, his obscure ancestry, 173

Cybele, mother-goddess, worship of, 231

Dasumius, L., consul AD 93(?), his testament, 239, 246, 252

De Sanctis, G., views on Roman nobility, 37, 52

Didius Julianus, emperor (AD 193), and gladiatorial shows, 20

Dio, Cassius, consul AD 229; historian: attitude to equestrians, 182–3; present at games and public demonstrations, 15–17; on political role of games, 19; on access to senatorial order, 151, 158–9

Selected index of proper names

Parentalia, religious festival for the dead, 233–4

Paul, lawyer, early 3rd century AD, 24

Paulinus, of Pella, 5th century AD, his estates, 190

Pedius, Q., knight, 1st century BC, his marriage, 111

Perpetua, Christian martyr, early 3rd century AD, 5

Pertinax, emperor (AD 193): abilities, 182; humble background, 173

Petronius, novelist, 1st century AD, on gladiatorial shows, 24–6

Phaedrus, author of fables, 1st century AD, 15

Plautius Silvanus, M., consul 2 BC, family tomb of, 206

Pliny the Elder, natural historian, 1st century AD: on legacy-hunting, 242; on luxury at Rome, 79

Pliny the Younger, senator, writer, friend of Trajan: on aristocratic childlessness, 96; on commemorative memorials, 250; ghost story of, 234–5; on gladiatorial shows, 2; on influence of ex-slaves, 177; on legacy-hunting, 239–40; on senatorial order, 151–4, 166

Plotina, wife of Trajan, her influence, 155

Plutarch, essayist and biographer, c. AD 100: on marriage alliances, 87–8, 97; on mourning, 218, 225–6

Polybius, Greek historian, 2nd century BC: on costs of gladiatorial shows, 8; on fertility and marriage, 78; on funerary rites, 201–2; on honesty at Rome, 80; on luxury at Rome, 79; on Roman military behaviour, 207

Pompeii, near Naples, gladiatorial barracks at, 23–4; gladiatorial shows at, 7, 12, 21–2, 25–6; graveyards at, 233; literacy at, 236

Pompeius Magnus, Cn., leading senator and general, 1st century BC, 41; civil-war with Caesar, 54; marriage alliances of, 48, 87

Pompeius, Sextus, son of Pompeius Magnus, 28

Popillius, P., legate 210 BC, his ancestry, 65

Popillius, Laenas, M., consul 316 BC, his family, 65

Porcius Cato, M., consul 195 BC, censor: new man, 50; on divination, 82; on female emancipation, 92

Porcius Cato, M., leading conservative senator, 1st century BC, marriage and political alliances of, 87–8

Procopius, historian 6th century AD, his description of epidemics, 209

Propertius, poet, 1st century BC: on his dead lover, 229; love poetry of, 85

Quinctius Flamininus, T., consul 150 BC, gladiatorial games of, 4

Quintilian, orator, 1st century AD, ghost-story of, 235

Rome: career structure of senators at, 150–65; death at, 201ff; demonstrations at, 15–20; expectation of life at, 70–3, 147; gladiatorial shows at, 1ff; imperial court at, 174–5, 190–1; individuation at, 79–81; living conditions of poor at, 29, 208–10; political myths of, 114; political system of, 34–6, 42–5, 107–17, property rights at, 245–7; public disorder at, 29–30; secularisation at, 81–4; warrior state, 1–2, 29

Sallust, senator, historian, 1st century BC: on the *coup d'état* of Catiline, 92–3; on the nobility, 36; on Roman moral decline, 83

Scriptores Historiae Augustae (SHA), late 4th-century AD imperial biographies, historial fabrications in, 130

Scullard, H. H., views on Roman nobility, 36–7, 52

Sempronius Gracchus, C., populist tribune of the people (123/2 BC), 44, 114

Sempronius Gracchus, Tib., populist tribune of the people (133 BC), 44, 114

Seneca, senator, philosopher and essayist, 1st century AD: on the divinity of Claudius, 122; on gladiatorial shows, 3; on grief and mourning, 207, 218; on inheritances, 77; on legacy-hunting, 238–9; on paternal power, 244; on senatorial order, 153, 166; on sexual mores, 94–5; (his brothers, 167)

Septimius Severus, L., emperor (AD 193–211), and senatorial order 21, 146, 183

Serapis, Egyptian god, worship of, 231

Servilia, mother of Brutus (assassin of Caesar), as a political force, 93

Servius, literary critic, 4th century AD, 4

Spain, provincial senators from, 184–93

Spartacus, leader of slave revolt, 73 BC, 29

Statius, poet, 1st century AD, flattered imperial ex-slaves, 177

Stein, A., views on Roman senate, 126

Stone, L., on expression of grief in England, 222–3

275

SCIENCE, FOLKLORE AND IDEOLOGY

Studies in the Life Sciences in Ancient Greece

G. E. R. LLOYD

Taking a set of central issues from ancient Greek medicine and biology, this book studies first the interaction between scientific theorising and folklore or popular assumptions, and second the ideological character of scientific inquiry. Topics of current interest in the philosophy and sociology of science illuminated here include the relationship between primitive thought and early science, and the roles of the consensus of the scientific community, of tradition and of the authority of the written text, in the development of science.

'Geoffrey Lloyd in this book, then, opens new perspectives on the development of the life sciences in Greece and Rome, and frees them from a deadening historiographical tradition that presumes only a few great "rational" treatises worthy of study.' *The Times Literary Supplement*